FAN CULTURES

An unnervingly close reader and a sophisticated theorist, Hills is the best of a new generation of scholar-fans. Matt Hills's *Fan Cultures* is dynamite – and it's going to blast a hole through some of the roadblocks and dead-ends in previous theories of fandom.

Henry Jenkins, MIT

Fans are one of the most widely-studied groups of media consumers. Often knowing more about a character or TV series than the stars or programme-makers themselves, and ready to make surprising readings of plotlines and characters, they have been seen as the ultimate active audience.

Fan Cultures is the first comprehensive overview of fans and fan theory. Emphasising the contradictions of fandom, Matt Hills outlines the ways in which fans have been conceptualised in cultural theory and challenges many of these established paradigms. Hills draws on case studies of specific groups, such as Elvis impersonators, X-Philes and Trekkers, and discusses a range of approaches to fandom. Taking all of this into account, he ultimately questions whether the development of new media creates the possibility of new forms of fandom and explores the significance of the term 'cult' for media fans.

Matt Hills is Lecturer in Media and Cultural Studies at Cardiff University. He is co-editor of *Intensities: The Journal of Cult Media* (www.cult-media.com).

SUSSEX STUDIES IN CULTURE AND COMMUNICATION
Jane Cowan
University of Sussex

Books in this series express Sussex's unique commitment to interdisciplinary work at the cutting edge of cultural and communication studies. Transcending the interface between the social and the human sciences, the series explores some of the key themes that define the particular character of life, and the representation of life, at the end of one millennium and the beginning of the next.

Our relationships to each other, to our bodies and to our technologies are changing. New concepts are required, new evidence is needed, to advance our understanding of these changes. The boundaries between disciplines need to be challenged. Through monographs and edited collections the series will explore new ways of thinking about communication, performance, identities, and the continual refashioning of meanings, messages, and images in space and time.

CULTURAL ENCOUNTERS
Edited by Elizabeth Hallam and Brian Street

THE HOUSE OF DIFFERENCE
Cultural Politics and National Identity in Canada
Eva Mackey

VIRTUAL GEOGRAPHIES
Bodies, Space and Relations
Edited by Mike Crang, Phil Crang and Jon May

VISUAL DIGITAL CULTURE
Surface Play and Spectacle in New Media Genres
Andrew Darley

Forthcoming:

A NATIONAL JOKE
Andy Medhurst

FAN CULTURES

Matt Hills

London and New York

First published 2002
by Routledge
2 Park Square, Milton Park, Abingdon, Oxon, OX14 4RN

Simultaneously published in the USA and Canada
by Routledge
270 Madison Ave, New York NY 10016

Routledge is an imprint of the Taylor & Francis Group

Transferred to Digital Printing 2005

Typeset in Galliard by Taylor & Francis Books Ltd

British Library Cataloguing in Publication Data
A catalogue record for this book is available from the British Library

Library of Congress Cataloging in Publication Data
Hills, Matt 1971–
Fan Cultures / Matt Hills
Includes bibliographical references and index.
1. Fans (Persons) – Psychology. 2. Subculture. 3.Television viewers – Psychology. 4.
Celebrities in mass media. 5. Motion picture actors and actresses. I. Title
HM646 .H55 2002
306.1–dc21
2001051092

ISBN 0–415–24024–7 (hbk)
ISBN 0–415–24025–5 (pbk)

IN LOVING MEMORY OF ERNEST 'JIMMY'
HILLS, WINIFRED HILLS AND MARY LEWIN

I playfully invoke the *Star Trek* series ... because the crews of the Enterprise in both its old and new dispensations (as well as those of *Voyager* and *Deep Space Nine*), for all their highly visible 'multi-cultural' inclusiveness, project into the future the very problem that concerns me here: a 'community' which presents itself as a utopia of freedom and independence for its members, and yet seems capable of functioning only as a rigid hierarchy. Academic 'communities', like those of the *Star Trek* starships, often pride themselves on their ostensible enlightened distance from the rest of the universe ... *Freedom* (as in 'academic freedom') is one of the most bandied-about words in academic space. However, in actual practice this 'freedom' is predicated ... on deference to senior members of the profession.... Indeed, academic communities, like those of the military-modelled TV starships, are intensely devoted to rank, with the gulf separating the untenured from the tenured, the 'part-time' from the 'full-time', and the graduate students from the faculty, looming especially large, though they may all teach in classrooms right next to each other.... In spite of their supposed 'enlightenment', the capacity for – and accomplishment of – brutalities, from the petty to the severe, of such 'communities' are an open secret of academia. Yet the system persists ...

(Bartolovich 2000: 77)

CONTENTS

CONTENTS

PREFACE

On the lack of singular definitions

Everybody knows what a 'fan' is. It's somebody who is obsessed with a particular star, celebrity, film, TV programme, band; somebody who can produce
reams of information on their object of fandom, and can quote their favoured
lines or lyrics, chapter and verse. Fans are often highly articulate. Fans interpret
media texts in a variety of interesting and perhaps unexpected ways. And fans
participate in communal activities – they are not 'socially atomised' or isolated
viewers/readers.

Everybody knows what a 'fan' is, of course, but in an academic study dealing
with fan cultures and covering the issue of 'cult' media, the reader might still
expect a 'theorised' definition of what 'fandom' is, and what constitutes a fan
'cult'. Surely our common sense notions of fandom cannot be left untouched
by the need for academic rigour and conceptual clarity?

So, how have 'fandom' and the media 'cult' been defined academically?

To date, defining 'fandom' has been no easy task, despite (or perhaps
because of) the 'everydayness' of the term. Abercrombie and Longhurst (1998)
place the fan, the 'cultist' and the 'enthusiast' along a spectrum of identities and
experiences, distinguishing between them by linking increased specialisation of
interest, social organisation of interest and material productivity to the move
from 'fan' to 'cultist' to 'enthusiast'. Having made these distinctions,
Abercrombie and Longhurst then align prior literature on fans with their definition of 'cultist': 'Cultists ... are closer to what much of the recent literature has
called a fan. There are very explicit attachments to stars or to particular
programmes and types of programme' (1998: 138–9). The fan, for
Abercrombie and Longhurst, is characterised by a lack of social organisation
(they typically discuss young children as 'fans'). It seems faintly unhelpful to
produce a taxonomy in which the definition of 'fan' is at odds with the use of
this term in almost all other literature in the field. The attempt to separate
'cultist' and 'enthusiast' identities also causes problems given that, although one
key distinction is whether the fan interest is media-derived (= cultist) or not (=
enthusiast) (1998: 132), Abercrombie and Longhurst nevertheless align *Star
Trek* fans with enthusiasts.

Less contradictory attempts at definition occur in Tulloch and Jenkins (1995) and also in Brooker and Brooker (1996). Tulloch and Jenkins ignore the term 'cult' (despite its prevalence within fan groups and related niche media), but distinguish between followers and fans (1995: 23), again along a spectrum of increased involvement: the 'fan' claims a social identity which the 'follower' does not. Brooker and Brooker (1996: 141) also note that 'Tarantino's admirers might not all be fans ... and not all fans will be cult fans', marking a clear separation between the committed fan and the presumably even more knowledgeable and fan-community-oriented 'cult fan'.

However, I will use the term 'cult fan' interchangeably with 'fan' – typically using cult fan when the object of devotion has been specifically and repeatedly described as 'cult' within the fan group and/or related niche media[1] – such as *Cult Times*, *Cult TV*, *Cult Movies* – since it seems to me that attempts at the separation of terms have never been entirely convincing. (Tulloch and Jenkins (1995: 23) concede that the fan–follower distinction 'remains fluid and somewhat arbitrary'.)

Cult followings have built up around a diversity of media output such as *The Prisoner* (Gregory 1997), *The Avengers* (Miller, T. 1997 and Buxton 1990), *Star Trek* (Gibberman 1991), *Doctor Who* (Tulloch and Alvarado 1983; Tulloch and Jenkins 1995), *Batman* (Pearson and Uricchio 1991; Brooker 2000), *Twin Peaks* (Lavery 1995), *The X-Files* (Lavery, Hague and Cartwright (eds) 1996) and the films of Quentin Tarantino (Brooker and Brooker 1996). Classic cult films such as *Casablanca* (Eco 1995b; Telotte 1991), 'Midnight Movies' (Hoberman and Rosenbaum 1991), *The Rocky Horror Picture Show* (Austin 1981), and banned or restricted titles like *A Clockwork Orange* (Parsons 1997), all continue to attract intrigued, devoted audiences – as do a variety of contemporary horror titles (Conrich 1997; Dika 1990; McDonagh 1991), science-fiction films and writers (Bukatman 1993; French, S. 1996; Luckhurst 1997: 154), not to mention comics/manga (Bukatman 1994; Schodt 1996) as well as anime (Napier 2001) and Hong Kong cinema (An 2001). And fan-made digital cinema parodies of *Star Wars* have attracted 'enormous cult followings' in their own right (Jenkins forthcoming). A list of *contestably* 'cult' films, books, TV series, etc. could in fact fill a number of books all by itself (and this ongoing cataloguing process, which is also a process of ongoing argument, has been attempted by a number of authors: see, for example, Everman 1993; Peary 1981, 1983; Savage 1996; Lewis and Stempel 1993; Whissen 1992; French and French 1999).

Having said that fandom and cult fandom appear to overlap, 'cult fandom' *does* seem to imply a cultural identity which is partially distinct from that of the 'fan' in general, but I would suggest that *this relates not to the intensity, social organisation or semiotic/material productivity of the fandom concerned, but rather to its duration, especially in the absence of 'new' or official material in the originating medium.*[2] Thus *Star Trek* fans did not become 'cult fans' historically until the programme's intense popularity persisted after its cancellation, and

cult fans

cancelled

until a mythology of fan activism had thereby grown up alongside the programme's commercial regeneration as a contemporary transmedia 'franchise'. Likewise, I would suggest that *Doctor Who* fans only properly became 'cult fans' after the programme's cancellation, although given the show's extremely lengthy run, it is possible to argue that the durability of 'cult fandom' preceded cancellation. By this token, X-Philes (fans of *The X-Files*) should not be classified as cult fans given that they are intensely interested in an ongoing programme. And yet the intense devotion which many programmes now appear to inspire very shortly after their transmission calls into question any strict separation of 'fan' and 'cult fan', given that in almost all aspects other than longevity (and hence fan-interest despite the lack of new 'product') these fandoms may otherwise form part of an analytic whole.

Cult fandom can therefore be thought of as being made up of three dimensions which can, in specific cases, contradict one another:[3]

i   Tautological definitions – the use of 'cult' discourses within fandoms.
ii   Temporal definitions – 'cult' fandom as enduring (see Davidhazi 1998).
iii   Affective definitions – 'cult' fandom as an intensely felt fan experience.

I can only sympathise with the observation made by John L. Caughey (1984: 40): 'as ordinarily used, both in common parlance and in social analysis, the term "fan" ... does not do justice to the variety of attachments to media figures [and media texts] ... – and it does not do justice to ... these attachments.' My specific use of the term 'cult fan' is meant, then, to delimit more precisely a particular (enduring) form of affective fan relationship.

Inevitably contested terms ...

Given this sense that 'cult' and 'fandom' are contested terms both inside and outside the academy, I am not convinced that 'rigorous definitions' are the only way to proceed. I want to use this preface to spell out a few of the key arguments that follow from considering definitive 'definitions' to be an academic mistake. Attempts to define fandom, or cult media, in this way make a potentially fatal error; they assume that by fixing terms in place they can isolate an 'object of study'. I have made this assumption so far. But by fixing their terms of reference, these types of argument neglect to consider that terms such as 'fan' and 'cult' may not circulate simply as 'labels' for actual things or referents, but may instead form part of a cultural struggle over meaning and affect (by which I mean the attachments, emotions and passions of those who self-identify as 'fans', but who may also contest the description).

I want to suggest that fandom is not simply a 'thing' that can be picked over analytically. It is also always performative; by which I mean that it is an identity which is (dis-)claimed, and which performs cultural work.[4] Claiming the status of a 'fan' may, in certain contexts, provide a cultural space for types of knowledge and attachment. In specific institutional contexts, such as academia, 'fan' status may be devalued and taken as a sign of 'inappropriate' learning and uncritical engagement with the media (see Introduction). Fandom, then, is never a neutral 'expression' or a singular 'referent'; its status and its performance shift across cultural sites. What different 'performances' of fandom share, however, is a sense of contesting cultural norms. To claim the identity of a 'fan' remains, in some sense, to claim an 'improper' identity, a cultural identity based on one's commitment to something as seemingly unimportant and 'trivial' as a film or TV series. Even in cultural sites where the claiming of a fan identity may seem to be unproblematically secure – within fan cultures, at a fan convention, say, or on a fan newsgroup – a sense of cultural defensiveness remains, along with a felt need to justify fan attachments (see chapter 3). Viewing fandom as a 'thing' or 'object of study' has led previous studies of fandom to treat the ways in which fan identities are legitimated as authentic 'expressions' of a group commitment.

One important question which has not yet been adequately addressed is *what fandom does culturally* rather than how fandom can be fitted into academic norms of 'resistant' or 'complicit' readings. My approach is based on a refusal of what I would term, somewhat clumsily perhaps, 'decisionist' narratives. A 'decisionist' theoretical narrative seeks to attack or defend sections of fandom, or fandom taken in the abstract. 'Decisionist' narratives hinge on making political decisions as to the 'goodness' or 'badness' of fan cultures; should these fan attachments and interpretations be devalued as industrial complicity or valued as creative expressions of audience agency? Such approaches ultimately carve culture into good and bad objects, objects to be 'rationally' denigrated, ignored and despised, or objects to be 'rationally' applauded, celebrated and valued. This scenario produces a type of endemic 'moral dualism' within the academy in which singular definitions are constructed not only of objects of study, but also of 'good' and 'bad' instances of popular culture. At worst, this promotes a check-list mentality; at best it produces consistent and worked-through political commitments. All too often it avoids both abomination and apex, hovering around a mid-point of 'going through the motions', and producing *institutionally acceptable* forms of knowledge. The cultural politics of this 'critical' knowledge, contrary to stated aims, may well be blunted by issues such as the audience/readership for academic work, as well as being blunted by the ways in which academic knowledge remains permeated by forms of 'common sense', despite tacit 'subcultural' assumptions that academics somehow escape the ideological mechanisms that they otherwise unveil in popular culture. Where are the analyses of hegemony as it is reproduced through academic thought? Why has popular culture provided a space for the reiteration of this 'hegemonic' thesis, while academia has, by and large, been spared the same attentions?

Is there any way out of 'decisionist' thinking? There is a deliberate contradictoriness to my argument here; I am *opposed* to approaches which construct oppositions. Surely this must be a mistake which destroys the logic of my argument? Well, yes, if you expect an argumentative position to operate entirely without contradiction. Any reader firmly committed to a model of culture as non-contradictory, and who believes that 'the real world' is composed of clearly definable entities – either in advance of conceptual models, or through the action of conceptual models – will probably need to put this book down round about ... *now*.

For those still with me, one of the main points of this book – as you'll see from a brief glance at the chapter titles – is its 'suspensionist' position, a position which refuses to split fandom into the 'good' and the 'bad' and which embraces inescapable contradiction (the ugly?). This means approaching the contradictions of fan cultures and cult media as *essential cultural negotiations* that can only be closed down at the cost of ignoring fandom's cultural dynamics.

My argument is that fan cultures cannot be pinned down through singular theoretical approaches or singular definitions. Where I do favour a particular approach, then this is on the basis of revising previous 'schools of thought'.[5] Even here my argument lacks singularity, since chapter 4's rewriting of Winnicottian theory concludes that fan attachments cannot be reduced to any one 'explanation'. My use of Winnicott is motivated by the paradoxical possibilities that his work opens up, as is my use of Adorno's work in chapter 1, as is my sustained focus on fan cult(ure)s as part of a 'dialectic of value' in which personalised, individual and subjective moments of fan attachment interact with communal constructions and justifications without either moment over-writing or surmounting the other.

This reintroduces the 'subjective', something which has been very much written out of sociological versions of media and cultural studies – to their detriment – and something which has been written into psychoanalytic versions of media and cultural studies in very specific ways, again to their detriment. If this means, ultimately, that some of my arguments will be attacked for their naivety, then so be it. My aim is, quite deliberately, to illustrate the explanatory paucity and limits of sociological and psychoanalytic 'disciplinary' norms, in which staking out a certain argumentative orthodoxy seems to be more important than engaging with a sense of cultural dynamism. One occasionally has a sneaking suspicion that academic writers are more attached to their discipline than their 'subject'. As Graham McCann (1991: 337) has observed in his own sociological work on the biography of Marilyn Monroe: 'if I had to choose between betraying my discipline and betraying my subject, I hope I should have the guts to betray my discipline.' If I seem to reintroduce 'the subject' as something cut adrift from communal constructions and cultural configurations, then this argument should be read less as an embarrassing 'lapse' and more as an assault on disciplinary/institutional norms which work to limit, and sometimes rule out, the creative cultural and psychological spaces which may remain for us as subjects. Otherwise why do academics bother to write and publish impassioned arguments? Who do they suppose they are arguing with or persuading if their sense of 'the subject' is so severely curtailed?

Approaching fan cultures (Part I) and theorising cult media (Part II) obliges us to consider the creative spaces of fans as subjects with psyches as well as members of 'interpretive communities'. If, ultimately, the subjective is configured through forms of 'common sense', so that fandom has a certain 'subjective' authenticity, this subjective experience still cannot be entirely depicted as a reflection of 'discursive' or 'cultural' structures (see chapter 4). Otherwise the question of where fan cultures come from cannot be answered; fans are fans because fan communities exist and can be entered. How, then, do new fan cultures emerge? Previous studies have nothing to say on the *emergence* of fan cultures, precisely because they always assume a pre-constituted fan community and hence a set of fan 'norms' against which the fan as subject can be measured and placed, and through which the fan as subject can be determined.[6] By ignoring the fan as subject, previous studies have also neglected the 'multi-dimensionality' of fandom. Fan cultures are typically approached as isolated and singular 'things'; *Star Trek* fans, or X-Philes, or Elvis fans. This ignores the extent to which fans of one text or icon may also be fans of other seemingly unrelated texts/icons (see chapter 3), and again provides a rather unhelpful view of fan cultures as securely 'bounded' entities. Of course, these boundary-drawing exercises may also be a result of (academic) publishing and its economic imperatives rather than being 'purely' conceptual errors.

Notes

1 Based on the self-classifications adopted by fan groups, I have not included 'mystery' or detective fiction within my 'cult(ural) studies'. Despite rarely adopting the term 'cult', the diverse fandoms for mystery fiction, I would nevertheless argue, display many of the characteristics of the media cult discussed in chapter 6. The serial character occupying a detailed social world and providing a trusted focal point for fan sentiment (see McClure 1977) and the irresolvable speculation of fans (off- and on-line; see Kelly 1998) are common to texts and icons typically described as 'cult' and to mystery fiction and its fans. It could be argued that one of the most famous fictional cult icons ever devised belongs to the 'mystery' genre: one Sherlock Holmes of 221b Baker Street. However, according to the (contradictory) parameters of the media cult which I suggest here (parameters which must pay some attention to distinctions made within the cultures under consideration), the character of Holmes cannot be firmly classified as a media cult despite the existence of otherwise compelling formal similarities.

2 Despite failing to embrace the 'cult' epithet, Sherlockians have a head-start on the cult fandoms which have sprung up around 1960s TV programmes (see Penzler 1977 and Pearson 1997).

3 If we consider these three dimensions as triangulated rather than simply as a list then there are three possible forms of contradiction: tautological–temporal, temporal–affective and affective–tautological.

   The first (tautological–temporal) relates to the 'mystery' fans mentioned in note 1 above. It could also relate to sports or football fans (Redhead 1997); these fans do not use the term 'cult' but nevertheless show the enduring commitments of 'cult fans'. These types of fans will not be discussed here due to their lack of any tautological dimension; quite simply, they do not self-describe as cult fans. A further contradiction is possible: fans may self-describe as 'cult fans' without displaying any enduring fan commitment. This contradiction concerns the commodification of cult audiences (see chapters 1, 4 and Conclusion).

The second possible contradiction (temporal–affective) relates to pop/music fans. These fans may be very emotionally invested in their fandom, but the commitment to an object of fandom may not persist over time (Garratt 1984 and 1994). Clearly this is not so for all music fans; the Springsteen fans analysed by Cavicchi (1998) maintain their fandom over time, as do Gilbert's (1999) Velvet Underground fans, and the Deadheads analysed in Adams and Sardiello (2000).

The third type of contradiction (affective–tautological) covers the possibility that fans may self-describe as 'cult fans' without seeming to display emotional investments; this covers fan cultures where the accumulation of fan knowledge is most intently valued (see chapter 2 on fan cultural capital). This contradiction may relate to specific fan cultures where the display of emotion is devalued, e.g. male horror fans who perform their fandom as 'knowledge'-based rather than 'emotion'-based (chapter 4). Conversely, fans may display fan attachments without self-describing as cult fans, a situation which is similar to the mystery and sports fans described above.

4 And fandom may also do different cultural work in different cultural and historical contexts, as historical studies have demonstrated. For example, Fuller (1996) has examined early 'movie fan culture', while Studlar (1997) addresses fan magazines of the 1910s and 1920s. Robertson (1998: 231–2) has alleged that 'much ... research on fans ... is too narrow, being either of a presentist bent or of a restricted historical focus'. While I would accept this charge in relation to my own work here, presenting work of a 'presentist' nature in no way rules out considering the cultural and historical specificity of this 'present'.

5 Much of my work here can therefore be thought of as a type of 'metatheorizing', namely that which is 'done *after* theories have been developed. Such metatheorizing may seek a better understanding of those theories, or it may seek to create new theory' (Ritzer 2001: 15).

6 Or as Muggleton (2000: 23–4) puts it: 'The CCCS approach, in other words, falls into the trap of reifying the concept of subculture. It is treated, in effect, as a real, material entity that "acts". As such, the concept stands in for the individual members. Individuals appear in the analysis only as epiphenomena of essences, structures and totalizing theories.'

ACKNOWLEDGEMENTS

Directly and indirectly, many people have contributed to the writing of this book. Brett Mills helped with the fandom graph in chapter 3, and Tim Robins very graciously gave me access to a range of *Doctor Who* fanzines. All my colleagues at the University of Central England and Cardiff University have been helpful and supportive. At UCE, thanks to Julie Parry, Rod Pilling, Steve Spittle, Christine Tudor and Tim Wall. At Cardiff, thanks to Gill Branston, Glen Creeber, Beccy Harris, Sanna Inthorn, Justin Lewis, Jo Marshall, Maire Messenger Davies, Roberta Pearson, Terry Threadgold, John Tulloch, Karin Wahl-Jorgensen and Kevin Williams. Particular thanks go to Rebecca Farley and Sara Gwenllian Jones for welcoming me to Cardiff and for making *Intensities: The Journal of Cult Media* (*www.cult-media.com*) a reality rather than an idea.

I'd very much like to acknowledge and applaud my PhD supervisor, Roger Silverstone, for always setting the highest standards. At Sussex University I was also lucky enough to be in the company of Culcom postgraduates such as Caroline Bassett, Matt Bennett, Clare Birchall, Kay Dickinson, Jeremy Gilbert, Suzy Gordon, Irmi Karl and Jo Littler. Elsewhere in academia, thanks to Nick Couldry, Mark Jancovich, Cathy Johnson, Kurt Lancaster and Nickianne Moody.

The following people read and commented on the draft of *Fan Cultures*: Henry Jenkins, Una McCormack, John Tulloch, and an anonymous UK reader. I am enormously grateful for the support and constructive criticism that was offered by each of them.

Thanks to all (and I mean *all*) the students who have taken the module 'Cult Media and Fandom' at UCE and Cardiff University over the past two years. I can't list one hundred or so names here, but I'd particularly like to thank Chris Monk, Dean Murphy, Dean Reilly and Jo Wasilew, as well as Victoria Armstrong, Brett Morton, Adrian Smith, Laura Sykes, Ben Talbot, and the rowdy people. You all made teaching feel less like a paid job and more like something I'd choose to do with my time anyway.

Outside the academy, hello to Paul Martin and Helen Whitehouse, Russell Bradshaw, Nick Williams, and the international, jet-set Nicks. Thanks to Ben

Morgan for the postcards which always arrived at just the right time, and to James Welch for supplying vast amounts of fan knowledge and enthusiasm.

Heartfelt thanks to Roxanne Nichols for being there, beginning, middle and end. Thanks also to Brenda, Scott, Ryan and Audrey for welcoming me to Canada.

Lastly, although of course they are really first, love to Mum, Dad, Stuart, Grandpa and Nelson the brown tabby cat.

Matt Hills, Cardiff, 2001

INTRODUCTION

Who's Who? Academics, fans, scholar-fans and fan-scholars

This book could begin at any number of times and places, either personally or theoretically. Personally *and* theoretically, it could begin with my reading Henry Jenkins's (1992a) *Textual Poachers* as a media studies undergraduate. Unlike so many of the other books that filled my reading lists, this one I read in a single sitting, unable to put it down. The book provided a sense of recognition – my own experiences as a media fan seemed to be captured in its pages – and also a glimmer of dissatisfaction; the fans that Jenkins wrote about differed from my experiences of fandom, seeming to lack a sense of fandom's competitive, argumentative and factional possibilities.

Turning the clock even further back, I could begin with my precocious but aborted attempt to read John Tulloch and Manuel Alvarado's *Doctor Who: The Unfolding Text* at the age of twelve. Perhaps I wasn't ready for the 'semiotic "thickness"' of the book (1983: 249), even if Tulloch and Alvarado were later to be quoted in the very programme that they had analysed. Although *The Unfolding Text* proved to be too much for my pre-teen faculties to handle, it also gave me a glimpse of a different (theorists') world where television was something important and deserving of analysis. A world, in actual fact, which wasn't so very far away from the importance that I already attributed to *Doctor Who* as a devoted fan of the programme. At that time I was more interested in writing *Doctor Who* stories rather than analyses, but the presuppositions underlying both activities are closely related: both activities take the programme as a starting point for further creativity, and both assume that television is not ephemeral or trivial, and that a particular programme deserves detailed consideration.

A multitude of fan experiences – not only on the fringes of *Doctor Who* fandom – lie beneath and between the lines of this completed 'text', as do my experiences as a student and now as a lecturer in 'the academy'. In what follows, I will bring these submerged 'other texts' to the surface of this one, but my account is also intended to be a general introduction to, and indeed a synthesis of, the many different theories of fan culture which have circulated through media and cultural studies.

Perhaps unfashionably, I will suggest that a general theory of media fandom is not only possible but is also important; too many previous works

1

have focused on single TV series, singular fan cultures, or singular media ('TV fans' versus 'cinephiles'). But these distinctions are often produced through the institutional agendas of university departments, such as the need to establish 'film studies' in the 1970s, and the attempt to counter this with 'TV studies' as a rival field. By seeking to validate and valorise specific media as objects of study, theorists immediately cut themselves off from the transmedia and multimedia consumption of media fans. And the focus on singular fan cultures also presents the danger that fans' readings will be cut off from the wider consumption patterns that surround, and may help to make some sense of, their fan activities. All too often, my basic argument will run, theorists follow their own institutional or theoretical agendas, and use fandom within these theory wars and territorial skirmishes. And of course, if this is to be my argument then I too will have to defend myself from the very same accusations, or make explicit what my own institutional and theoretical agendas might be.

It is necessary to reflect on the ways in which media and cultural studies closes its seminar room doors on the figure of 'the fan' as an imagined Other, thereby constructing what is to count as 'good' academic work. Of course, this is only half of the story. It is equally important to consider the place of 'theorising' within fan cultures, and to consider what boundaries are imagined around 'good' fan practices. These boundaries may work to exclude 'the academic' as an imagined otherin fan writings and practices, providing the other half of what could be described as a torn social dynamic. Such mutual marginalisation would suggest that fandom and academia are co-produced as exclusive social and cultural positions. The categorical splitting of fan/academic here is not simply a philosophical or theoretical error, but is also produced through the practical logics of self-identified 'fans' and 'academics'.

However, this narrative of mutual marginalisation does not exhaust the approaches that can be taken to the relationship between fandom and academia. We can also consider alterations within cultural studies whereby the figure of 'the fan' has become a topic of debate, leading us into an examination of the academic who also claims a fan identity (just as I have already done in these opening pages). Alexander Doty has recently examined the problems and possibilities opened up by this hybrid 'scholar-fan', and I will compare his account with Henry Jenkins's earlier work as well as considering a very different account of the academic-fan set out by Richard Burt.

I will conclude this discussion of fandom versus academia by turning to the fan-academic, that is, the fan who uses academic theorising within their fan writing and within the construction of a scholarly fan identity, as opposed to the professional academic who draws on their fandom as a badge of distinction within the academy. For, curiously enough, while the academic-fan or 'scholar-fan' has become a highly contested and often highly visible topic for theorists, the fan-academic or 'fan-scholar' has been passed over in silence.

Why fans don't like academics, and vice versa

It might seem odd to describe something called 'academia' or 'the academy' as if this were some kind of monolithic or singular entity. I am not, of course, claiming that all academics are alike, or that all academic institutions are alike. This 'nightmare of sameness' would be an untenable position. Academia, in fact, works hard to produce difference. Differences of theoretical approach abound, as do differences in the selection of favoured theorists. Different interpretations of the same canonical films and television programmes are argued over and sometimes reproduced with minor variations; the similarities between interpretations are often downplayed in favour of an emphasis on the novelty of newer readings (Bordwell 1989). However, despite this multiplicity of theoretical approaches, I want to suggest that academia is nevertheless bounded by its own *imagined subjectivity*.

By this, I do not mean that academics imagine themselves as 'subjective' rather than as 'objective'. The subjectivity that is imagined is, rather, a certain *type* of subjectivity. And the imagined academic subject is imagined precisely because it does not relate to the actual subjectivities of embodied academics.

Barbara Herrnstein Smith has examined how idealised or 'imagined' versions of subjectivity are linked to the establishment and maintenance of a community and its system of value:

> [I]t is assumed or maintained ... that the particular subjects who constitute the established and authorized members of the group are of sound mind and body, duly trained and informed, and generally competent, all other subjects being defective, deficient, or deprived: suffering from crudenesses of sensibility, diseases and *distortions of perception*, weaknesses of character, impoverishment of background-and-education, cultural or historical biases, ideological or personal prejudices and/or underdeveloped, corrupted or jaded tastes.
>
> (Smith 1988: 41; my italics)

Imagined subjectivity, we might say, attributes valued traits of the subject 'duly trained and informed' only to those within the given community, while denigrating or devaluing the 'improper' subjectivity of those who are outside the community.[1]

I want to focus on academia as a system of value, following the work of Barbara Herrnstein Smith. The 'good subject' of the 'duly trained and informed' academic is a resolutely rational subject, devoted to argumentation and persuasion. The possibility that this intense valuing of rationality is imagined is evident from the fact that different theoretical approaches within the academy cannot be brought together via rational activity, nor can the truth-claims of any one theory be rationally adjudicated on the grounds of pure 'evidence', whatever such a thing would look like. In short, academics have no choice, when all is said and done, other than to *believe* in their favoured theories. But, at the same time, the possibility that faith is the ultimate glue within academic argument is typically disavowed and ignored in favour of the imagined subjectivity of the rational academic.

A different narrative of academic work has been considered by a number of writers, among them Stanley Cavell and Randall Collins. In 1981, Cavell addressed the place of 'Film in the University', wondering whether film cults were invading the humanities curriculum. In part, this fear depended precisely on the rational imagined subjectivity of the academic supposedly being threatened by the passions and commitments of 'irrational' cinephiles or film fans. But Cavell goes on to challenge this value system, in which the 'good' rational academic is placed under threat:

> I have spoken of a university, with its commitment to rational discourse toward some public goal, as if it too is an agent of the destruction of cults; but I have also admitted its own propensity to cultism. And I have spoken as if, for example, Wittgenstein and Heidegger ... were clear candidates for a university curriculum, yet I know that each of them is mainly the object of a cult.
>
> (Cavell 1981: 273)

Questioning the separation of 'good' rationality and 'bad' cultism, Cavell brings cultism and fandom back into the heart of academic work,[2] suggesting that it is indeed a type of faith which underpins the academic's 'commitment to rational discourse'. And although he does not use the term 'faith' to cover this phenomenon, Randall Collins refers instead to the 'emotional energy' which he sees as a vital component of academic work, along with cultural capital (i.e. knowledge):

> When a group has a high degree of agreement on the ideas put forward by some intellectual leader, that person becomes a sacred object for the group. Thus arise the cult figures of intellectual life: ... Hegel, Marx, Wittgenstein. ... [I]ntellectuals are highly aware of the cult heroes of the past.
>
> (Collins 1998: 36)

Possessing their own cult heroes and cult theorists of the past, academics are – in terms of their embodied and actual subjectivities – out of alignment with the imagined subjectivity of 'good' rationality. It might equally be said that the university is not always aligned with its idealised commitment to rational discourse, for as at least one cultural critic has argued, albeit provocatively: 'The university was designed to generate and contain the ... fandom of adolescents' (Rickels 1999: xiv). However, whether the university and the academic measure up to the idealisations that are established for them is not the problem.

The real problem is that *despite* consistently failing to measure up to the 'good' imagined subjectivity of the rational self, this idealisation continues to carry such cultural power and effectiveness. By regulating what counts as the 'good' subject, i.e. the authorised and competent self, this highly limited version of imagined subjectivity acts as an extremely powerful cultural device. It can be used to restrict and pathologise specific cultural groups, while promoting the achieved 'normality' and 'legitimate' authority of others. Imagined subjectivity is hence not just about systems of value; it is also always about who has power over cultural representations and cultural claims to legitimacy, and who is able to claim 'good' and moral subjectivity while pathologising other groups as morally or mentally defective. As Blackman and Walkerdine have commented: 'the normal/pathological distinction underpinning the construction of Otherness plays a specific role in the ways we relate to, understand, and act upon ourselves as subjects of particular kinds' (2001: 115).

Academic practice – regardless of its favoured theorists and theoretical frameworks – typically transforms fandom into an absolute Other. For example, Barker and Brooks (1998) were confronted by a fan of Sylvester Stallone in their research into audiences of *Judge Dredd*. This fan's behaviour did not seem to fit into Barker and Brooks's theoretically-favoured version of subjectivity (in which cinematic pleasure is experienced according to routine and self-conscious 'scripts' of cinema-going). Rather than functioning as a challenge to this theoretical assumption, the fan's experience was instead described according to its 'absolute distinctness' (*ibid.*: 67) from the types of cinema-going which the study otherwise examined (including those of *Judge Dredd* fans).

Possibly the most famous academic 'othering' of fandom is Simon Frith's (1990) review of Andrew Ross's *No Respect* and Morag Shiach's *Discourse on Popular Culture*. Frith's work elsewhere has sought to break down barriers between fandom and academia by considering how 'many fans of pop music who are not academics are certainly intellectuals ... [and] they're involved in the same sort of fantasizing that academics ... are also involved in' (1992: 183). But this later emphasis on the continuity between fandom and academia in terms of shared cultural fantasies and shared anxieties about what it means to be a fan (1992: 182) presents a very different account of the fan–academic relationship to that which is embedded in Frith's review from 1990. Although Doty (2000) refers to Frith's attempt to explode the binary between fans and academics, it is Frith's stringent (1990) review piece which has surfaced most frequently in academic accounts of the 'fan problem'. For example, the exact same quote from Frith's (*ibid.*) review is repeated in Rowe (1995) and then again in Brunsdon (2000), giving the impression that thinking on the 'fan problem' did not move on much across the 1990s:

> [M]y conclusion is that 'popular culture' just isn't a political site. It is, indeed, a fantasy land, but the fantasies are those projected onto it by (male) intellectuals themselves: intellectuals longing, daring, fearing to

transgress; intellectuals wondering what it would be *not to be an intellectual.*

(Frith 1990: 235)[3]

In this statement it is clearly the case that fans and intellectuals *cannot* share the cultural fantasy referred to, since the fan cannot fantasise 'not being an intellectual' in the same way that an academic might. And this remains true even if you accept Frith's 1992 separation of 'intellectual' and 'academic', a splitting of terms which is promptly lost given that he appears to use the two interchangeably (Frith 1992: 183). Frith's chastening words seem to call for an acceptance on the part of academics that they are academics, and that as a result there are inevitable limits to their possible transgressions.

Rowe's commentary appends Frith's words to a discussion of the irony that 'those who have chosen the formal written word ... are also seeking to evade the burdens of rationalism' (Rowe 1995: 14) by seeking to align academics with fans. Brunsdon, meanwhile, quotes Frith amid a discussion of doubts 'about the necessity and value of an academic engagement [with popular cultural objects]. These doubts come from a range of positions, including, for example, both high cultural dismissals of popular culture and fans' dismissals of academics' interpretations of their enthusiasms and activities' (2000: 212). In Brunsdon's account, too, there is little to be gained from aligning academics with fans: instead, the feminist-intellectual must fight to construct a value system within which her work can function. For Rowe, it is ironic that academics might want to think of themselves as fans. For Brunsdon, this is seemingly a distraction from the feminist struggle to legitimate new (popular cultural) objects of study within the academy. Both of these academic accounts, however, make use of Frith's work to demarcate a boundary around the 'good' academic, positioned as the bearer of a 'commitment to rational discourse toward some public goal', to reiterate Cavell's formula.

Brunsdon mentions fans' dismissals of academic accounts. Such dismissals may be overstated (something which I will explore in section 3 of this introduction), but for now I want to consider the contrasting boundaries which fans draw around their own imagined subjectivities. Fans' own accounts of how they entered the world of fandom, referred to as 'becoming a fan' stories, have been explored by Cavicchi (1998):

> Becoming a Springsteen fan ... entails a radical, enduring change in orientation. It is not simply a matter of acquiring a new taste but is the development of a complex relationship with Bruce Springsteen through his work, *a dramatic opening of oneself to another's experience. While fans often have trouble articulating exactly why they became fans, in their stories they dramatically portray the process of becoming a fan as a journey from one point to another,* they indicate that it is a lasting and

profound transition from an 'old' viewpoint ... to a 'new' one, filled
with energy and insight.

(Cavicchi 1998: 59; my italics)

These fan accounts are similar to the hesitancies and inarticulacies of soap fans
(see Harrington and Bielby 1995), similar to the 'it completely took me away'
and 'it just started from there' of Barker and Brooks's Stallone fan (1998: 67),
and similar to Mark Kermode's account of becoming a horror film fan:

> I ... sensed from the very beginning that there was something incom-
> prehensibly significant about the actions being played out on-screen,
> something which spoke to me in a language I didn't quite understand.
> ... I felt from the outset that beyond the gothic trappings these movies
> had something to say to *me* about *my* life. I just didn't have any idea
> what.
>
> (Kermode 1997: 57)

In each case, the fan's accounts can be described as strikingly *self-absent*.[4]
Exactly at the point where we might – in the terms of an academic imagined
subjectivity – expect a rational explanation of the self's devotion and fandom,
we are instead presented with a moment of self-suspension and radical hesitation. We are confronted by a moment where the subject *cannot* discursively and
'rationally' account for its own fan experience, and where no discourse seems to
be available which can meaningfully capture the fan's 'opening of oneself to
another's experience', or, indeed, to a mediated text.

The 'good' subjectivity imagined within fandom is, therefore, not a resolutely rational subjectivity. Rather, it is radically 'open'; 'bad' or denigrated
subjectivity, in this case, is a passionless, hyper-rational, intellectualising subjectivity. Academia is implicitly made other through a denigration of forms of
knowledge which are divorced from passion and commitment, as well as
through a distaste for the specialist jargon of the academic. In this way, the fan
can also present the non-fan academic as being 'defective, deficient, or deprived:
suffering from ... distortions of perception', although in this instance the
'defects' are constituted by academic language, while deprivation and distortion
arise through the rational detachment of the academic's imagined subjectivity.

Just as academia cannot be thought of as a singular entity, fandom also
cannot be depicted as a univocal site or as one 'thing'. Subjectivity is argued
over here too. Fans can – and do, as Cavicchi (1998) illustrates – draw on
discourses of subjectivity which have moved beyond academic specialisation,
such as versions of Freudian thought. Therefore within the 'common senses' of
fandom, academic debates (sociology versus psychoanalysis) find themselves
curiously paralleled (in Freudian versus social explanations of fandom, e.g. the
'fandom is just a way of making friends' approach).[5]

From this initial sketch it should, I hope, be clear that the clash between fandom and academia is less a matter of what fans and academics actually *do* as subjects, and more a matter of the imagined subjectivities – the different guiding discourses and ideals of subjectivity which are adopted by fans and academics – which are linked to cultural systems of value and community.[6]

While cultural studies theorists such as Jenkins (1992a) and Tulloch and Jenkins (1995) have started to extend the imagined subjectivity of the academy into the cultural spaces of fandom via discussions of fan knowledge and expertise, it is only recently that a self-reflexive recognition of this strategy has occurred (see Jenkins 1996). Green, Jenkins and Jenkins (1998) argue that:

> Fan criticism does differ from academic criticism in significant ways: the subjective and impassioned engagement with the material, the rejection of specialized technical language and theoretical authority, and the tendency to focus on personal rather than institutional explanations ... [but t]aking fans seriously means critiquing academic modes of thinking and writing *and recognizing our own blind spots, silences, and failures to rise above 'confusing struggles'*.
>
> (Green, Jenkins and Jenkins 1998: 13; my italics)

These authors 'urge a more open dialogue between academic writing and other modes of criticism' (*ibid.*: 14). It is the possibility of this hybridisation (see also Tulloch and Munro 1999) that I want to pick apart in the next section.

How might the imagined subjectivity of fandom be extended into the cultural spaces and institutions of academia, rather than vice versa? What 'silences and failures' can be admitted into the imagined subjectivity of academia, and how can the mutual marginalisation of fandom and academia's imagined subjectivities be challenged?

Textual poachers and academic tactics ...

What concerns me here is the extent to which specific academic agendas have tended to dictate the conceptual shape of fandom within cultural studies. This process, where certain aspects of fandom are emphasised and other aspects are downplayed, is evident in the polemical defence of fandom mounted by Jenkins (1992). Just as Barbara Herrnstein Smith's theory of good and bad imagined subjectivities would predict, Jenkins splits fans and non-fans into very different types of subjectivity, creating a *moral dualism*, by which I mean a view of the cultural world which constructs and focuses on two clear sets of 'good' and 'bad' phenomena.

Jenkins expresses an anti-psychological stance on many occasions, and his commitment to a social rather than psychological explanation of fandom is a major component in his programme. And yet, at the very moment that he examines the fan as a cultural rather than psychological entity, Jenkins explicitly describes the non-fan in psychological terms:

> [T]he fan still constitutes a scandalous category in contemporary culture, one alternately *the target of ridicule and anxiety, of dread and desire....* The stereotypical conception of the fan, while not without a limited factual basis, *amounts to a projection of anxieties* about the violation of dominant cultural hierarchies.
>
> (Jenkins 1992: 15 and 17; my italics)

That this is a type of moral dualism is clear from the fact that the 'good' fan is cleansed of aberrant psychology while the 'bad' non-fan responsible for reproducing negative stereotypes of fandom is given the psychological attributes of 'dread and desire'. Such moral dualisms are, in fact, common in everyday discourse, but have been repeated in influential forms of sociological theory such as the work of Anthony Giddens and Jurgen Habermas (see Barnes 2000: 32n10, 87). Whenever we discuss an unwanted or negative event as being caused externally (i.e. we are not responsible for it) while seeking to take credit for a desired or positive event (i.e. we are responsible this time) then we are drawing on an implied moral dualism where 'externalities are evil and inner states are good' (*ibid.*: 87). The links between seemingly complex social theories and everyday discourses should therefore not be discounted or overlooked, especially as these links suggest that theories are often powerful narratives in which 'good' is pitted against 'evil' without any kind of rigorous theoretical rationale behind this 'systematic partiality' or bias (*ibid.*).

It is not difficult to assess why Jenkins splits the fan and non-fan into nonpsychological and psychological components respectively. This manoeuvre allows him to do away with the fan-as-obsessed-weirdo stereotype. Indeed, this pathologising view of the fan is dismissed as the projection of non-fans who are outside the experience of fandom and so cannot comprehend its pleasures and logics. However, Jenkins complicates the moral dualism that he has constructed by conceding that negative stereotypes of the sad, geeky fan are 'not without a limited factual basis'. This is a puzzling admission, because although it disrupts the moral stance which Jenkins has asserted, he makes no attempt to address this contradiction or difficulty in his own argument. The force of a moral dualism is therefore left in place despite the possibility that a 'factual basis', however limited, may call for a more complex and less celebratory model of fandom than that offered by Jenkins.

Fandom, I would suggest, deserves to be represented more on its own terms (in which the limits of this 'limited factual basis' are explored and made explicit) rather than being used to form part of a moral dualism. The task which confronts cultural studies at this moment in time (and it is a task which is relevant given the historical state of the field, and not as a matter of theoretical dogma) is to theorise the media cult and its fandoms through a primary allegiance to the role of 'fan' and a secondary allegiance to 'academia'. These priorities have been tactically reversed in Henry Jenkins's work, as he has acknowledged in interview:

> [A]t the time at which I wrote the book [*Textual Poachers*], academic discourse on fandom was predominantly negative. The negative stereotypes were so strongly in place that I didn't feel comfortable attacking fans. ... Raising the negative in that space would have been ... destructive to the creation of a dialogue that makes us rethink what fandom is. ... *I chose to tell a story that accented the positive rather than the negative, but I think it was tactically necessary at that point and I stand behind that.*
>
> (Jenkins 1996: 274; my italics)

Jenkins's work therefore needs to be viewed not simply as an example of academic-fan hybridity, but also as a rhetorical tailoring of fandom in order to act upon particular academic institutional spaces and agendas. Fandom, for Jenkins, does not play the role of a cultural object which is to be understood and represented; instead, it is a community and a term which must be translated into the shape which will allow it to act on the academic community. Fandom is *used.*[7] However tactically, it is cut to the measure of the space which cultural studies' discourses allow it; a space which is 'utopian' insofar as it stresses – or stressed in 1992 – audience activity, and a space which in the early nineties also disqualified forms of psychoanalytic theory as well as marginalising the heritage of the Frankfurt School (see chapter 1). John Michael has recently offered a critique of Jenkins's work on fandom which reinforces my point:

> Jenkins is intent on proving that Trekkies [*sic*] are not a collection of alienated and maladjusted cultural dupes but a sort of peaceable kingdom operating without the impositions of intellectuals. Surprisingly, however, as he describes the Trekkie [*sic*] 'community', it begins to resemble a sort of idealized research seminar engaged in a fairly traditional form of literary study.
>
> (2000: 120)

The academic's institutional and political use of fandom, where fans are represented as miniaturised academics, must not be disavowed any longer. It has operated behind the scenes of the academic's engagement with fandom for long enough. Michael criticises Jenkins for projecting the values of the academic community onto fan culture: 'Describing fan culture in the idealized terms of a perfected university seminar – a place in which cultural products and the issues they entail are subjected to widespread and lively debate and a multitude of decodings – is to pay fan culture a very high compliment. *But we should never forget that this is a compliment within a value system that particularly or most*

10

reliably pertains to academic intellectuals who have internalized these ideals? (2000: 122; my italics). Again, as per Barbara Herrnstein Smith's linkage of value systems with types of imagined 'good' and 'defective' subjectivities, Michael reads Jenkins's rationalisation of the fan as a product of the 'academic intellectual' value system.

Couldry (1996: 326) notes that 'Jenkins ... is explicitly both an analyst and a fan (of the type he analyses). He is therefore required to recognise that the fan and the analyst have skills in common, even though earlier analytic practice would not have recognised the significance of fans' work.' Such a narrative places Jenkins, as an academic-fan, squarely within a 'progressive' framework. It assumes that Jenkins's hybrid identity allows a more adequate 'recognition' of a basic similarity between 'fans' and 'academics'. But it could equally well be argued that this is a constructed pseudo-similarity aimed at legitimating academic practice by projecting this onto a *rationalisation* of the fan.

I have so far evaluated the scholar-fan as a hybrid identity which has negative consequences for representations of fandom because fan culture comes to resemble the 'perfected university seminar' (Michael 2000: 122) at the very moment that it is allowed into academic discussion. This is a rather costly price to pay for fandom's appearance within the seminar room, since it tends to leave the imagined subjectivity of the rational academic firmly in place, simply extending this to cover the cultural practices and experiences of fans.

There are a number of alternative considerations of the position of the scholar-fan. It is to two further analyses of the academic-fan that I will now turn: Alexander Doty's broadly optimistic view of the scholar-fan, and Richard Burt's pessimistic alignment of the academic-fan with fantasies of cultural omnipotence.

'So what's a scholar-fan to do?'[8]

Both Doty's and Burt's accounts of the scholar-fan are concerned with the cultural practices which regulate academic work – what I have termed the 'imagined subjectivity' of academia. Doty poses the following question:

> Why shouldn't readers know something about a critic's personal and cultural background and training? Why is hiding or suppressing information like this still considered more professional and scholarly by most people? ... The result of a couple of decades of ignoring or hiding personal and cultural investments in our ... academic writing, however, has been to squeeze much of the life out of it in many senses.
>
> (Doty 2000: 11)

The scholar-fan must still conform to the regulative ideal of the rational academic subject, being careful not to present too much of their enthusiasm while tailoring their accounts of fan interest and investment to the norms of 'confessional' (but not overly confessional) academic writing. For Doty, the problem which remains is how to pull off the trick of merging fan and academic identities without 'coming off as embarrassingly egotistical or gee-whiz celebratory' and thereby 'losing the respect of the reader/student' (2000: 12). This fear of a loss of respect is crucial. Such respect, I would argue, is an effect of the cultural system of value at work here. Respect is aligned with, and given to, the imagined subjectivity of the 'good' and rational academic who is expected to be detached and rational, even about his/her own investments in popular culture. Respect is not to be given lightly to those subjects who are 'deficient' or 'defective' and who deviate from the regulatory norms of academic writing or performance.[9]

The regulatory power of imagined subjectivity, and its myriad effects of respect, status and threatened pathologisation, means that where academics do take on fan identities, they often do so with a high degree of anxiety:

> I'd always felt awkward about studying Madonna and her fans (as if I wasn't one of them). Sometimes I worried that my job as an academic cultural critic disqualified me from real fandom ... I also knew that being a Madonna fan in the context of the academy, especially as I was working on Madonna, would for some, disqualify me as a member of the real academy.
>
> (Schulze cited in Doty 2000: 12–13)

It might be easier to play safe, and to 'never let ... slip a too-revealing or embarrassing enthusiasm' (Branston 2000b: 116). But the more awkward and anxiety-inducing challenge to the norms of academic writing and representation is to try to separate out analytically the 'embarrassment' and the 'enthusiasm'. For this seemingly 'natural' conjunction marks the 'common sense' cultural categories which operate in academic practice. Why is respect forfeited and embarrassment generated by the scholar-fan? It is in these moments that we can see the mechanisms of a cultural (not merely subjective) system of value at work. It is a system of value which powerfully compels subjects to strive to work within the boundaries of 'good' imagined subjectivity, or face the consequences of pathologisation. Attempts at rewriting this situation as a clash between 'modernist' and 'postmodernist' sensibilities miss the point that regulatory frameworks of imagined subjectivity are no less present in accounts of postmodernism.[10] Cultural systems of value which have a bearing on how we think about and present ourselves as 'good' subjects cannot be reduced to points of 'modernist' or 'postmodernist' logic.[11]

In contrast to Doty's discussion, Richard Burt perceives the scholar-fan to be part of a very different project. Burt considers the scholar-fan not to be a challenge to normative academic subjectivity. Instead, the academic-fan represents a disguised continuation of academic norms: 'this kind of cultural politics isn't real politics; rather, it's only academic politics' (1998: 22). Burt focuses on the work of Constance Penley and Andrew Ross, suggesting that these academics' attempts to identify as fans goes so far but no further: '[t]he perceived lack of political consciousness in *Star Trek* slash fandom ... [means] critics such as Penley and ... Ross who want to deconstruct the distinction between the fan and the intellectual also want to keep that distinction at least faintly in place' (1998: 15). Rather than being a figure of embarrassment, Burt analyses the academic-fan as a figure of perverse plenitude. He suggests that the position of the academic-fan indicates an academic fantasy of 'having it all', and of being 'the one who can cross over, do it all' (*ibid.*). Burt takes issue with this fantasy, suggesting that the academic-fan can never finally draw fans and academics into full alignment. This is primarily so because academics insist on reserving, for themselves, the ability to determine political significance. As Burt rather scathingly puts it: 'all other critical [i.e. fan] perspectives can be read from the master perspective of the academic insofar as the academic is defined as the political' (1998: 17). It supposedly becomes the academic's privilege and prerogative to decide upon the political worthiness of fan cultures and practices.

Burt's critique therefore focuses on two issues. Firstly, his work participates in a pathologisation of academic-fans as 'deficient' subjects who are unable to accept the limits of their own cultural context. These poor deluded creatures are swept away by their desire to 'have it all'. Secondly, these academic-fans only pretend to be interested in surrendering their interpretive power and authority, since they retain the right to judge the fandoms they engage with and to find them politically lacking. Here, yet again, is a version of moral dualism, this time played out idiosyncratically across 'academic-fans' and 'fans' rather than, as is more usually the case, in terms of 'academics' versus 'fans'. In Burt's moral dualism, the 'bad' and 'deficient' academic-fan is contrasted with the 'good' fan. The academic-fan lacks *lack*, while the fan is viewed through the perspective of imagined fan subjectivity, being immersed and passionate rather than hyper-rationalised. Intriguingly, Burt sides with the imagined subjectivity of fandom, seeing fandom as self-absent while positioning 'legitimate' academic criticism as over-rational. His work ultimately and conservatively restores fandom and academia to their fixed places as absolutely Other:

> The range of what the fan hears or doesn't hear is the effect of not only the dispersal of sites of fan criticism but of the fan's multiple, excessive positioning, a positioning that can never be fully rationalized, explained or excused by being defined as the site of legitimate criticism.
>
> (1998: 20)

Despite the intricacies of many of his insights, then, Burt's moral dualism is one which values the fan's self-absence above the academic's attempts at rationalisation. Burt turns the fan's 'excessive positioning' into a romanticised virtue rather than a vice. This is a challenge to the imagined subjectivity of the academic's rational self, but it is a challenge which leaves the terms of the debate in place, simply reversing sides and trying to argue from within the fans' defence of their own community and system of value.

A more interesting moment of fan-academic undecidability is apparent in Will Brooker's admission of academic-fan status in *Batman Unmasked*. Brooker states that '[a]s a white, male, heterosexual and middle-class researcher, I love that man: I love Batman' (Brooker 2000: 8). Brooker's declaration of love for his subject matter is aimed at disrupting the norms of 'distanced' academic investigation by placing the researcher within the frame of his own research. But such a naked declaration, which lacks even the academic propriety of the question posed to Alexander Doty by the co-editors of *Hop on Pop* (namely, 'what's your investment?'; see Doty 2000: 13) is complicated by Brooker's discussion of his childhood Batman stories. He describes his first ever Batman story as a case of 'working "in the gaps" as Michel de Certeau would put it' (Brooker 2000: 5).

This complex layering of self-accounts strains 'common sense' notions of fan and academic imagined subjectivities. A public declaration of love is presented in the 'here and now' of Brooker's academic writing, while his childhood (and very much non-academic) Batman story is analysed within an academic framework. The expected co-ordinates of a 'fan' versus 'academic' moral dualism are hence confused. The child-fan becomes the site for theoretical projection, while the projecting academic self seeks refuge in a statement of love rather than in an analysis of 'affect'.[12] Yes, the academic's specialised language intrudes rather comically on the child's love of comics. And yet, the academic self refuses to fall back on a specialised language, using 'love' as a common sense marker of 'authenticity' which is in line with the fan's 'self-absent' imagined subjectivity.

A further example of an interesting but flawed attempt to destabilise 'writing as a fan' versus 'writing as an academic' is I.Q. Hunter's contribution to *Unruly Pleasures: The Cult Film and its Critics*. Hunter's piece deals with his fandom of the film *Showgirls*, and is provocative in its attempts to undermine academic interpretation in favour of Hunter's private or unarticulated investment in the film: 'why I like the film has little bearing on whether I get the meaning of it right *in public*, although as an academic I am obliged (i.e. paid) to pretend that this matters very much indeed' (2000: 195). The public circulation of meaning and interpretation is relatively unimportant to fandom; this is Hunter's heretical suggestion. He goes on to use a pragmatic approach to interpretation derived from the work of philosopher Richard Rorty. Rorty has asked whether 'good' interpretations should be persuasive or somehow 'correct', concluding that a 'good' interpretation should simply be one which makes a difference to the reader concerned. This approach 'discards for good the line between academic interpretation and the unruly pleasures of fan activity. Interpretation under this description is a series of quirky, unpredictable, self-pleasuring experiments in disguised autobiography' (Hunter 2000: 201). Like many an academic before him, then, Hunter plays with abolishing the difference between fan and academic. He also applies certain theories to his own fandom and then (mock) bemoans the result: '[r]ather than being an engaged, active and freethinking cultist, I am cruelly redescribed as a case study ... Exhibit One: the postmodern white male academic' (*ibid*.: 197). The outcome of this academic play with fandom, however, is rather predictable. When the chips are down, Hunter backs off from Rorty's work, dismissing this with the ultimate academic insult that it is a 'non-theory' (*ibid*.: 201).

In his conclusion to *Watching Television Audiences*, John Tulloch examines three different studies of fandom:

> [O]nly two of the three researchers would self-describe as a fan of cult media [Henry Jenkins and Matt Hills]. The third saw the cult of *90210* as something that others (mainly the young women she taught ...) were into [E.G. McKinley]. What difference did this make, theoretically and methodologically, to these research projects and their 'audience' findings? What can we learn about cultural and media studies from a study of academic fans (and non-fans) writing about other fans?
>
> (2000: 202)

My own answer to this question is fourfold. Studying academic-fans studying fans (or themselves as fans!) can, all too often, reveal the ways in which an academic imagined subjectivity triumphs over a fan imagined subjectivity. First, academic accounts consistently produce a version of fandom which seems indistinguishable from the interpretive, cognitive and rational powers of the 'good' academic (Jenkins 1992; McLaughlin 1996). Second, in a petulant revolt aimed at building 'symbolic capital' (i.e. securing a reputation for one's self), academic accounts throw their lot -in with the imagined subjectivity of fandom and seek to emphasise the limits of rationality, thereby romanticising the fan's 'affect', 'love', or 'excessive positioning' (Burt 1998; see also Hills 1999a for an example of this). Or, third, academic accounts toy with the idea of magically abolishing the difference between 'fan' and 'academic' knowledges before finally retreating to the superiority of an academic position (Hunter 2000; Hartley 1996). And finally, recent academic accounts have started, deliberately and purposefully, to confuse fan and academic subjectivities (e.g. Doty 2000; Brooker 2000; Green, Jenkins and Jenkins 1998).

But all these accounts – my own previous PhD work included – show a certain disregard for fandom. All are focused on the 'scandalous' (by now, in fact, rather conventional) figure of the academic-fan. All pick away at the consequences for academics who declare their own fandoms, asking if this is a move which challenges academic norms or one which produces a new brand of academic authority.[13] But by focusing so intently on the academic-fan, academic accounts show a rather dismaying short-sightedness. What they consistently neglect is the possibility that fan and academic identities can be hybridised or brought together not simply in the academy but also outside of it, in the figure of the fan-scholar.

Street smarts … and the great British amateur: the fan-scholar

The first two words of my title here are borrowed from an intriguing book by Thomas McLaughlin – *Street Smarts and Critical Theory: Listening to the Vernacular*. McLaughlin argues that although academic theories and the 'ordinary language' of fans possess different amounts of cultural prestige, this difference in status is really the only distinction between the two (1996: 5, 10). Of course, the notion of 'ordinary language' is loaded from the outset. Do we ever think of our everyday speech and writing as some homogeneous thing called 'ordinary language', against which heroically transcendent 'theory' can be positioned? 'Ordinary language' constructs a moral dualism between forms of knowledge so that the 'ordinary expertise' of fans can never be the same as the 'theoretical expertise' of academics. This split is also produced in Branston (2000a). In Branston's case, an initial sense of theory as 'ordinary' and as culturally omnipresent gives way at almost exactly the same time as the figure of the fan is introduced: 'our students, as audiences, fans, are sometimes the object of studies which celebrate their powers to remake and resist almost any media resource … But we still need to equip students with some sense of what is specific and special to the activity of theorising' (2000a: 25). Strangely, then, theory is ordinary only until the student-fan speaks up, and then this imagined other needs to be quickly set back on the straight-and-narrow of 'specialised' theory.

McLaughlin is caught up in the same problem: he wants to value theory outside the academy but isn't prepared to surrender the privileges and power of academic authority. His own academic language therefore works against his conscious aim of focusing on and valuing fan theory. This is an inevitable self-contradiction: McLaughlin is still writing as an academic even while seeking to examine non-academic 'theories'. Nevertheless his work possesses a number of strengths which merit discussion.

First, while McLaughlin accepts that there are differences in cultural prestige between academic and 'ordinary' theories, he does not build a whole series of distinctions on top of this basic difference. For example, he refutes the idea that academic theory is somehow 'general' and able to escape the contexts of its production. This means that both academic and fan theories are the product of local norms and interpretive disputes: 'Any intense fan experience – whether it's being an opera aficionado or a Deadhead – provides opportunities for vernacular theory. Local information and local interpretative practices and disputes make theory possible' (1996: 24). And 'the same must be said about critical theory as an academic discipline: it also speaks from and is implicated in a specific social discipline, one that enforces rules of analysis, argumentation, and articulation' (*ibid.*: 10). This means that, for McLaughlin – regardless of matters of cultural prestige – *all* theories are 'vernacular' or ordinary/localised. It also means that 'critical theory' cannot claim superiority over fans' own understandings of the industries and cultural worlds in which they are implicated.

This levelling of the cultural playing field carries a number of conditions and provisos. Presumably not all fans are the 'elite fans' that 'must ... at times come to the defense of their obsessions, and so have to articulate their values, their sense of why *Star Trek* or ... splatter movies are important enough for obsessive attention' (1996: 24). These fans, who provide satisfying explanations of their fandom which may then be taken up by their respective fan cultures, are seemingly 'elite' because they articulate communal values which would otherwise remain implicit. They are also the 'elite' because they possess 'so much information on their chosen topic' (1996: 24). Since not all fans will be the 'elite', it could be argued that McLaughlin solves the problem of aligning fans and academics by focusing on the most 'intellectual' fraction of fandom, examining those fans who seek to explain their fan culture to and for itself, and who also criticise and analyse the media industry. These elite fans are so very knowledgeable, and so committed to accumulating further fan knowledge, that for McLaughlin '[e]lite fans become in effect scholars of their idols ... Because of this fanatical knowledge, elite fans can come to theoretical questions in ways similar to those of academic cultural critics ... Vernacular cultural theory lacks the systematics of academic theory: it occurs in flashes, in local circumstances, rather than in sustained analysis' (1996: 58–9).

Elite fans are scholars,[14] yes, but they are still *not quite* academic scholars: they are not systematic or sustained enough, being only capable of flashes of theory. Again, the choice of words here comes close to damning fandom with faint praise. McLaughlin is clearly operating within an academic imagined subjectivity. 'System' and 'rigour' are therefore valued terms, while the occasional 'flash' is definitely less impressive. From within the imagined subjectivity of fandom these terms would be valued and constructed very differently: the academic would be 'long-winded' or 'boring', whilst fan knowledge would be 'to-the-point' rather than being represented as a 'localised flash'. Or as Gill Branston has put it: 'popular cultures ... themselves imply that "intellectualising" is unnecessary, or that "theories" simply serve a callow kind of "political correctness" – even while quantities of style journalism, cultural comment and public relations proliferate in precisely those areas broached by the questions posed in theories' (2000a: 18).

Although McLaughlin concludes that the 'culture of everyday life is a critical culture, and the [fan]zines get that culture into print' (1996: 69), his 'elite fans' are 'scholars' who do not use the same language as academics. But the fan-scholars I want to consider briefly are fans who do exactly that:

> Thomas Noonan was the first New Fanboy. ... He was one of the first fans to take litcrit techniques and terminology, ally them to a sense of theatre and throw them at the wall of conventional fandom. The reaction to his work at the time was explosive. He was called 'pretentious' a lot, which is still a word used quite randomly by those fans for whom the joy of *Doctor Who* is that they don't have to think about it. These days it seems to mean 'anything I don't immediately understand'.
>
> (Cornell 1997: 127)

This account comes from Paul Cornell's history of *Doctor Who* fandom. Although Cornell's history has been challenged within *Who* fan culture, it is useful because it draws attention to the overlap of fan and academic analyses. Fans do not just write 'fan fic' (fan fiction), they also produce their own critical accounts of the programme's texts. And they do so using the theoretical approaches of academic media studies and literary criticism: 'Recently, a number of academics have started to examine programmes like *Who* in books like *The Unfolding Text* and ... *Textual Poachers*. But it takes critics from inside, who know the ropes, to do it really well' (Cornell 1997: 12).

These 'insider critics' are usually ex-media studies or ex-Eng Lit students. Cornell lists fan-scholars such as Tat Wood, Nick Pegg, Dave Hughes, Alec Charles and Martin Wiggins. The blurring of fan and scholarly identities occurs in the very language that Cornell uses: 'the practice [of fan crit] reached its zenith with *Spectrox*, Tat Wood's irregular book-length dissertation in the form of a fanzine' (Cornell 1997). Bizarrely, the fanzine-as-dissertation has been entirely ignored in academic work on fandom. Zines have been examined as sources of 'critical' fan knowledge (McLaughlin 1996; Duncombe 1997; Niedzviecki 2000), but not as a site where academic knowledge may also circulate outside the academy.[15]

Some fan-scholars have in fact actually moved into professional academic careers. For example, Tim Robins was the first and founding editor of what later became the *In-Vision* fanzine series (a critical history of *Doctor Who* carried out story-by-story). Robins went on to become a media and cultural studies lecturer at Glamorgan University. The fanzine that Robins was involved in setting up, *Doctor Who – An Adventure in Space and Time*, is referred to on page 2 of *The Unfolding Text*:

> [T]he programme's own scholars ... cherishingly and with painstaking accuracy have revealed and debated it in all its minutiae during the last few years. ... For absolute archivist competence in the intensive history of *Doctor Who*, this work [*Doctor Who – An Adventure in Space and Time*] is second to none.
>
> (Tulloch and Alvarado 1983: 2)

But even while accepting that fans are scholars, Tulloch and Alvarado mark a distinction between their *extensive* academic work and the fans' *intensive* programme research:

> [T]he intensive approach investigates *Doctor Who* as a found object, with its own 'essence' which is the source of analysis [while] the extensive approach [i.e. the 'proper' academic approach] examines the programme as a site of intersection, a nexus, where codes ... meet. Hence the object of analysis ... is not cherished as a personal posses-

sion, domesticated, loved for the comforting store of intimate secrets it
reveals to the aficionado.

(*ibid.*)

And yet, looking back at some of the analyses presented in *An Adventure in
Space and Time*, as well as browsing through Paul Cornell's (1997) edited
collection of fanzine writings, *Licence Denied*, it is difficult not to view some fan-
scholarly work as being clearly 'extensive' rather than 'intensive'. However,
rather than revaluing the work of fan-scholars, what I want to suggest is that the
circulation of 'litcrit' and media studies terms outside the academy threatens the
very opposition of intensive/extensive or fan/academic knowledges. And even if
the collapse of this opposition is only relevant for certain, well-educated sections
of a fan culture,[16] it remains a significant and under-researched fact that fan-
scholars have directly drawn on academic knowledge in order to express their
love for a text. So, not all fans have viewed academic analysis as an alternative to
'cherishing' the text as a 'personal possession'. As Branston has observed: 'the
boundaries between the academy and this ... "outside" [are] far from water-
tight' (2000a: 25), even if academic imagined subjectivity continues to draw
lines between its own 'good' community and the 'bad' fan-outsider as Other.

One possible objection to my argument so far would be the following: if
academics and fans imagine their subjectivities in opposition to one another (the
'rational' academic versus the 'self-absent' fan) then how can it be the case that
scholar-fans and fan-scholars are all busily working away on their favoured objects
of fandom? Such an objection would allege that I have overstated my case, and
that fandom and academia are not as mutually antagonistic as I have suggested.
However, the considerations of writers as diverse as Branston (2000a), Brunsdon
(2000), Burt (1998), Cornell (1997), Frith (1990 and 1992), Hartley (1996)
and Michael (2000) all suggest that fans are wary of academics, and that
academics cannot simply assume the mantle of 'fan'. Discussing such tensions,
Pamela Church Gibson has recently observed that some

of the fans of these films [the *Alien* franchise] may actually be antago-
nized by the activities of academics. The best-selling British film
magazine *Empire* is aware of 'fandom' in a way that official scholarship
is not ... [and] it regards some academic work as risible.... 'The *Alien*
franchise has been at the centre of more egghead pontificating than
any other movies in cinematic history. And all of it is absolute arse ...'.

(Church Gibson 2001: 43–4)

Leaving aside such incisive commentary, it becomes apparent – given
fan–academic tensions – that the scholar-fan and the fan-scholar are necessarily
liminal in their identities (that is, they exist between and transgress the regulative norms of academic and fan imagined subjectivities). This 'between-ness' is

what underpins the defensiveness and anxiety of both groups, since both are marginalised within their respective primary communities. Equally, neither fan-scholars nor scholar-fans can 'properly' belong to the other, secondary community unless they temporarily adopt its institutional norms of writing and practice. For example, I am able to work as an academic, despite (or rather, because of) having been a fan of cult TV and science fiction all my life only because I present an identity which conforms to institutional expectations. I give lectures which refer to academic books (most of the time), I offer arguments for and against theoretical positions, I use a specific academic language, and I possess the qualifications which are required of me professionally. My cultural practice, then, is shaped and delimited by institutional constraints, and my fandom can only emerge in the lecture theatre or seminar room if it is appropriately channelled through these norms of academic practice: 'Academics ... [operate] ... within particular institutional and historical contexts which in fact strongly form ... the kinds of theories and publications' that they are able to produce (Branston 2000a: 20).

Any and all attempts at hybridising and combining 'fan' and 'academic' iden-tities/subjectivities must therefore remain sensitive to those institutional contexts which disqualify certain ways of speaking and certain ways of presenting the self.[17] Of course, the same problems would work in reverse if I tried to speak as an academic at a fan convention; in that venue, with its own rules of conduct, the use of academic language and academic self-presentation would seem equally out of place and inappropriate. It has recently been suggested (for example, by Peter Hutchings at the 'Defining Cult Movies' conference held at Nottingham University in November 2000) that differences between fans and academics have typically been overstated. But while *differential institutional constraints* act on fan and academic cultural practices (and I can see no way that these institutional differences can be dissolved for as long as the university remains a residual site of cultural authority) then fans and academics will remain opposed. Indeed, even academics who appear keen to value the expertise of 'popular readerships' are also keen to preserve their own authority, kept safely above and beyond the reach of fans.[18] I concur with Pamela Church Gibson when she writes that it 'is time ... to acknowledge the activities of fans – and possibly to learn' (2001: 50). But the fan/academic binary and its related moral dualisms may not be so easy to defuse or refuse. And, of course, even the notion of 'learning' from fans remains framed by the academic's 'imagined subjectivity' ...

Summary

Academics and fans both value their own institutionally-supported ways of reading and writing above those practices which characterise the other group. This creates a type of mutual marginalisation.

Moral dualisms are created and sustained by systems of cultural value which defend communities against others. These moral dualisms are made to appear natural by their reliance on imagined subjectivities, so that 'we' are 'good' while 'they' are 'bad'. Academics draw on an us/them distinction which maps onto the 'common sense' separation of rational/immersed, while fans defend their activities by drawing on a 'common sense' distinction between immediacy/over-rationalisation. The important fact here is that both fans and academics defend and seek to value their activities by using common sense (i.e. ideologically loaded and pre-theoretical) categories:

- Imagined subjectivities and their simplistic moral dualisms possess cultural power. This means that scholar-fans are typically looked down on as not being 'proper' academics, while fan-scholars are typically viewed within fandom as 'pretentious' or not 'real' fans.
- Imagined subjectivities are imagined because they do not correspond with the actual, embodied subjectivities of either fans or academics. *Academics are not resolutely rational, nor are fans resolutely immersed.* Academic knowledge is not always meaningfully 'testable', nor is fan knowledge always 'informal' or 'experiential'.
- Academic work has focused on scholar-fans rather than fan-scholars, possibly because the academic-fan allows academic authority to be reconstructed and preserved in the face of a challenge from fan knowledge. The fan-scholar, on the other hand, exacerbates this challenge, suggesting that academic language and expertise cannot be kept safely 'in' the academy. Although academics – especially those in cultural studies – often profess an interest in 'organic intellectuals', they seem remarkably happy to ignore the prime candidates for this role within fandom.

The rest of this book ...

Part I: Approaching fan cultures

This examines the various theories that academic studies of fandom have employed. Along the way, it suggests problems and limits to these theories, and begins to build up a new model for academic work on fandom.

Having already considered some of the difficulties involved in writing academically about fans, and the problems of claiming both 'fan' and 'academic' status, I will move on to examine the issue of consumption in the next chapter. There I will suggest that the moral dualism I have started to explore in this opening section is not the only opposition which structures fan and academic identities. For, as well as constructing themselves against 'bad' academics, fans also construct themselves against 'bad' (mindless or undiscriminating) consumers. By returning to the work of the Frankfurt School theorists, in particular the much-maligned work of Theodor Adorno, I will reopen the topic of the fan-as-consumer.

This will then lead into a discussion in chapter 2 of sociological theories of fan culture which draw on the work of Pierre Bourdieu. Bourdieu's approach to the distinctions of consumption has proved to be highly influential in studies of fandom, and I will examine Jeffrey Sconce's work on fans of 'trash' cinema as an exemplar of this approach.

Chapter 3 returns to the work of Henry Jenkins, comparing this with Camille Bacon-Smith's more traditionally 'ethnographic' approach to *Star Trek* fan culture. My key question here will be whether involved/traditional fan ethnographies are able to deliver the types of understanding that they promise. I will suggest that more explicitly auto-ethnographic work is called for, rather than academics' fan experiences being implied in their work. To attempt to combat these 'containments' of fandom in academic writing, I will argue that the cultural identities of lecturers and students who are fans need to be examined more carefully so that 'theory' and 'experience' can be brought closer together.

Chapter 4 closes the first part of the book by addressing an approach to fan culture which stands accused of pathologising fans: psychoanalysis. I will suggest in this chapter that certain psychoanalytic approaches can, in fact, be usefully applied to fandom, provided that these approaches are respectful of fans' everyday creativities and 'little madnesses'. Given that 'love' and 'affect' have been used to characterise fans' attachments to their texts, and given hegemonic-stereotypical accusations of fan 'irrationality' or 'arationality', it seems impossible to take fandom seriously without taking fan psychology seriously.

Part II: Theorising cult media

This part of the book focuses on the practices which are associated with 'cult fandom'. Chapter 5 examines the thorny topic of fan religiosity – something which is especially pressing given that the term 'cult' is embraced by many fans. This term provides a category which seems to make sense of fans' diverse objects of fandom. And yet, while the term 'cult' has become increasingly significant to fans, as well as within consumer culture, its links with religious discourses have been ignored by academics. 'Cult' media has largely been treated as an 'embarrassment' to the 'good' rationality of the academic subject, or as a term cleansed of any religious connotations.

Chapter 6 will explore the extremely wide range of texts and icons which have had 'cult' status attributed to them. It will pose the following questions: what, if anything, links the cult text and the cult icon? And can 'cult' be thought of as a genre?

The key idea running across all the chapters in Part II is that we cannot consider the cult fan simply to be a 'reader' of texts or icons. An important part of being a cult fan, I want to argue, involves extending the reader–text, or reader–icon, relationship into other areas of fan experience (cf. Lancaster 2001).

To emphasise that reading-based metaphors are inadequate, I will focus on a series of case studies in chapters 7 and 8, as well as in the concluding chapter.

Chapter 7 will consider how cult fandom moves beyond the text to take in practices of fan tourism and cult geography (visiting locations and sites linked to the fan's favoured text or icon), and will feature a case study of *X-Files* fans, or 'X-Philes' as they are known. Contrary to the more usual academic discussions of *The X-Files*, conspiracy theory and postmodernism, this chapter will examine the significance that Vancouver played in establishing the programme as a cult.

Chapter 8 will focus on the fan-impersonator, considering how the fan's body can be used as a site for the display of their devotion to texts and icons. I will examine Elvis impersonators as a case study here, focusing on the work done by Lynn Spigel and Lynne Joyrich (who both attended the same Elvis Presley International Impersonators Association annual event and then published very different academic articles discussing it).

The concluding chapter will consider how new media technology has affected cult media and fan cultures, unpicking some of the celebratory rhetoric which has accompanied the migration and movement of fan culture on to the web.

Part I

APPROACHING FAN CULTURES

1

FAN CULTURES BETWEEN CONSUMERISM AND 'RESISTANCE'

It is not just the imagined subjectivities of the 'fan' and the 'academic' which clash and imply different moral dualisms, i.e. different versions of 'us' (good) and 'them' (bad). The imagined subjectivity of the 'consumer' is also hugely important to fans as they strive to mark out the distinctiveness of fan knowledges and fan activities. This chapter will therefore examine how 'good' fan identities are constructed against a further imagined Other: the 'bad' consumer. My aim is to explore how cultural identities are performed not simply through a singular binary opposition such as fan/academic, but rather through a raft of overlapping and interlocking versions of 'us' and 'them'. This makes locating cultural 'power' or cultural 'resistance' in any one group (fans/producers/academics) extremely difficult.

First, though, I want to examine the role that theories of consumption and 'the consumer' have played in accounts of fandom, and in fans' own practices. In the second section of the chapter I will go on to argue that the work of Theodor Adorno has been greatly simplified in cultural studies' accounts which have sought to value and celebrate the activities of fans.[1] However, it is not my intention to return to a notion of the fan as 'cultural dupe'. Instead, I aim to place fan cultures squarely within the processes and mechanisms of consumer culture, given that fans are always already consumers. The third section of the chapter then presents a case study in which I examine what happens to notions of the 'fan-consumer' and the 'fan-producer' when fan cultures are themselves directly targeted as a niche market. Finally, I examine recent work on *Babylon 5* fandom which has been carried out by Kurt Lancaster, work which draws on performance studies rather than cultural studies.

The consumer as other

[F]ans are not true cultists unless they pose their fandom as a resistant activity, one that keeps them one step ahead of those forces which would try to market their resistant taste back to them.

(Taylor 1999: 161)

What has given rise to the notion of the 'resistive' fan or cultist? I will not argue that this is entirely a fiction of cultural studies researchers seeking to romanticise active audiences; specific attributes of cult TV fandom would seem to support the 'resistive' label. The dedicated commitments of cult TV fans typically continue long beyond the cancellation of their favoured programmes. This tension between the fans' enduring devotion and the rapid turnover in TV productions is one way in which the cult TV fan can be said to act against the expectations of the TV industry. The fan's emotional investment also results in (and is compounded through) an attention to detail and programme continuity which is often at odds with the producers' need to tell new stories over the duration of a TV series. Fans expect adherence to established tenets, characterisations, and narrative 'back-stories', which production teams thus revise at their peril, disrupting the trust which is placed in the continuity of a detailed narrative world by these 'textual conservationist' fans.

It is primarily these qualities – as well as an expressed hostility within cult fandoms towards commercialisation and commodification – which have led to the theorisation of cult TV fandom (and other related media fandoms) as somehow anti-consumerist.[2] This rather one-sided view of fandom (see Cavicchi 1998, especially chapter 3) has tended to minimise the extent to which fandom is related to wider shifts within consumer culture, such as the increase in consumption-based social and communal identities. It has also reduced the significance of consumption and commodification within fan cultures, for example in the potentially curious co-existence within fan cultures of both *anti-commercial ideologies and commodity-completist practices*.[3]

As part of this one-sided academic view of fandom, in which fan identities are typically viewed against consumer identities, the place of the specialist retail outlet within fan culture has not been examined. This prior neglect is now receiving some belated correction, for example in the work of Kurt Lancaster (1996). However, it is worth noting that even in his fascinating discussion of the New York branch of Forbidden Planet, Lancaster continues to betray an anxiety over the commodity-status of its contents, moving all too rapidly from the ('bad') fan-commodity to the ('good') fan-community:

> Forbidden Planet is a 'clearinghouse' for science fiction commodities that allow people to enter worlds of fantasy ... the objects purchased in this store become a means for branching out into other worlds (by reading and fantasising), the participants of which come together in a setting at this bookstore, online, or at a convention.
>
> (Lancaster 1996: 34–5)

As well as Lancaster's work on the place of merchandise within fandom, Taylor and Willis (1999: 192) include a photograph of the Stoke-on-Trent store 'Fantasy World' in their account of fan culture as a type of 'minority audience'. They observe that 'within fan cultures there are certain modes of behaviour that are acceptable ... activities that are not acceptable are more clearly linked with ... dominant capitalist society' (*ibid.*). However, this commentary is placed directly below a caption which reads 'fan groups often consume in specialist shops such as this one' (*ibid.*). On the one hand, we are presented with a view of fans as (specialist) consumers, whose fandom is expressed through keeping up with new releases of books, comics and videos. On the other hand, we are told that fans whose practices are 'clearly linked with' dominant capitalist society (e.g. they may be trying to sell videos recorded off-air) are likely to be censured within the fan culture concerned. This is not simply a theoretical contradiction; it is an inescapable contradiction which fans live out. While simultaneously 'resisting' norms of capitalist society and its rapid turnover of novel commodities, fans are also implicated in these very economic and cultural processes. Fans are, in one sense, 'ideal consumers' (Cavicchi 1998: 62) since their consumption habits can be very highly predicted by the culture industry, and are likely to remain stable. But fans also express anti-commercial beliefs (or 'ideologies', we might say, since these beliefs are not entirely in alignment with the cultural situation in which fans find themselves).

Can this contradiction be resolved by a 'better' theory of fan activity? My argument in the next section of this chapter will suggest not: the best we can hope for is a theoretical approach to fandom which can *tolerate* contradiction without seeking to close it down prematurely. Nor am I suggesting that fans are somehow 'deluded' in their anti-commercial beliefs. This would also collapse the fans' cultural contradiction into a smooth instance of logical good sense by judging the 'fan-as-consumer' position to be true and judging the 'fan-as-anti-commercial' position as false. Conventional logic, seeking to construct a sustainable opposition between the 'fan' and the 'consumer', falsifies the fan's experience by positioning fan and consumer as separable cultural identities. This logic occurs in a number of theoretical models of fandom, particularly those offered up by Abercrombie and Longhurst (1998) and Jenkins (1992).

Abercrombie and Longhurst present a 'continuum' of audience experiences and identities, ranging from the 'consumer' at one end, to the 'petty producer' at the other end of the scale, and taking in the 'fan', the 'enthusiast' and the 'cultist' along the way (see 1998: 141). Abercrombie and Longhurst's model reproduces exactly the type of moral dualism which places 'good' fandom in opposition to the 'bad' consumer. They view 'the consumer' as somebody who has the least amount of each type of skill that they define and study.[4] This view of the consumer is an essentially negative one: consumers lack the developed forms of expertise and knowledge that fans, enthusiasts and cultists all possess in ever-increasing and ever-more-specialised forms. Consumers are at the bottom of the pile. Petty producers, for whom 'the previous enthusiasm becomes a full-time occupation' (1998: 140), are involved in market-organised relations and are able to use their finely-honed skills to produce material professionally which can then be marketed back to their own fan culture.

It might seem odd to suggest that Jenkins's work on fandom participates in a moral dualism of 'good' fandom versus 'bad' consumption, especially since Jenkins has addressed television fan culture through what he concedes is a 'counter-intuitive' lens, beginning from the position that '[m]edia fans are consumers who also produce, readers who also write, spectators who also participate' (1992b: 208). This reads like a definite end to any fan–consumption opposition. However, Jenkins's position is complicated by the fact that he revalues the fans' intense consumption by allying this with the cultural values of production: they are 'consumers who also produce'. But what of fans who may not be producers, or who may not be interested in writing their own fan fiction or filk songs? Surely we cannot assume that all fans are busily producing away? The attempt to extend 'production' to all fans culminates in John Fiske's categories of 'semiotic' and 'enunciative' productivity (1992: 37–9) in which reading a text and talking about it become cases of 'productivity'. This raises the suspicion that the term is being pushed to do too much work, since, short of not watching a programme at all, there appears to be no way of not being 'productive' in relation to it (and presumably even the decision not to view would retain an aspect of productivity). What this blanket extension of 'productivity' does away with semantically is the tainted and devalued term of 'consumption'.[5] But by switching one term for the other, or revaluing fan activities by stressing that fans are consumers who are also (unofficial) producers, the basic valuation of 'production' and the basic devaluation of 'consumption' continue to be accepted. Fandom is salvaged for academic study by removing the taint of consumption and consumerism.

This type of academic work seemingly colludes with 'half' of the fan experience (anti-commercial ideology) by writing out or marginalising the other, contradictory 'half' (that of the commodity-completist). The contradictoriness of fandom within consumer culture has been examined by a number of writers (Cavicchi 1998; Barker and Brooks 1998; Brooker 1999a, 1999b). But rigid assumptions that fandom and production are valuable, whereas consumption is somehow secondary and lacks value, still need to be contested rather than being used to underpin academic interventions in this area of study.[6] For as Cavicchi has rightly noted, choosing to discuss fandom either as 'dependence on, or resistance to, or negotiation with ... business' amounts 'as in the parable of the blind men and the elephant [to] mistaking the part for the whole, and would [seem to] have more to do with the interpreter's interests than with fan interests' (1998: 63). Janet Staiger has similarly cautioned against cultural theorists' tendency to split fandom into 'good' and 'bad' components: 'While most studies of fans emphasize the positive features of exchange and empowerment ... I would point out that scholars may need to shift their presumptions even here – although not back to the days when fans were considered pathological spectators ... Fandom ... cannot be easily bifurcated into good and bad' (Staiger 2000: 54).

Toying with the work of Theodor Adorno ...

The work of Theodor Adorno is regularly criticised and dispensed with in academic and academic-fan accounts of fan culture. It is Adorno's perspective on 'overconsumption' which is set up and knocked down by Henry Jenkins as the lead-in to his own account of 'how texts become real' for their fans (Jenkins 1992: 51). Similarly, it is the work of Adorno which is despatched early on in the co-authored work of Tulloch and Jenkins: 'most of the textual accounts of popular science fiction are embedded in the tradition of the Frankfurt School (Adorno, Horkheimer, Marcuse, Habermas, etc.), with their pessimistic stress on popular culture's tendency to communicate the "common sense" of social order rather than "fantasies" of social change' (Tulloch in Tulloch and Jenkins 1995a: 25).

Adorno and the Frankfurt School theorists are recurrently depicted as elitists, as pessimists, and as 'unsophisticated' thinkers intent on demonising mass culture and denying any power or agency to its audiences: 'Today many people tend to believe that other, more sophisticated approaches to the issue have superseded the Frankfurt School's conception of mass culture as a monstrous and monolithic ideological machine' (Modleski 1986: 156). Open any contemporary textbook and you are likely to be confronted with a statement on the Frankfurt School's arrogance and their view of the 'passive' mass audience. This received wisdom is extremely useful for media studies scholars. It allows researchers to preserve the fiction of 'linear progress', i.e. that we definitely now know better than the misguided theorists of the past. However, this version of moral dualism (past views of the passive audience = bad; current views of the active audience = good) resembles an academic version of 'popular memory'.[8] Acting as a conservative form of 'popular memory', that is, defending the status quo of current theorists' interpretive authority, dismissals of the Frankfurt School carve the history of media studies into a highly reductive 'then' and 'now': 'the Frankfurt School and its project are what many in cultural studies feel they must resist in order to consolidate their project' (Michael 2000: 112).

I am not convinced that the simplistic version of Adorno's work which retains wide currency in media studies is particularly useful, beyond its function of legitimating current and 'superior' thought.[9] The selective reading of Adorno means that many helpful links which could be made between Adorno's approach to consumption and the position of the fan as a consumer have been blocked off.

As a starting point to my use of Adorno's work, I will briefly consider how Henry Jenkins (1992a) links Adorno to the 'toymaker' in Margery Williams Bianco's fable *The Velveteen Rabbit*. Jenkins uses the tale of the Velveteen Rabbit as an example of how fans' love for a text can make that text significant in their lives:

Seen from the perspective of the toymaker, who has an interest in preserving the stuffed animal as it was made, the Velveteen Rabbit's loose joints and missing eyes represent vandalism ... yet for the boy, they are traces of fondly remembered experiences, evidence of his having held the toy too close and pet it too often, in short, marks of its loving use.

(Jenkins 1992a: 51)

In *The Velveteen Rabbit*, then, the moral battle is one of the toymaker's authority versus the child's love for his toy rabbit. And in Jenkins's commentary, which takes off from his retelling of the Velveteen Rabbit's tale, it is Adorno's work which stands as the theoretical version of the 'toymaker':

Adorno ... takes the toymaker's perspective when he describes how prized cultural texts are 'disintegrated' through overconsumption as they are transformed from sacred artefacts into 'cultural goods' ... Adorno suggests that musical texts become mere background, lose their fascination and coherence, when they are played too often or in inappropriate contexts, while popular texts are made simply to disintegrate upon first use and therefore have little intrinsic worth. What Adorno's account of repeated consumption misses is the degree to which songs, like other texts, assume increased significance as they are fragmented and reworked to accommodate the particular interests of the individual listener.

(Jenkins 1992a: 51)

The heartless 'toymaker' Adorno is hence positioned as the villain of the piece. Jenkins's explicit link between tale and theory makes plain the narrative and moral structure of his account. And yet, although Jenkins's summary of a specific article by Adorno is perfectly fair, Jenkins rather curiously neglects – given his theme – to cite an entry from Adorno's *Minima Moralia* which is entitled simply 'Toy shop'. In this fragment of thought, Adorno addresses the playing child in terms which are perhaps no less sentimental than *The Velveteen Rabbit*, and also in terms which are not so very far away from Jenkins's use of theorist Michel de Certeau:

Play is their [children's] defence ... In his purposeless activity the child, by a subterfuge, sides with use-value against exchange value. Just because he deprives the things with which he plays of their mediated usefulness, he seeks to rescue in them what is benign towards men and not what subserves the exchange relation that equally deforms men and things ... the unreality of games gives notice that reality is not yet real. Unconsciously they rehearse the right life.

(Adorno 1978: 228)

This statement requires some unpacking. Adorno is drawing on the Marxist terms of 'use-value' (what we can actually use a cultural object for: i.e. we can use soap to wash ourselves) and 'exchange-value' (the 'exchangeable' value that an object has when mediated through money: i.e. how much a bar of soap costs). From a Marxist perspective, it is 'exchange-value' which destroys the uniqueness of objects while also fixing them with a cost which is always inflated above the actual costs of production and labour (this 'surplus value' being extracted as capitalist profit, and thereby estranging workers from their own labour). In other words, exchange-value is the unnatural imposition of a capitalist system, while use-value is its alibi, and the remnant of non-capitalist practice. Exchange-value deforms both 'men and things' since it suggests that all objects are interchangeable through the medium of money, and also, ultimately, that men (and women) become objects that can be bought and sold under capitalism. As exchange-value colonises social and cultural relations, it reduces everything to a logic of purchasing power, including education (pay-per-view lectures?) and love (we start to think of ourselves as competing for a partner on the 'love market': see Cameron and Collins 2000).

Adorno's 'Toy shop' entry therefore suggests that the playing child is not entirely resigned to, and caught up in, the capitalist world. The child is able to side with 'use-value' against 'exchange-value', using his or her toys in seemingly 'purposeless ways' unanticipated by the toymaker. The child's play rehearses the 'right' (i.e. better/utopian) life in which the evils of 'exchange-value' are temporarily done away with. This resistance, this imagination of a better life, and this temporary deviation from the 'expected' or 'anticipated' use of a cultural object all correspond to, and predate, the work of Michel de Certeau (1988) which forms the theoretical centrepiece of Jenkins's *Textual Poachers*. Adorno's work is thus not limited by its 'pessimism'; as I have started to demonstrate, his approach to 'mass culture' is, in fact, not unremittingly pessimistic. Rather, as I will now outline, the limit to Adorno's work lies in his adherence to the Marxist 'laws of value' that I have summarised above.

Adorno adopts a 'dialectical' approach to culture. This means that he refuses to accept that logical concepts adequately capture reality, believing instead that material 'reality' is essentially contradictory, and remains outside the mastery of traditional logic. However, this approach does not imply that theoretical under-standing is therefore pointless or worthless; instead critics must attempt to work with concepts which can contain contradiction, or concepts which can 'sublate' contradiction (meaning that contradictions are both preserved and surpassed by systems of thought). Adorno's most rigorous statement of his approach comes in his book *Negative Dialectics* (1996). Dialectics must remain 'negative' for Adorno because the process of conceptualising our material world can never reach an ultimate conclusion. It is for this reason that Adorno criticises Hegel (1977) for cutting short dialectics in the moment of a final synthesis (i.e. a final and complete fit between concepts and the world). Adorno suggests that dialectical logic is more respectful of its objects of study than other, more 'positivist' approaches (which emphasise the non-contradictoriness and self-evidence of the world) because dialectical logic is 'more positivistic than the positivism that outlaws it. As thinking, dialectical logic respects that which is to be thought – the object – even where the object does not heed the rules of thinking' (1996: 141).

This respect for the object's contradictoriness, however, is barely evident in Adorno's reliance on Marx's categories of 'use-value' and 'exchange-value'. This Marxist 'law of value' is treated non-dialectically, as a 'factual' object which occurs behind the back of the subject and confronts it precisely as a 'law'. Miklitsch (1998: 84) has noted the lack of interest shown by Marx in 'individual consumption' (i.e. what people actually do with what they have 'consumed'), and suggests that it is important to account for this moment of consumption, or what Miklitsch terms 'final consumption' (*ibid.*: 92) rather than remaining fixed at the level of supposedly 'objective' laws of value. Adorno, following Marx, shows a general theoretical lack of interest in what consumers actually do with their objects of consumption, although this is contradicted by his specific investigations of 'final consumption' such as the 'Toy shop' example where 'what defies subsumption under identity – the "use-value" in Marxist terminology – is necessary anyway if life is to go on at all, *even under the prevailing circumstances of production. The utopia extends to the sworn enemies of its realisation*' (Adorno 1996: 11, my emphasis).

Adorno, hence, produces a theoretical approach which can be read against itself, and where 'pessimism' at the level of general theory gives way to an awareness of contradiction and complexity in specific cases such as the playing child (taken as a model for fandom by both Jenkins and myself). Unfortunately most cultural studies accounts of Adorno's work remain fixed at the level of his general pronouncements rather than investigating how these pronouncements are undermined in the details of Adorno's thought. And few seek to explore the tensions which exist between Adorno's dialectics and his own reinstatement of a subject/object binary: 'The polarity of subject and object may well appear to be an undialectical structure in which all dialectics take place' (Adorno 1996: 174).

It is important to pick up on Adorno's anxious defence of the subject/object split, challenging his general dualism of consumer-Subject and law-of-value-Object, as well as that which is constructed between Adorno as philosopher-Subject and the culture industry as administered-Object. Both are moments in which the subject and object become absolutely opposed, and where dialectics thus forgets both itself and the possibilities of 'final consumption' (Miklitsch 1998: 83–4). Restoring dialectical thinking to the consumer (subject) and the law-of-value (object) means constructing a 'dialectic of value' in place of this 'dialectic of enlightenment'. This means making Adorno's 'Toy shop' example more contradictory – more dialectical – than it is in Adorno's own formulation. For how is the child able to 'side with use-value against exchange-value' unless these terms are opposed, just as conventional logic opposes subject and object? My argument here is that 'use-value' and 'exchange-value' cannot ever be fully separated out from one another. Even as the playing child, or the fan, appears to depart from the perspective of the 'toymaker' (or producer) and find their own use for a text, they still remain simultaneously caught up in the system of exchange-value. The fan's appropriation of a text is therefore an act of 'final consumption' which pulls this text away from (intersubjective and public) exchange-value and towards (private, personal) use-value, but without ever cleanly or clearly being able to separate out the two. It is for this reason that fan 'appropriations' of texts or 'resistances' to consumption can always be reclaimed as new instances of exchange-value.

Appadurai (1986) comes close to recognising the dialectic of value when he notes that things can 'move in *and* out of the commodity state ... [S]uch movements can be slow or fast, reversible or terminal, normative or deviant' (cited in Miklitsch 1998: 88). However, Appadurai's theory relies on the passing of time to defuse the dialectic of value and restore a logic of non-contradiction. A logic of identity is restored because at point 'a' in time the object is purely a commodity, whereas at point 'b' in time this same object is viewed purely as a non-commodity. The awkward question which would remain, is how and where could the definite division between these events be located?

An excellent example of the 'dialectic of value' is the existence of a market for media tie-in memorabilia or 'collectibles'. This market can be examined easily enough by looking at the Internet site ebay.com. Many commodities offered for sale on Ebay should, according to the conventional logic of use and exchange-value, be almost worthless. However, due to many of them having been intensely subjectively valued by fans, such commodities take on a redefined 'exchange-value'. But this new exchange-value is not predetermined by any 'law of value'. It is created through the durability of fans' attachments, and through the fans' desire to own merchandise which is often no longer being industrially produced. This is not 'exchange-value' in any classical, Marxist sense. It emerges only through *a process of localised (fan-based) use-valuations* (which are not entirely reducible to 'economic' models, being intensifications of personalised 'use-value'). These fan-based 'use-values' interact with systems which belong to the economy 'proper', meaning that the existence of a marketplace for media-related collectibles is underpinned by the lived experiences of fandom. *Even if this implies that the 'law of value' returns in a more coercive manner, then this process does not, after all, go on behind the backs of social agents (fans), but goes on instead through the historically specific, embodied and lived experiences of these fans.*

This section has been predominantly theoretical. In the following case study of fans of 'cult television' (this being a self-description within the fan culture concerned), I want to show how the 'dialectic of value' can illustrate the cultural and economic processes in which fan cultures are implicated. I will then conclude the chapter with a brief examination of Kurt Lancaster's (2001) work on fans of *Babylon 5*, also asking how 'cultural power' can be conceptualised in relation to fan cultures.

Textual poachers turned textual gamekeepers?

In this section, I want to focus on *Cult Times*, a monthly UK broadcast-listings magazine which resembles a post-Fordist version of *The Radio Times* (an identification which it signals through its very title). Despite the deconstruction of the 'production/consumption' binary that I have examined above, I want to suggest that we should not view the leaking-together of these terms through rose-tinted glasses. Viewing cult TV fandom as a niche market does not mean discussing the simplistic 'empowerment' of fans. Target marketing also involves the cultural and economic disempowering of cult audiences via their niche isolation from wider 'coalition audiences' and via the related decline in the wider economic viability of the fans' favoured media text(s). That fans appear to 'get what they want' is only the beginning of a more complex situation. Cult TV fandom, which has been discussed as a matter of 'grass roots' consumption versus preprogrammed 'top-down' commodification (see Feuer 1995), therefore needs to be approached without the imposition of such a rigid binary opposition, being viewed as more essentially contradictory. Having already agreed that there may be a variety of reasons to consider fandom as 'resistive' or as operating through a set of 'unruly' consumption practices, I want to set these practices within the context of commodification. My argument is that initially unexpected consumption practices, far from challenging the interests of TV producers, and the power relationships through which capital circulates, are rapidly recuperated within discourses and practices of marketing. Fandom has begun to furnish a model of dedicated and loyal consumption which does, in point of fact, *appeal* to niche and non-terrestrial TV producers and schedulers[10] operating within a fragmented multi-channel media environment.[11]

Fan-consumers are no longer viewed as eccentric irritants, but rather as loyal consumers to be created, where possible, or otherwise to be courted through scheduling practices. Consider, for example, the interest which 'minority' or niche UK 'narrowcasters' such as satellite/cable channels have shown in the programmes which make it into the pages of *Cult Times*. Sky One has been the first-run channel for *The X-Files*, for *Star Trek: Deep Space Nine* and *Voyager*, and is currently showing *Buffy the Vampire Slayer* ahead of the BBC and *Angel* ahead of Channel 4, while Bravo was, for a time, known as 'the cult channel', and promoted itself along these lines with its 'timewarp television' slogans. Where such channels were, and are, unlikely to reach anything resembling a mass audience, they have used financial clout (in the case of Sky) and the cannily themed scheduling of cheap reruns (Bravo) to secure loyal fan audiences. In such cases, it is clear that cult TV fans are being directly targeted as a niche market, rather than emerging unexpectedly through 'grassroots' movements of TV appreciation. The supposedly 'resistive' figure of the fan has, then, become increasingly enmeshed within market rationalisations and routines of scheduling and channel-branding.[12]

The case of Bravo (which has now moved away from programming 'cult' material) is particularly intriguing. Its 'Vice-president of Programming Yoni

Cohen' was interviewed in 1995 as part of a magazine article dealing with cult television (see Green and Bodle 1995). Cohen is quoted as follows:

> Yoni Cohen is wary of defining what makes its [Bravo's] output 'cult'. 'That's defined by the audience', he says. However, he stresses that these programmes have both a distinctiveness (there's never been anything like them) and an internal consistency (from week to week, they create a coherent framework, within which their stories take place). Cohen knows that keeping on the right side of cult TV's fans is important in his line of broadcasting. 'You can get in terrible trouble with them if you show the programmes in the wrong order. So we listen to fans, try to find out what the original transmission or production order was for each series, then present the programmes respecting the original details as much as possible.'
>
> (Green and Bodle 1995: 19)

What is significant within this interview is its discursive characterisation of cult TV as a grassroots or fan-owned phenomenon ('defined by the audience') and its simultaneous emphasis on 'keeping on the right side' of the fans. What this demonstrates is the extent to which, when approaching the fan audience as a target market, the fan culture's values of authenticity must be mirrored (whether these are transmission dates or – a yet more extreme form of authentication – production dates). At the same time, this observance of fan 'authenticity' masks the extent to which 'fan-ownership' acts as a rhetorical device aimed at promoting the notion that target marketing merely 'reflects' values and distinctions which are already operative within the cultural worlds of dedicated cult TV fandom. This discursive construction purposefully neglects the agency and intervention of the cult narrowcaster who is able to identify and schedule cult programmes which will deliver the desired audience, thus reconstructing the fan culture as a niche market which is isolated from the 'mainstream'. Following Collins (1992), 'coalition audience' rather than 'mainstream' is probably a more accurate identification of the situation where fandom is able to occupy a space within a series of other audience fragments gathered around a single programme.

John Tulloch's discussion of *Doctor Who* fans as a 'powerless elite' (in Tulloch and Jenkins 1995: 144–72) hinges on the subordinated position of TV fans within a wider coalition audience, and hence requires rethinking in relation to fandom as a niche market. Any immediate assumption of fan 'power' within this altered narrowcasting context is, I think, extremely problematic – despite the cult-audience-friendly discourse of those such as Yoni Cohen. While the 'power' of fandom as a niche market is, in part, the power to see its own values of 'authenticity' mirrored, there is also a contradictory limit to the niche market's assumption of 'power' which has been usefully identified by Will Brooker in relation to the fans of Batman comics:

Within a narrower market, such as direct-to-video animation or half-hour cartoons, we may find a genuine 'adaptation' ... Purists might temper their protests with the reflection that their hero would, had he not been subjected to each of these mutations, be now far less complex, far less significant, far less rich in meaning; if indeed, that is, he had lasted this long. Like the work of Austen and Shakespeare, Conan Doyle and Fleming, it is through being adapted that Batman has survived.

(Brooker 1999a: 197)

The contradictory limit to the power of the niche market is, then, precisely that through seeing its own agenda on screen, fandom loses any possibility of creative textual mutation and thus becomes locked into its own rigidly maintained sets of values, authenticities, textual hierarchies and continuities. And as Brooker rightly points out, had the comic fans' agenda been allowed to dictate the 'good' Batman and thus disallow the 60s TV programme, or the Burton and Schumacher films, then the character of Batman would be unlikely to retain the resonance and cultural hold which it continues to possess within contemporary culture. In short, capitulating to the fans' agenda as a target market ('empowering' the fans) potentially spells the end of the text which has inspired their very fandom, since the isolation of the fan audience from any wider coalition audience effectively terminates any economic viability for the text beyond its fan-ghetto of 'preaching to the converted'.

As Brooker also illustrates, the rationalisation and routinisation of cult fandom has not been limited to the thematic buying-in of programmes aimed at securing loyal audiences. Cult fan-consumers have also been targeted and reconstructed as a niche market through non-broadcast means: via the ruses of direct-to-video releases, or through direct-to-audio 'adaptations' of TV programmes such as the current range of original *Doctor Who* audio stories produced by Big Finish Productions, under licence to the BBC, and marketed and distributed through specialist outlets (e.g. via mail order advertised in niche magazines such as *Cult Times* or *Doctor Who Magazine*, and via distribution to specific stores such as the Forbidden Planet chain). Unlike the BBC's attempts to produce the cult TV programme *Blake's 7* as two radio shows, subsequently released as BBC Audio Cassettes, the Big Finish productions have not been conceived as material for broadcast. They are solely aimed at distribution and consumption within the relevant fan culture as a niche market. Stephen Brown, in *Postmodern Marketing*, has identified a related move towards 'authenticity' in branding:

[L]ongevity is considered to be all-important ... [and] ... long established brand names are *extremely* precious commodities. It would appear that in an increasingly uncertain, fragmented, disorienting and fast-changing world, they provide consumers with a point – an oasis –

> of marketing stability. They are imbued with an evocative patina of the
> past ... [and] many products, whose life cycles have long since run
> their course, have been successfully raised from the dead ... not least,
> the tie-in products from re-runs of old television series such as
> *Thunderbirds, Stingray, Batman, Captain Scarlet* and *Joe 90*.
>
> (Brown 1995: 116–18)

Were adaptations such as the *Blake's 7* radio dramas aimed primarily at a
'nostalgic' wider audience, then Brown's point might well have some force.
However, his chosen examples seem to work, in part, against the 'nostalgia'
narrative, since each TV programme he cites is recognisable as part of the intertextual cult ensemble gathered within the listings of *Cult Times*, and is thus
recognisable as having an enduring and attached fan audience rather than an
audience which is purely recruited through brand-reinvention which carries a
'patina of the past'. Furthermore, although one may quibble over the extent to
which *Blake's 7* constitutes a 'nostalgically' resurrected brand, the niche-
marketed Big Finish productions of *Doctor Who* cannot be taken to follow
Brown's neo-nostalgic 'point of stability' argument, since they are not 'reinven-
tions' of a brand; the 'brand' of *Doctor Who* has, quite simply, never become
absent for the programme's cult fans.

The creativity of the cult fan as a producer (within the supposedly 'free'
space of leisure practices) has formed the basis for theorisations of fandom
which celebrate this 'activity', whether it be video editing, costuming/imper-
sonation (see Nightingale 1994, 1996), filk songwriting and performing or
fanzine production (Jenkins 1992a). Jenkins's work is heavily indebted to that
of Michel de Certeau (1988), and I want to discuss this debt briefly.

For de Certeau, consumption is theorised within a model of consumer
appropriation. This depends upon a rigid separation of producers (who are
those who 'own' space or the apparatus of production, and who are thereby
able to pursue powerful 'strategies' marked out through their ability to antici-
pate trends) and consumers (who own no 'proper' space of their own, and
hence 'poach' on the producer's territories or through 'appropriating' the
producer's products. This 'improper' and despatialised activity is described by
de Certeau as a form of 'weak' tactics operating in opposition to strong
'strategy'). This model may appear persuasive when applied to fanzine production which rewrites characters and situations from 'official' TV texts within
(feminist or queer) cultural politics, given that fanzine producers have no 'space'
of their own (i.e. they are not able to produce the show which they love, or
directly influence its direction). And yet the difficulty with de Certeau's model
is that it seems too rigid to deal helpfully with any blurring of consumer and
consumer-as-producer identities. De Certeau denies the possibility that the
consumer can occupy an official and production-based space (since spatialisation
belongs to strategy, while 'tactical' consumption strays across the territory of
the otherwithout making any space or place of its own). Are professionalised

fans writing for *Cult Times* exercising strategy, tactics, strategic tactics or tactical strategies? Is the fan-producer of a BBC-licensed *Doctor Who* audio drama occupying a tactical or strategic space? Rick Altman has taken issue with the cultural stasis which is implied by de Certeau's approach to consumption:

> Stressing localised reception (in time as well as space) of texts produced by someone outside the reception sphere, critics have never taken seriously the ability of audiences to generate their own texts and thus to become intenders, mappers and owners in their own right. ... When we take a wider view, we easily recognise that ... [w]ith each cycle, the nomadic poachers become property owners, and thus authors, map-makers and intenders, thereby establishing the capital that attracts still others' poaching activity.
>
> (Altman 1999: 212)

However, set against de Certeau's and Jenkins's romanticisation of powerless fan 'poaching'[13] – and Altman's seemingly essentialist counterstatement that poachers somehow inevitably become powerful owners[14] – it is worth considering that the supposed 'empowerment' of textual poachers who are able to turn 'textual gamekeepers' does not occur within a transhistorical or essentialist space. Rather, it occurs quite precisely within the economic and cultural parameters of niche marketing whereby fan-consumers and producers are more closely aligned within a common 'reception sphere' or 'interpretive community' (see Amesley 1989).

The movement from 'hobbyist' to paid 'expert' depends less on general processes of capital (which are posited by Adorno 1991) than upon specific leisure 'pursuits' being reconstructed as niche markets. The possibility of cult TV fan-consumers becoming producers, either working as professional writers/editors for *Cult Times*, or producing audio dramas for Big Finish Productions, for example, hinges not simply on Adorno's 'totalistic' culture industry, but requires the more precise mechanisms of market segmentation, in which fans' values and authenticities are, equally precisely, sold back to them. And thus who is better placed to produce this material – which by definition must draw on immersion in fan culture and its forms of knowledge and competence – than the fans themselves?[15]

The cult TV audience's reconstruction as a target market hence allows for the possibility that boundaries between 'work' and 'play' – objectified labour and creative labour respectively – might be more thoroughly destabilised through the figure of the 'professionalised fan' (see also Thornton 1995: 153), though absolutely without cause for the simplistic celebration of this highly contradictory 'empowerment':

> Watching *Doctor Who* was a serious business for me as a kid. ... I'd be in front of the television at least half an hour before the scheduled

transmission time. I'd have certain special foods arranged in front of me. I'd make sure I was comfortably dressed and positioned on the sofa ... In retrospect, all this seems to suggest a seriously dysfunctional child – at best, a dangerously anal-retentive one. But it *was* only once a week, and nowadays I can at least justify this former obsessiveness as early vocational training.

(Gillatt 1996: 3)

Textual poachers turned textual performers?

My focus in this chapter has been on the ways in which fans have, and in fact often *haven't*, been addressed as consumers. I have already noted a tension surrounding this issue in Kurt Lancaster's work, but my observations so far don't do justice to the originality of Lancaster's approach. Much like the earlier work of Jenkins, Lancaster develops his theorisation of fan culture around a central and dominating metaphor. In place of the poacher – although this motif returns in chapter 5 of *Interacting with Babylon 5* (2001) – we have the fan as textual performer (see also Lancaster 1999 and Lancaster and Mikotowicz 2001). This doesn't mean that fans start to appear as actors in their favoured shows; Lancaster focuses on *Babylon 5*'s online fans and fan fiction writers as well as players of the *Babylon 5* role-playing game, collectible card game, an 'interactive' CD-ROM, and a starship war game. As Lancaster observes:

> [I]t is important to examine these various fantasy games [related to popular cultural and 'cult' texts] ... in order to show how they create immersion through performance in the minds of their players. [C]ultural studies texts ... do not elucidate the performance structures of the imaginary entertainment environment, and they do not describe the formal performance qualities arising out of the mise-en-scenes of these various sites.
>
> (Lancaster 2001: xxviii)

By focusing on the individual fan's experience of immersion, Lancaster temporarily suspends many of the cultural studies' questions of 'gender, race, and class' (2001: xxvii), although he acknowledges that such questions cannot be altogether removed from a performance studies paradigm. Thinking of fans as performers means displacing an emphasis on the text–reader interaction, and focusing instead on the myriad ways that fans can engage with the textual structures and moments of their favoured cult shows, reactivating these in cultural practices of play. For example, Lancaster analyses how *Babylon 5* fans use the *Babylon 5* collectible card game to 'touch' their affectively valorised programme:

> [T]hey want to attain haptic-panoptic [touching-seeing] control over images (and perhaps feelings) that formerly sped past them during the

41

viewing of *Babylon 5*. They can now slow these images down and manipulate them for their own purposes (limited as this is by a structure of game rules). ... Where before the show could only be seen, now it can be both observed and touched.

(Lancaster 2001: 102)

Lancaster emphasises fans' imaginative and emotional engagements with a meta-textual terrain of images, images that come to carry subjective significance as well as being embedded in the narrative 'arc' of the originating programme. Although Lancaster's version of the individual fan appears to possess no explicitly theorised psyche, these fans nevertheless 'try to capture – through participation and immersion – the original cathartic moment felt during the first viewing of a story' (2001: 155).[16] Lancaster's work undoubtedly goes a long way towards reintroducing moments of the 'individual' and the 'subjective' that have been neglected in cultural studies approaches, since as Henry Jenkins notes in his foreword to *Interacting with Babylon 5*: '[p]erformance studies ... tends to focus more fully on personal rather than subcultural meanings' (Jenkins 2001: xx).

Lancaster's work anticipates and makes many of the steps that I am calling for and defending in this book. Impressively, Lancaster implicitly questions the text–reader model that has dominated cultural studies work on media audiences; he does not replay the theoretical problems associated with CCCS (Centre for Contemporary Cultural Studies) work on subcultures; he explicitly emphasises and prioritises the study of fan emotion; he sidesteps the issue of fan ethnography, presenting a new theoretical take on fandom; and he considers fan culture to be made up through creative self-expression as well as communal activities. On the debit side, Lancaster also replays some of the problems associated with earlier work. For example, his focus on fans of a single programme tends to suggest an overly bounded fan 'group'. And his use of a performance studies approach leaves somewhat unclear what, if any, theoretical model of subjectivity is being drawn on in his work. The fact that fans try to relive and re-embody 'cathartic' moments of emotion long after the experience of the original emotion implies some kind of residual depth-psychology, or at the very least some sense of experiential 'holding' or conservation. But although this fan experience is described and posited as a key part of Lancaster's work, it is never placed within a theoretical framework which might explicate how or why such an emotional 'holding' or 'reliving' could become important to fans.[17]

By focusing on the subjective and the imaginative, Lancaster therefore arguably under-emphasises two processes alluded to in the previous indented quote (Lancaster 2001: 102). These processes are, firstly, how rule-based structures act on fan-performers or players, a matter referred to in the parenthetical aside '(limited as this is by a structure of game rules)'. And, secondly, there is the question of how fans' feelings come to be attached to specific texts or images. This is captured in Lancaster's supplementary commentary, again placed in brackets: '(and perhaps feelings)'.

Taking up the latter point, I would argue that Lancaster, like much of fan studies before him, marginalises fan psychology even while making fan emotion central to his enterprise.[18] Direct references to the 'psychological' in *Interacting with Babylon 5* occur most frequently in discussions of RPG characters and their 'psychological profiles' (see Lancaster 2001: 38, 42 and 106). Where the issue of *fan* psychology is explicitly raised rather than implied in discussions of fan emotion, we are informed that this psychology has to be bracketed off when thinking about performance (see 2001: 146). Alternatively, fan psychology appears when Lancaster quite rightly defends RPG gamers against accusations of 'emotional instability' or 'escapism' (2001: 158). And while mounting this defence, Lancaster distinguishes between fans, who have 'a refined sense of viewing ... and ... are not just consumers of fantasy but active producers and creators of it', and those who are 'dangerously or deliriously *fanatical* like a right-wing cult organization (for science fiction fans are not cultic)' (*ibid.*). While marking many developments in fan studies, and being state-of-the-art in almost all respects, Lancaster's work hence continues to struggle with the notion of the fan-consumer. Like Jenkins before him, Lancaster deals with the taint of fan consumption by recuperating fan-consumers as 'producers' and 'creators'.[19]

The subject of cultural power has continually run beneath my arguments here, becoming more prominent in the previous section 'Textual poachers turned textual gamekeepers?' where I took issue with the relevance of viewing fans as a 'powerless elite' when they are no longer an elite fraction of a coalition audience, but instead make up the entirety of a niche audience. Given the importance of the issue of cultural power – who has it and who doesn't – I want to conclude with a note on this.

The problem with arguments about cultural power is precisely that they often assume (a) that power can be located in one group or another, and/or (b) that power operates systematically. In fact, I would suggest that the notion that 'academics' are culturally powerful while fans are not, or indeed that media producers have cultural power where fans do not, are little more than reassuring myths.

The difficulty in assuming the systematic or locatable operation of power is that these two principles have the potential to disturb and disrupt one another rather than being logically or materially harmonious. Take the example of 'fans' versus 'academics'. It has been claimed that a 'system of bias ... debases fans and elevates scholars even though they engage in virtually the same kinds of activities' (Lewis cited in Hunter 2000: 196). But the systems of cultural value occupied by fans and academics are not part of a single 'system': fans seek to value their own activities, as do academics, and aspects of the self-valuations of each community will tend to be related to the wider cultural circulation of meaning. In terms of their media representation, academics can expect to be subjected to common sense norms of 'clear communication', meaning that the fans' critique of 'bad' academic subjectivity has a wider cultural efficacy (see

Murdock 1994). Meanwhile, fans can expect to be pathologised in media repre-sentations, meaning that the academics' critique of 'bad' fan subjectivity also carries cultural weight outside this specific community (Tulloch 2000; Lewis 1992; Jenkins 1992a). It is thus not simply the case that fans are debased and scholars are elevated: in specific ways, the 'common sense' of a shared culture is partially opposed and partially drawn on by *both fans and academics*. This suggests that 'power' is not wholly locatable in either one group.

Since neither fan nor academic identities are wholly constructed against one another, but are also built up through the relay of other identities such as the 'consumer', any sense of a singular cultural system of value is deferred yet further. Fans may secure a form of cultural power by opposing themselves to the bad subject of 'the consumer'. Academics may well construct their identities along this same axis of othering, meaning that in this case both fans and academics may, regardless of other cultural differences, be linked through their *shared* marginalisation of 'the consumer' as Other. Once again, this suggests that cultural power cannot be located in any one group, nor can it be viewed as the product of any singular system. If anything, the emergence of cultural power can be viewed as the effect of an interference between, and an amplifica-tion of, different moments of othering and different moral dualisms. It should not be assumed that these different dualisms simply line up in some type of overall 'structural homology' (where 'fan' would be to 'academic' as 'fan' would be to 'consumer'). The fact that dualisms may cut across or disturb one another – as do fan/academic and fan/consumer dualisms – means that they are at best *relatively homologous* since the fan/academic binary does not map onto a fan/consumer one; instead fans and academics are typically united against the figure of the 'bad' consumer.

Summary

- In this chapter I have focused on the fan experience as inherently contradic-tory: fans are both commodity-completists and they express anti-commercial beliefs or 'ideologies'. However, I have sought to preserve this cultural contradiction rather than explaining it away and restoring a sense of pure 'logic'. I have suggested that any academic approach to fandom which favours one side of this contradiction inevitably falsifies the fan experience.
- To avoid this danger, I returned to the work of Adorno and introduced the idea of the 'dialectic of value'. This considers fans to be simultaneously inside and outside processes of commodification, experiencing an intensely personal 'use-value' in relation to their object of fandom, and then being re-positioned within more general and systematic processes of 'exchange-value'.
- I have argued that niche marketing – while seeming to reflect authentic values of fan culture back to the fan, and thus to align production and

44

consumption values – nevertheless does so at a cost. The fan-consumer niche market becomes almost entirely insulated from any wider market. It is therefore cut off from the 'mass' cultural circulation which generated the existence of such a fandom in the first place. As Virginia Nightingale (1996: 124) has noted, fans 'remain the target for renewed managerial activity to contain the quixotic preoccupations which become pretexts for the development of new and commercially exploitable fan communities'.

2

FAN CULTURES BETWEEN COMMUNITY AND HIERARCHY

In the last chapter, I suggested that we can use Adorno's work to think through the fan–consumer contradiction rather than trying to resolve it. In this chapter, I want to examine another theorist whose work has played an important part in fan studies: the French sociologist Pierre Bourdieu. His work on processes of cultural distinction offers a way for theorists to analyse how fan 'status' is built up. It allows us to consider any given fan culture not simply as a community but *also as a social hierarchy* where fans share a common interest while also competing over fan knowledge, access to the object of fandom, and status.[1] It is this emphasis on competitiveness which provides my title and the image of fans as 'players'. According to Bourdieu and his followers, fans play in the sense that they tacitly recognise the 'rules' of their fan culture, attempting to build up different types of fan skill, knowledge and distinction.

In the first section of this chapter, then, I will introduce and explore Bourdieu's work, examining what it can offer fan studies and also pointing out some of the limits to this approach. In particular, I will illustrate how Bourdieu's work – unlike that of Adorno in chapter 1 and Winnicott in chapter 4 – closes down the contradictions of fandom, ultimately producing a hyper-rational view of the 'calculating' fan. I will also explore how Bourdieu's work is unable to account adequately for the moral dualisms and the broadly 'moral' struggles over cultural value and legitimation that fandom is always caught up in.

I will then address the work of theorists who have adapted and criticised Bourdieu's work on distinction, applying it to specific fan cultures and fans of popular culture more generally. Finally, in the third section of this chapter I will present a case study focusing on fans of what has been termed 'psychotronic cinema'.

A powerful metaphor: the work of Pierre Bourdieu

The central concept employed in Bourdieu's model is a metaphor. Just as the behaviour of an enterprise is determined by the nature and loca-

tion of its physical plant or 'capital', that of the individual is determined by the nature and location of their 'human capital' ... perhaps
economic ... or perhaps 'social capital' (i.e. a personal network of
friends and acquaintances), or 'cultural capital' (the general information about cultural artefacts absorbed as a by-product of daily life), or
else 'educational capital' acquired through schooling.

(Gershuny 2000: 84–5)

As Gershuny usefully notes, Bourdieu's work is rooted in a central and guiding
metaphor. Bourdieu supposes that cultural life can be modelled by taking an
'economistic' approach. This treats all social relations as if they are economic;
people invest in knowledge (reading the right books), in social contacts
(networking and knowing the right people) and in culture (having knowledge
of appropriate cultural works and how to respond to them). Bourdieu argues
that different types of capital as well as 'economic capital' (money) are
unequally distributed across society. The amounts of different capitals that we
possess (economic; social; cultural) are not random, but relate to our place in a
class system. The dominant bourgeoisie possess relatively high levels of
economic capital, social capital (the old boys' network) and cultural capital
(having been well-educated at the right schools). The dominated bourgeoisie,
on the other hand, have high cultural capital, but possess lower economic
capital than the 'dominating' fraction. The dominated bourgeois can be
thought of as bohemians, scholars and intellectuals; they value 'culture' and
'learning' over financial rewards, and seek to legitimate their class position and
tastes by viewing the dominant bourgeoisie as vulgar and as lacking in cultural
discrimination. Bourdieu also identifies other class fractions: the petit bourgeois
(who possess mid-range levels of forms of capital) and the working class (who
possess low levels of forms of capital).

Bourdieu (1984, 1990) goes on to offer a monumental cataloguing of social
practices and activities, including cultural consumption. His work attempts to
account for the reproduction of cultural identities by examining the objective
social and economic conditions in which people find themselves (see Robbins
1991: 131). But while the bourgeoisie is supposedly split in two (into 'dominant' and 'dominated' fractions), Bourdieu's analysis assumes a more
homogeneous petit bourgeoisie and a more homogeneous again proletariat or
working class.

Bourdieu's work presents an interesting challenge to fan studies since it
suggests that fandoms may be thoroughly reducible to the practices of specific
class fractions. Bourdieu discusses 'fandom' in four different ways, in line with
his four major categorisations of cultural groups:

The dominating fraction of the bourgeoisie can depend on economic and (to a
lesser extent) cultural capital in its pursuits: it is thereby typified in the ostenta-
tious display of 'expensive' works of art. According to Bourdieu's argument,

this class fraction would never correspond to, or participate in, the cultural activities of fan culture. Strictly speaking, Bourdieu does not attach the label of 'fandom' to the dominant bourgeoisie; there is something always culturally 'improper' about the notion of fandom in his account.

The dominated fraction of the bourgeoisie relies on (and seeks to increase) its highly developed cultural capital by 'liking the same things differently, liking different things, less obviously marked out for admiration':

> Intellectuals and artists have a special predilection for the most risky but also most profitable strategies of distinction, those which consist in asserting the power, *which is peculiarly theirs*, to constitute insignificant objects as works of art or, more subtly, to give aesthetic redefinition to objects already defined as art, but in another mode, by other classes or class fractions (e.g. kitsch).
>
> (Bourdieu 1984: 282, 283)

The petit bourgeois lifestyle, however, is caught up in the resolute impropriety of fandom that is identified by Bourdieu. The petit bourgeois is able to recognise 'legitimate culture', but does not possess sufficient knowledge of it. This gap between recognition and knowledge results in the petit bourgeoisie's perversely misplaced fan knowledge which cannot bring the rewards or the legitimacy of official cultural capital:

> [T]he petit bourgeois, always liable to know too much or too little, ... is condemned endlessly to amass disparate, often devalued information ... The stockpiling avidity which is the root of every great accumulation of culture is too visible in the perversion of the jazz-freak or cinema-buff who carries to the extreme, i.e. to absurdity, what is implied in the legitimate definition of cultivated contemplation, and replaces consumption of the work with the consumption of the circumstantial information.
>
> (1984: 329, 330)

Working class tastes actually merit the debasement of the term 'fan' itself in Bourdieu's account (1984: 386). Bourdieu views this fandom as an 'illusory compensation' for the working class fan's lack of social and cultural power.

The flaw with this argument is that it simply *assumes* the legitimacy of a fixed and monolithically legitimate 'cultural capital', rather than considering how 'cultural capital' may, at any single moment of culture-in-process, remain variously fragmented, internally inconsistent and struggled over. Does the 'cultural capital' of an IT specialist have the same 'value' as the 'cultural capital' of a scholar of Latin? How can a single thing called 'cultural capital' exist even in a 'single' culture? Our objects of cultural knowledge and education are various and are themselves caught up in networks of value which may vary between communities and subcultures as well as across class distinctions. Such a fixed model also neglects the possibility that struggles over the legitimacy of 'cultural capital' may occur both between and *within* class fractions, communities and subcultures.

Bourdieu's model also implies that moral evaluations stem from struggles over class difference and distinction. But as Honneth has put it: '[t]he central economic concepts upon which ... [Bourdieu's] cultural analysis is based, compel him to subsume all forms of social conflicts under the types of struggles which occur over social distribution – although the struggle for the social recognition of moral models clearly obeys a different logic' (cited in Robbins 2000: 126). Given that fandom is so often placed within a moral dualism, then it is quite likely that any moral devaluation of 'the fan' (as a deficient subject) cannot entirely be explained through Bourdieu's model. (And this is especially so given that Bourdieu himself appears to adopt a moral position in relation to 'the fan', albeit under the guise of 'neutrally' explicating different class fractions.)

Applying Bourdieu's model means treating popular culture and media fandom as a 'scandalous category' which opposes notions of 'proper' cultural capital and 'proper' aesthetic distance or appreciation (see Jenkins 1992a: 16–19). In Henry Jenkins's account, this also means reading an attributed lack of morality off from 'fans' transgression of bourgeois taste and disruption of dominant cultural hierarchies' (1992a: 17). Jenkins notes that 'aesthetic distaste brings with it the full force of moral excommunication and social rejection' (1992a: 16). This cultural linkage of (alleged) immorality and 'bad' or improper tastes is undeniable, but I would argue that the moral dualism at play here cannot simply be subordinated to Bourdieu's master-narrative. Of course, moral dualisms and distinctions may well operate to naturalise and shore up dominant (bourgeois) aesthetics. But having said that, the legitimacy of 'bourgeois' aesthetic values can equally well be challenged if these values are recontextualised within negatively evaluative moral dualisms (i.e. where detached appreciation is deemed 'bad'). This altered moral dualism may also, as Jenkins notes, be adopted by 'highly educated, articulate people who come from the middle classes, people who "should know better"' (1992a: 18). But despite this fact, Jenkins closes down his interpretation in line with Bourdieu's ideas. By consistently reading morality off from aesthetics (i.e. cultural and educational capital) he privileges cultural capital, suggesting that it is automatically a source of cultural legitimation. This type of account cannot explain, for example, why fan-scholars using the language of media studies and writing about a television programme such as *Doctor Who* are marginalised and stereotyped within their own fan culture *as well as being marginalised and stereotyped outside of it and in academia*. These fan-scholars possess the trappings of 'proper' cultural capital/educational capital and certainly do not present themselves as 'immersed' or non-analytical readers. They may also belong to the dominant as well as dominated bourgeoisie. And yet their 'detached' work is seemingly valued neither by academics (anxious to differentiate themselves from this all-too-close fan shadow) nor by fellow fans (keen to preserve a separation from overly-rationalising and jargon-heavy academics). Although we could argue that these fans are marginalised within fan culture because they are too close to displaying 'proper' cultural capital, this does not adequately account for their simultaneous 'othering' within academia where we might expect their work to be welcomed. In the absence of differences in cultural capital and aesthetics, fan-scholars remain marginalised here by the need to preserve a moral dualism between 'good' accredited and 'duly trained' professional academics and 'bad' amateur fan-scholars practising 'wild' analysis outside the academy. This indicates that rather than reading morality off from cultural capital, we should, at the very least, view the two as being non-coincident, although I would argue that *moral dualisms logically precede the valorisation of cultural capital rather than vice versa as Bourdieu (1984) and Jenkins (1992a) seem to imply*. The assumption that cultural capital is unquestionably 'good', and that more is unquestionably socially and culturally better is perhaps itself the product of a grounding and preceding moral dualism which belongs to academic imagined subjectivity.

Bourdieu's account therefore seems to run aground when confronted by the powerful moral dualisms which structure imagined fan and academic subjectivities. Because his work tacitly assumes that the 'cultural capital' embedded in a sociological and self-reflexive worldview automatically carries cultural legitimacy and authority, Bourdieu's theory has little purchase on the possibility that 'cultural capital' (whether this is in its incorporated, objectivated or institutionalised states: see Robbins 2000: 34) can fragment along subcultural (Thornton 1995) lines as well as being subjected to recontextualising moral dualisms.

In the rather mechanical world of Bourdieu's *Distinction* there can only be as many different types of fan culture and fan activity as there are class fractions or relevant distributions of forms of capital. Either that, or any one fan culture can only represent in microcosm the same four class-based spaces allotted by Bourdieu's thought. Although Henry Jenkins uses the work of both Bourdieu and de Certeau in *Textual Poachers* (see, for example 1992a: 61–2), he does not consider de Certeau's own criticism of Bourdieu's master-narrative of distinction: 'Bourdieu ... gives the impression of *departing* (of going towards these tactics [the multiplicity of cultural distinctions]), but only in order to *return* (to confirm the professional rationality)' (de Certeau 1988: 60).

Post-Bourdieu: fandom and the diversifications of cultural capital

Bourdieu's 'capital' metaphor has been developed by revisionists of his work. Later theorists have coined the term 'popular cultural capital' (Fiske 1992), and minted the concept of 'subcultural capital' (Thornton 1995). In this section I want to explore the critiques of Bourdieu which these theorists have offered.

John Fiske's (1992) piece 'The Cultural Economy of Fandom' presents two critiques of Bourdieu:

- Bourdieu emphasises 'economics and class as the major (if not the only) dimensions of social discrimination' (1992: 32) thereby neglecting gender, race and age in Fiske's view (although Bourdieu has consistently related social discrimination to age through his concern with 'inter-generational' differences and struggles; cf. Garnham with Williams in Garnham 1990: 87n2).

- Bourdieu fails 'to accord the culture of the subordinate the same sophisticated analysis as that of the dominant' (Fiske 1992: 32).

Fiske then partially misrepresents the concept of habitus, suggesting that 'losing capital of either sort [cultural/economic] changes ... one's habitus' (1992: 33). This seems mistaken, since one's habitus is not merely a product of types of capital, it is a product of early (i.e. childhood) socialisation (see R. Jenkins 1992: 76; Garnham with Williams in Garnham 1990: 75). Fiske also develops the concept of habitus, but again with limited reference to Bourdieu's use of the term. Fiske suggests that fans occupy a 'popular habitus' as opposed to a 'dominant habitus' (1992: 43). The latter leaves the logic of Bourdieu's work in place, but the former creates a new type of unclassed habitus seemingly linked only to the consumption of popular culture. Fiske contrasts the 'dominant' to the 'popular' habitus in a number of ways. First, the popular habitus promotes participation in the text, whilst the dominant habitus promotes discrimination between texts. Second, the popular habitus allows fans to 'see through' the text to production information, while the dominant habitus 'uses information about the artist to enhance or enrich the appreciation of the work' (1992: 43). Neither of these two distinctions is convincing. Selecting *Rocky Horror* fans as an example of participation smacks of selecting an example to bolster one's argument, while the contrasted discrimination of the 'buff' ignores the fact that *Rocky Horror* fans may well discriminate between different stagings of the show, evaluating them in relation to an ideal or in relation to the film version. Fiske's second contrast seems similarly weak: 'enriching appreciation' (dominant) and 'seeing through the text' (popular) sound suspiciously like rephrasings of the same thing, since both are concerned with the use of extra-textual information which acts as a supplement to the consumption of the text, and both provide a sense of 'expert' knowledge and hence greater pleasure for the fan or the 'appreciator'. Sconce (1995: 389) appears to accept Fiske's separation here, but then demonstrates that Fiske's 'opposed' notions are brought together by 'paracinema' fans, a move which still suggests that Fiske's initial binary opposition is flawed. Furthermore, the binary opposition of the 'popular' versus the 'dominant' habitus seems to resemble a moral dualism desperately seeking some kind of stable theoretical distinction between 'good' popular culture and 'bad' high culture, but unable to alight on anything substantial enough to divert attention from its incessant splitting of terms, cultures and experiences.

Remaining focused on Fiske's separation of 'popular' and 'official' culture, this distinction is explained by the fact that 'popular cultural capital, unlike official cultural capital, is not typically convertible into economic capital, though ... there are exceptions' (1992: 34). The exception to the rule proves to be fan-artists, able to sell their work at conventions, but just as Fiske announces this exception he seems to introduce a further distinction between 'more mundane popular cultural capital, which is never convertible to economic capital, and fan cultural capital which, under certain conditions, may be' (1992: 40). Just as popular cultural capital becomes tainted by the possibility of being exchanged for hard cash, Fiske temporarily carves it away from 'fan cultural capital' (the terms are otherwise used interchangeably throughout Fiske's essay). This has the curious effect of maintaining popular cultural capital's anti-economic purity, something which Fiske returns to twice in the course of four pages: 'the fan's objects of fandom are, by definition, excluded from official cultural capital and its convertibility, via education and career opportunity, into economic capital' (1992: 42), and again: 'It is the exclusion of popular or fan cultural capital from the educational system that ... disconnects it from the economic' (1992: 45). But what of media and cultural studies? Do these new disciplines not allow one route through which fan cultural capital can – admittedly when allied with 'official' cultural capital – make it into the realm of employment? Other possibilities for the exchange of fan cultural capital into economic capital include writing for niche or genre magazines such as *Cult Times* (discussed in the previous chapter), as well as the examples of 'music and style journalists and various record industry professionals' given by Sarah Thornton (1995: 12). Fiske's cleavage of popular cultural capital and economic capital also appears to defend some imagined 'pure' use-value against the predatory iniquities of 'exchange-value'. This particular splitting falsifies the 'dialectic of value' that I have identified as centrally important because it allows us to think about fans' 'sense of possession' (Fiske 1992: 40) of their object of fandom as feeding back into a redefined exchange-value. (While also reminding us that we cannot split apart use-value and exchange-value, or 'the fan' and 'the consumer', but should view these terms and identities as always being interlinked in contradiction.)

Sarah Thornton (1995) offers a further supplement to Bourdieu's work. Thornton suggests a further series of problems which need to be addressed in any media or fan studies application of Bourdieu:

• Bourdieu does not relate the circulation of cultural capital to the media (television/radio), meaning that the media are seemingly neutral or inconsequential within the processes of accumulating different types of capital.
• Bourdieu's view of cultural capital focuses on subcategories of capital which 'are all at play within Bourdieu's own field, within his social world of

players with high volumes of institutionalised cultural capital. However, it is possible to observe subspecies of capital operating within other less privileged domains' (Thornton 1995: 11).

Addressing these blind spots, Thornton conceives of the 'hipness' of clubbers as a form of 'subcultural capital' which 'confers status on its owner in the eyes of the relevant beholder. ... Just as books and paintings display cultural capital in the family home, so subcultural capital is objectified in the form of fashionable haircuts and well-assembled record collections' (*ibid.*) Thornton suggests that subcultural capital does not correlate with class distinctions in any one-to-one way, although she is careful to note that this does not mean that class becomes wholly irrelevant.

Thornton's account also focuses on how what I have termed 'moral dualisms' can be constructed and sustained through imagined subjectivities. She describes how previous academic studies of youth have 'relied on binary oppositions typically generated by us-versus-them social maps ... Inconsistent fantasies of the mainstream are rampant in subcultural studies' (1995: 92–3). Thornton attempts to set aside these us-versus-them otherings in order to investigate how the clubbers' subculture constructs its own moral dualism between a 'good' and authentic in-group and a 'bad' and deficient out-group which lacks taste and knowledge in relation to dance music. Thornton recounts how clubbers disparaged 'raving Sharons and Techno Tracys' as representatives of 'handbag house' (1995: 100). This feminised and classed 'mainstream' works to support the value system of the clubbers: 'whether these "mainstreams" reflect empirical social groups or not, they exhibit the burlesque exaggerations of an imagined *other*' (1995: 101).

Thornton therefore *locates moral dualisms and processes of othering both in previous academic studies and in the subculture under analysis* (see 1995: 115), but she has relatively little to say about the moral dualisms which allow value to accrue to her own work. Thornton meticulously relates subcultural capital to media circulation, arguing that the mass media circulation of subcultural information causes this subcultural capital to plummet in value (being viewed as a form of 'selling out'), while moral panics cause subcultural capital to rise since the youth culture concerned can then construct itself in celebratory and rebellious opposition to the 'cultural status quo' (1995: 129). But academic publishing is not discussed or considered (and would this count as mass media, niche media or micro media?). Academic studies of youth and fan culture may well be of interest to the cultures analysed, but Thornton devotes all of half a page to this possibility (1995: 162). How can we explain this notable absence given Thornton's eagerness to question and analyse cultural systems of value where 'nothing classifies somebody more than the way he or she classifies'? (Bourdieu 1990: 132 cited in Thornton 1995: 101).

I would argue that Thornton's critiques of previous work in the field of subcultural studies fit into the practices of academic imagined subjectivity. In order to demonstrate the 'originality' of one's work it is necessary to clear a space' in the field of academic argument. This is therefore an activity which strives to construct cultural capital (as symbolic capital) in one's academic field, while preserving a sense of argument via disinterested and logical reason. (And this clearly applies as much to my own work here as to Thornton's.) Playing by the rules of the academic game also requires, then, a sense of the lofty and disinterested imagined subjectivity of the academic who is not placed within his or her own object of study, and who is not implicated in the conclusions that can be drawn about this 'other'. By cutting academic publishing off from discussions of industry, authenticity and subcultural value, Thornton is able to maintain a 'detached' and implicitly 'universal' academic position. The value system of the cultural studies academic is tacitly assumed but never subjected to the same analysis as that of her respondents. This doesn't simply leave Thornton as *participant*-observer out of the equation, as Gilbert and Pearson (1999: 18–19) have noted, it also leaves Thornton's specific brand of 'academic capital' – and the distinctions which may have accrued to her by way of coining 'subcultural capital' – in the privileged position of remaining unspoken. In part, then, Thornton seems to over-correct Bourdieu's focus on the forms of capital which circulate in his own academic field, since her focus on 'subspecies of capital operating within other less privileged domains' neglects her own investments and capitals as a Lecturer in Media Studies at Sussex University (at the time of the publication of *Club Cultures*). In short, Thornton rails against 'us' versus 'them' accounts, but then reconstructs precisely such a moral dualism by writing out her own (academic) writing and its position within a series of over-lapping cultural fields and struggles over cultural value. While 'they' are caught up in subcultural classifications, 'we' seem able to document such struggles serenely and without being implicated in them.

And yet the 'universal' academics of cultural studies have shown a remarkable propensity to return time and time again to the study of subcultures, fan cultures and youth cultures. I wonder if this is because cultural studies, with its own authenticities and its own well-practised sense of existing as a 'good' moral campaign or inter-discipline rather than as a 'bad' institution or industry, is caught up in some of the same us-versus-them distinctions which it keeps redis-covering in 'subcultural capital'. Indeed, it is tempting to suggest that the predilection for studies of subculture and fan culture has emerged through a partial (but projected outward) recognition of academia as a subculture and 'critical industry'. Perhaps when academics describe subcultural capital and its authenticities (and the subcultural dislike of 'the mainstream') they are, in part, describing a cloaked version of themselves: 'The traditional dilemma of ... an account of the culturally different is contained in the postulate of authenticity which, explicitly or implicitly, underlies it. In this context the word "postulate" should be taken quite literally: *a moral demand is made of the group being inves-tigated*, that it keep as far away as possible from worldly influence' (Lindner

2001: 81, my italics). Locating games of authenticity and their moral dualisms 'out there' is one way of safely leaving these issues silent in relation to the self.

Bourdieu has used the term *illusio* to describe the loss of self-awareness which is necessary to keep players in a 'game' of cultural distinction: '*Illusio* in the sense of investment in the game doesn't become illusion ... until the game is apprehended from the outside, from the point of view of the impartial spectator, who invests nothing in the game or its stakes' (Bourdieu cited in Dreyfus and Rabinow 1999: 90). This is a problematic statement, since it assumes that the rules of a game can only be analysed when we are fully 'outside' the game in question. It therefore relies on an inside–outside binary opposition which ignores the possibility that cultural distinctions can be accrued by analysing one's own game while still remaining *sufficiently* within its terms (i.e. Bourdieu writes his own position out of his argument here!). However, Thornton's veiling of her own investments in analysing club cultures does seem to correspond to the notion of *illusio* in its academic form. Inside the game of subcultural analysis, and accepting its rules, Thornton unselfconsciously reproduces those distinctions which accrue to the 'invisible' and 'detached' academic.

Having considered two post-Bourdieu accounts of fandom, I have shown how Fiske's work moves away from the subtleties of Bourdieu's formulations and towards an insistent use of binary oppositions, despite aiming to restore the complexity of popular cultural capital to Bourdieu's insistently 'legitimate' (and legitimating) account of cultural capital. And I have shown how Thornton's later account reworks Bourdieu more effectively, but remains caught within a logic of academic distinction. However, both Fiske's and Thornton's accounts preserve and re-emphasise a central logic of Bourdieu's argument: the economic metaphor assumes a type of calculating subject, intent on maximising the return of their investment in forms of capital. For example, Fiske observes that within 'such a local or fan community the pay-offs from the investment are continuous and immediate' (1992: 39). Investment in fan knowledge, and hence fan cultural capital, is represented as a compensation for low achievement at school (1992: 33) or as a way for young fans to challenge their elders and betters. And Thornton notes that 'subcultural capital ... has long defined itself as extra-curricular, as knowledge one cannot learn in school' (1995: 13). This type of knowledge brings with it the rewards of subcultural 'authenticity' (1995: 26; see also Lindner 2001: 81).

In each case, then, Fiske and Thornton reconstruct a calculative rationale for the investment in fan or subcultural capital. Proto-fans, fans in the making, are therefore represented as committed utilitarians, assessing the options that are open to them before deciding where to put their time and energy in order to reap certain rewards, and occasionally getting it wrong by 'trying too hard' (Thornton 1995: 12). Now, while this account may well accurately represent sections of fandom, it seems unlikely that such a calculative model will account for all fans, especially given the 'becoming-a-fan' stories which I considered in the Introduction. If many fans emphasise being transformed by their emerging fandom, suddenly being swept away by a need to know more, then it is difficult to see how these 'self-absent' and self-transformative accounts can be squared with Bourdieu's model. It may well be the case that Bourdieu's model functions more adequately for fans who are already securely placed within the institutions, organisations and social networks of fan cultures (being inside the 'rules of the game' of fan distinction) while nevertheless failing to capture the processes at work in fans' initial 'conversions' to their fandoms.

Assuming that Bourdieu's model accounts for organised fandom, we would also expect to uncover some discussion, however minor or brief, which applies (or reworks) the concept of 'social capital' in relation to fan cultures. However, despite the rewritings of Bourdieu offered by Fiske and Thornton, both of these revisionists focus on the concept of 'cultural capital'. Why should this concept have proved so alluring to academic critics, whilst social capital languishes in neglect? There are, I think, two plausible explanations. One is that the concept of cultural capital is exaggerated in Bourdieu's work, with social capital being subordinated to this. These tendencies are then reproduced in later work: 'Erickson (1996), accusing Bourdieu of neglecting social capital ... [argues] that social networks play a much stronger role in the maintenance of social position than does the possession of cultural capital' (Bennett, Emmison and Frow 1999: 268).

A further possibility is that cultural capital has proved more appealing to academic followers of Bourdieu because of its resonance with the concerns of *cultural* critics. In other words, it is possible that a relative homology occurs between the substance of Bourdieu's account and the inculcated predispositions (dare I say the habitus?) of academic critics, who tend to value the possession of culture as a primary source of distinction, since their professional and institutional identities are, to a large extent, premised on this type of distinction. As Carol A. Stabile has usefully commented:

[A]s critics we are implicated in a logic of distinction that ... is at once ideological (a tacit acceptance of the rules of the game) and economic (if we do not 'contribute' to our fields, that is, play by the rules, we are less likely to get jobs ... thereby risking exclusion from the game itself).

(Stabile 1995: 417)

The curious neglect of social capital among Bourdieu's revisionists reinforces Stabile's cautionary note to the effect that '[i]n order to understand the homologies between and among fields, then, media analysts must understand the logic of the field occupied by their object of study as well as the logic structuring their own field' (1995: 418).

Against Fiske and Thornton, I would suggest that the social hierarchy of fandom needs to be more explicitly analysed. John Tulloch has referred to 'executive fans', by which he means 'fans who are executives of the fan club and its magazines' (Tulloch in Tulloch and Jenkins 1995: 149). And Andrea MacDonald has suggested that:

> Fandom, just like the legitimate culture Bourdieu (1984) describes, is hierarchized. ... Fans do not explicitly recognise hierarchies [within their fan cultures; this is not always the case], and academics also hesitate to recognise hierarchies in fandom. Jenkins (1991, 1992), although never specifically denying the existence of hierarchies in fandom, does not address them, and implies that they do not exist by focusing on the grass roots production of fan culture.
>
> (MacDonald 1998: 136)

Neither Tulloch nor MacDonald, then, go on to relate their discussions of fan hierarchy to Bourdieu's concept of social capital, although MacDonald nevertheless develops a sensitive and detailed account of the multiple dimensions of fan hierarchies, which she identifies as hierarchy of knowledge, hierarchy of fandom level, hierarchy of access, hierarchy of leaders and hierarchy of venue (see MacDonald 1998: 137–8). Following Fiske's coinage of 'fan cultural capital' (the knowledge that a fan has about their object of fandom), I would suggest that 'fan social capital' (the network of fan friends and acquaintances that a fan possesses, *as well as* their access to media producers and professional personnel linked with the object of fandom) must also be closely investigated in future analyses. Of course, fan social capital cannot be entirely divorced from fan cultural capital, since it is likely that fans with a very high fan cultural capital will become the 'executive fans', and will therefore possess high level of fan social capital. But while high fan social capital is likely to be predicted by high fan cultural capital, this relationship need not follow. Extremely knowledgeable fans may also 'lurk' or refuse to participate in organised fandom. One highly unlikely combination of these forms of capital would, however, be high fan social capital and relatively low fan cultural capital. It is difficult to imagine how this fan would move through fan circles without betraying their lack of knowledge, and hence their lack of prestige within the fandom.[2]

This raises a further possible absence: 'fan symbolic capital'. Bourdieu uses 'symbolic capital' to refer to 'capital with a cognitive foundation, which rests upon knowledge and recognition' (cited in Earle 1999: 183). It is not at all clear that 'symbolic capital' is actually a type of capital, since elsewhere Bourdieu has written that symbolic capital is 'commonly called prestige, reputation, fame, etc., which is the form assumed by these different kinds of capital [economic, cultural and social capitals] when they are perceived and recognised as legitimate' (Bourdieu 1991: 230). In its apparently variant forms, then, symbolic capital is both a form of recognition (fame, accumulated prestige) and the specific 'legitimation' of other conjunctions of capitals which are themselves 'known and recognised as self-evident' (*ibid.*: 238). A possible instance of 'fan symbolic capital' would be Andrea MacDonald's example of those fans who are nominated as spokespeople for their fandom:

> [O]utsiders to fan discourse (such as journalists and academics) will usually be directed either by fans or by production people to fans who have achieved a certain level of recognition or authority. ... Only authorities are allowed to speak uncontested to outsiders such as journalists.
>
> (MacDonald 1998: 138–9)

Having considered some of the reworkings of Bourdieu, I have suggested in this section that cultural capital has been overly emphasised in later accounts, while other types of capital (social and symbolic) have been underplayed in studies of fan culture. I have also suggested that Bourdieu's work cannot account for non-calculative moments of fan subjectivity such as the fan's initial entry into their fan culture. I will close this chapter by examining a particular fan culture – that surrounding psychotronic cinema – and the issues of fan distinction which it gives rise to.

A psychotronic case study

The pages of *Psychotronic Video* (hereafter *PV*) focus on a wide range of films; exploitation, cult film, the *giallo*, mondo, horror, blaxploitation, science fiction, porn, trash, as well as including music reviews. In many ways the readers and writers of *PV* appear to form a textbook example of the processes of cultural distinction analysed by Bourdieu. Here are film fans who contest 'the notion of "good taste", which functions as a filter to block out whole entire areas of experience judged – and damned – as unworthy of investigation. The concepts of "good taste" are intricately woven into society's control process and class structure' (Vale and Juno 1986: 4).[3]

Vale and Juno's introductory 1986 statement has rebounded through academic studies of psychotronic cinema. The privileging of such a statement is easy enough to explain. Academic preoccupations with the politics of taste are mirrored in this section of critical popular culture, allowing academic commentary the rare luxury of citing a highly articulate and politicised statement which makes its own arguments for it. However, while proving all too tempting to academics (this account included), Vale and Juno's statement then presents something of a problem for academic studies of paracinematic fan culture; namely, how can academic work go on to legitimate itself by presenting a meta-account which develops out of 'psychotronic' politics? Unless academic work is content simply to announce the discovery of a 'good' and critical area of fan culture (Lindner's 'moral demand' all over again), academia must continue to mark out and legitimate its own strategies of distinction. Admittedly, the first strategy is pursued by McLaughlin (1996):

[F]or all of its vigorous bad taste and offensive material, *PV* treats these films in a serious and scholarly way. Its audience is clearly the collector – reviews give straightforward plot summaries, sometimes of amazingly perverse stories, that provide a prospective collector with a good clue about whether the film would interest him.

(McLaughlin 1996: 71)

McLaughlin's account strikes a tone of bemused tolerance: never mind the bad taste, feel the scholarship. By seeking to value *PV* solely for its 'serious and scholarly' fan knowledge, he marginalises the issue of 'amazingly perverse' taste as if it were faintly embarrassing, or worse, as if it might taint or counteract his own political and moral claim for *PV*'s status as an example of 'good' vernacular theory. Given that it could be argued that 'psychotronic criticism' runs 'counter to dominant streams of political correctness in the academy' (Chibnall 1997: 85), McLaughlin's apparent unease is unsurprising. At the very least, his reading strategy illustrates the interaction of different taste cultures, with the 'good' liberal academic seeking to find value in the 'bad taste' of a subculture which is otherwise seemingly alien to him, and therefore separating out what can be tolerated and counted as a source of value within his own academic culture.

Other critics have not split off 'good' knowledge from 'bad' bad taste. Using Bourdieu's work, Sconce relates his account of the distinctions of trash cinema to the field of academic distinction. Following Fiske and Bourdieu, Sconce considers how alternative forms of cultural capital are likely to appeal to those who either lack official cultural capital, or those who have yet to convert high levels of cultural and educational capital into economic capital: 'fans, as exiles from the legitimising functions of the academy, and many graduate students, as the most disempowered faction within the academy itself, both look to trash culture as a source of "refuge and revenge"' (Sconce 1995: 379). This situation could, perhaps, also be linked to Bourdieu's argument that it is (only) the dominated bourgeoisie who look to maximise a return on their cultural capital by making 'risky' investments in new forms of cultural distinction and hence in new fields of cultural value ('trash cinema' in this case). Bourdieu notes that such risky investments bring the greatest rewards, and indeed the earliest explorers of 'psychotronic cinema' seem to have accrued considerable cultural and symbolic capital: 'Michael Weldon, with ... his excellent *Psychotronic* magazine, was a trailblazer to whom we are all indebted' (Ross 1993: xii).

Having usefully linked his field of study to the academic field which he occupies, Sconce then goes on to view *PV* as an example of 'paracinematic' distinction:

[P]aracinematic viewers ... use [these films' textual] excess as a gateway to exploring profilmic and extratextual aspects of the filmic object itself. ... Whereas aesthete interest in style and excess always returns the viewer to the frame, paracinematic attention to excess seeks to push the viewer beyond the formal boundaries of the text.

(Sconce 1995: 387)

Sconce argues that it is through a focus on the 'non-diegetic' aspects of 'psychotronic' films – 'unconvincing special effects, blatant anachronisms or histrionic acting' (*ibid.*) – that their fans are able to revalue 'bad film'. He consistently contrasts paracinema fans to cinematic aesthetes, suggesting that paracinema fans are dedicated in their opposition to 'legitimate' cinematic tastes. Sconce also notes that this opposition cannot be thought of as static: 'the paracinematic sensibility has recently begun to infiltrate the avant-garde, the academy, and even the mass culture on which paracinema's ironic reading strategies originally preyed' (1995: 373). It seems that the challenge of paracinematic taste has been so successful that it is now no longer clearly 'oppositional', while the previously 'legitimate' taste (while still culturally powerful) is certainly not monolithically dominant, if indeed it ever was. This dynamic process formed the subject matter of one of publisher/editor Michael Weldon's *PV* intros:

> Have you noticed how many more magazines are out there – all covering the same (new) releases? I saw a whole display of Scream Queen magazines in a store recently. Things have changed a lot, haven't they? Who could have guessed when this zine started that we'd see a major movie about ED WOOD JR? It's real good too!
>
> (*PV* No. 19 1994: 3)

Weldon's use of a single word in brackets here is interesting. His addition of '(new)' marks out one line of cultural distinction; as a 'good' object for academic valorisation, *PV* values psychotronic and trash film history (and for an academic version of this historical valorisation see Schaefer 1999). Film summaries are presented under headings such as '70s Adult', 'Sick 70s', '40s' and '60s NYC', as well as by country ('Australia/New Zealand'), actresses (e.g. 'Bonet') (all in *PV* No. 19 1994: 54–61) and directors (e.g. 'Franco' and 'Woodsploitation' for material relating to Ed Wood Jr. are given in *PV* No. 18 1994: 57 and 60). A further category for reviews is 'More Sequels Nobody Wanted', which states *PV*'s anti-commercial ideologies very succinctly, even while the zine's commodity-completist/archivist tendencies are simultaneously evident.

Sconce points out the existence of rival 'trash' aesthetics. He compares *PV* to a competing fanzine-turned-magazine *Film Threat*: 'while *Psychotronic* concentrates on the sizable segment of this community interested in uncovering and collecting long lost titles from the history of exploitation, *Film Threat* looks to transgressive aesthetics/genres of the past as avant-garde inspiration for contemporary independent film-making' (Sconce 1995: 375). This difference in emphasis resulted in *Film Threat* depicting a 'typical' reader of *PV* as 'passive, overweight and asexual, with a bad complexion' on one of its subscription forms (*ibid.*). Sconce curtly describes this as an effort 'at generating counter-distinction within the shared cultural project of attacking "high-brow" cinema' (*ibid.*), but promptly displaces this rift by focusing instead on the separation of paracinematic fans and 'the cineastes they construct as their nemesis' (1995: 375). The latter separation would be predicted by Bourdieu's model (cleaving along a 'dominated' and 'dominating' axis of the dominant class fraction high in educational capital), but the former bid for 'counter-distinction' remains problematic. It is not clear in this case how the variant 'trash aesthetics' of *Film Threat* and *PV* can be related back to a class or generational differential or to a differential distribution in economic, cultural, social or educational capital. In short, rather like the example of *Doctor Who* fan-scholars that I gave earlier in the chapter, there is a problem here for any interpretation which seeks to ground 'moral dualisms' (the 'hip' us versus the 'geeky' them) either in class differences or in differences of generational trajectory. Sconce does not, in my opinion, sufficiently explore the contradiction that opens up in his account at this point. How can we then account for internal fan-cultural struggles over distinction which would not be predicted by Bourdieu?

Rogers Brubaker has observed that '[h]aving thoroughly "objectified the objectifiers", Bourdieu might now usefully "subjectify the objectifiers"' (1993: 225). Although Brubaker is referring to sociologists and their moments of reflexivity and non-reflexivity, this could also be usefully applied to those subjects involved in the *Film Threat/PV* cultural distinction. How can we explain such fine-grained moral dualisms and constructions of an imagined other? Thornton considers an imagined other to be projected outside the subculture or fan community concerned, and I have followed this logic on a number of occasions so far. But here is an example of an imagined other being projected *within* a fan culture or subculture. 'Subjectifying' this distinction – which is in any case inevitable because we have no 'objective' class, cultural, gender or generational differences to hang on to – this resembles what Freud has termed the 'narcissism of minor differences' whereby in the case of 'two neighbouring towns each is the other's most jealous rival; every little canton looks down upon the others with contempt. Closely related races keep each other at arm's length, ... the Englishman casts every kind of aspersion upon the Scot, the Spaniard despises the Portuguese' (Freud [1921] 1991: 131). Or the 'underground-indie' trash cinema fan despises the 'archivist' trash cinema fan.

The 'narcissism of minor differences' indicates that moral dualisms can be constructed at two levels; both in terms of legitimating one's own cultural practices against other imagined subjectivities, and also in terms of legitimating one's own cultural practices against imagined others whose very cultural proximity also threatens the project of distinction. Cultural closeness and distance can, it seems, both produce mechanisms of cultural distinction. Bourdieu's model seems to be premised only on more-or-less 'distant' mechanisms of cultural distinction, where classes (or fields) defined by their habitus seek to ward off the values of other classes/fields. Such a model therefore cannot account convincingly for the threats to cultural value which are posed by 'close' or culturally proximate mechanisms of distinction.

The moral dualisms produced by cultural proximity are abundant in academic (sub)culture, where intellectual formations fragment along the lines of fiercely defended and supposedly theoretically-pressing 'differences' such as that of 'cultural studies' versus 'political economy'. These fine-grained 'fractal distinctions' (see Abbott 2001: 10–21) also operate in fan cultures, which typically segment along the lines of favoured characters, actors, periods in a series, films in a franchise, or according to differences in fans' interpretive strategies (McCormack 2000; Lindlof *et al.* 1998). Frow (1995) and Bennett, Emmison and Frow (1999) have offered a critique of Bourdieu's work which can allow us to make further sense of these types of cultural distinctions. Frow (1995) characterises Bourdieu's work as doubly essentialist: it assumes 'a single class "experience" common to the sociologically quite distinct groups Bourdieu includes in the dominant class' and it 'posits a single aesthetic logic which corresponds to this experience' (1995: 31). To counter these problems, Frow introduces the concept of the regime of value: 'every act of ascribing value ... is specific to the particular regime that organises it ... Regimes of value are relatively autonomous of and have no direct expressive relation to social groups' (1995: 145). This raises the possibility that a 'regime of value' may, under specific circumstances, be shared by academic-fans and non-academic fans, or by academics and fans. It also loosens cultural value and moral dualisms from the iron grip of a class determinism. The concept is developed in Bennett, Emmison and Frow (1999) where it designates:

> those normative organisations of the proper which specify what counts as a good object of desire or pleasure; a proper mode of access or entry to it; and an appropriate range of valuations. ... The concept designates a convergence of lines of force which is discernible in its effects and which can be subsumed within larger conceptual structures or broken down to smaller, more specific levels ... [A] distinction ... can ... always be ramified, according to the context of meaningfulness, into a finer web of distinctions.
>
> (1999: 260)

The first part of this definition is not so different from Tony Bennett's concept of the 'reading formation' (see Frow 1995: 145). But the second part of this definition means that the concept can account both for culturally 'distant' and culturally 'proximate' moral dualisms. The same 'regime of value' can break down into a fine web of distinctions while retaining effects at the level of 'larger conceptual structures'.

But, as I will demonstrate over the course of the next two chapters, any 'single-lensed' theoretical approach (i.e. 'sociological' or 'psychoanalytic') to fandom remains incapable of accounting:

1   for the social and cultural regularities of fan cultures, and
2   for fan cultures' dialectic of value, and thus for the fans' intensely felt 'possession' and 'ownership' of their fan object.

The point we have reached thus far tackles point (1) reasonably well, but is unable to address point (2) other than by viewing this fan sentiment as the construction of a specific regime of value. And this ignores the 'experiential chronology' of fan cultures. The generation of a fan community depends on fans from different walks of life gathering together to share their fandoms. In other words, the fans' sense of possessiveness, ownership and textual attachments are already in place *before* 'normative organisations of the proper which specify what counts as a good object of desire or pleasure; a proper mode of access or entry to it; and an appropriate range of valuations' can be said to act on fan interpretation. But all previous approaches to fan culture which stress the 'interpretive community' (Amesley 1989; Jenkins 1992), the 'reading formation' (Bennett and Woollacott 1987; Tulloch and Jenkins 1995) or even the 'regime of value' (as I have done here) are forced – through theoretical necessity – to treat fan communities as already established communal facts rather than accounting for their generation and formation.

Summary

- In this chapter I have examined Bourdieu's model in some detail, suggesting that it offers a significant and important metaphor when thinking about fan cultures. However, it is important not to lose sight of the fact that Bourdieu's complex theoretical engagement is based on one guiding metaphor ('the economy' of culture), and may therefore remain unable to deal with aspects of fandom which do not fit into models of competitive and calculative 'play'.
- I have also examined later readings of Bourdieu which apply his work to fan culture. Although Fiske and Thornton develop Bourdieu's work in helpful ways, both view fan culture as functional. Both also focus on 'cultural capital', I would argue as a result of their places within the academic field.
- Also, neither Fiske nor Thornton reflect on the moral dualisms (us-versus-them) that are constructed within their own academic accounts. Fiske pits 'good' popular cultural capital against 'bad' economic capital, and Thornton writes her own bid for cultural distinction out of her account. Bourdieu, it seems to me, is guilty of the same writing-out of the self through his insistence on an *illusio* which is total when 'in' the game and which can be seen as 'illusion' only when one is totally 'out' of the game.
- I have suggested a further problem with Bourdieu's work, which is the highly systematic and ultimately deterministic nature of its 'professional

rationality'. This means that Bourdieu and his followers all have a tendency to read moral and aesthetic differences off from the master-grid of class difference, or through a limited 'dominant'/'subordinate' model.

- By examining work on psychotronic film, I have considered how Bourdieu's model is unable to account for the moral dualisms which emerge within class fractions and within fan (sub)cultures.

3

FAN CULTURES BETWEEN 'KNOWLEDGE' AND 'JUSTIFICATION'

> [I]f I have not sought to get people to speak about ... [their passion or fandom], it is not just because the subject 'speaks for itself', but also because in matters of admiration and celebration every request for justification produces a backlash. For, in inducing interviewees ... to provide an account of their experience, one forces them out of their participatory stance ... and throws them into a position of justification.
>
> (Heinich 1996: xiii)

My focus in this chapter on ethnographies of fandom will lead me to suggest that all too often fan 'justifications' are accepted as cultural facts by ethnographers, rather than being subjected to further analysis. I would argue that the recent boom in 'fan studies' has produced the figure of 'the fan' within a highly specific cultural studies' narrative. Work on fandom has formed a key part of the move towards valorising active audiences, and this use of the fan has resulted in an extremely partial and limited examination of fan practices. Fandom has been curiously emptied of the dimensions which, I would suggest, most clearly define it: dimensions of affect, attachment, and even passion, as well as, crucially, the dimensions of commodification through which these processes are enabled and constrained.

Fan ethnographies: emphasising the knowledgeable fan

The significantly affective nature of the fan's attachment renders ethnographic methodology problematic in this context; it cannot be assumed (as is so often the case in cultural studies) that fandom acts as a guarantee of self-presence and transparent self-understanding:

> We should emphasise from the outset that the pleasure can be so intense that it almost cannot be articulated by those experiencing it. We were struck repeatedly in our interviews and informal conversations with fans by the strength of their passion for, devotion to, and sheer

love of daytime television, *to an extent often beyond their own compre-hension.*

(Harrington and Bielby 1995: 121, my italics)

The ethnographic process of 'asking the audience', although useful in many cases, constitutes a potentially reductive approach. It assumes that cultural activities can be adequately accounted for in terms of language and 'discourse', rather than considering how the question 'why are you a fan of ... ?' itself causes the fan to cut into the flow of their experience and produce some kind of discursive 'justification'.

Cultural studies' 'ethnography' has rarely pursued this insight, failing to consider processes of auto-legitimation within fan culture, and instead depicting these processes as fan 'knowledgeability'. This emphasis on the fan's knowledge, and on the display of knowledge, acts, in part, as an alibi for the ethnographic process: given the fan's articulate nature, and immersion in the text concerned, the move to ethnography seems strangely unquestionable, as if it is somehow grounded in the fan's (supposedly) pre-existent form of audience knowledge and interpretive skill. And yet this grounding figure of 'the fan' is itself a reduc-tion of subjectivity; a reduction which operates as a foundational legitimation of, and for, ethnographic methodology. Fandom is largely reduced to mental and discursive activity occurring without passion, without feeling, without an experience of (perhaps involuntary) self-transformation. This ethnographic version of fan culture seems to have no inkling that discursive justifications of fandom might be fragile constructions, albeit socially-licensed and communal ones. This is *not* to argue that fans *cannot* discuss their feelings, passions and personal histories of fandom in any meaningful manner. Far from it. Instead I am trying to emphasise that *fan-talk cannot be accepted merely as evidence of fan knowledge. It must also be interpreted and analysed in order to focus upon its gaps and dislocations, its moments of failure within narratives of self-consciousness and self-reflexivity, and its repetitions or privileged narrative constructions which are concerned with communal (or subcultural) justification in the face of 'external' hostility.* Previous fan-ethnography has largely erred on the side of accepting fan discourse as interpretive 'knowledge'. My aim here is to reconsider fan discourse as a justification for fan passions and attachments.

Analysing the affective nature of the fan-text attachment means that 'asking the audience' cannot act as a guarantee of knowledge. As Michael Haslett discusses in the *Doctor Who* fanzine *Skaro*, *Who* fandom as a community typi-cally presents particular justifications of its collective love for the programme, but these justifications are – to a great extent – merely a way of defending the fan's attachment against external criticism:

> Harken to ... some stirring rhetoric about 'WHO' having the most flexible format on British television, something about its narrative range incorporating horror, sci-fi, fantasy, historical adventure and

comedy, to name but a few of its multiple genres. 'This is what makes *Doctor Who* so great' they all say, from haughty academics, drawing their fan pensions, to members of the greedy brat-pack. Alas, these are often merely the empty homilies of unimaginative plodders, with most of us doubtless having succumbed to using this stock favourite slice of hyperbole in the past ... It is no more than a cloud of smoke, a cult phrase repeated parrot-fashion, perhaps to hide the fact that we cannot agree on what *Doctor Who* is or should be.

(Haslett 1994: 10)

Fan-ethnography would readily uncover this *discursive mantra*, by which I mean a relatively stable discursive resource which is circulated within niche media and fanzines and used (by way of communal rationalisation) to ward off the sense that the fan is 'irrational'.[1] If *Doctor Who* fandom relies on the justification of a 'cult phrase' stressing the format's flexibility, then an equivalent defence for *Star Trek* fans would concern the progressive politics and multiculturalism of the original crew. However, if 'asking the audience' is sufficient in itself, then such discursive structures and repetitions would tend to be accepted at face value rather than being considered as defensive mechanisms designed to render the fan's affective relationship meaningful in a rational sense, i.e. to ground this relationship solely in the objective attributes of the source text and therefore to legitimate the fans' love of 'their' programme.

Addressing the question 'why are you a fan of this particular text?', it seems that fans typically register some confusion or difficulty in responding, before then falling back immediately on their particular fandom's discursive mantra. This process – the marked absence of an explanatory framework for one's intense devotion which immediately shifts onto the firmer ground of discussing textual characteristics – is neatly encapsulated within (then-President of 'Six of One', *The Prisoner* Appreciation Society) Roger Langley's contribution to *The Prisoner: A Televisionary Masterpiece* (Carraze and Oswald 1990):

> *Why has a television series ... played a big part in my life of over 20 years? I still do not know!* ... If you are reading this new book, you must already be interested in *The Prisoner!* So, what do we share? Is it the acting of Patrick McGoohan, the beauty of Portmeirion, the excitement of the episodes or the strange atmosphere of the episodes as a whole? Is it the issues raised by the stories, the strange happenings in the Village, the unusual music or the striking costumes? These things, and many more, are all vital ingredients of *The Prisoner*, providing many reasons for its appeal.
>
> (Langley in Carraze and Oswald 1990: 12, my italics)

The fan cannot act, then, as the unproblematic source of the meaning of their own media consumption. This is not necessarily to recap the 'fallacy of meaningfulness' uncovered by Hermes (1995) – which emphasises the ritualistic rather than primarily semiotic use of media such as women's magazines. Instead I would describe the belief that fans can fully account for their fandoms as a 'fallacy of internality'. The assumption here is that sense and understanding are securely present inside the fan community, whereas external academic narratives – whether they are psychological, psychoanalytic or sociological – are somehow fraudulent or imposed upon the phenomenon that they attempt to explain away (see, for example Bacon-Smith 1992). This 'fallacy of internality' neglects the extent to which internal fan community understandings are collectively negotiated precisely in order to ward off the taint of irrationality, and in order to present a public and rationalised face to the world outside the fan culture. The fallacy of internality assumes that the 'in-group' is a source of pristine knowledge. It neglects the sociological dynamics whereby the culturally devalued 'in-group' of media fandom is compelled to account for its passions.[2]

I am hence refuting the adequacy of ethnographic methodology *in this precise instance* (and not across all instances of media consumption in all contexts and modalities) on the basis that the positivism of such empirical work is *insufficiently positivist*: it typically ignores the structured gaps and replications within the discursive frameworks which are used by fans to account for and justify their fandoms.

But what of the various fan-ethnographies that have been produced, and which form the canon of 'fan studies'? Henry Jenkins (1996: 263) contrasts his own *Textual Poachers* to more 'traditional participant-observer approaches'. This is because Jenkins's work doesn't present an 'outsider' entering into – and discovering the cultural truth of – the 'field' of fandom. The term 'ethnography' is often used rather loosely in media and cultural studies, sometimes indicating little more than hour-long interviews with respondents. In its original anthropological context, the term implies a lengthy immersion in the field being studied. (And this 'field' is typically thought of as being alien to the analyst, who has to come to understand a different way of life.) On the basis of these definitions of the term 'ethnography' as it has been used in classical anthropology, Jenkins argues that another study of fandom, published in the same year as *Textual Poachers* and written by Camille Bacon-Smith, more fully deserves the label of a *traditional* 'fan-ethnography'.[3] This is because Bacon-Smith presents a participant-observation of sections of *Star Trek* fan culture in which she self-consciously represents herself as 'the ethnographer' entering an unknown subcultural field, determined to understand its practices and activities.

Bacon-Smith's conclusions validate her methodology very precisely and without remainder: she veritably scrapes away at the layers and layers of misdirection which the fan community presents to her as an initial 'outsider' who gradually, over the course of years of research, learns the ropes. Indeed, the power struggle between insider and ethnographer-outsider is explicitly depicted by Bacon-Smith in terms of her own ethnographic quest narrative:

as an ethnographer, I found myself searching for the heart of this community: what made it tick? ... The deeper I penetrated the community, the more elusive my goal became.

Of course, a community gives certain signals when an outsider approaches the heart of its culture. In the beginning the heart is hidden – often in plain sight – passed over, casually dismissed by those in the know. Later, as the importance of the practice ... starts to emerge from the dense fog of apparent communal indifference, the intrepid ethnographer finds herself swamped with data – explanations that agree too closely with one another, that offer tidy answers to her questions with no loose ends to unravel.

When the investigator gets too close, the community sidetracks with something of value, something that conserves the risk the ethnographer knows is present but that does not expose *too* much.

(1992: 224 and 226)

Bacon-Smith is clearly highly aware of the self-mythologising narrative of her account,[4] hence the overwritten 'intrepid' ethnographer struggling on bravely through the 'fog'. Despite her exaggerated presentation of such a narrative, Bacon-Smith nonetheless relies on it to determine her account of the 'evasive' fan community. She concedes her desire to 'jump up and down and scream "Look what I found! A conceptual space where women can come together and create – to investigate new forms for their art and for their living outside the restrictive boundaries men have placed on women's public behaviour! Not a place or a time, but a state of being" ' (*ibid.*: 3). This introductory admission is presumably intended to reassure the reader: Bacon-Smith *wants* to jump up and down, but 'a colder mind prevails' and we are returned to the hallowed halls of strictly objective and affect-less academia. As such, Bacon-Smith's presentation of the fan community plays its own narrative games of expectation, disruption and delay with the reader. Bacon-Smith chides Jenkins for using the fan community to further his own 'political agenda' (*ibid.*: 282), but it is hard to see how her own account could refute such an accusation.

Bacon-Smith announces her academic identity as 'Ethnographer' (see also Bacon-Smith 2000). By doing so, she positions herself as a kind of detective, using the conventions of the murder mystery or detective-thriller to frame her account of fandom. She is the seeker of knowledge, the character who will prevail. It is her 'colder mind' which is able to circumvent the stalling tactics, distractions and diversions of the fan community. Bacon-Smith's account is one of a world of clues and misdirections, a subcultural fan world charged with meaning. This narrative construction resembles the principles of Sherlock Holmes's 'empirical imagination' where 'the truth is right there to be read on the surface of things, had we the wit to see. Mundane facts become marvels and wonders – clues, evidence, proof' (Atkinson 1998: 109). And Bacon-Smith's version of events, which I have quoted above, fits entirely and uncannily into

Pierre Bayard's analysis of the detective novel. Where the truth of a fan culture is always in plain sight, but where fans attempt to distract the detective-ethnographer, we find: 'the principle of truth hidden by its obviousness ... [and the second mechanism, that of] [d]istraction. ... This time we are dealing with a negative disguise. It is not that the truth is made unrecognisable, but that the false ... is dressed up to draw attention to itself' (Bayard 2000: 21, 24).

This highlights a further problem with fan-ethnographies; the extent to which they use narrative conventions from popular fiction, thereby allocating certain narrative functions to their respondents and the fan community. It may be impossible to avoid writing academically without providing a narrative shape to one's 'theoretical' account (meaning, non-judgementally, that all theories are also stories). It is still a problem for ethnographers, however, that their accounts may so closely resemble the conventions of certain genres. This resemblance means that such accounts are unable to construct more complex characterisations of fan culture beyond a sense of 'communal conspiracy' to be battled by the detective-ethnographer (Bacon-Smith), or a sense of 'communal creativity' to be recognised and valued by the scholar-fan (Jenkins). As Van Maanen has observed: 'literary tales [ethnographies using the conventions of literature] may be so tied to the representational techniques of realistic fiction that they distort the very reality they seek to capture' (1988: 135).

My own narrative of fandom is less detective-based and is equally less concerned with depicting fan cultures as inherently positive or as miniaturised models of academia. In my own rather less heroic narrative template, the character of 'the academic' abandons the construction of easily legible moral dualisms (thereby creating a meta-dualism between those who champion a cause or a fan community and those who refuse to draw moral and communal lines clearly around 'us' and 'them'). This abandonment of moral dualism is perhaps an academic version of 'anti-hero' fiction in which characters we are expected to sympathise with ('the academic' and 'the fan') may also possess unwanted or undesirable attributes. The work of Jenkins and Bacon-Smith seems to embody two sides of the same coin: both refuse to let go of one-sided views of fandom. Jenkins sees Bacon-Smith as presenting a falsely negative view of fans (Jenkins in Tulloch and Jenkins 1995: 203), while, in turn, she castigates his work for presenting a falsely positive view (Bacon-Smith 1992: 282). And oddly enough, the 'reality' of fandom that each seeks to capture in broadly ethnographic terms may well exist *between* their respective moral positions.

My own position here is close to that established by Jensen and Pauly (1997). They decry the way that theories of media audiences tend to construct these audiences as 'other' to the investigating academic (*ibid.*: 195). However, Jensen and Pauly conclude that 'if subjects are imagined as deficient in their articulation of their own experience, then there is not much chance that the researcher will learn anything from those subjects' (*ibid.*: 166). This, however, is a view which assumes that 'learning' is only possible on the basis of the other's full or 'non-deficient' self-articulation. On the contrary, I would suggest that what academics need to learn is that their own accounts are also 'deficient', meaning that this cannot be used as a way of (morally) devaluing other subcultures and communities.[5] What academics can learn from subjects who are unable to articulate their own experiences is that they, too, may not be able to articulate the full meaning of their own experiences, therefore no longer existing in a fantasised 'authoritative' space outside any cultural struggle over meaning. This possibility is closed off by Jensen and Pauly's assumption that the 'good' subject is self-present, articulate and always capable of full self-explanation without remainder; a perfect restatement of academic imagined subjectivity.

Another related and very real problem for fan ethnographies is what they assume will count as 'the real'. Although few fan ethnographies dwell on this question, what counts as the 'field' to be observed will differ if a psychoanalytic critic is interpreting ethnographic 'data' as opposed to a sociologist. The notion that these sorts of problems of academic knowledge and interpretation can be 'put ... to one side', seems, to my mind, faintly optimistic (Couldry 2000b: 14). This suspension of theoretical debate in favour of 'getting on with things' also implies that what counts as the 'real' is self-evident and can be detached from arguments over its interpretation. However, rather than accepting the narrative of ethnography as an encounter with the 'real' (which is superior to the 'abstract' and supposedly 'unreal' space of overly-generalising Grand Theory), I would argue that ethnography needs to be based on a reconceptualisation of empiricism so that 'the real' consistently encompasses not only the discourses and routines of everyday life (Silverstone 1994), but also the possible absences in discourse, and the potential gaps in both academics' and fans' reflections on their own identities and cultures. By way of illustrating these possibilities, I will now turn to the practice of autoethnography in which 'ethnographies of the self' are produced.

Autoethnography: narratives of the fan, narratives of the self

In acquiring one's conception of the world one always belongs to a particular grouping which is that of all the social elements which share the same mode of thinking and acting. We are all conformists of some conformism or other, always man-in-the-mass or collective man. ... The personality is strangely composite: it contains Stone Age elements and principles of a more advanced science ... The starting point of critical elaboration is the consciousness of what one really is, and is 'knowing thyself' as a product of the historical process to date which has deposited in you an infinity of traces, without leaving an inventory. The first thing to do is to make such an inventory.

(Gramsci 1971: 324)

If fan-ethnography has typically been limited by its view of 'the real' as a matter of discourse and articulation, or by its one-sided accounts of fandom either as a social coping mechanism (Bacon-Smith 1992) or a valuable 'interpretive community' (Jenkins 1992; Amesley 1989), then how can the limits of both fan and academic self-expression be explored differently?

A useful exercise here is autoethnography, in which the tastes, values, attachments and investments of the fan and the academic-fan are placed under the microscope of cultural analysis. Autoethnography aims to create a partial 'inventory' of the 'infinity of traces' deposited within the self by cultural and historical processes. Autoethnography also displaces the problems of assuming that the 'real' is always primarily discursive. This is possible because autoethnography asks the person undertaking it to question their self-account constantly, opening the 'subjective' and the intimately personal up to the cultural contexts in which it is formed and experienced. As a form of voluntary self-estrangement, autoethnography confronts the subject with a variety of possible interpretations of their self-accounts, and their self-accounts of their self-accounts. This process of persistent questioning throws the self into the realisation that explanations of fan and consumer activity are themselves culturally conventional. This realisation can open up the possibility of inscribing other explanations of the self; it can promote an acceptance of *the fragility and inadequacy of our claims to be able to 'explain' and 'justify' our own most intensely private or personal moments of fandom and media consumption*. The fragility of discursive accounts is exposed by this persistent questioning, provoking an investigation of why we stop self-analysis at a certain point by refusing to challenge privileged discourses. This endpoint of self-analysis does not reveal the 'true' discourse through which we can account for own cultural practices. Quite the reverse; these limits reveal that certain discourses are powerful because of the (non-discursive) investments that we make in them, and because of their structuring absences and familiar repetitions.

Autoethnography does not simply indicate that the 'personal is political'.[6] Instead, it indicates that the personal – the heart of the self and the core of our cultural identity as we perform it – is always borrowed and alien. The logic of that borrowing is rarely evident to us, which is where the question of cultural politics can enter the equation, but the key statement of any autoethnography is that the 'personal is cultural'; our identities are constructed through *relatively homologous* systems of cultural value. This means that no single 'system of value' can be isolated, only the interference pattern produced by multiple systems of value which cannot readily be made to line up and which are, equally, not entirely unrelated.

I will now demonstrate what this can mean in more practical terms by examining a number of academic-fan autoethnographies and showing how they are 'deficient' in their self-accounts. All refuse to question aspects of identity which the writer is attached to and which 'self-reflexivity' therefore cannot easily dislodge. Hollway and Jefferson refer to these moments as the 'discursive investments' of the 'defended subject' (2000: 19). These are moments when a core of self-identity is protected by an investment in a particular discourse. However, the radical component in Hollway and Jefferson's work is that they view themselves, as researchers, as equally 'anxious, defended subjects' (2000: 45). Their work therefore meets with the key criteria of 'accountable theory' suggested by Nick Couldry:

> Quite simply: the language and theoretical framework with which we analyse others should be always be consistent with the ... language and theoretical framework with which we analyse ourselves. And, equally, in reverse ... The reversibility of the principle is crucial: it is what prevents us from falling into a spiral of endless self-interrogation, never to resurface.
>
> (Couldry 2000b: 126)

However, I am not convinced that the problem of 'endless self-interrogation' expressed here is a pressing one. For me, the real problem is the absolute reverse; when and why do we call a halt to our self-interrogations? What cultural categories, common sense narratives and systems of value do we leave in place by assuming that we have reached rock-bottom in our self-justifications? I am not at all interested in initiating some endless and narcissistic navel-gazing. But I am concerned by the possibility *that narcissism emerges at precisely the place where we stop self-interrogation*, leaving a comfortable sense of our own cultural value(s) and identity fixed in place as somehow authentic. And it is this sense of narcissism – not navel-gazing but instead complacently calling a day on the analysis of how the self is formed inside culture – that I will examine in four autoethnographies: Fiske (1990), Bukatman (1994), Wise (1990) and Wolff (1995). I will then conclude this chapter by presenting my own autoethnography.[7]

In 'Ethnosemiotics: Some Personal and Theoretical Reflections', John Fiske sets out to explore his own responses to *The Newly Wed Game*. Fiske's aim is to consider how social discourses in the text link into the social discourses which he draws on to construct his sense of self. Fiske identifies three discourses: the professional, the popular and what he terms the 'semantic'. The last type covers all topics 'that both infused ... daily life and were called up by the program' (1990: 86), while the first two types cover Fiske's work as an academic and his sense of himself as a fan of the popular with 'vulgar tastes: the garish, the sensational, the obvious give me great pleasure, not least because they contradict the tastes and positionings of the class to which, objectively, I "belong"' (*ibid.*). Fiske notes that, in his article, a professional discourse is dominating 'popular' and 'semantic' discourses. In other words, he is writing as an academic, producing an article which has to meet the standards expected of a major international journal. So far, so good. Fiske does not claim that his own audience responses are in any way 'typical'. Instead, he observes that self-introspection based on cultural theory is important because although '[n]either I nor my readings are typical ... the process by which I produced them is evidence of a cultural system' (*ibid.*).

Examining this supposedly singular 'system', Fiske then broadens the scope of his study to take in his living room. The objects contained in the room are analysed in relation to the discourses through which Fiske realises his sense of self: the 'cheap plastic toy TVs' (1990: 88) on top of his actual TV are linked to a 'popular' discourse, while Fiske analyses both his antique furniture and his homemade TV stand and cheap technology as examples of his 'reluctance to enter uncritically into the capitalist commodity economy' (*ibid.*). The same anti-capitalism 'semantic' discourse is therefore reflected in a variety of different cultural artifacts. Fiske also observes that the same object can operate 'multidiscursively', meaning different things in different discourses. Both the physical environment in which media consumption takes place, and the types of texts that are consumed, can therefore be linked to the 'cultural system'(s) through which the self is constructed.

Fiske claims that autoethnography, where he as the ethnographer 'is both producer and product' (1990: 90), can be used to 'open up the realm of the interior and the personal, and to articulate that which, in the practices of everyday life, lies below any conscious articulation' (*ibid.*). The approach is therefore justified on moral grounds: autoethnography does not privilege 'the theory and the theorist' by assuming that the theorist has a privileged insight into the experiences of his or her respondents. Instead, Fiske's version of autoethnography is one where the subject is able to participate in their own construction of meaning, coming to view their sense of self in an altered and expanded way through the use of theory, but not through subordination to theory.

What, then, are the limits to Fiske's autoethnography? Where, as a 'defended subject' does he demonstrate an investment in certain discourses and identities which prevents any further self-reflection? I would argue that this occurs primarily in Fiske's account of his political position: 'my call for an extension of this methodology (with its politics, ethics and theory) comes from a left-wing, progressive academic (albeit a male, though hopefully not too masculine a one)' (1990: 91). Although Fiske's work presents a number of points which allow theory to illuminate experience and vice versa, his political stance remains outside the frame of self-reflexivity, remaining seemingly unquestioned and unchallenged. Fiske's narrative of himself as 'critically resisting' capitalism is left firmly in place, and the contradiction between his own ('duly trained' and privileged) ability to manipulate theory and a sense of autoethnography being 'non-imposed' is not uncovered and explored. Instead, autoethnography is contrasted to psychoanalytic and ideological approaches, since these are viewed as approaches where theory is imposed on experience. This moral dualism, and Fiske's attachment to his own 'good' and apologetically 'masculine' leftist subjectivity, is never questioned; it is an element of Fiske's self-identity and his experience of self which is not sufficiently 'opened up' as part of a cultural system of value.

I would argue that this is the narcissism inherent in Fiske's autoethnography. His analysis of his own living room and his own subjectivity is not inherently narcissistic, but the narrative closures of his account are. These premature closures put an end to self-reflexivity, allowing the 'good' self to settle into its habitual boundaries, and leaving this routine 'below any conscious articulation' rather than 'raising' it into the space of theoretical reflection. By contrast, the next male author whose work I would describe as 'autoethnographic' seems intent on confessing all, and risking the embarrassment and loss of (student) respect which this might involve.

Scott Bukatman's 'X-Bodies (the torment of the mutant superhero)' begins with a provocative set of statements. Rather like Fiske, Bukatman also sounds a faintly apologetic note when discussing his masculinity: 'I don't read superhero comics anymore. I'm probably not as worried about my dick as I used to be. Well, *that* isn't exactly true – but I no longer deal with it by reading about mutant muscle men and the big-titted women who love them' (Bukatman 1994: 93). Superhero comics are immediately proposed as some kind of compensatory reading, something vaguely dysfunctional that can be used to assuage a sense of not matching up to a masculine ideal. And the doubt, the fragility and the impossibility of any sustained identification with this ideal does not, after all, come to an end in Bukatman's account. He explicitly comments that perhaps not all of his early (adolescent) anxieties have been entirely left behind (*ibid.*: 125).

Bukatman's account is autoethnographic because it combines a thorough critique of the cultural positions which he adopts as a cultural critic and a fan. Unlike Fiske, Bukatman worries away at his sense of self, constantly refusing to allow a stable narrative of the 'valued' and 'secure' self to emerge. Layers upon layers of self-exploration are revealed. Bukatman is 'forced to realize that the autobiographical subject isn't me, the adolescent dreaming of bodily strength and cosmic consciousness, but me, the adult academic who feels compelled to write about comic books' (1994: 96). But this investment in a controlling academic identity which magically displaces his adolescent lack of control is not taken for granted. Bukatman questions this separation of identities, suggesting that the adult academic identity and the adolescent superhero comic book reader can't be separated out (1994: 126). Neither identity is automatically the 'good' counterpoint to the deficient or 'bad' other. Academic identity is a threat as well as a form of salvation; its desire to control causes it to become overly narrow and overly disciplined: 'the academy keeps refusing to tell me about *my* self' (*ibid.*). Nor does Bukatman's self-reflexivity end here, because he then confesses that this unending struggle of good–bad 'academic' versus good–bad 'fan' identity is itself a version of the comic book narratives he is analysing, being '[v]ery heroic ... My writings validate my own past, and thus my own self. Superheroes, science fiction, Jerry Lewis – I'm the emperor of the nerds, the god of geeks' (*ibid.*).

Unlike Fiske, Bukatman ruthlessly exposes the cultural value systems which operate within his work. He arrives at a sense of having validated his own identity, something which Fiske does by positioning himself as the left-wing academic, but without reflecting on this. Is Bukatman's account therefore a better autoethnography? Yes, in a sense, but it too fails to build up a wider inventory of the self. Bukatman's investment is in a discourse of the 'proud academic – still committed to rigorous intellectual inquiry and supportive pedagogy despite the narrowness of so many of the "approved" academic discourses' (*ibid.*). Like Fiske, Bukatman ultimately has no option other than to subordinate fan discourses to academic discourses. The limits to his self-exploration are reached when a final commitment is uncovered which cannot be called into question. And this commitment – the rigour of the intellect – is little more than an idealisation and a 'common sense' cultural category. Intellectual rigour cannot form the unchallengeable alibi for autoethnography. Continuing to question the investments of the self must also call into question this very investment in the process of 'questioning' as essentially 'rigorous'.

The 'critical' academic opposed to narcissistic 'common sense' is certainly a very useful legitimation for this type of academic thought. But it is a validation which must ultimately come into conflict with its own principles. Perhaps, therefore, autoethnography achieves its fullest aims only when:

(a) it refuses to stop questioning the narcissism of 'common sense' and its narrative closures, while
(b) simultaneously acknowledging that 'infinite traces' of the self cannot ever be fully enclosed by any alternative narrative, whether this is a narrative of 'critical elaboration', secure left-wing politics or 'intellectual rigour'. All such terms merely expose the non-discursive and affective investments in discourses of 'us' (cultural critics) and 'them' (fans).

This seems to imply that the best autoethnographies should succeed in a type of self-deconstruction and self-destructiveness in which all possible grounds for legible cultural value are eroded. But even this sounds rather optimistically avant-garde, recapping the banality of the bohemian mind.

Perhaps the more useful implication is that a good autoethnography should reveal the narcissistic limits of 'intellectual rigour' as well as the narcissistic limits of 'common sense'. For while the latter leaves our sense of self securely in place, the former not only disrupts usual common sense categories, it also needs to be disrupted when it becomes the 'common sense' of academia.[8] This means that by travelling through the widest variety of discursive battles and legitimations that scholarly thought can offer, we arrive at the point where self-reflexivity proves to be an idealisation, sustaining the fantasy that words and thought alone can change the world. Autoethnography therefore goes on questioning, necessarily moving beyond the point where it can defend its own value as an exercise, but also moving beyond the point where 'critical' thought has any relevance, running up against and exposing its own affective roots.

Another false ending. Even this convenient twist, this juxtaposition between critical thought as ideal and affect as material, cannot remain fixed in place as a surreptitious restoration of the value of autoethnography. By running into its own final limits, autoethnographic thought is not heroically elevated into a new realm of emotional awareness and material struggle. By running into its own final limits, far past the safety of the narcissistic, autoethnography exposes academic thought as embedded in one industry among others. Autoethnography leaves behind the concept of the 'culture industry' and cuts through to the 'critical industry'. This is a cultural space intent on producing novel versions of thought's limited repertoire and intent on promoting and validating 'intellectual rigour' as an authentic subcultural value. But, rather curiously, the excessive 'intellectual rigour' proposed by autoethnography exposes the fact there can never be enough 'intellectual rigour'. As long as critical thought operates as a commodity, as a marker of academic reputation, and as a token of 'academic' versus 'fan' cultural difference, then the same old 'common sense' oppositions and moral dualisms will be reproduced through discourses of, and investments in, the rigour of the 'critical' versus the laxity of the 'untutored'.

Although both Fiske and Bukatman seek to distance themselves from 'bad' masculinity, both also reinstate the figure of the authoritative academic which autoethnography aims, ultimately, to undermine. Autoethnography should demonstrate instead the cultural contexts through which the self is constructed, examining how *processes of 'common sense', commodification and self-justification/rationalisation structure both fan and academic identities.*

I want to move on to discuss autoethnographies which deal with issues of feminist identity and fandom.[9] Sue Wise (1990) has reflected on her Elvis fandom, while Janet Wolff has written about her 'personal music history' as a fan of American rock 'n' roll singer Eddie Cochran (Wolff 1995: 23).

The tone of Wise's account is what immediately strikes the reader. We are not confronted with an analysis of cultural order (as in Bukatman 1994) or discussions of cultural agency (as in Fiske 1990). Wise does not immediately adopt a highly academic writing style which is peppered with technical terms. She begins very conversationally: ' "Whose are all those ELVIS records? Argh!" is a commonly heard question in my home, and always has been ever since it has been regularly frequented by feminists' (1990: 390). The puzzle which this generates is how Wise was able to be both 'a feminist and an Elvis fan' (1990: 391). These identities are felt to be mutually exclusive: liking Elvis is a badge of otherness for Wise's right-thinking feminist friends. It is a taste and an attachment which doesn't belong within their cultural distinctions, discriminations and values. Elvis is too securely placed within a particular version of cultural history, a narrative in which his female fans were 'overwhelmed by his animal magnetism' (1990: 392). This narrative contrasts Elvis as a 'butch God' to his passive female conquests, and it is therefore viewed as highly patriarchal and ideologically suspect ('deficient') by 'duly trained' feminists. In order to revalue her Elvis fandom, Wise attempts to defuse the 'butch God' narrative, recounting that for her, Elvis carried a very different set of meanings:

> mostly my interest in Elvis took the form of a solitary hobby, *a private thing between 'him' and me* ... I had never analysed my fondness for or interest in him as I grew up. He was just there as an important part of my life – *he had always been important to me and I had never questioned how or why* ... as the years went by echoes of my past (in the voice of Elvis?) have from time to time surfaced ... Such a thing occurred in 1977 when Elvis died. I was surprised at how much his death touched me ... As I listened to records and delved into clippings ... the memories that were evoked had nothing to do with sex, nothing even to do with romance. The overwhelming feelings and memories were of warmth and affection for a very dear friend.
>
> (Wise 1990: 393, 394, 395, my emphasis)

For Wise, Elvis is represented and experienced as more of a 'teddy bear' than a 'butch God'; her solitary fandom as an adolescent provided her with a way of securing her own personal space within 'an overcrowded household which was accepted as legitimate by my family' (1990: 393). Elvis was her friend, and a source of solace, comfort and security.

However, when Wise 'gets feminism' gradually in her early twenties, she realises that her Elvis fandom will have to be rejected. It does not seem to fit with the cultural pressures which are brought to bear on her by her new cultural context: 'I don't remember reading or hearing any specific feminist analysis which said that "Elvis can seriously damage your health" ... But the main pressure came from incredulous friends, who were always quick to point out the ideological impurity of Elvis' (1990: 394). This autoethnography places fandom squarely within the cultural and personal setting of networks of friends and family, unlike Fiske's and Bukatman's accounts where the academic-fan tends to appear as a lonely but heroic central figure. Wise partially displaces the idea of the heroic academic-fan by focusing on her own susceptibility to cultural influences and pressures. Fandom may well be experienced as intensely personal (having a kind of intensified use-value) but if this sentiment cannot return to the cultural space of exchange-value (carrying shared, intersubjective value) then it is likely to wither or to be temporarily abandoned. Fandom does not seem to flourish in a resolutely hostile environment; its passions and attachments have to be linked to a localised sense of cultural value and legitimacy, even if this occurs only within a household or a small circle of friends rather than the 'imagined community' of a fan subculture.

Wise therefore offers a practical illustration of Fiske's argument that the self is an 'agent of culture in process'; she was not free to express her fandom as she 'personally' wished to. She was enabled to be a fan (by her family's acceptance of this) but was later constrained by a different (1970s feminist) cultural context. Expressions and experiences of fandom cannot, therefore, be assumed to be entirely 'internal' to the 'expressive' self. Experiences of fandom always have to be negotiated between the internal self and its experiences and the external self and its cultural context, meaning that distinguishing between the 'internal' and the 'external' ultimately becomes impossible (see the next chapter).

Wise uses her 'personal experience of a public phenomenon as an example of a totally taken-for-granted view of reality which is open to a different interpretation' (1990: 398). This follows autoethnography's aim of questioning 'common sense' assumptions and categories, especially since Wise is arguing against a certain 'dominant' view of Elvis which is not simply 'out there' in the media: 'feminists have gone along with this – the media hype has succeeded, the image swallowed, the feminist reworking left undone' (*ibid.*).

What are the limits to Wise's autoethnography? She very acutely illustrates how constructions of 'us' and 'them' can be falsified, drawing attention to the possibility that feminist 'critics' of patriarchal popular culture may well reproduce '*male* ideas about rock music' (1990: 397). The 'good' object of feminism is shown to be more complicit with what it opposes than its own self-legitimation would indicate. Wise also avoids the technical and specialised academic language which is favoured by Fiske. If anything, her account forms the reverse image to Fiske's: both writers are concerned with autoethnographically placing the personal within the cultural, but where Fiske subordinates his fan discourse to an academic one, Wise seems to subordinate academic discourse to fan discourse. In this case, it is feminists – rather unusually – who are represented as cultural dupes, and as the passive victims of 'media hype'. It is feminists' discussions of 'ideology' which are shown to be out of step with the consumer and fan experiences of the pre- or proto-feminist. This reversal of the typical academic account, where critical activity dispels audience passivity, remains trapped in its terms of reference. For example, a more complex reworking could have examined the contextual agency of the feminists opposed to Elvis, rather than figuring them as passive. Whenever agency is selectively attributed to one group or character (the autoethnographer as Elvis fan) and denied to another group (the feminist opposition), then we are dealing with an unsustainable moral dualism.

Given Wise's critique of feminism, we can hardly expect later feminist cultural critics to respond kindly to her work. Sure enough, Janet Wolff writes: 'Wise ... feels obliged to justify his appeal by rejecting Elvis the "butch God"(an image, she says, constructed by men) in favour of Elvis the "Teddy Bear"' (1995: 26). This brief commentary carries two implications. First, Wise's autoethnography functions as self-validation, just as Bukatman validates his own experiences, and Fiske validates his own politics. Second, Wolff seems to imply in the interjection 'an image, she says, constructed by men' that Wise herself is avoiding the complexities of interpretation by neatly aligning one interpretation of Elvis with a dominant sense of male 'media hype' while leaving her own interpretation supposedly outside the cultural system of power and dominance that her narrative constructs. This should remind us once more that good autoethnography should attempt to be multivocal; it should not operate as a legitimation of the investments of the academic-fan self which are dressed up as theoretical 'critique'.

Wolff's own account of her Eddie Cochran fandom also raises a number of useful points, dwelling on problems with fans' justifications of their fandom. Wolff begins by writing as a fan, indicating that Eddie Cochran was important to her because of his music, before suddenly varying her account and adopting an academic perspective:

> I have been talking as though the appeal of rock 'n' roll (of Eddie Cochran) is simply *there*, in the music – in the beat, the body and the voice. Work on youth culture has shown, of course, that music, like other aspects of fashion and style, operates in conjunction with a complex process of individual and social identities, and may therefore be selected on the basis of affective criteria other than the sound itself.
>
> (Wolff 1995: 26)

In true autoethnographic style, Wolff immediately reverses her position again, and also acknowledges that this reversal is contradicted elsewhere in her study: 'I do want to argue that there is something in the music of early rock 'n' roll which constitutes a direct appeal – to the body, to the emotions' (1995: 27). Her admission that this is contradicted elsewhere returns her work to the predictable academic norms of cultural studies which suggest that 'the imme-diacy of the body' (1995: 38n23) cannot be trusted or assumed. Wolff does indeed toe this line in a chapter on dance criticism (1995: 68–87). Why, then, does this writer accept the disciplinary norms of cultural studies and feminism in one instance, but break those norms in her discussion of Eddie Cochran?

I would like to view this as a challenge to academic assumptions. But it seems to replicate exactly what Wolff has criticised in relation to Wise's account: the investment of the fan-self is protected from the intruding discourses of academia. Cochran's music, as the 'good' object of a teenage fandom, is split off from academic norms which refuse to allow value to emerge automatically from texts. Wolff therefore makes a theoretical exception for her object of fandom, refusing to have its personal significance undermined, and holding on to a sense of her possession of Cochran's music. Thus, for all her claims to be 'working on the assumption that ... preferences are not purely personal or idiosyncratic, but can be used to explore more general features of a cultural moment' (1995: 28), Wolff still preserves a privileged status for the cultural moment of her Cochran fandom. She focuses on the 'role of culture in the formation of identity: the ways in which we use certain cultural events, practices, objects in the continual process of our own production of self' (*ibid.*), but shifts the terms of her argument in order to disguise her personal investment in late 1950s rock 'n' roll as a matter of theoretical argument and cultural/musical specificity.[10] Wolff describes her work as an 'ethnography of the self' (*ibid.*: 29), arguing that this does not substitute autobiography for theory. I would characterise her account of Eddie Cochran, at least, as autobiography which distorts theoretical logic. Personal investment masquerades as theory, and academic discourse is again subordinated to fan discourse.

Self-imaginings: autoethnography as an escape from singular fan culture

All of which sets up the ground which my own autoethnography must traverse. Through the preceding discussions I have established four key principles for autoethnography:

1   Autoethnography must constantly seek to unsettle the moral dualisms which are thrown up by the narcissism of 'common sense' and its narrative closures. This requires the constant use of self-reflexive questioning.
2   Autoethnography must constantly seek to unsettle the use of theory as a disguise for personal attachments and investments; good autoethnography does not simply validate the self and its fandoms by twisting theory to fit the preferences of the self. Again, this requires the constant use of self-reflexive questioning.
3   Self-reflexivity cannot legitimate autoethnography as an exercise. The concepts of 'intellectual rigour' and heroic reflexivity act as another form of academic 'common sense' which sustains the critical 'us' versus the duped 'them'. When self-reflexivity is subjected to 'self-reflexive' critique then it becomes apparent that this term supports a fantasy of academic power and a fantasy of the idealist transformation of society. At this point, self-reflexivity acts as part of academia's 'critical industry'.
4   Autoethnography should treat self and other identically, using the same theoretical terms and attributions of agency to describe both.

Autoethnography can also achieve something which fan-ethnographies to date have neglected. That is, rather than isolating single fan cultures (e.g. the study of *Star Trek* fans as in Bacon-Smith 1992 and Penley 1991, 1992, 1997) or specific intertextual networks of 'cult TV'/'telefantasy' (Jenkins 1992), autoethnography can chart how multiple fandoms are linked through the individual's realisation of a self-identity. These multiple fandoms and interests in different media forms may cohere in intriguing ways. Particular discourses might be shared across what, at first glance, appear to be very different objects of fandom. Of course, different fandoms may also not clearly relate to one another, allowing different aspects and dimensions of self-identity to be realised through various cultural materials. Autoethnography offers one possible solution to the problem identified by Nick Couldry, namely, the problem of 'too many texts', and of how we, as media consumers and fans, construct a sense of those texts that are relevant and meaningful to us. Couldry rightly observes that 'we should know more about what individuals' "textual fields" are like – how do people select from the myriad texts around them, what common patterns are there in what they select? Yet this is an area where cultural studies has done very little research' (Couldry 2000b: 73).

Beginning an autoethnography, it is pragmatically useful to attempt to chart all one's objects of fandom, both past and present. This allows the autoethnographer to get a sense of the variety and possible coherence of their fan objects, as well as asking the question: *why do various fandoms become relevant and irrelevant to cultural identity at specific times?* These could be moments in a life-story (leaving home but using fandom to remain connected with a family-based identity); moments in the construction of age-based identities ('child'/'teenager'/'youth'/'adult'); moments when different cultural identities and contexts become dominant ('fan'/'academic'); or moments which emerge through the popular construction of cultural history ('the 1970s', 'the 1980s').

I would also suggest charting one's fandoms by subject matter, indicating where there are intertextual or generic links, and then over time, indicating when fandoms became less or more significant. Although this type of self-reporting cannot be assumed to be infallible or 'correct', this is not really a problem since we will return to the issue of self-reflexivity to examine how the *autoethnographer constructs a certain sense of self in their own account.* My own autoethnographic diagrams of my fandom are presented below (Figures 3.1, 3.2). Clearly an issue the autoethnographer confronts when drawing up these

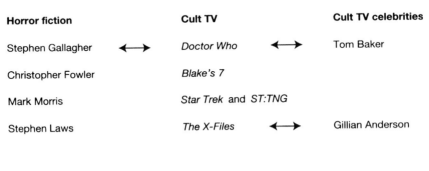

Figure 3.1   Fandoms grouped by subject matter, intertextual links indicated.

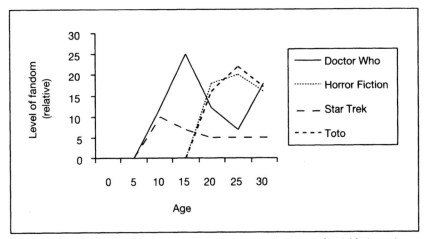

Figure 3.2   Significant fandoms over time, with subjective sense of variable intensity

diagrams is what he or she is prepared to count as a 'fandom'. I would suggest taking as broad a view of 'fandom' as possible, and including any devoted media consumption as well as non-media-based passions, enthusiasms or hobbies which may have led to specialist media consumption. These diagrams can very quickly become overly-simplified, but an awareness on the part of the autoethnographer of what is being left out, and what is being fitted in, can provide the basis for later discussion.

These diagrams can be analysed autoethnographically in a variety of ways. First, what common discourses are shared by my objects of fandom? 'Britishness' seems to be important: *Doctor Who* is often favourably contrasted with 'US'-style telefantasy by its fans, carrying positive values of 'story/intellect/eccentricity' versus 'production values/action/formula' (see Tulloch and Jenkins 1995). Equally, the type of horror fiction that I became interested in during my teens was, although this was not a calculated decision at the time, British horror. The writers whose work I followed all tended to use English settings (northern England in the case of Gallagher and Laws; London as a focus in Fowler's work). I seem to have avoided obviously 'bestselling', 'mainstream' and American horror writers, having little interest in Stephen King, and never following the work of James Herbert and Clive Barker with the same energy that I devoted to reading Gallagher, James, Laws, Morris *et al.*

Another discourse which is shared by all my objects of fandom, even though there are no obvious intertextual links between my music and television fandoms, is that of 'cultishness', by which I mean a marginality constructed against the tastes and practices of the 'mainstream'. My tastes in music, fiction and television share a common thread: I tend to value bands and programmes which lack obvious 'credibility' but which nevertheless appeal to highly insular fan cognoscenti. Level 42, while typically being mocked as a product of 1980s pop by non-fans, were and are valued by their fans through discourses of musicianship, with band member Mark King being referred to as one of the world's best bass players in niche magazines such as *Guitarist* and *Bassist*, as well as having featured in the 'musos' magazine, *Making Music*. King's playing was deliberately showy, but this was on an instrument usually considered to be the workhorse of a pop/rock band rather than a solo instrument. In other words, his showiness was revalued by fans through concepts of the 'underdog'; the bass player, who would usually be in the shadows, here takes centre-stage.

Toto, although an American AOR/MOR band, are largely ignored in their home market; their fan culture is predominantly European and Japanese. (This also places them within an 'anti-American' discourse even while they cannot be aligned with 'pro-British' discourses.) Also, Toto are again valued by their fans through discourses of musicianship, with guitarist Steve Lukather being thought of as a virtuoso player who retains an individual playing style even in sessions. Lukather, unlike other guitar heroes, is not linked with values of speed and obviously 'flash' playing; instead his style is discussed as a matter of chameleonic skill which never surrenders its individuality.

Alongside pro-British, anti-American and 'cult' discourses which are shared across my objects of fandom, it is also worth noting that my fan tastes are almost unremittingly masculine, developing around male horror writers and male guitarists. And this despite, or perhaps because of, my lack of any real sporting fandom. My fan objects therefore allow me, rather anxiously, to construct a sense of masculine power and agency, since I actively seek out value against the perceived 'norms' of the mainstream and, equally, against the norms of subcultural credibility. I could, at the age of fifteen, and later while I was at university, have immersed myself in the credible bands of the time. Instead I steadfastly refused to fall into what I viewed as the 'fashion' of the moment, remaining interested in Toto and Level 42. There is therefore also a constant sense of seeking (more or less consciously) not to fit into expected patterns of media consumption and expected patterns of taste. Indeed, this type of unthinking opposition to the 'conventional' is itself a set of conventions, as is clear from the cultural discourses which structure all my fandoms. This taste for the 'oppositional' may also have followed me into my academic career. I now construct a sense of self-identity at least partially through identifying with critics whose work I value (Adorno, Winnicott, Bollas), retaining the same structural opposition to theorists whose work is deemed too 'obvious' or too 'mainstream' (e.g. Foucault and Melanie Klein). And when the theorist's work I value threatens to go mainstream, as has Christopher Bollas's since I first wrote about this in my PhD, then I feel a sense of loss. As Scott Bukatman reports: 'there's my irrational fear of losing my self by joining a community (*any* community)' (1994: 126). The theorist is no longer my cult possession; their work is, instead, part of a cultural canon, and part of a wider 'movement' or moment in thought.

Despite having excluded academic theorists from my autoethnography, by analysing the common aspects of my declared fandoms I have been able to perceive links with these other areas. I have suggested, through self-analysis, that certain aspects of my cultural identity are produced by and through my fandoms:

cultishness (i.e. 'discerning' consumption/musicianship/not obvious best-sellers/eccentricity), masculinity (the virtuoso/the underdog/intellect/agency) and Britishness (typically realised against the 'bad' other of America).

However, what does this account leave out? First, I present myself as a cultural agent, as somebody who actively makes use of his media fandoms. This reinforces a sense of my cultural power and, as a narrative of self, can certainly be challenged. Second, I have not discussed my class position, my ethnicity and my sexuality, leaving these as unspoken and invisible categories. This absence can also be challenged. Third, I have constructed what seems to be an overly coherent account of my 'unified' subjectivity: do my fandoms really all line up so tidily along certain axes, or have I excluded more problematic and disruptive fandoms?

So far, I have not focused on the temporal shifts in my fandoms. Opening up this topic can allow for a less 'active' and heroic view of my media consumption. For example, a major shift in my fandoms occurred at around the age of fifteen. As my interest in *Doctor Who* waned then new fan objects started to become important to me. The music of American AOR/MOR band Toto became important, and my interest in *Doctor Who* seemed to be transferred, via the mediating intertextual link provided by Stephen Gallagher's work, into British horror. Although my interest in Gallagher's writing initially depended on my *Doctor Who* fandom, this became less important as I started to read other horror writers. But why this shift in fandoms? Why did I start to move away from *Doctor Who*, only to return to this fandom in my mid-twenties? In this case, I cannot present myself as an active cultural agent. My fandoms here were subjected to the pressures of cultural context. I drifted away from *Who* fandom because of a teenage estimation that if I continued with this all-consuming passion I would never, in a million years, have any chance of getting a girlfriend. Now, whether or not this was true, the fact that this decision made cultural sense to me indicates the operation of one aspect of a cultural system of value whereby media fandom is/was linked to a sense of 'failed' or inadequate masculinity. Living within this dimension of cultural value, I was not able simply to pursue my fandom. Like Wise, I felt under pressure to reject it, even if I cannot recall any direct challenge to my sense of masculinity. My sensed need to alter my fandom, possibly also linked to an urgent teenage need to separate my identity from that of the 'child', therefore produced a shift from TV sf fandom to horror fandom. Horror, in this case, provided a clearer sense of 'enduring' masculinity and an imagined 'toughness' through which my cultural identity could be reconstructed. If I used horror to perform a different type of masculinity, I also used more marginal forms of horror literature rather than 'mainstream' film, retaining a sense of unease with 'good' masculinity and tempering this with an 'anti-mainstream' cultishness and an 'anti-physical' bookishness that I possess in an exaggerated and 'vocational' (i.e. professionally legitimated) form today.

What are the other problems with my autoethnographic account? I have considered how my self-identity remains highly gendered, albeit via an 'intellectual' and masochistic masculinity. The cultural resources which I have used to construct my sense of self cannot be separated from my class position; as a middle-class academic, I bid for alternative cultural capital in precisely the way that Bourdieu's (1984) model describes the dominated bourgeoisie. However, unlike I.Q. Hunter (2000: 197), I am not particularly distressed at being reduced to my class position, or at having my fan 'authenticities' recontextualised as part of a system of value. This shuttling between experience and theory illustrates how well theory can sometimes fit with our experiences, making a new form of sense out of untheorised life.

However, it is also vitally important not to lose sight of the ways in which 'theory' fails to fit with 'experience'. As Wolff rightly observes: 'cultural studies is not just about texts or theories: it deals with lived experiences, and with the intersections of social structures, systems of representation, and subjectivities ... Here it *does* matter if the [theoretical] interpretation does not fit experience' (1995: 35; see also Miles 2001: 165). Although through autoethnography we can never entirely 'disprove' a theory, we can suggest that the ideal-types of theory possess a limited scope in the face of our own inhabitations of culture. For example, I was both a *Star Trek* fan and a *Doctor Who* fan up until about the age of twelve, when *Doctor Who* became far more important to me. (Why this should have been so, I am unable to recount.) Theoretical accounts have tended to emphasise hostilities between these two fandoms (Tulloch and Jenkins 1995). And although my *Star Trek* fandom has not been greatly active since my childhood, I still retain an affection for the programme, having been a *Doctor Who* fan and a *Star Trek* 'follower' at the same time (see also Tulloch and Jenkins 1995). Theoretical accounts have tended to emphasise singular fandoms (where horror fans aren't also fans of guitarists, or where *Doctor Who* fans aren't also fans of D.W. Winnicott's writing, and so on), and my own autoethnography has sought to expose the limitations of studies which focus on single fandoms. This autoethnography also opens up a further challenge to 'fan studies': how can we theorise the cultural activities of fans who are not institutionally aligned, and who refuse to attend conventions or take part in 'stereotypical' fan activities? I would describe myself as always having existed on the fringes of organised fandom: whenever it seemed that I was close to properly entering an organised fandom, somehow or other I recoiled from this possibility. Whether this was writing fan fiction for the *Doctor Who* Appreciation Society or reviewing for the horror fan magazine *Samhain*, the threat of being 'absorbed' into an organised community was always sufficient to send me scurrying back under cover as a solitary fan, or at best as a fan who shared his knowledge and enthusiasm only with a highly localised and limited set of fellow fans (see Bacon-Smith 1992). Organised fandom, conventions and all, always seemed like a bridge too far. Of course, this statement is a type of self-legitimation which fails in the very moment of its performative claim. 'I'm not one of those sad fans who hangs out at conventions' this claim attempts to announce, trying to ward off pathologising fan stereotypes by constructing a 'self'/'other' split. But this attempt at self-legitimation simultaneously reveals that I cannot sustain this moral dualism: I am far inside the fan stereotype (given my self-construction as 'bookish', as 'different', as 'intellectual', as inadequately 'masculine') whether I like it or not, and whether I argue my case or not. In short, I can't rationally dispel the force of this fan stereotype, or the possibility of it being applied to me, simply by wishing it away or by creating moral dualisms to do this work for me magically.

What other lapses have I uncovered in my account? In terms of my ethnicity, my whiteness has largely been mirrored back to me through the texts that I have been a fan of, forming a shared cultural discourse. This type of reflection may seem too crudely fixed at the level of 'observable' ethnicity, but it nevertheless serves to emphasise how cultural discourses have a powerful effect on our judgements of whether media texts are relevant to us. Clearly fans can identify across ethnicity, but often only the basis of a shared authenticity such as a celebratory 'anti-mainstream' stance (which takes me back to my point about relative homology at the end of chapter 1).

With regards to sexuality, my objects of fandom have not always clearly mirrored my own lived heterosexuality. *Doctor Who*, as Cornell (1997) notes, has always had a sizeable gay following. And horror fiction, my attempt at bolstering my masculinity, is hardly alien to concepts of 'polymorphous perversity' or to transgressions of the codes of heterosexuality. Although I have included Gillian Anderson as one of my fan 'objects', I have refrained from discussing this until now, perhaps through a class-based sense that issues of sexuality are not a 'proper' topic of discussion. I remain highly uneasy about professing that any element of sexual attraction enters into my appreciation of female cult celebrities. This unease may stem from an investment in a broadly feminist academic position which disagrees theoretically with the objectification of women while continuing to participate practically in these 'bad' cultural mechanisms. It may well be the case that what I would prefer to pass over in silence is an aspect of my cultural identity which begins to problematise my 'unified' self, threatening to fragment the self into a series of contradictory investments and attachments.

Despite my criticisms of Fiske and Bukatman above, I also find upon rereading this account that I, too, have produced a structuring absence: my family.[11] I have completely failed to address the household and other cultural contexts in which my early fandoms were formed. 'Common sense' cultural categories – markers of 'privacy' – therefore intrude multipally on this account, since I have absented both my sexuality and my family, presumably feeling these are too close to home to be subjected to 'analysis'. But, unlike Wolff (1995), I must seek to avoid drawing arbitrary lines between naturalised 'immediacy' and mediated 'cultural systems'.

I would never have embarked upon the life of a fan, nor that of an academic, had it not been for the encouragement, indulgence and tacit legitimation offered by my family. This household context did not simply enable certain fan meanings or interpretations, instead it allowed the significance of my fandom to

87

be preserved and trusted, no matter what. My media consumption was regulated by my parents when I was a young child, but regardless of the (then culturally acceptable) use of corporal punishment, and the often used threat of being sent to my room, I was never banned from watching my favourite TV programmes and objects of fandom. My fandom was respected by my parents, and formed part of my distinctive identity in the family: I was the *Doctor Who* fan. This defined my 'uniqueness' in the family.

This familial idealisation raises the question of the 'origins' of my *Doctor Who* fandom. Was this, like Nick Hornby's account of his Arsenal fandom, a way of communicating with my father which then became my own private 'possession'? The beginnings of fandom can sometimes seem very clear to us; we become fans of something because our friends are, or because our brothers and sisters are. But this associative 'contagion' of fandom's attachments and affects – either through social networks or through intertextual networks – also poses a challenge to cultural theories of fandom. How can such intense fan experiences of subjective 'ownership' and 'possession' of the text emerge through 'cultural systems'? How does the contingency of this cultural system (i.e. a different associative link could have been made from text to text or from other to self) become transformed into the fan's insistence on the necessity of *this* text or *this* icon? Both fan-ethnographies and autoethnographies have a highly limited purchase on these questions, and on how fan desire becomes stuck in the form of an enduring media attachment which persists over time and in different cultural contexts and stages of life.

Given the questioning spirit of autoethnography, I want to round up with a further question. Does my academic discourse construct a sense of the contemporary 'I' as knowledgeable in comparison to my past fan self? My account so far seems to assume just such a division. Here is *the* academic moral dualism *par excellence*: the assumption that illuminating theoretical eyes can perceive the cultural order which is otherwise buried in the unthought routines of everyday life. But I have already suggested that self-reflexivity cannot form the ultimate legitimation of autoethnography. Taking this point seriously, even while becoming caught up in a performative contradiction, I am methodologically and theoretically obliged to concede that my account of my own fandoms arrives at a point of narcissistic and narrative closure which privileges (present) academic reflection on the non-academic (past) self. The only possible way to disrupt this narrative closure may be to interpret fan culture (and the self) through alternative theoretical positions, employing psychoanalysis rather than cultural studies. I will address this in the next chapter.

Summary

- Fan-ethnographies have been limited by a number of recurring problems such as the narrative structures that they have used, and the moral dualisms that they have played out in terms of 'pained' fan-victims (Bacon-Smith 1992) versus 'poaching' fan-victors (Jenkins 1992).

- Fan-ethnographies have focused on fans of single texts or narrow intertextual networks, treating these fans as naturally-occurring (and spectacular) communities. This tends to close down the investigation of how we may, as subjects, negotiate our way through multiple fandoms of varying intensities at different times.
- Fan-ethnographies have assumed that both fans and academics can fully account discursively for their cultural practices. The fans' discursive mantra which works to justify their fandom is therefore accepted at face value. So is the academic's discursive mantra which works to justify academia: the notion of 'critical' or 'self-reflexive' thought.
- The turn to autoethnography has sought to address some of these problems. I have examined four autoethnographies of different fandoms. Through this process I arrived at four key aspects of autoethnography. I then applied these ideas in my own autoethnography.

4

FAN CULTURES BETWEEN 'FANTASY' AND 'REALITY'

In this chapter I will approach fandom as a form of cultural creativity or 'play' which moves, non-competitively, *across* the usual boundaries and categories of experience rather than being caught up within any particular 'field':

> Play enables the exploration of that tissue boundary between fantasy and reality, between the real and the imagined, between the self and the other. In play we have a license to explore, both our selves and our society. *In play we investigate culture, but we also create it.*
>
> (Silverstone 1999: 64, my italics)

My central concern here will be with the broadly emotional experiences of fans. Without the emotional attachments and passions of fans, fan cultures would not exist, but fans and academics often take these attachments for granted or do not place them centre-stage in their explorations of fandom.

In the first section below I will consider non-psychoanalytic versions of fans' affective 'play'; I will then move on to consider how different fan cultures (horror fans; *Star Trek* fans; soap opera fans) have been psychoanalysed by critics. I will develop an approach to fandom – based largely on the work of psychoanalyst Donald Woods Winnicott – which takes into account both the 'structural'/historical dimensions of fan cultures and the 'lived experiences' of fans, without subordinating either one to the other. This will retain and develop my focus on fandom's 'dialectic of value'; I will argue that we cannot focus simply on the fan's experience or on the cultural determinations of fan 'readings' of texts. An approach is needed which preserves space both for the individual fan's psychology and for the cultural 'context' in which fan cultures exist.

Fandom as 'affective play'

The question of affect in cultural studies is particularly evident in the ongoing work of Lawrence Grossberg (1988, 1992a, 1992b, also 1997a, 1997b): 'If affect cannot be "found" in the text or read off its surfaces (any more than meaning can), it is also the case that affect is not something that individuals put into it. Affect is itself articulated in the relations between practices' (1992a: 83). Grossberg's focus on fandom and affect is useful because it promises to over-come the split whereby de Certeauesque theory deals with fan 'interpretation', while non-theoretical understandings of fan 'love' persist alongside this more dense theoretical material (Jenkins 1992a; Brooker 2000). Grossberg refuses to leave fan 'affect' outside the scope of theorisation:

> Affect is not the same as either emotions or desires. Affect is closely tied to what we often describe as the feeling of life. You can under-stand another person's life, but you cannot know how it feels. But feeling, as it functions here, is not a subjective experience. It is a socially constructed domain of cultural effects ... different affective relations inflect meanings and pleasures in very different ways. Affect is what gives 'colour', 'tone' or 'texture' to our experiences.
>
> (Grossberg 1992b: 56–7)

But Grossberg's model of affect lacks 'playful' potential (i.e. movement across boundaries of 'inner' and 'outer', 'real' and 'fantasy') because the boundaries of affect are firmly established. For Grossberg, scrupulously observing the disci-plinary norms of cultural studies, there must be no suggestion that feeling is 'subjective'. No one else can get inside the 'colours', 'tones' and 'textures' of my life, but those colours, tones and textures can nevertheless be analysed as 'socially constructed' *effects* that I am subjected to. But if this is so, then my fan investments, passions and attachments are never really 'mine'. Any sense of self is merely inscribed according to cultural rules, and the self is thus seemingly an effect of cultural context and its 'mattering maps' (Grossberg 1992b: 57). Any sense of self experienced and inscribed through fandom can only appear to be false:

> [f]ans ... circulate and also consume particular types of information as a kind of personal/collective property. Fan websites present this infor-mation in largely standardised formats which are personalised by the individual fan primarily through the interpolation of autobiographical example ... [implicitly declaring] this is my site, my contents, ... my way ... Fan sites endlessly rewrite from this finite base of factual knowl-edge, and they do so from the first person.[1]
>
> (Hoxter 2000: 174–5, 178)

Clearly the 'first person' is not to be trusted. And yet how is this lived self-inscription any different to the self-inscription which is practised by academics? Cultural studies academics also read a limited number of (canonical) books, and the purpose of a well-turned bibliography is to display one's learning in a 'stan-dardised format'. Just as the fan produces a sense of self through displaying their personalised knowledge, then so too does the academic build up a notion of their work as 'personal/collective'. According to the principle of 'self and other equality' established in the last chapter, any implied criticism of the fan's 'false' subjectivity must also rebound on the academic's similarly 'false' self-inscriptions. And yet this does not occur; despite academics' and fans' shared 'romanticism' – both are committed to their 'authentic' selves – cultural studies retains the guiding (inter)disciplinary norm of excluding the subjective. At best, this can result in a misrecognition of the emotional processes of the academy, taking us back to a particular imagined academic subjectivity which supposedly transcends the 'subjective'. At worst, this commitment to cultural construction rather than the 'subjective' can actually cut cultural studies off from the lived experiences of those that it seeks to engage with.

The disciplinary importance of warding off the subjective is also testified to in Brian Massumi's (1996) critique of Grossberg's work. Massumi suggests that 'Grossberg slips into an equation between affect and emotion at many points, despite distinguishing them in his definitions' (1996: 237n3). Both Grossberg and Massumi are, in different ways, concerned with establishing that affect can be analysed, and that it is not unstructured, unformed or unobservable in its effects. Both are concerned, in different ways, with separating 'affect' from 'emotion'. For Grossberg, this move establishes the authority of a cultural studies' 'structural' perspective influenced by Deleuzian thought, while for Massumi it legitimates a Deleuzian/Spinozist reading of affect as 'effect'. In part, Massumi's criticism of Grossberg resembles a fan's claim of 'possession' or 'ownership' over their favoured text, seeking, as it does, to reinstate a more 'correct' or 'proper' reading and thereby laying claim to 'Deleuze [as] ... the great white hope of a non-Saussurean cultural theory' (Osborne 2000: 46).

Is it possible to avoid wholly reproducing 'common sense' categories (e.g. fans' 'love' for a text) while also respecting the fan's 'affect' as subjective, and therefore as meaningfully 'possessed' by a self? Roy Boyne has recently observed that sociological thought is foundationally committed to the 'denial of the subject', although he notes that 'the subjective moment ... remains residual and obdurate even after the fiercest dilutions, deprivations and denials to be found within social science' (Boyne 2001: x). If this 'subjective moment' is to be taken seriously without entirely falling back into 'common sense' (see also Blackman and Walkerdine 2001) then this would mean presenting an account of fandom which meets both of the following criteria:

1   It must display continuity with fan experiences (of 'possession' and 'owner-ship'), and

2   It must re-present these emotional experiences within a consistent theoretical framework.

A number of recent theorists of emotion such as Campbell (1997), Lupton (1998) and Williams (2001) have all sought to move away from the constructivist position which has dominated cultural studies. Each of these theorists has emphasised the importance of 'outlaw emotions' which do not simply reflect culturally constructed categories (Campbell 1997: 162), the extra-discursive and discursive nature of emotions (Lupton 1998: 38), and the sheer 'slipperiness' of emotions: 'Our discourses and constructions of emotion ... are never simply the end of the matter. ... The multi-dimensional nature of emotions should ... be stressed here, "over-spilling" a range of disciplinary borders and boundaries along the way' (Williams 2001: 135).

However, a persistent 'tailoring' of affect to a singular and bounded position has occurred not only in constructivist cultural studies but also in much recent film studies work which has taken up a 'cognitivist' position.[1] Carroll (1990) has offered a summary of the basic assumption driving this work: 'What ... identifies and individuates given emotional states? Their cognitive elements. Emotions involve not only physical perturbations but beliefs and thoughts ... about the properties of objects and situations' (1990: 26). This work repeats the boundary-building of Grossberg's constructivist approach, albeit in a different guise. The issue this time is not (structured) affect versus (unstructured) emotion, but is instead affect versus cognition.[2]

The notion of 'affective play' does not simply transgress the ordered accounts offered by different disciplines; it also necessarily transgresses cultural studies' affect/emotion binary by reintroducing the subjective into cultural studies (Campbell 1997; Lupton 1998). And it transgresses cognitive film theory's affect/cognition binary by refusing to view these as useful alternatives (Buckingham 2000: 112; Barbalet 1998: 45). This results in a situation where:

> we need theories that allow for the creation of affective meanings that are new and potentially liberatory. I question whether the notion of oppositional subcultures serves this purpose. ... [T]hat I must belong to and reflect the values of an oppositional subculture to express outlaw emotions potentially *restricts possibilities for expressing personal significance as it is reflective of the pattern I make of my life and experiences.*
>
> (Campbell 1997: 162, my italics)

In short, neither constructivist nor cognitive theories can account for the formation of fan cultures through the expression of 'personal significance'. Sharing the problems of the 'regime of value' examined in chapter 2, any approach which reads affect off from a cultural context implies that affect cannot underpin the generation of new cultural formations and contexts. The fans' 'oppositional subculture' must always precede and culturally support fan interpretation and affect, rather than vice versa. Taking this latter view means considering affect as playful, as capable of 'creating culture' as well as being caught up in it.

What I have already termed the 'dialectic of value' (within which the fans' intensely felt and personal 'possession'/ownership of the text is important) therefore seems to be deflected by Grossberg's framing of 'affect' within a model of cultural construction. For Grossberg, fans' sense of textual 'possession' and 'ownership' can only appear as delusional effects of cultural positioning, as seems to be the case in Hoxter's account of online *Exorcist* fans.

Grossberg's model of affect has perhaps been most usefully extended in Dan Fleming's (1996) study, *Powerplay: Toys as Popular Culture*. Attempting to draw together cultural studies and psychoanalysis Fleming arrives at a view of 'object relational interpellation' (1996: 199) which stresses the non-alignment of different planes of subject-positioning, namely the 'object-relational' and the 'ideological'. He illustrates this notion through the series of *Star Trek: The Next Generation* figures produced by Playmates, considering the extent to which object-relational interpellation may *not* fall into 'ideological interpellation'. Fleming's argument hinges on the child's developmental capacity to 'play the other' through playing with toy characters; it is this playful capacity for fluid identification and self-objectification which the 'adult' is deemed to lack in his or her absorption into more fixed subject positions. Fleming thereby suggests that the hegemonic dominance of the masculine identity of Captain Jean-Luc Picard, which he argues is central to the televised narrative of *ST:TNG*, is unlikely to retain such a centrality within the child's play. Whereas televised narrative opens a space for the other only to close it off again, 'the toys are not the TV series. The child who carries around a little plastic Borg as an object of totemistic attachment is identifying with the monster, the "inhuman", in a way that is never explicitly allowed by the conventions of the TV series' (1996: 201). For Fleming, 'ideological interpellation' implies a fixing of the subject from 'outside'; it is a matter of compliance. 'Object-relational interpellation', on the other hand, reserves greater space for the subject in terms of this positioning being navigated from the 'inside':

> To suggest that some objects hold us enthralled, not just because they are conduits for delivery of an ideological 'summons', a fix, but also because we summon forth from them a function as devices of enthralment, *is to propose a more interested role for the subject than has been allowed in most cultural studies to date* (and evokes the notion from psychoanalytic object-relations theory that pleasure is not an end in itself but a 'signpost' to a meaningful object).
>
> (1996: 196, 197, my italics)

The question which then remains is the following: if a 'more interested role for the subject' can seemingly only be introduced by drawing on object-relations psychoanalysis, then can this 'subjective move' be developed by moving cultural criticism further towards the principles of psychoanalysis? Given my own call here for a more fully 'subjective' rather than constructivist or 'discourse-determinist' cultural studies,[3] this is a possibility that I will address in the next section.

Psychoanalysing fan cultures

It would be a mistake to assume that psychoanalysis can offer up a singular theory of affective play which can then simply be 'applied' to fan cultures.[4] For one thing, there are probably almost as many schools of psychoanalysis as there are fan cultures, and no two psychoanalytic approaches completely share a view of affect. Psychoanalyses of fandom have been thin on the ground, but have tended to predominantly use the work of object-relations theorist Donald Woods Winnicott (Randolph 1991; Stacey 1994; Harrington and Bielby 1995), or the post-Freudians Jean Laplanche and Jean-Bertrand Pontalis (Penley 1992; Creed 1993), with references also being made to Melanie Klein's work (Elliott 1999; Hoxter 2000; see also Stacey 1994 and Dawson 1994).

There has been a confluence of *theoretical* and *ethical* opposition to psychoanalysis within cultural studies. Theoretical opposition focuses on the accusation that psychoanalysis is a transhistorical and universal model of subjectivity (i.e. it fails to be historically sensitive). Ethical opposition focuses on a number of charges. First, it supposes that psychoanalysis is an elitist form of cultural criticism since it claims to be able to 'read' the unconscious of the 'other' (Fiske 1990). Second, it supposes that psychoanalysis inherently pathologises fan cultures (i.e. fans are treated as psychologically aberrant or as disturbed in some way). Andrew Tudor, for example, has questioned the specific predominance of psychoanalytic theory in work on horror fiction (and its fans) in just these terms:

> perhaps ... psychoanalytic theories of horror gain credibility from the widespread belief that horror fans are a peculiar bunch who share a perverse predilection. A taste for horror is a taste for something seemingly abnormal and is therefore deemed to require special explanation in terms of personality features not usually accessible to the casual observer. How could anyone want to be horrified, disgusted even, unless there was some deeply hidden reason of which they were not aware?
>
> (Tudor 1997: 446)

However, by considering the psychoanalytic work which has been done on fan cultures I will demonstrate that ethical objections are occasionally misplaced, while theoretical objections can be meaningfully addressed. I will consider Kleinian-influenced work first. Next I will examine work which draws on Laplanche and Pontalis, and finally I will conclude this chapter by considering Winnicottian interpretations of fan culture.[5]

Klein: containing (horror) fans

[I]n the process of identifying with a celebrity, the fan unleashes a range of fantasies and desires and, through projective identification, transfers personal hopes and dreams onto the celebrity. In doing so, the fan actually experiences desired qualities of the self as being contained by the other, the celebrity. In psychoanalytic terms, this is a kind of splitting: the good or desired parts of the self are put into the other in order to protect this imagined goodness from bad or destructive parts of the self. There is, then, a curious sort of violence intrinsic to fandom.... The relation of fan and celebrity is troubled because violence is built into it.

(Elliott 1999: 139)

This quote is taken from Anthony Elliott's account of Mark Chapman, the fan who shot and killed John Lennon. Although Elliott is concerned with Chapman's mental health (and justifiably so), his account also implies a number of things about 'fans' more generally. Elliott draws on Melanie Klein's work on the paranoid-schizoid position, as well as referring to 'projective identification'. The latter, as Elliott's account demonstrates, is a psychical process whereby dangerous or disavowed aspects of the self are projected onto somebody else. But this attempt at 'getting rid' of part of the self is not entirely successful, as the self then identifies with what has been cast out:

Klein follows the bizarre logic of this process to show how the interior which is expelled and located in others is still attached to the self. What is projected is also identified with so that all that has been thrown out returns, and the violence of the expulsion ... is matched by the violence of the invasion of the self when the bad objects strike back.

(Parker 1997: 100)

The 'paranoid-schizoid' position, on the other hand, is a position which is never surmounted in our psychological health, and which we return to in times of stress and anxiety. This is important as it means that the 'paranoid-schizoid' position cannot be linked to some kind of definitive 'developmental' narrative. And if it is never clearly 'left behind' then its functioning cannot be viewed as 'regressive'.

The 'paranoid-schizoid' position involves a 'splitting' of the self into 'good' and 'bad' parts, something which becomes necessary because the goodness of the self cannot be accepted or secured in times of great stress and internal self-division: 'Paranoid-schizoid mechanisms come into action when anxiety is high: they provide a kind of "first aid"; in particular, by separating out goodness from badness, they function to "protect" the goodness' (Segal 1991: 179).

This, like many psychoanalytic accounts, can sound very counter-intuitive:

what are these 'bad' and threatened 'good' parts of the self? Surely our 'selves' are not internally torn apart in such violent ways? But object-relations theory is always concerned with how our identities are made up out of 'the relations of the self to external others or "objects"' (Stacey 1994: 228), and therefore how we 'introject' (take inside the self) aspects of others while expelling or 'projecting' out elements of our internal self. This ongoing process of exchange between 'inner' and 'outer' is what characterises any broadly object-relations perspective: the self is always related to, and realised in, a particular environment. These exchanges of self and environment occur, however, at the level of unconscious fantasy: we are not aware of their dynamics. It is this emphasis on identity as a process related to social and cultural others/objects which makes this approach valuable to cultural studies.[6]

Kleinian approaches to fandom have tended to focus on star–fan relationships, as do both Elliott (1999) and Stacey (1994). Elliott deals with the pathology of this relationship by emphasising projective identification, while Stacey emphasises the more 'normal' processes of projection and introjection. And yet Elliott's account does not seem to contain the 'violence' of fandom that it broaches as a topic. Spilling out of the pathological figure of Mark Chapman, Elliott's account implies that 'fandom' (which he contrasts to 'fanaticism') is also marked by a deeply buried violence of idealisation. This 'violence' of fandom seems to slip from detailed psychoanalytic reasoning and towards the stereotype of the 'deranged' fan, causing clinical terms to bleed into a 'common sense' devaluation of fandom. This is one of the key dangers of psychoanalysing fandom; *contra* Elliott's work (in this case, at least), it is important not to allow psychoanalytic readings to 'over-step' their bounds. In short, the use of psychoanalytic interpretation needs to be carefully monitored and contained by the 'analyst'. This 'containment' is important because it should strive to prevent a form of psychoanalytic 'authority' from writing its 'knowledge' over common sense categories. Just as I have observed that narrative and 'common sense' closures in autoethnographies are narcissistic, so too are all types of psychoanalytic closure which are achieved by surreptitiously filtering psychoanalytic expertise through 'common sense'.

Ironically, Kleinian accounts of fandom seem unable to recognise fan culture as anything other than a confirmation of key Kleinian terms. There is little or no creative 'object-relationship', one might mischievously suggest, between a Kleinian critic and their object of study. Instead, the theory concerned is projected onto the object (fan culture), blanketing it without remainder or resistance. This problem is less evident in Stacey (1994) and Dawson (1995), as both of these cultural critics offer astute and related critiques of Kleinian work. Stacey notes that object relations theory remains 'problematically universalistic' (1994: 232); despite its attempts at situating the self in an external environment, this 'environment' is still a psychoanalytic model rather than a sociological version of the 'outside'. Dawson reiterates this criticism, suggesting that Klein's work shows a disregard for the politics of the external world: 'real effects on others ... are subordinated to a concern for the inner drama' (1994: 45).

This concern with the 'inner drama' is replayed in Julian Hoxter's (2000) Kleinian-influenced account of *Exorcist* fans. Following on from a detailed and intriguing engagement with Kleinian theory (see Hoxter 1998), Hoxter shifts tack to psychoanalyse horror fans rather than horror films. The resulting work is marked by the recurrent problem of psychoanalytic accounts of fan culture: 'common sense' stereotypes of fandom are once again mapped onto and conflated with psychoanalytic conceptual distinctions. 'Expert' accounts therefore reproduce a sense of the aberrant fan who somehow 'lacks' a proper engagement with culture. To be fair, Hoxter is well aware of this possibility. Following on from a specific interpretation of *Exorcist* fans' 'acquisition of fan knowledge' he comments that:

> This is not to suggest for one moment that ordinary film fans – even horror fans – are in some way 'disturbed'. It is rather that in the kind of informational acquisitiveness, in the reification of facts as facts that their websites present, we can ascribe a certain eloquence to the self-regulation of the field of enquiry of cult.
>
> (Hoxter 2000: 180)

Unfortunately, it is necessary to distinguish between the logic of Hoxter's account and his claim here. For, having linked these *Exorcist* fans to post-Kleinian accounts of 'intellectual consumption as defence' (2000: 179), Hoxter can hardly then claim that his account lacks implications of pathologisation. He implies that the fans' knowledge is a way of displacing 'a sense of insecurity and anxiety regarding the status of the fan before his object' (2000: 178) rather than a valid expression of learning. There is thus something eternally 'improper' about fan knowledge; this status of 'knowledge as defence' does not seem to apply, for example, to the post-Kleinian critic who is securely contained by his theory. Fan knowledge is supposedly a compensation for a type of powerlessness, just as it was for Bourdieu-influenced critics in chapter 2. This time, however, the fans' powerlessness is related to subjective anxiety rather than to an exclusion from official cultural capital or economic capital.

The issue of containment forms part of Hoxter's argument. He states that 'containment' is an important psychical process because it allows the child to internalise (take in from the maternal other) an ability to process and transform bad feelings into more tolerable states.[7] Hoxter then links this process of projection and introjection to the fans' relationship with *The Exorcist*:

> To express this in Kleinian terms, one would suggest that the fan imbues the film with the function of a kind of knowing container and the spectator's fear is projected with the expectation of a moderated

return, enabling the spectator successfully to introject and safely to enjoy the film-as-fiction.

(2000: 181)

Hoxter then goes on to conclude that it is 'doubtful whether Internet fan networks currently function as truly receptive containers which can understand and return and therefore strengthen the fan's (infant's) own capacity to contain' (2000: 185). This argument therefore sets up a Kleinian-influenced ideal which the fan culture does not live up to. Hoxter's qualifying statement that this 'is not to suggest that they perform no useful purpose' (*ibid.*) is therefore rather redundant. The fact of the matter is that whatever this 'useful purpose' is defined as, it can only be a 'lesser' function than the idealised strengthening of the fans' own 'containment' of emotional experience. These fans are never viewed as possessing advanced forms of emotional literacy; they are consistently viewed as second-rate, and as failing to measure up to the 'good' objects and demands of post-Kleinian theory. As such, this work corresponds to the second of the ethical objections raised against psychoanalysis: despite explicitly seeking not to, it continues to view fandom as aberrant or, at the very least, as 'deficient'.

Laplanche and Pontalis: fantasising (horror and *Star Trek*) fans

The work of Jean Laplanche and Jean-Bertrand Pontalis has been highly influential in film theory as well as trickling through into work on fan cultures:[8]

> Fantasy, in Laplanche and Pontalis' account, has a number of characteristics which are suggestive for ... a reworking of psychoanalytic film theory. The first is ... its existence for the subject across a number of subject positions. 'A father seduces a daughter', then, is the 'summarised version of the seduction fantasy', but the actual structure of the fantasy offers 'a scenario with multiple entries, in which nothing shows whether the subject will be immediately located as daughter; it can as well be fixed as father, or even in the term seduces' (Laplanche and Pontalis 1986: 22–3). Identification in fantasy, then, is shifting, unconfined by boundaries of biological sex, cultural gender or sexual preference.
>
> (Thornham 1997: 95)

This loosening of identification in fantasy promised to extricate psychoanalytic film theory from the problems created by seeing identification as rigidly structured by gender. It provided 'an alternative to [an] emphasis on cinema's power to fix or "position" both the female characters within a narrative and also the

99

female spectator in the cinema' (Donald 1989: 137). Laplanche and Pontalis's work thus held out the promise of more 'mobile' subject positions being taken up in fantasy.

However, a number of factors complicate this celebratory narrative of progress (from 'bad' fixed subject positions to 'good' fluid subject positions). I will consider only one here: the issue of 'primal fantasies' or 'fantasies of origin'. Laplanche and Pontalis argue that there are three, and only three, types of primal fantasy. Each fantasy works, like a myth, to explain the mysterious origins of the subject, and each has its roots in 'childhood theories', in other words, in the child's attempts to account for 'his' existence. These fantasies are therefore structurally limited to the sets of questions which confront the child: 'The originary fantasies are limited in kind to castration, seduction, and the primal scene of coitus between the parents' (Rapaport 1994: 87). Seduction fantasies explain the origin of sexuality (this is mistakenly conceptualised by the child as a kind of intrusion from outside; see also the related criticisms of Laplanche's later theory of the 'primal situation' in Campbell 2000: 8). Primal scene fantasies explain the origin of the individual (the primal scene is often mistaken in a number of ways in childhood theories of sexuality: either sexual intercourse is represented as an act of violence, or the child imagines intercourse and birth to operate through oral and anal mechanisms rather than through genital activity). And castration fantasies 'explain' the origin of sexual difference, again mistakenly since – assuming a one-sex model – the woman's genitals are misrecognised as a 'lack'.

Such a theory becomes incapable of explaining historical and generic 'fantasy', i.e. the fantasies of film and forms of fiction, other than as reworkings of a limited repertoire of 'primal' or 'original/originary' fantasies. As Linda Williams has put it: 'the most difficult work ... will come in the attempt to relate original fantasies to historical context and specific generic history' (1999: 279).

The difficulties involved in linking original/primal fantasies to media texts as fantasies have arguably been glossed over and potentially wished out of the theoretical frame: 'other questions can be posed and "answered" in fantasy but these [the primal fantasies] are the most basic ones' (Penley 1992: 493; see also Laplanche 1989: 163 for a defence of the primal fantasies as open to 'culturalist' explanation and discussion). Other cultural critics respond to the problem of the primal fantasies by rejecting their structural limitation and adding 'new' primal fantasies (Lebeau 1995: 80–1), and some rely on the very primacy of the 'primal fantasies' to validate and value their area of research:

> The horror film ... continually draws upon the three primal fantasies ... in order to construct its scenarios of horror. Like the primal phantasies, horror narratives are particularly concerned with origins: origin of the subject; origin of desire; origin of sexual difference.
> (Creed 1993: 153; see also the mapping of primal phantasies onto 'body genres' in Williams 1999)

It is also important to note that discussing horror, for example, as especially close to primal fantasies carries an implication for fans of the genre. These fans are supposedly caught up in specific scenes of fantasy, unable to process and transcend childhood theories of sexuality, and unable to adopt the more 'knowing' position of the psychoanalytic theorist. Horror fans are again denied a position of meaningful 'knowledge', supposedly being caught up in the affective 'body genre' of horror (Williams 1999). This ignores horror fans' own construction of a counter-moral dualism which contrasts 'good' fan knowledge to the 'cringing' of the 'bad' non-fan, or non-(true)-fan:

> We understood that when special-effects maestro Tom Savini popped up on-screen as 'third bystander from the left' ... it was the film-maker's way of winking at the fans in the audience, to which the correct response was a knowing laugh. I remember forming a fleeting bond with a fellow movie-goer at a screening of *The Fly* ... when an on-screen doctor preparing to abort Geena Davis' insect foetus turned out to be director David Cronenberg. While everyone else cringed, the two of us chuckled smugly from opposite sides of the auditorium, like ships signalling each other in deep fog.
>
> (Kermode 1997: 60)

While (academic-)fans such as Kermode discuss their fan knowledge in terms of genre 'literacy' (1997: 65) and fan 'education' (*ibid.*: 58), in psychoanalytic accounts of the horror genre and (by implication) its fans, any possibility of fan knowledge is at best dismissed as a gendered/ideological construction, and at worst, denied altogether. In contrast to this position, I have so far sought to illustrate the limits to fan knowledge, given that this is contained by fan imagined subjectivities and moral dualisms, and also given that fan knowledge is marked by absences and communal legitimations. But I have also indicated the limits to academic knowledge, which needs to be similarly situated within its own proliferating moral dualisms, absences and communal legitimations. I have suggested that any 'good' psychoanalytic account of fandom – to follow the principle of self–other equality established in the previous chapter – must rebound on academic 'epistemophilia' and hence on academic knowledge/affect. If the 'knowing' fan may be defending aspects of their subjectivity and their tastes, then the same may be true for the 'knowing' critic.

The apparent need to maintain a moral difference or dualism between academic and fan is evident in Penley's psychoanalysis of *Star Trek* fans as 'slash' writers. Slash is a type of fan fiction (or fan art) which depicts male characters such as Captain Kirk and Mr Spock as sexually and romantically involved with one another, while (usually) maintaining that the characters concerned are still 'heterosexual'. Slash writing has also extended to cover female/female slash, although this type of slash has yet to be meaningfully examined psychoanalytically in fan studies.

Slash has, perhaps, been disproportionately focused on by academic writers working on fandom, probably because it offers an example of 'tactical' fan reworking which can be fitted into a de Certeau-derived model. For Penley, psychoanalysis is once again important because the activities of these slash-writing fans seem to resist any other 'logic' of explanation: 'I agree with Lamb and Veith's argument, although I think it helps us more to understand the sociological question of "why Kirk and Spock?" than the perhaps more psychical question of "why two men?"' (Penley 1992: 490–1). But this comparison of explanations is telling: why is the 'psychoanalytic' question purely a matter of gender rather than referring to the actual characters? Can 'Kirk' and 'Spock' not form the objects of psychoanalytic investigation? This must, in some sense, remain a possibility given that Penley wants to emphasise 'the fans' identification with the whole *Star Trek* universe' rather than 'just the characters' (*ibid.*: 491).

Penley also offers the standard justification for using Laplanche and Pontalis (1986 [1968]): their account allows that 'the subject can hold a number of identificatory positions' (1992: 480). The 'complexity' of Laplanche and Pontalis's account is therefore assumed to make sense of the 'complexity' of slash writing and fan identification. But by separating off the issue of 'gender' from the issue of characterisation (Kirk/Spock), albeit temporarily, Penley enacts the same type of splitting that marks Creed's account of the horror film. For Creed surface details (secondary fantasies) are reduced to 'primal' or original fantasies, and for Penley the seemingly incidental (K/S) is subordinated to the essential (slash as male/male). This shift is not absolute; Penley does pay attention to the specificity of K/S and *Star Trek* fandom, and oscillates productively in her own identifications between 'sociologist' and 'psychoanalyst'. Ultimately, Penley's moral dualism is thus distinctive from those offered by Creed and Hoxter. For Penley, the 'good' fans that she identifies with 'show a strongly psychoanalytic understanding of the relation of the unconscious to everyday life' (1992: 491). But these fans are also a 'bad' object. They also trouble Penley by refusing to identify as feminists: 'I cannot tell you how many times during the three slash conventions I have attended that I heard the phrase, "I'm not a feminist, but ... "' (*ibid.*: 491). This is actually a more intricate moral dualism than those usually inhabited by academic writers. On the axis of psychoanalytic understanding Penley perceives herself and the fans as engaged in a communal activity, while at the level of self-declared politics the fans remain, rather disappointingly for Penley, adrift of her own position, which is nevertheless assumed to be morally superior to the fans'. Burt (1998: 15) does not quite seem to capture the intricacy of Penley's position when he castigates her work for reinstating the academic's superiority over fans. And Michele Barrett certainly misses this intricacy altogether in the following rather bizarre comment:

It is a shame that the image of *Star Trek* in cultural studies is so coloured by Constance Penley's rather bizarre enthusiasm for the sexual fantasies of a tiny group of fans. As an increasing literature on 'The Metaphysics of Star Trek', 'Star Trek in Myth and Legend', 'Star Trek and History' and so forth demonstrates, there are more serious things to say about this huge phenomenon.

(Barrett 1999: 181)

Barrett succeeds in superimposing a new and highly rigid moral dualism onto Penley's work ('serious' versus 'frivolous' work), while simultaneously displaying an apparent ignorance of the fact that 'Penley's' enthusiasm for slash has been shared by many other scholars.[9] Barrett also neglects to consider that her 'more serious' examples are also products of the 'Star Trek industry' (Westfahl 1996) as well as of 'serious' or 'disinterested' reason.

Penley may be overstating her own case when she argues that she has given up 'the righteous rush of the negative critique' (1997: 3), since there is more than a tinge of righteous disappointment in her 1992 conclusions. But the moral dualism enacted by Penley's work does not align psychoanalysis/sociology with academic/fan or knowledge/affect. In this case, the academic is both within the space of knowledge and affect, going 'completely ga-ga over this fandom' (1992: 491, contra Burt's 1998 reading), as well as working within the spaces of psychoanalysis and sociology. My own disappointment with Penley's disappointment stems from the fact that her work ultimately continues to use a 'psychoanalysis' versus 'sociology' binary to reinstate a moment of 'us' ('good' feminist academics) versus 'them' ('bad' non-feminist-identifying fans). Fans and academics can be united in psychoanalytic alliance (unlike all the previous accounts I have examined here), but they remain sociologically divided. Of course, this division could also be read as a criticism of feminist academics who are too distant from the fans' concerns. But this possibility is foreclosed by the details of Penley's discourse: 'they [the fans] perceive ... a middle-class feminism that disdains popular culture and believes that pornography degrades women' (1992: 492). The implication is that these fans – caught up in a 'common sense' equation of feminism with anti-populist subjectivities and agendas – misrecognise the fact that feminism is actually what they are doing, and what they should declare themselves in alliance with. Penley's psychoanalytic/sociological split could also be defended as a realist representation: i.e. it simply is the case that fans and academics are socially divided groups and communities. But this (relatively naive) empiricism would neglect the dynamics of any such division, failing to consider how this division is reproduced through the torn halves of fan and academic imagined subjectivities rather than through the fans' ('deficient') inability to perceive the ('objective') superiority of academic accounts.

If I began this examination of psychoanalysis hoping to find a more 'interested' role for the subject, then it has to be noted at this point that this has hardly been forthcoming. Psychoanalytic accounts have generally been tailored to the cut of (ideological) academic arguments and moral dualisms, constantly placing fans as deficient, and constantly decrying the possibilities of fan 'knowledge' in favour of an emphasis on fan affects, emotions or fantasies (which, of course, do not possess the status of 'knowledge'). I have suggested that the splitting of emotion or fantasy from cognition or knowledge forms a typical part of many moral dualisms (and this splitting is indeed shared by academic accounts of academic moral superiority and some fan accounts of fan moral superiority such as Kermode 1997). To find a way out of this particular type of splitting it is necessary to turn to a psychoanalytic model which refuses to prioritise system-building 'knowledge' over emotion, and which refuses to split 'fantasy' from 'reality'. The seeds of such an approach, I will suggest, are given in D.W. Winnicott's account of play.

Winnicott: the 'little madnesses' of (soap opera) fans

The first useful convergence between Winnicott's work and fan culture lies in the notion of the 'transitional object': '[t]o get to the idea of playing it is useful to think of the *preoccupation* that characterises the playing of a young child. The content does not matter. What matters is the near-withdrawal state, akin to the *concentration* of older children and adults' (1971: 60). Within this withdrawn state the child enacts delusions of omnipotence, *assuming rights of control and possession over the object which is paradoxically both created and found.* The most significant feature of the transitional object is that it opens and occupies a 'third area' in the child's experience, belonging neither in the realm of inner and outer reality but being instead a 'resting place for the individual engaged in the perpetual human task of keeping inner and outer reality separate yet interrelated' (1971: 3). Winnicott persistently stresses the continuity which this third space possesses with cultural experience, believing that the initial transitional object is decathected when its creative mediation has spread out over the whole cultural field. Elsewhere this play–culture continuity is presented like so: '[o]ut of ... transitional phenomena develop much of what we ... greatly value under the headings of religion and art and also the little madnesses which are legitimate at the moment, according to the prevailing cultural pattern' (1988: 107).

So, the transitional object must always have some kind of physical and intersubjective existence; it cannot be some kind of imagined entity or hallucination. But at the same time, the transitional object forms part of the young child's initial separation of subjective and objective spheres, being the first me and not-me object. It is through the transitional object that the child recognises the existence of a world outside him- or herself. By taking on this role, the child's transitional object opens up a space between internal and external which 'religion and art' will later come to occupy. The transitional object also preserves a crucial contradiction:

> the child jumps from a perceived world to a self-created world. In
> between there is a need for all kinds of transitional phenomena ...

[where] there is a tacit understanding that no-one will claim that this
real thing is a part of the world or that it is created by the infant. It is
understood that both these things are true: *the infant created it and the
world provided it.*

(Winnicott cited in Phillips 1988: 117, my italics)

Harrington and Bielby (1995), in a rather under-cited but major study of soap
fans, apply Winnicott's work on the 'transitional object' to this fan culture.
Their account is a rich and powerful use of psychoanalysis which refuses to
denigrate fan 'knowledge' and which also preserves a sense of the 'personal'
significance which favoured texts can hold for their fans. Harrington and
Bielby's account therefore meets both the criteria established (in the first part of
this chapter) for the psychoanalysis of fan culture. It respects the fans' sense of
textual ownership (i.e. it leaves a place for the interested subject rather than
reducing this to an effect of social or cultural structure) while also repositioning
this 'ownership' within a consistent theoretical position (i.e. it doesn't simply
replay 'common sense' accounts of fannish 'love' for a text, despite coming
close to this in its accounts of fan 'limerence'). Furthermore, Harrington and
Bielby do not replicate some of the tensions and problems in Kleinian and
'fantasy'-based approaches to fan cultures, since their work avoids imputing a
'deficient' lack to the soap fans that they study. So far, so good, *contra* the
ethical objections of sociological-cultural studies critics. However, my chief criticism of Harrington and Bielby's work would be that although they move
towards avoiding a universal or transhistorical position (the sociological-cultural
studies 'theoretical' objection to psychoanalysis), they do not sufficiently rework
Winnicott's own arguments. Their wholesale 'application' of Winnicottian
psychoanalysis leaves their argument stuck with problems which are unresolved
in Winnicott's work.

Harrington and Bielby argue that soap fans' pleasure in viewing is usually
explained *away* by theoretical accounts; it is viewed as escapism, as identification, as resistance to dominant ideology, and so on (1995: 130). This results in
a situation where fans' enjoyment is 'rationalised' in academic accounts rather
than being explored as an event in and of itself. Harrington and Bielby emphasise that popular culture is experienced by its fans, and that this experience
should not be over-rationalised by theory. This argument has also been more
recently picked up by Michael Real: 'In the effort to hyper-rationalise culture
through theory, we create false hope and a false goal if our theoretical rationality
attempts to convert all cultural experience into elite culture or folk culture or
some other rationally approved alternative' (2001: 176). In Harrington and
Bielby's account, however, it is the notion of 'ludic reading' which both respects
the fans' intense pleasure and provides a theoretically consistent interpretation:
'a key form of pleasure is rooted in activities that allow individuals to challenge
the boundaries between internal and external realities' (1995: 133). Through
affective play, soap opera becomes a 'transitional object' for its fans. Soap texts

105

therefore no longer belong purely in 'external reality', nor are they entirely taken in to the fans' 'internal reality'. Instead these texts can be used creatively by fans to manage tensions between inner and outer worlds. If any one of us became caught up purely in our inner world of fantasy then we would effectively become psychotic; if we had no sense of a vibrant inner world and felt entirely caught up in 'external' reality then, conversely, we would lack a sense of our own uniqueness and our own self (a sense which, I would suggest, is lived and experienced even by sociologists wanting to argue that this is an ideological/constructed effect of social structures). It is therefore of paramount importance for mental health that our inner and outer worlds do not stray too far from one another, and that they are kept separate but also interrelated. That fans are able to use media texts as part of this process does not suggest that these fans cannot tell fantasy from reality. Quite the reverse; it means that while maintaining this awareness fans are able to play with (and across) the boundaries between 'fantasy' and 'reality' (1995: 134). As I have already mentioned, it is also important to realise that this process is ongoing and does not correspond to a childhood activity which adults are somehow not implicated in. All of us, throughout our lives, draw on cultural artefacts as 'transitional objects'.

Roger Silverstone (1994, 1999) has also applied Winnicott's work in television studies and cultural studies. Winnicott's emphasis on the always unfinished task of reality acceptance, and on the continuity between culture and the child's first act of play both lend a considerable degree of legitimacy to this exercise. Problems arise from the fact that Silverstone appears to concede too readily that 'the implication of my argument ... is that television must offer a regressive experience, if by regressive is understood a return to some earlier phases of an individual's development or to a withdrawal to a dream-like state' (1994: 18). But this concession can only be mistaken given the logic of Silverstone's own borrowings from Winnicott. Regression to infantile identifications cannot find a role within the creative and affective 'play' of the media fan. This is due to the fact that play and its cultural derivatives form part of the 'perpetual human task of keeping inner and outer reality separate but inter-related'. That this project is necessarily and inevitably *an on-going dynamic* means that its manifestations can in no way be tied to implications of blanket regression. Such pathologising inferences stem in part from Silverstone's uneasy oscillation between identifying television *per se* with the transitional object while at the same moment allying it with the 'potential space released by' the child's first transitional object (1994: 13; Silverstone (1999) avoids these problems).

Silverstone (1994) and Harrington and Bielby (1995) both seem to replicate a confusion which is inherent in Winnicott's own account of the transitional object. A distinction needs to be made between the transitional object-proper (an actual physical object which the child both finds and creates, originally through fantasies of destruction) and the cultural field which is said to displace the transitional object through the natural decathexis of the object-proper. But in neither account is such a distinction drawn. Harrington and Bielby differentiate between 'child' and 'adult' experiences of transitional phenomena (1995: 134) but simultaneously collapse this distinction by using the term 'transitional object' to cover each type of play experience. I suspect that this problem occurs as a result of Winnicott's own argument, given its stress on a lived *continuity* in the use of transitional phenomena and its *differentiation* between the transitional object-proper and the 'transitional space' of the cultural field.

Admittedly, Harrington and Bielby devote considerable attention to the cultural contexts within which the 'little madnesses' of different transitional objects can be tolerated:

> What, then, divides what is acceptable as a transitional object from what is unacceptable? ... [D]imensions of fiction/nonfiction and high-brow/lowbrow intersect in complex ways, making it difficult to reach only one conclusion as to why some forms of play are socially accept-able while others are not. By all accounts, though, soap operas are both lowbrow and fictional. Fans use them as transitional objects, even though it is socially unacceptable to do so.
>
> (Harrington and Bielby 1995: 136)

This further complicates their account, as they start to relate Winnicottian theory to systems of cultural value, inter-relating psychoanalytic and cultural explanations of the fan experience. Their argument also begins to relate the fans' experience of playful pleasure to industrial and social-historical contexts: '[industry] changes [such as increased space for viewer letters in commercial fan magazines] break down the barrier between the fictional and the real by fostering an illusion of intimacy between celebrities and fans ... and create space for this type of play to flourish' (1995: 152). But this specific point is highly problematic: ludic reading is viewed here as something which can be directly encouraged by industry machinations, despite that fact the transitional phenomena are both 'created and found'. This contradiction – which is central to Winnicott's account – is therefore overruled in Harrington and Bielby (1995) by a logic of ideological coercion where 'an illusion of intimacy' is created by TV industry strategies. And this occurs despite the authors' earlier statement that 'ideological' explanations of play and fan pleasure should be avoided. There is a shift in the logical model that Harrington and Bielby use; at moments they remain focused on affective play, but then fall back into a model of theoretical over-rationalisation.

I have suggested that difficulties arise in Silverstone (1994) and Harrington and Bielby (1995) because of both accounts' allegiance to faithfully repro-ducing or 'applying' Winnicott's work. One of the major problems with Winnicott's narrative is how the movement from the *proper transitional object* (*pto*) to the objective (or at the least, intersubjective) world of the cultural field might be accomplished. Elizabeth Wright (1987: 96) has criticised the lack of clarity in this move, as has Adam Phillips:

[U]nlike later and more sophisticated cultural objects, like works of art, the first Transitional Object is essentially idiosyncratic and unshareable. Winnicott, however, never makes clear how the child gets from the private experience to the more communal experience, from a personal teddy bear to a pleasure in reading Dickens.

(Phillips 1988: 115)

Or, we might add, from a private experience playing with a *Star Wars* toy figure to a communal pleasure in attending *Star Wars* conventions. And this addition also gives the game away: Phillips's assumption is that 'personal' and 'communal' pleasures will adopt different objects, implying a high/low culture distinction in which 'sophisticated' texts replace 'unshareable' teddy bears. But as I will go on to show, this distinction cannot operate in relation to contemporary *ptos*.

Silverstone is absolutely correct in his statement that 'television will become a transitional object in those circumstances where it is already constantly available or where it is consciously (or semi-consciously) used by the mother-figure as a baby sitter' (1994: 15). Silverstone points out, furthermore, that television also displays the material trustworthiness needed to qualify as a transitional object, because this object must survive the child's fantasised destructions of it. In this carefully delimited sense, then, television *can* act as the *pto* but only insofar as it interacts appropriately with the biography of the child concerned. Television's texts can be used as a child's *pto* but can also be interpreted later by that same child as part of their cultural experience (functioning both as *pto* and as decathected *pto*). The possibility of this biographical continuity between *pto* and cultural experience represents a sociohistorical shift, the significance of which cannot be overstated.

I therefore want to suggest a psychoanalytically-derived definition of fan culture. This definition ties in with the 'dialectic of value' because it views cultural contexts and affective play as inter-linked, rather than reading affect off from a 'determining' cultural context:

A fan culture is formed around any given text when this text has functioned as a *pto* in the biography of a number of individuals; individuals who remain attached to this text by virtue of the fact that it continues to exist as an element of their cultural experience. Unlike the inherently private but also externally objective *pto*, this 'retained' object must negotiate its intensely subjective significance with its intersubjective cultural status. It is this essential tension which marks it out as a *secondary transitional object*. This process illustrates that the *pto*'s movement into the cultural field may not be one of pure diffusion, but may imply a residual kernel or preserved distribution of interest which corresponds to a subjective location of the third space.

The secondary transitional object is therefore always an idiosyncratic local-ising of Winnicott's 'third space' ('space' which is neither purely internal nor external, being a mediating point between internal and external forces acting on the self). Although the secondary transitional object cannot be 'possessed' in quite the same way as the *pto*, and must therefore be viewed as a communal/intersubjective fact or experience, many fan cultures nevertheless testify to the original creativity of the subject via their idiosyncratic cultural location. In this case, the 'third space' which interests Winnicott cannot be viewed as synonymous with 'culture', religion or art *tout court* but should be perceived instead as a region of 'personalised' culture.

This takes us towards a definition of the secondary transitional object. Such an object can be arrived at in two ways: first, it may be *a transitional object which has not altogether surrendered its affective charge and private significance for the subject, despite having been recontextualised as an intersubjective cultural experience* (whereas the *pto*'s subjective significance does not translate into an intersubjective experience). It is this struggle between intersubjective cultural experience and personal significance which helps to explain fans' seemingly irra-tional claims of 'ownership' over texts and icons. However, the secondary transitional object may not be a *pto* which has directly been 'retained' by the fan, but may instead be arrived at by virtue of its absorption into the subject's idiosyncratically-localised third space. In this case, the secondary transitional object enters a *cultural repertoire which 'holds' the interest of the fan and consti-tutes the subject's symbolic project of self.* This helps to explain how fans' interests can be extended and relocated by the contagion of affect, with fan interest being channelled through intertextual networks of texts and icons. The first definition of the secondary transitional object emphasises the psychical processes of early experience, whereas the second definition accepts that subjec-tive 'third space' cannot be reduced entirely to psychical processes, being capable of extension and redefinition according to the objects which are encountered socially and historically by the subject.

Such a revisionist Winnicottian definition poses the related question as to whether all televisual or filmic *ptos* are inevitably retained within the adult's cultural world. I would suggest that matters of generic identification and cultural value could determine whether or not object-relationships are retained, depending on the cultural 'appropriateness' of this retention (in line with aspects of Harrington and Bielby's (1995) discussion).

Attachments to generically-identified 'children's programmes' may not be retained (see Messenger Davies 1989: 179) due to the child's perception that to do so would be inappropriate. This may occur as a matter of parental deval-uation of the text, or it may arise through any number of social pressures acting on the child to take heed of these generic markers. Texts which are more likely to be retained would seem to be those which appeal from the very beginning to both children and adults, either through a form of double-coding or through an emphasis on sociological dislocation/fantasy which can support both child and adult engagements. The generic marking of these programmes is hence sufficiently imprecise so as to permit a fluid combination of adult and child viewer demographics (see Buxton (1990); Spigel and Jenkins (1991); Tulloch and Alvarado (1983); Carpenter (1977); Pearson and Uricchio (eds) (1991)). The 'structural integrity' of many cult texts will therefore tend to support an intergenerational mix of fans (see Taylor (1989) on the intergenerational role of the film *Gone With the Wind* for its female fans; see also Dolan (1996: 11) on the rise of generational identities within culture).

Another issue introduced by the contemporary intersection of 'developmental' biographies and the media is that of the 'quality' of transitional objects which start their cultural lives as manufactured media commodities. While we cannot contrast commodified texts to somehow non-commodified teddy bears, and while the element of commodification may be deemed irrelevant to the child who will always both find and create the *pto* (Winnicott 1971: 104) it may nevertheless be the case that, as Dan Fleming testifies:

> To go fast is to forget fast: in the present context this evokes all too clearly the relationship between children and toys today. In writing this book I have been keenly aware of writing about the quickly abandoned. I have seen Transformers or Turtles lying apparently unwanted even while I was struggling to understand their appeal.
>
> (Fleming 1996: 198)

What, then, can be the quality of a transitional object which is so quickly seized on and equally quickly decathected and disregarded?

It seems to be the case that many fan cultures, and especially those surrounding cult texts, stand as the precise antithesis to the 'quickly abandoned' Turtles and Transformers. Where the affective relationships of fan culture preserve an attachment which challenges the disposability, pre-programmed obsolescence and contained innovation of the commodity, the readily forgotten 'Mutant Ninja/Hero Turtle' appears to be far more thoroughly integrated within the circuits of capital and consumerism. Indeed, as Alex Geairns, 'Cult TV expert' for the magazine *Infinity* has noted:

> There's ... one type of TV appreciation which has yet to gain a name. This is when a TV series gains a huge following for a very short time over its run, and is very quickly discarded upon cancellation or conclusion. The usual symptoms of Cult TV appreciation are there – the merchandise, the various art and craft skills, even in some cases the conventions. But the appreciation is not ongoing – it dies with the programme. To be a fully sanctioned cult show, the life of a programme must continue through the fans after its death.
>
> (Geairns 1996: 21)

Geairns's suggested label of 'Fad TV' might seem appropriate for the accelerated production-consumption cycle of toy manufacture and transmedia 'synergy'. If the structural integrity of the commodified *pto* is such that it imposes social pressure upon the child to move on to the next object-experience then we might ponder its trustworthiness as a transitional object. For in one sense the commodity *pto* does *not* resist the child's fantasies of destruction: the programmed commodity cannot be trusted (cf. Bettelheim (1978) on the value of the fairytale's trusted repetition). It vanishes at the whims of the culture industry. The structural integrity of the object is hence weakened by the reliance of actual, physical toys on the overarching meta-narrative of an accompanying TV series. Kinder (1991: 35) has pondered 'whether early exposure to television accelerates the process described by D.W. Winnicott of "decathecting transitional objects"', placing the child more rapidly in a situation whereby shared cultural experiences – in the form of commodity 'supersystems' (*ibid.*: 122) – must be acknowledged.

Robert M. Young (1989) presents the argument that contemporary consumption – especially that based around the experience of 'high-tech' – rediscovers the transitional object in adult life, such that a Walkman, a car stereo or in-dwelling earphones can all 'enfold' the consumer in a womb-like protected, trusted and intense space. But Young's introduction of the 'transitional object' into arguments surrounding consumption ignores the difficulties implied by combining processes of consumption and object-relating; difficulties which surface in the idea of 'Fad TV' and in the reality of discarded toys with whom an object-relationship has been broken off according to the psychically colonised rhythms of production and consumption.

Affective play 'creates culture' by forming a new 'tradition' or a set of biographical and historical resources which can be drawn on throughout fans' lives. This produces an enduring affective 'structure' which corresponds to the subject's personalised third space. However, it cannot be absolutely recovered *as a structure* precisely because it can be extended as new cultural objects enter the subject's 'third space' over time and according to a 'logic' of association. Cultural tradition and reproduction hence emerge from the idiomatic location of the space of play within the cultural field. Winnicott is very clear on the attributes which are taken on by this space. Phenomena of the play area take on 'infinite variability, contrasting with the relative stereotypy of phenomena that relate either to personal body functioning or to environmental actuality' (1971: 116). That 'infinite variability' can be produced through play may go a long way towards explaining the apparent fixity and repetition of fans' media consumption. Adam Phillips notes the conscious fixity of interest which fandom represents, although for him this is a problem to be solved rather than a lived experience to be respected:

> Psychoanalysis is the art of making interest out of interest that is stuck or thwarted. It doesn't, in other words, believe that the football fan

isn't really interested in football: it believes that he is far more interested in football than he can let himself know ... [W]e treat the objects
of interest as clues, as commas that look like full stops.

(Phillips 1998: 14)

Interest may well become 'stuck' – this seems to capture the situation of the
cult fan all too well – but does this imply that the fan must be released from
their interest? Such an argument replicates the Winnicottian notion of the
decathected transitional object, positing a total diffusion of cathexis (and hence
the mobility of free-floating interest) as an ideal which is rarely, if ever, reproduced given the actuality of the *pto*'s residue. We are, perhaps, all 'stuck' on
something, whether that thing is the dogma of Lacanian lack, sociological anti-
subjectivism, Deleuzian philosophy, or the dogma of a specific fandom. I would
suggest that it is whether or not our 'stuckness' can act as a personal and good
enough 'third space' for affective play that is significant, and not whether or not
we – or our interests – are 'stuck' *per se*.[10]

Summary

- In this chapter I have argued that it is important to view fans as players in
the sense that they become immersed in non-competitive and affective play.
I have suggested that what is distinctive about this view of play is that (i) it
deals with the emotional attachment of the fan and (ii) it suggests that play
is not always caught up in a pre-established 'boundedness' or set of cultural
boundaries, but may instead imaginatively create its own set of boundaries
and its own auto-'context'.

- I have criticised previous considerations of fan affect for their lack of play-
fulness; that is, for reducing affect to an effect of pre-existing structures or
conventions. Fans, I am suggesting, create the conventions that they attend
(to), through subjective and affective play. This opposes my account to
many strongly anti-subjective sociological and philosophical currents in
cultural studies.

- I then examined a range of psychoanalytic accounts of fan culture, aiming
to explore psychoanalysis as a space in which the 'subjective' could be theorised or restored. However, many of these accounts conflicted with the
criteria for work on fan cultures which had been set out both in this and
the preceding chapter. Kleinian and fantasy-based approaches tended to
position fans as 'deficient', thereby recreating an academic moral dualism of
'us' versus 'them'.

- Winnicottian accounts, I have argued, offer the clearest potential for a
psychoanalytic interpretation of fan cultures. This is so because Winnicott
suggests that our emotional attachments within culture, or 'little
madnesses', continue throughout our lives as a way of maintaining
mental/psychical health. In this reading, fandom is neither pathologised

nor viewed as deficient; instead it can be theorised psychoanalytically as a form of 'good' health. Such an account can also be turned on the figure of the academic, for whom theory and theorists can provide a personal and idiosyncratic 'third space' for play activity. Just as fans create the contexts of their fan cultures, so too do academics create new contexts for future work through the interplay of affective play and 'tradition' (producing academic movements such as 'deconstruction' or even something called 'cultural studies').

- I then concluded by suggesting that Winnicott's work cannot simply be adopted wholesale: to address theoretical charges of universalism it is necessary to introduce a new conceptual distinction between 'proper' and 'secondary' transitional objects.

This detour through the space of the subject brings Part I of this book to a close. It develops out of the autoethnography of the previous chapter, and builds on my arguments against ethnography as a privileging of the always 'articulate' fan subject. It also presents a counter-argument to much of chapter 2 and its anti-subjective 'sociological' stance. In my reworking of Winnicott, I have sought to preserve the contradictoriness that I observed as an important aspect of fan cultures in chapter 1. Winnicott, much like Adorno, refuses to close down contradiction in favour of a purely 'logical' resolution. This allows us to view Adorno and Winnicott's work as curiously complementary. Through a reworking of Adorno in chapter 1, I focused on the fan's 'dialectic of value' where fandom is both a product of 'subjective' processes (such as the fans' attribution of personal significance to a text), and is also simultaneously a product of 'objective' processes (such as the text's exchange value, or wider cultural values). My reworking of Winnicott in this chapter contributes to a dual-lensed approach which does not view the 'dialectic of value' as resolutely sociological. My use of Winnicott circles around the same 'dialectic of value' of fandom, providing a different perspective on the same cultural and psychical process. In this case, however, my attention has been much more closely and minutely directed towards thinking about fans' 'concentration' on their favoured texts. Through Winnicott's interest in keeping open the question 'did you find this or did you make it?', I have not had to close down the dialectic of value prematurely. Fan cultures, that is to say, are neither rooted in an 'objective' interpretive community or an 'objective' set of texts, but nor are they atomised collections of individuals whose 'subjective' passions and interests happen to overlap. Fan cultures are both found and created, and it is this inescapable tension which supports my use of Winnicott's work, as well as supporting what I have termed the 'dialectic of value' that is enacted by fan cultures.

In Part II I will continue to develop these arguments by focusing on the cultural world of 'cult' fandom and its associated texts and icons in more detail. The question I will begin with is this: why the term 'cult'?

Part II

THEORISING CULT MEDIA

5

FANDOM BETWEEN CULT AND CULTURE

> There is nothing intrinsically pathologizing about comparing media fans to religious devotees, since in both instances the roots of devotion are remarkably similar, and the texts produced by *Star Trek* fans and the like ... are not unlike the religious texts of the Middle Ages, which had a similar degree of reinterpretation and turned the authors and translators into famous figures, often drawing attention away from the spiritual content of the work that they were analysing.
>
> (Giles 2000: 135)

In this chapter I want to explore Giles's contention that 'there is nothing intrinsically pathologizing' about linking fan cultures to notions of religious devotion. However, I am highly aware of the fact that such interpretive links run the risk of seeming absurdly insensitive to cultural and historical contexts. For example, is it really helpful to compare fan-produced texts to the 'religious texts of the Middle Ages'? Rather than making such leaps of logic, which seemingly require a faith all of their own, I will instead examine why discourses of 'cult' are used within various fan cultures. Despite the label of 'cult' media occurring in a secularised and commodified context, I will argue that media 'cult' discourses form part of a fan experience which retains elements of 'religiosity'.[1] My point of departure will be that fan cultures, especially those self-identifying as 'cult' fandoms, cannot usefully be thought of as religions. I will argue that *neoreligiosity, not religion* is what we must consider when thinking about cult fandoms.

This approach to cult fandom may appear odd, but all it really does is open up a metaphor that is employed by fans. Rather than 'imposing' an academic metaphor (as in chapter 2 and Bourdieu's work), we can explore the languages that fans use to characterise the 'self-absent' imagined subjectivity of fandom. In other words, in fan accounts which work to articulate the reasons for any given fandom, what justifying discourses can be used to render fandom 'objective' and/or legitimate? As I pointed out in chapter 3, aesthetics offers one possibility, with fandom becoming rooted in the 'objective' qualities of a text. But another possibility is for fans to use the languages of religion and devotion to seek to explain their fandom:

> The correspondences between narratives of religious conversion and becoming a fan can easily devolve into pat generalisations about 'media idols replacing religious figures' ... That is not my intent, here, and I think we ought to be careful about such inferences. I do think, however, that while religion and fandom are arguably different realms of meaning, they are both centred around acts of devotion, which may create similarities of experience. In fact, fans are aware of the parallels between religious devotion and their own devotion. At the very least, the discourse of religious conversion may provide fans with a model for describing the experience of becoming a fan.
>
> (Cavicchi 1998: 51)

By emphasising that cult fandoms may display a type of religiosity without forming 'religions' I am, to an extent, following Cavicchi's lead: I, too, can see little to be gained from producing a broadly functionalist narrative in which the fan-star or fan-text relationship replaces the role of traditional 'organised religion'. However, Cavicchi is not willing to dismiss the language of religion as wholly inappropriate to fandom; there remains, he suggests, a 'similarity of experience' which the discourse of 'cult' may capture. There is a hesitation here, which it is important to preserve, just as I have sought to preserve specific moments of contradiction in previous chapters. Fandom both *is* and *is not* like religion, existing between 'cult' and 'culture'. 'Cult' discourses are thus not entirely hollow and empty (i.e. a kind of 'discourse determinism' which cleanses 'cult' of any experiential dimensions), but neither do these discourses quite 'fit' fan cultures.

Undoubtedly one of the major problems with linking fan cultures either to religion or religiosity – and this is a problem for both fans and academics – lies in identifying what is actually meant by 'religion' in the first place. It is hardly the case that this provides a stable reference point or referent:

> We act as though we had some common sense of what 'religion' means ... We believe in the minimal trustworthiness of this word ... Well ... nothing is less pre-assured ... An analysis above all concerned with pragmatic ... effects ... would not hesitate to investigate the usages or applications of the lexical resources [such as 'cult'], where, in the face of new regularities, of unusual recurrences, of unprecedented contexts, discourse liberates words and meaning from all archaic memory and all supposed origins.
>
> (Derrida 1998: 1, 35)

Hence my approach in this chapter cannot be to identify 'religion' or 'religiosity' as essential things, then suggesting that fan cultures somehow share this 'essence'. This is why I have already suggested that it is the *neoreligiosity* of fandom that is important, and which fans' appropriated discourses of religion might testify to and produce. Neoreligiosity implies that the proliferation of discourses of 'cult' within media fandom cannot be read as the 'return' of religion in a supposedly secularised culture, nor as the 'social relocation' of religion, both of which would assume religion's essential stability. Instead, the neoreligiosity of cult fandom is pragmatically produced through the 'new regularities' of 'cult' as a label for types of media texts and media consumption, as well as through the 'unusual recurrences' of such religious discourses within fandom. Fan culture's neoreligiosity occurs as an *effect* of fan discourses and practices, rather than relying on a preceding *essence/*'ontology' of religion and its supposed functions in society. Discussing the connotations of 'cult' also allows a consideration of the extent to which 'cult' discourses reflect emotional and affective processes in culture, processes which cultural studies has tended to marginalise via its anti-religiosity:

> *Religion is an embarrassment to us; it's an embarrassment to me, and above all because we Western intellectuals are so deeply committed to the secularisation thesis which makes of religion an archaic remnant which ought by now to have withered away. This thesis ... is plainly wrong.* It is wrong ... both because organised religion is flourishing in many parts of the world, and because religious sentiment ... has migrated into many strange and unexpected places, from New Age trinketry to manga movies and the cult of the famous dead ... [A]mong the things we need to know about ... is the history and sociology of religion ... we need to take religion seriously in all of its dimensions because of its cultural centrality in the modern world.
>
> (Frow 1998: 208–9, my italics)[2]

This 'embarrassment' has been clearly on show in recent studies of fandom (Jenkins 1992a; Tulloch and Jenkins 1995) which have notably neglected the analysis of 'cultishness' (Jewett and Lawrence 1977) by virtue of defusing any religious connections and connotations in 'cult' fandom. Other studies (Jensen 1992) have considered the etymology of 'cult' as a 'cultural symptom' attached to fandom rather than as a substantive feature of fan activity. 'Cult' is hence assumed to speak more to a series of theoretical and practical anxieties surrounding 'the fan' rather than to the actual practices of fan cultures.

However, the neoreligiosity of the fan experience must be taken seriously without seeking refuge in evaluative terms which would link this to pathologising notions of 'obsessional neurosis' (Freud 1907) or psychosis (Robins 1996). Equally, scholarly work must refrain from reproducing the 'moral panics' of the mass media (Cohen 1987), replete with pathologised representations of the cultist-proper (Barker 1984) and the fan/cultist-metaphorical.

Jindra (1994, 1999), Frow (1998) and Doss (1999) have all suggested that the sociology of religion can shed light on the phenomenon of fandom. Jindra (1994 and 1999) focuses specifically on *Star Trek* fandom as a religious phenomenon, and his discussion overlaps in part with my own use of Luckmann's work – although Jindra (1994) relies on a 1991 essay by Luckmann which restates his 1967 position and thus fails to locate this within the 1967 Berger–Luckmann debate which I will examine below. More importantly, however, Jindra fails to address the significance of the term 'cult' within *Star Trek* and related fandoms, discussing *Star Trek* fans as if they constituted a unique phenomenon (see 1994: 27) rather than forming part of the wider discourses and experiences of cult fandom. In the following section, however, I want to explore how discourses of 'cult' may operate more generally within fan cultures. I will then move on to consider how the sociology of religion might help to build up a general theoretical approach to the media 'cult'.

Connotations of 'cult'; considering an 'alien' discourse

We might suppose that all religious sentiment has been cleansed from the word 'cult' in its 'unprecedented contexts' of media consumption. This would certainly tie in with a vast body of sociological theory which argues that processes of secularisation are characteristic of 'modernity' (Lyon 1985; Beckford 1989). However, many writers in the sociology of religion focus on distinctive possibilities for the reconstruction of religion in new social contexts. Organised religion may have declined through a process of 'differentiation' (i.e. it is increasingly separated from state mechanisms), but a privatised and individualised space remains open to voluntary adoptions of sacred themes and ideas, while the 'secularisation' thesis itself has been contested and complicated (Lyon 1985).

For our purposes, though, it may be enough to note that the etymology of 'cult' has certainly not lost all force; etymology, sociology and history have proceeded through a series of interconnections, rather than the first being overtaken and obliterated by the latter two forces. 'Cult', in other words, does not surrender all religious force when used by fans, even if this use may also be ironic or humorous (see Hills 2000a: 81–2). But within a predominantly secular environment this fan neoreligiosity is perceived as alien and as other in media coverage of fan cultures.

While New Religious Movements (NRMs) are deemed to act as some kind of threat to the rationalised 'modern' self (as Eileen Barker (1984) illustrates in *The Making of a Moonie*) this depiction resonates with anxieties which have found a place in media analysis (Winn (1985) being indicative) as well as in the common image of the 'fan' as absorbed in a fantasy world. Whether or not it is used in properly 'religious' or metaphorical and fan cultural senses, then, the term 'cult' remains highly negatively-charged within current constellations of meaning (see Wright 1995). Karen Fields, in her introduction to *The Elementary Forms of Religious Life* (1995: lvi), notes that: '"Cult" now connotes not just feasts and rites but excessive and perhaps obsessive ones, attached to beliefs assumed to be outlandish'. Fields supports this observation by reference to the survey carried out by James Richardson in 'Definitions of Cult: From Sociological-Technical to Popular-Negative', noting also that a strong case has been made for the excision of the term 'cult' from serious scholarship due to the extremely negative connotations which it has acquired. If 'cult' remains a useful term within both practical and theoretical systems (i.e. for both cult fans and within theories of cult fandom) it must be precisely *because* of the cultural conflicts and sociological processes which are inscribed across its varied usage and connotative elements, and not in spite of these complexities. In other words, why would fans make use of a term which may well be culturally devalued outside fan cultures? What cultural work can the discourse of 'cult' be made to perform for fan cultures?

Considering the term 'cult' in relation to media forms and modes of reception immerses any such undertaking in a thoroughly Bakhtinian worldview:

> [a]ny concrete discourse finds the object at which it was directed already as it were overlain with ... the 'light' of alien words that have already been spoken about it. It is entangled, shot through with shared thoughts, points of view, alien value judgements and accents.
>
> (Bakhtin 1981: 276)

Analysis of the 'cult'-proper in the sociology of religion could be deemed to be wholly irrelevant to the study of media processes and fan cultures in contemporary society. However, from a Bakhtinian perspective, we need to consider how 'cult' discourses may circulate across and between these different contexts of use. And when both journalistic coverage and academic 'imagined subjectivity' tend to treat fandom and the 'cult'-proper as structurally identical phenomena (as common instances of modernity's other)[3] then we might reasonably posit an underlying ideological process. Michael Jindra observes that a stigma is shared by cultists-proper and *Star Trek* fans:

> Religious movements often have a sense of being persecuted or looked down upon because of their zealousness. And indeed, there is a stigma associated with *ST* fandom. The stigma is quite real and is one of the most controversial aspects of the phenomenon. Disclaimers on the part of fans that they are not 'hardcore' fans are common.
>
> (1994: 47)

However, despite linking religious movements and *Star Trek* fans, Jindra does not investigate this as a structurally meaningful connection. His argument hinges on viewing religion-proper and *ST* fandom as similarly liminal, since both supposedly exist in the interplay 'between seriousness and diversion' (1994: 48). But this hardly seems an appropriate 'identity' to draw between the two phenomena; however much religion-proper may operate as entertainment or 'diversion', it could hardly be argued that this is its primary function as compared to popular culture. In short, Jindra moves from observing that religion and fandom are similarly stigmatised to assuming on this basis that they must be the same thing. Instead, my interest here lies in how one stigmatised group (fan culture) may draw on the discourses of an already stigmatised group (religion and new religious movements). Such a set of concerns is a world away from arguing that media 'cults' must be akin to NRMs by virtue of their common nomination as 'cults'.

The move from 'cult' NRMs to 'cult' media can hence only occur on the basis of considering how 'cult' discourse is made to work in a new context while remaining 'shot through with shared thoughts, points of view, alien value judgements and accents' which stem from its prior religious uses. Although fans can seek to anchor their 'self-absent' imagined subjectivity through aesthetic discourses, such attempts remain problematic because they require reassertion in relation to every new textual instance (or they require a single programme or film series to be aesthetically ranked for moments of 'authenticity' and 'inauthenticity' which may then threaten the expressed fandom). Religious discourses and metaphors, however, possess a virtue which aesthetic discourses singularly lack: religious discourses are not called upon to defend the precise qualities of the 'inspirational' text. Whereas aesthetic discourses remain open to counter-bids and assertions (McKee 2001), religious discourses are more transparently based on expressions of communal faith which do not allow notions of 'proof' or 'evidence' to come into play. By surrendering norms of 'proof' for expressions of fandom,[4] fan cultures are able to sidestep the 'why are you a fan of this?' question which would otherwise pose extreme problems for self-absent imagined subjectivity. Religious discourses therefore allow for a particular relaxation of 'rationalisations' and 'justifications' which fans may otherwise be called upon to produce, converting the fans' lack of a response to the 'why?' question into a positive expression of faith and attachment rather than a lack of fan rationality.

And yet, at the same time such discourses cannot simply be reworked by fans, or entirely converted into functional moments within fan culture. As Bakhtin indicates, this is because words can never be 'owned' by their users; they remain somehow 'alien', entangled in the social networks and contexts which they traverse. And so it is with fans' 'cult' discourses. These discourses remain caught up in secular/academic contexts in which religion is devalued as irrational, and where it is considered to be a superstition that should have 'withered away'. By discursively producing a relaxation in norms of self-accountability and self-articulation (a relaxation which would no doubt puzzle many media ethnographers), fans are able to safeguard what might be called their 'practical consciousness' in the face of calls to 'explain' their 'excessive' or 'obsessive' fandom:

For Giddens, practical consciousness 'consists of all the things which actors know tacitly about how to "go on" in the contexts of social life without being able to give them direct discursive expression'. One can perform a whole series of social activities without knowing how to describe them in verbal or written language. For example, when one watches a film or reads a book, one can interpret them without necessarily being able to describe the process of interpretation in discursive terms.

(Jancovich 1990: 17)

This definition of 'practical consciousness' is perhaps too broad to cover the type of self-absence which is linked to expressions of fandom. Both fans and non-fans will 'interpret' and 'read' films and books without being able to articulate these processes discursively. But only fans – as part of the cultural stigmatisation of 'excessive' fandom – will be called upon to account for their pleasures and attachments. Rather than this simply being an example of 'practical consciousness', then, I would suggest that the fans' imagined subjectivity of self-absence which falls back into discourses of aesthetics and religion is an example of *practical unconsciousness*. This consists of all the things that actors tacitly *do not know* (i.e. fans cannot ultimately answer the question 'why this text?') but which nevertheless still allow them to 'go on' in their subcultural and subjective activities.[5]

This 'practical unconsciousness' cannot univocally achieve the legitimation of fan culture. By seeking to leave open the undecidability of fan pleasures and simultaneously avoid the taint of irrationality, it uses religious terms which themselves remain (partially or ambivalently) culturally devalued. Being 'shot through' with the negative connotations of 'cult' (cut off from reality; immersed in false beliefs; emotional; manipulated; weak-minded), these discourses cannot simply be revalued or rearticulated by fans. Such discourses remain embedded in a network of other cultural contexts. This leaves open the possibility that non-fans may (re)stigmatise fan culture. And it is this potential restigmatisation which could account for the fact that while using 'cult' discourses, fan cultures as diverse as those surrounding Elvis and *Star Trek* also seek to ward off the 'alien' connotations of the devotional terms they are deploying:

> What does it mean when adherents [in this case, Elvis fans] deny the religiosity of something that looks so much like a religion? Yet their resistance begs consideration. Some fans object in order to avoid charges of heresy or iconoclasm, because their religion [i.e. religion-proper] forbids sacred status for secular figures ... *But most do so to avoid being ridiculed as religious fanatics.*
>
> (Doss 1999: 74, my italics)

Or:

> *Star Trek* fan discourse often takes place on the boundaries between
> religion and the denial of religion. Many *Star Trek* fans, though
> denying that their adherence to *Star Trek* is religious, still use religious
> language to express their fandom.
>
> (Jindra 1999: 220)

These disparate fan cultures may well use religious metaphors and devotional
discourses, as do the fans in Cavicchi's (1998) study of Springsteen fan culture,
but all these fan cultures nevertheless deny their 'religious' status in order to
avoid a stigmatisation which is potentially re-introduced, paradoxically and
dialogically, through their very attempts at evading fan stigma. As Ted Harrison
has observed, in a study which comes dangerously close to simply aligning 'cult'
fandom with religion:[6] 'Elvis fans insist that they mean no disrespect to Jesus ...
Nevertheless, they persistently borrow the language of Christianity to express
their devotion to Elvis. Perhaps this is because it is the only spiritual language
they have to hand' (1992: 12).[7] Again, I would emphasise that this 'borrowing'
cannot merely be accidental, nor can it occur simply because religious terminology is 'to hand'. Either explanation ignores the cultural devaluation which
accompanies 'cult' discourses in secularised cultural contexts. For the fan appropriation of cult discourses to make sense, we have to argue one of two things:

1   Discourses of 'cult' media which operate in fan accounts share no links or
    connections with 'cult' discourses in religion-proper, or
2   Discourses of 'cult' operate culturally to safeguard fan accounts which are
    marked by 'self-absence', while also being dialogically linked to 'cult'
    discourses in religion-proper.

So far I have suggested that the former argument is unlikely to hold up
because of the semiotically inter-linked stigmatisations of fandom and religion-
proper within secular/academic contexts. However, it could be argued that
'cult' discourses are cleansed of religious connotations within fan cultures, with
these discourses only being reproduced as connotatively 'religious' in cultural
pathologisations of fandom. This more complex restatement of position (1)
remains open to the powerful objection that it positions fan 'rationality' and
non-religiosity definitively within the valued in-group of fans, while attributing
'religious' interpretations of cult media solely to non-fans. Such a reading
depends on a water-tight separation of interpretive communities (fan/non-fan)
which recreates the type of moral dualism that I have tracked throughout this
book. It may well be no surprise, then, that such a moral dualism structures
and legitimates fan accounts of the 'good' (non-religious) 'us' versus a 'bad'
(pathologising) version of 'them'.

It seems to me that argument (2) is a more complex, contradictory and likely account on the basis that it seeks neither to 'exonerate' fan cultures of the (secularised/academicised) taint of neoreligiosity, nor does it consider religious discourses as 'empty' vessels whose 'religious'/'non-religious' sentiments and meanings can be univocally tied to discrete moments in their discursive circulation. In the following section I want to consider how, given this statement, the sociology of religion might provide a useful way of forging a route through the media 'cult' in all its neoreligious, commodified and charismatic forms.[8]

'Cult' media and the sociology of religion[9]

Emile Durkheim's work (1964 and 1995) provides a valuable resource here.[10] For Durkheim – in one of the classic sociological definitions of religion – religion and society are seen as essentially linked. The 'elementary form of religion' is none other than society mistaking its own forces for those belonging to something external and other to it. This misrecognition of social forces results in a religious sphere of the 'sacred' which is set apart from day-to-day 'profane' existence. Elementary religion therefore operates, in Durkheim's account, through the production and the regulation of detached spheres of social existence. The 'sacred' is a realm of public ritual in which social gatherings of co-present actors enact their belief systems and hence subordinate themselves to a powerful external force. The existence of this force is subjectively confirmed by virtue of the uplifting and transcendent feelings which are engendered in the individual:

> Religion ceases to be an inexplicable hallucination of some sort and gains a foothold in reality. Indeed, we can say that the faithful are not mistaken when they believe in the existence of a moral power to which they are subject and from which they receive what is best in themselves. That power exists, and it is society.
>
> (Durkheim 1995: 226–7)

It follows from Durkheim's intimate connection of society and religion that 'there is something eternal in religion that is destined to outlive the succession of particular symbols in which religious thought has clothed itself. There can be no society which does not experience the need at regular intervals to maintain and strengthen the collective feeling and ideas that provide its coherence and its distinct individuality' (1995: 429). Durkheim's distinctive formulation views sociality and 'the passions' of the individual as necessarily interconnected; sociality, we might say, occurs here on the basis of a particular irrationality and ritualised misrecognition. These irrational and identificatory processes are then subsequently legitimated through sets of rationalisations, e.g. that the 'place' of the Royal Family is to aid tourism, and it is thus a rational economic element in contemporary society (see Billig (1992) for a brilliant discussion of these protective 'commonplaces', analogies of which exist in the discursive mantras and the practical unconsciousness of fan cultures).

However, there is a strong connection between Marty's (1969) definition of a religious-proper 'cult' and the media 'cult'. Marty distinguishes the 'sect' and the 'cult' on the basis of positive and negative sociality: the 'sect' aims at negatively bracketing off the social world and providing the individual with a pure and integrative set of beliefs and practices. By contrast, 'positively-oriented cults, usually gathered around charismatic persons or clans, succeed to the extent that they provide surrogates for interpersonal relations or attachments to significant persons in an apparently depersonalised society' (Marty 1969: 391). Cults are hence integrative against the backdrop of a 'depersonalised' society, and are not necessarily ideologically opposed to the value systems of this society. Cults also operate through the creation of interpersonal relationships, especially those of a powerfully affective and hence 'significant' nature. One could observe that the 'auteur' provides this locus of 'charisma' and coherence in terms of the media cult, and although the construction of such a figure varies according to specific media, this does seem to be a near-universal feature of the media cult.[11] Of course, we must refrain from easily equating 'religious-proper' definitions and issues with those of media cults. Such a move would generate the danger of a facile agreement with Durkheim's sociological functionalism, a factor which needs to be carefully tempered by considerations of historical specificity.

The difficulties and the advantages of applying a Durkheimian perspective on religion and sociality are made clear in the 1967 exchange between Berger (*The Sacred Canopy*) and Luckmann (*The Invisible Religion*). Luckmann argues for an examination of the 'anthropological condition of religion' (1967: 41) rather than focusing on particular institutionalised and organised forms of religion:

> It may be said that calling the processes that lead to the formation of the Self religious does, perhaps, avoid a sociologistic identification of society and religion but also fails to provide a specific account of the 'objective' and institutional forms of religion in society. We plead guilty to this charge. The analysis so far did no more than identify the general source from which spring the historically differentiated social forms of religion.
>
> (1967: 49)

Berger opposes Luckmann's seemingly universalist approach to religion, commenting that he cannot perceive the efficacy of equating the religious with the 'human' *tout court*, since this leaves only the biological or 'animalistic' functions of the subject outside religion. Religious functionalism of Luckmann's type appears to be purchased, therefore, at the cost of all-inclusive conceptualisation.[12] 'Religion' is disconnected from organised and institutional forms and rediscovered in a variety of unexpected and increasingly individualistic locations:

> Friends, neighbours, members of cliques formed at work and around hobbies may come to serve as 'significant others' who share in the

construction and stabilization of 'private' universes of 'ultimate' significance. If such universes coalesce to some degree, the groups
supporting them may assume almost sectarian characteristics and
develop what are called secondary institutions.

(Luckmann 1967: 106)

And yet, intriguingly, the media cult appears to fulfil Luckmann's predictions
regarding novel religious forms which are assumed to supersede organised religion. Luckmann, writing extremely presciently in 1967, predicted a move from
socially-organised religion to 'individual religiosity' revolving around loosely
connected themes and deriving from the individual's experiences (both familial
and consumerist) in the private sphere. As Beckford notes: 'Luckmann ... criticised the taken-for-granted identification of religion exclusively with what
happens in formal religious organisations; and he denied that rituals and
doctrines exhausted the category of religious phenomena' (1989: 102). This
critique led Luckmann to examine the possibilities for non-institutionally
specific religious activity which would continue to co-ordinate the efforts of the
individual to create, or find himself created within, a 'symbolic universe' which
could act as a sacred context through which everyday practical actions could be
legitimated or regulated. Luckmann therefore predicted the emergence of an
historically novel form of religion:

lacking an over-arching coherence or structure ... it will consist of an
assortment of sacred themes chosen by the individual ... the selections
will express flexible and unstable arrangements of personal priorities
which have little or no backing from public institutions ... They represent consumer preferences and are therefore congruent with the
individual's sovereign status and location in modern society.

(summary from Beckford 1989: 103)

For Luckmann the neo- and 'invisible' religion of modern society (1967) is
hence to be found through the selections of the individual, selections which
occur in the private sphere as a matter of consumption: these selections, and not
the social groupings of Durkheimian rites, are what confer an attenuated
'sacredness' upon a hotch-potch and contingent grouping of 'themes' and,
potentially, commodities.

In many ways, this conclusion is in fact not so different from that arrived at
in Berger's work (1967 and 1971), although the position of religion as a hence-
forth privatised and commodified form is evaluated negatively through Berger's
eyes, set as it is against a prelapsarian world of religious–social unity. The
collapse of the 'sacred canopy' of the *nomos*, that which shields against the
terrors of meaninglessness, supposedly removes defences against meaninglessness. This exposes those living through modernity to a greater level of anxiety
surrounding the continuity of self:

The world is built up in the consciousness of the individual by conversation with significant others (such as parents, teachers, 'peers'). The world is maintained as subjective reality by the same sort of conversation, be it with the same or with new significant others (such as spouses, friends or other associates). If such a conversation is disrupted (the spouse dies, the friends disappear, or one comes to leave one's original social milieu), the world begins to totter ... In other words, the subjective reality of the world hangs on the thin thread of conversation.

(Berger 1967: 17)

These 'conversational' processes take on a new centrality within the modern world, where the previously effective *nomos* of organised religion has been eroded by instrumental rationality and the extension of the capitalist drive for economic growth. This destabilisation of the *nomos* results in the fatal weakening of both organised and functional religion: 'insofar as religion is common it lacks "reality" and insofar as it is "real" it lacks commonality' (*ibid.*: 133). For Berger, then, privatised religion is barely a religion at all, offering no real scope for 'world-building' or 'world-maintenance'.

Berger and Luckmann agree, however, that the 'sacred' is not essentially bound by content: the 'totemic object'/animal investigated by Durkheim is deemed to occupy its privileged position for no other reason than the fact that: 'the things had to be from among those with which the men of the clan were most closely and habitually in contact. Animals met this condition best. For these hunting and fishing populations, animals were in fact the essential element of the economic environment' (Durkheim 1995: 235).

The production of sacredness, then, depends precisely upon the everyday and proximate form of the 'profane' world: the seeds of the sacred are contained within the most available, unremarkable and habitual aspects of the profane world, and the eventually rigid separation of the two bounded spaces must be seen as, in part, a defence against the self-evidence of this very reality. What is 'sacred' must be protected from collapsing back into the 'profane': hence the rituals which allow the transition between states. It is the very arbitrariness of the 'sacred' which produces the force of social convention. This arbitrary nature of the 'sacred' allows for the possibility that, historically, new sacred forms may emerge from new sociohistorical contexts and objects. Emergent neo-sacred spaces may be split apart from what was previously 'profane': indeed, a multiplicity of such 'sacred themes' may be generated by the inter-locking of individual/subjective and social/objective projects (e.g. nascent fan cultures and socially-organised fan cultures). Of course, if the 'sacred' hinges upon what is closest to hand for the individual, being built out of material encountered regularly and in a bounded manner, then media consumption suggests itself as an obvious candidate for any such process.

And yet, the media 'cult' is emphatically *not* a 'religion' in the traditional sense of the word, despite possessing elements of 'religiosity', as this is defined and contested within literature in the sociology of religion. If not truly an 'invisible religion', given the unacceptable equation of 'religion' with culture which this seems to imply, then the media 'cult' may at least remain partially within Durkheim's model, particularly with reference to the arbitrary nature of the sacred and the protection of the sacred/profane boundary. However, as I have shown in this chapter, the media cult can be better thought of as *neoreligious*. It does not simply indicate the collapse of religion into privatised expressions of faith or sentiment (Berger 1967) or the cultural relocation of something essentially described as 'religion' (Luckmann 1967). Instead, religious discourses and experiences are re-articulated and reconstructed within the discursive work of fan cultures, meaning that cult fans cannot ever 'cleanse' cult discourses of religious connotations, but neither can fans' use of religious terminology be read simply as an indication that fan cultures *are* fan 'cults' or 'religions'. Between religiosity and discourse – between cult and culture – there lies the dialogism of the media cult's neoreligious devotion. Cultic in the sense that its fan objects are perhaps ultimately arbitrary, fandom is also cultural in the sense that it seeks to account for its attachments by drawing self-reflexively and intersubjectively on discourses of 'religiosity' and 'devotion'. Eugene Halton has observed that 'the word cult, despite its obvious relation to culture, seems worlds apart from its meaning in everyday language' (1992: 44). But these apparent 'worlds apart' also enjoy a certain continuity: 'Human reason, in all its fullness, is in living continuity with the cultic roots of culture and is much more than merely rational' (1992: 62). Halton suggests that the rationalities and rationalisations of culture emerge out of 'playful, dreamlike, inquisitive, and ritualistic forms of conduct' (*ibid.*). It is in this sense that fandom exists between and betwixt culture and cult: not as pathologised or irrational, but as 'more than merely rational'. Cult discourses are drawn on in many fan cultures because they indicate that fandom is about more than just 'interpretive community' or a rational(ised) system of meaning; it is also about the dialectic of value – the interplay between intensely subjective, personalised value and objective/communal accounts.

Summary

- In this chapter I reopened the question posed in chapter 3: why this text/icon? I have argued that fans make use of religious discourses of 'cult' for specific reasons. First, this discourse lacks the restrictively text-specific nature of aesthetic arguments. Second, it preserves a space for 'self-absence' which means that the fan is not obliged to present a fully 'rational' explanation of his/her fandom. Third, despite avoiding the over-rationalisation which fandom attributes to academia, religious discourses still allow accusations of complete fan irrationality or arationality to be warded off.
- I then went on to argue that discourses of 'cult' are dialogic. In other words, their connotations are not exhausted by the situated contexts in

which media fans use them. This means that while defending against the continual need to 'justify' fan activities, fans also become enmeshed in unintended connotations such as 'religious fanaticism' or 'detachment from reality'. The discursive defence of fandom which draws on religious terms hence reintroduces the possibilities of stigmatisation which it seeks to evade.

- I considered the counter-argument that fan discourses of 'cult' are wholly non- or anti-religious. Such arguments seem motivated by an interest in characterising fans as univocally 'rational'. This position also assumes that religiosity is an intrinsically pathologising term, rather than viewing this as one aspect within the dialogic circulation of 'cult' discourses. I have suggested that any position which wholly severs cult discourses from religious sentiments (as do many fan accounts) relies on yet another simplistic moral dualism.

- Finally, I considered key readings of Durkheim's sociology of religion, e.g. the Berger–Luckmann (1967) debate. I used these to argue that the media cult's 'sacredness' for its fans may well be arbitrarily produced out of the everydayness and ready availability of media texts. This arbitrariness of cult artefacts would explain the difficulties that fans encounter when seeking to justify their fandoms.

6

MEDIA CULTS

Between the 'textual' and the 'extratextual'

In this chapter, I will consider how the 'cult' status of texts[1] and icons hinges both on audience distinctions/valorisations *and* upon textual and iconic characteristics. Rather than existing as a genre, cult texts and icons can be more usefully analysed via Wittgenstein's notion of 'family resemblances': 'a complicated network of similarities overlapping and criss-crossing: sometimes overall similarities, sometimes similarities of detail' (1988: 32).

I would suggest that there can be no final and absolute classification of the media cult (see Jerslev 1992), for just as different generations within the 'family' may recombine qualities and attributes, then so too may new 'media cults' produce further recombinations of family attributes, or even the generation of new 'basic' traits. However, the notion of 'family resemblances' has the benefit of allowing for this flexibility, rather than implying an absolutely fixed definition of 'cult'. The fact that many cults possess 'sometimes overall similarities, sometimes similarities of detail' also leads us to consider the possibility that certain textual and iconic forms predispose their audiences toward cult 'devotion'.

The cult object is hence neither textually programmable nor entirely textually arbitrary. The media cult is paradoxical (Winnicott (1971); see chapter 4) in that it is *both* 'found' (consisting of textual qualities and properties) *and* 'created' (in the manner of Durkheimian 'sacredness' discussed in the previous chapter) by the viewer.

In the next section I will consider the 'family resemblances' of cult texts: *auteurism*, *endlessly deferred narrative*, and *hyperdiegesis*. I will then move on to address cult icons in the second section of the chapter. Icons, I will argue, combine endlessly deferred narrative with qualities of 'denarration'.

The family resemblances of cult texts

Eco (1995b) lists three primary conditions of the cult text:

1   The furnishing of an entire narrative world which the fan can return to as if it were a private, sectarian space ... (198).

2   detachability or non-organic 'ricketiness' such that phrases, scenes and feel-
    ings can be lifted out of the text ... .
3   'living textuality', by which Eco means that the cult text exists beyond the
    legislation of an author, being a 'text of texts' which has no origin other
    than pure textuality (199).

The third attribute becomes the basis for Eco's discussion of *Casablanca*, which
he distinguishes from *Raiders of the Lost Ark* and *ET* on the basis that these are
intertextually self-conscious, and 'programmed' in terms of their heritage
(1995b: 210–1). By contrast, *Casablanca* is praised as belonging to a lost
moment, one in which intertextuality was more spontaneous, unthought and
naively 'authentic'.[2] This is one of two romantic binary oppositions in Eco's
work. Distrusting postmodern intertextuality, Eco also seemingly distrusts the
film in relation to the book. Given the latter's potential for re-reading and
reader activity, cult books supposedly manage to combine organic wholeness
with cult status (*ibid.*: 198). Film is viewed as a medium in which cult status is
irreconcilable with organic unity, since this filmic unity would prevent the
detachability necessary to the existence of the cult (*ibid.*).

Though ground-breaking, Eco's work has not aged well.[3] Its notion that a
film has to be watched all the way through in one sitting makes little sense in
video or DVD-based fan cultures, while its insistence that the films of Lucas and
Spielberg do not merit cult consideration alongside *Casablanca* suggests a
matter of generational taste weakly disguised as a theoretical distinction (see
chapter 3). Eco's concern with 'detachability' and 'living textuality' is also
complicated by the auteurism which many media cults display.[4]

If, *contra* Eco, *Star Wars* can be considered as cultish (see Brooker 1997,
1999b) then this status cannot be divorced from the fantasised 'presence' of
George Lucas as creator-*auteur*, and as a romanticised and 'revolutionary'
figure in the history of film. In his introduction to *Cult TV: The Essential
Critical Guide* (Lewis and Stempel 1993: 7), Patrick McGoohan distinguishes
the 'revolutionary' creators of cult shows:

> [Cult programmes] attract a fanatical following. They have something
> which fascinates their acolytes who view favourite shows time after
> time without diminishing enjoyment. Why? Perhaps the answer is that
> these programmes were made by enthusiasts who believed passionately
> in their work, and the energy of their belief is transmitted to a select
> audience sympathetic to the theme and themselves hungry for an
> enthusiasm.

In such accounts, it is the *auteur* which acts as a point of coherence and continuity in relation to the world of the media cult.[5] In production terms,
televisually this is likely to be the Executive Producer-Creator-Writer figure or
'hyphenate' (Thompson 1990: 36), for example *The X-Files*' Chris Carter, *Star*

Trek's Gene Roddenberry, *Blake's 7*'s Terry Nation, *Babylon 5*'s J. Michael Straczynski. Although the *auteur* figure is problematised by the collaborative nature of industry creation, fans continue to recuperate trusted *auteur* figures (see Lavery (1995) and Nochimson (1997)). A similar game of textual authorisation has been played out across *The X-Files*, where 'stand out' episodes are often marked as such by the writing/directing of Chris Carter.

Auteurism brings with it an ideology of quality: if much mass culture is supposedly unauthored – supposedly being generated according to formulaic industrial guidelines – then 'high culture' reading strategies intrude on this space through the recuperation of the trusted Creator.[6] Where no obvious candidate for the role of *auteur* is apparent, then the functions of authorial discourse can, as *Doctor Who* illustrates, be split across personnel (the typical triumvirate would be one of producer-director-star). The line between creator and audience is blurred by the fact that the former supposedly communicates an intense private vision to the latter.

The *auteur*'s extratextual 'presence' is in part produced by the fans themselves, but its legitimacy always predates fans' involvement through being offered up as an official extratextual/publicity narrative. A designated 'author' is hence likely to be offered up by shows which aspire to any sort of cult status. In contrast, forms close to 'cult' such as soap opera are far more likely to be non-authored within official publicity discourses, although fans may contest this non-authorisation.[7] It has been suggested by Jenkins (1992a) that the *auteur*/non-*auteur* distinction between, say, *Twin Peaks* and more traditional soaps is a matter of gendered reading practices, with male followers of Lynch's master-puzzle focusing on hermeneutic readings, i.e. attempting to 'crack' the narrative enigmas of the programme by referring to Lynch's supposed intentions. This rests uneasily alongside Jenkins's own discussion of '*Star Trek*, genre and authorship' (1995) which examines the extratextual Roddenberry-as-Creator narrative, and yet at the same time admits that *Star Trek* has a huge female following. This popularity can only imply that the officially licensed and extratextual view of Gene Roddenberry plays its part independent of gendered reading practices. Similarly, in the case of *Twin Peaks* the Lynch-as-*auteur* micro-narrative was licensed by pre-broadcast publicity (particularly magazine and newspaper adverts) and would therefore seem likely to have represented a frame of reference for both male and female fans (see Brown 1996: 60), even if the intensity of certain fans' engagement with the notion of Lynch-as-*auteur* (i.e. on alt.tv.twinpeaks) may have been gendered.

That both film and TV media cults consistently possess an author-creator suggests that what John Ellis neglected in his analysis of television (Ellis 1982) was the ability of cult TV to recuperate the author-function (Foucault 1977). This recurring construction of the *auteur* (Andrew 1993) indicates the indivisibility of romantic ideologies of authorship and the inscription of cult status. Shakespearean texts, for instance, boast immense longevity, enduring interest in the absence of 'new' Shakespearean works, complex audience (reader) demographics, and a very loyal and vocal readership. Equally, Shakespeare's texts have been reworked by devotees and have been reinvented across media as a myriad of modern restagings, film adaptations and books-of-the-film. In this sense 'Shakespeare', and the minutely detailed attention which many (academic) readers bring to these texts, could be identified as the perfect media cult (*Star Trek* is but a blip on the cultural timeline by comparison) in terms of its expansion beyond an original point of textual and historical context (see Bristol (1996: viii–ix) for a consideration of Shakespeare alongside the Beatles and the Elvis cult; see also Davidhazi (1998) on 'the romantic cult of Shakespeare').

The comparison between media cults and 'the Shakespeare myth' (Holderness 1988a, 1988b) is instructive: despite commonalities,[8] cult forms differ from this 'cult of Shakespeare' in that their 'creator function' is linked to a specific form of narrative; one which continues without end but which, unlike soap opera narrative, remains focused on particular themes and issues of (character) identity. The issue here is the extent to which media cults thereby display a characteristic narrative form, which I will term 'perpetuated hermeneutic' (Tulloch and Alvarado 1983: 133) or 'endlessly deferred narrative'. Recognising this form means recognising the textual determinations of cult status, and the sense in which the cult text is *found* rather than purely created by the cult audience. At stake is the identification of the cult as a set of inter-related forms which are common across different media. Cult TV; cult films; cult books – these all display combinations of 'endlessly deferred narrative' and 'hyperdiegesis' (see, for example, Hills (2000b) on the Discworld novels of Terry Pratchett).

Cult texts differ crucially from cultish objects of enduring fascination and affection such as the saga of the Royal Family. Since this tabloid drama is encoded as 'real' (or at least possesses actual referents) it can offer no 'author-function' or creator-auteur: there is no 'subject-who-is-supposed-to-know', no guarantor of trust underlying the open-ended royal tale. The narrative in this instance is 'endlessly deferred' simply by virtue of its realism.[9]

The cult's 'endlessly deferred narrative' is distinct from Barthes's 'hermeneutic code' (1974) since this operates across a single narrative.[10] 'Endlessly deferred narrative' is also distinct from the decentred narrative non-resolution of soap operas, which always continue to pose a number of questions, none of particular priority or significance, even while (temporarily) resolving elements of ongoing stories. The cult form, by contrast, typically focuses its endlessly deferred narrative around a singular question or related set of questions. This 'endlessly deferred narrative' typically lends the cult programme both its encapsulated identity and its title; consider, for example *The Prisoner* (where and why is Number Six imprisoned? Did he escape?) and *The Hitch-hiker's Guide to the Galaxy* (in which we get extracts from 'the Guide' but are never privy to its entirety, leaving it open to reinvention as a source of narrative information and revelation). Another example of this process is *Doctor Who*, which is actually a question as well as a title: the show's central character was not latterly called 'Doctor Who' but 'the Doctor'. 'Doctor *Who?*' is thus the question addressed throughout the programme's history in a variety of ways. The central character is therefore offered up as a mystery, or as 'unfinished'/unknown. Over 26 years a fairly comprehensive sense of the Doctor's identity was eventually arrived at, only to be destabilised in the final few seasons (1988–89) where it was hinted that previous programme knowledge was only partial. Threatened with narrative exhaustion, the programme struggled to find a way to 'regenerate' the sense of mystery which it had carried since its inception. *Doctor Who* projects its endlessly deferred narrative almost entirely upon the (non-) identity of its (anti)hero: other cult series have displayed similar tendencies with regards to particular characters.

'Classic' *Star Trek*, for instance, offered the character of Mr Spock, who as the only alien aboard the *Enterprise* presented an opportunity for endlessly deferred narrative. Spock's status as a half-Vulcan introduced an ongoing question regarding the nature of this difference which was addressed in particular episodes as well as being developed by Leonard Nimoy (see Nimoy 1995: 66 and 71). Over time – and across many episodes scattered throughout *Star Trek*'s transmission sequence – the character of Spock is 'unfolded' in terms of a familial history, sexuality, mating rituals, culture, beliefs and distinctive skills. Thus the 'mystery' of the character's identity is not considered as part of one distinct storyline but functions across the entirety of the meta-text that is *Star Trek*.

The collapse of an endlessly deferred narrative – whether by design or exhaustion – can signal a crisis point for any cult form: *Moonlighting*, for instance, enjoyed a dedicated, involved and loyal audience (and is featured as a 'cult' show in the niche magazine *Cult Times*) until it fatally resolved the sexual tension which existed between its co-stars. The 'will they, won't they' tease which had stretched across the 'episodic but non-discrete' paradox of the programme then ceased to act as a lure. *Moonlighting* entered the world of soap opera, in which the resolution of one narrative thread opened up a new set of possibilities, and thereby sacrificed the focal point of its own endlessly deferred narrative.

Identifying 'endlessly deferred narratives' in *The X-Files, Babylon 5* [11] and *The Fugitive,* Craig Hinton illustrates the commonality which fan writers perceive across the network or cluster of shows considered to be cults:

> In the same way that *Babylon 5* has garnered popularity, *The X-Files* is doing the same: they both give the audience a definite goal and they'll stay for the duration. It worked in the sixties with *The Fugitive,* and it still works today. We know that Scully and Mulder will eventually stumble on the truth, and we're all more than happy to hang around for the duration … Everyone likes a secret.
>
> (Hinton 1995)

This cultish intertextuality is repeatedly evident when scanning *Cult Times*: *Nowhere Man*, for example, is described in terms of two previously successful cults: '*Nowhere Man* creator and executive producer Lawrence Herzog is a pretty hip individual who can quote you chapter and verse [note the self-conscious presence of a religious discourse] on such cult fare as *The Prisoner* ... [but] *Nowhere Man* ... goes beyond the easy tag of *The Fugitive* meets *The X-Files*' (*Cult Times*, no author credited, November 1995: 10). *Nowhere Man* would appear to be an almost perfect cult object in that it echoes previous cult successes, has a creator-*auteur* responsible for writing key episodes which develop the show's mythology, boasts a lead character named Tom Veil (the veil of mystery and obscurity?) and has production personnel in common with other cult shows. It also offers the drip-feed of piecemeal revelation and the persistent opening up of further speculation which together create the powerful drive of the endlessly deferred narrative, possibly the most powerful of all audience-hooking narrative forms.[12]

This brief summary could be taken to indicate that *Nowhere Man* is a *self-consciously designed cult text*, and that therefore this cult text is purely 'found' (i.e. it exists objectively through production decisions) rather than being para-doxically both (subjectively) 'created' and (objectively) 'found'. This apparent resolution of what I have posited as an essential paradox is, however, itself a falsification: despite securing coverage in *Cult Times*, *Nowhere Man* failed to secure a dedicated cult following; it was deemed by fans to be too pre-programmed, i.e. it did not leave enough space for subjective 'creation', and hence could not function as a viable cult form. In this sense, then, neither coverage in cult 'niche media' (Thornton 1995) nor production strategies and extratextual publicity regimes can successfully anchor a media cult: audience engagement – which *can* be textually inferred, but which cannot be wholly read off from the text – remains the acid test of the media cult. Inferring a cult audi-ence on the basis of textual evidence remains problematic precisely because any such inference must take into account how the given text can be fitted into an intertextual network of existing cult texts by fans' extratextual valorisations.[13] If the text concerned is highly likely to be perceived as a 'clone' of a preceding cult text (e.g. *Dark Skies* as an imitation of *The X-Files*) then this factor will severely impair its cult potential and its incitement of audience attachment. Extratextual publicity regimes and niche media coverage therefore threaten the cult status of the text in the same moment that they assist in the realisation of this status; by aligning a text too firmly with cult precedents, cult potential can be clearly signalled, but simultaneously destroyed through the very transparency and clarity of this interpellation. '*Nowhere Man* ... goes beyond the easy tag of *The Fugitive* meets *The X-Files*', insisted *Cult Times*, but the anxiety raised by this disclaimer was clearly enough to more than hint at its reverse. The potential cult text is, in this instance, too clearly commodified, i.e. it functions to recruit an overly specific audience (the 'cult audience' as a defined subculture).

Arguably, cult shows win most of their popularity with audiences while they exist in the phase of directed and focused narrative enigma: the survival rate beyond this is limited, as *Twin Peaks* discovered to its cost. The endlessly deferred narrative of 'Who killed Laura Palmer?' provided an audience-winning focus around which surreal 'clues' and potentially meaningless/meaningful characterisation could proliferate. However, when the 'identity' of Bob – the spirit presence – was revealed and precipitated hermeneutic collapse, the series struggled to redefine a focused position from which to regenerate mystery. The ongoing battle between Agent Cooper and his nemesis Windom Earle proved to be too detached from the hook of season one to hold a wide audience, and the show entered a terminal decline. In spite of this, or rather because of it, *Twin Peaks's* final episode managed to produce the 'Grand Non-narrative' through which martyred cult shows strive to ensure their immortality: had Agent Cooper, our one (relatively) stable point of identification himself been possessed by 'Bob'? This 'Grand Non-narrative' has also been enacted by cancelled shows like *Quantum Leap* (has Sam met the 'person' or God-like entity who has been leaping him through time?), *The Prisoner*, and *Blake's 7* (has Avon been killed? In this case the desire to know is pointedly frustrated by virtue of the fact that the final moments of the soundtrack – a number of gunshots – play over a blacked out screen and then the end credits). This posing of a mystery even in the face of cancellation may help to explain the enduring presence of many cult shows. Sometimes the most endlessly deferred narrative of all is that which will never *officially* be answered or closed down, remaining open to multiple fan productions, speculations and recreations.[14]

The media cult also tends to focus on issues of 'epistemological eclipse' and 'ontological operation', i.e. the problematisation of (outer) knowledge and the realisation of (inner) self-knowledge. Other contemporary forms do not address these topics in so ready a fashion.[15] Diegetic mechanisms prevalent within the majority of popular culture do not operate in the manner of 'epistemological eclipse': the narrative game of the cult form is thus distinct from that of soap opera (unfinished-unfocused/'realist'); the detective novel (finished-focused/ 'revelatory') and the avant-garde (finished-unfocused/'suprarealist') in terms of its *unfinished and focused* narrative expanse (which could, especially in the light of the previous chapter, be dubbed 'religious').

Another defining attribute of the cult text is *hyperdiegesis*: the creation of a vast and detailed narrative space, only a fraction of which is ever directly seen or encountered within the text,[16] but which nevertheless appears to operate according to principles of internal logic and extension:

> It was a *World*, the thing George Lucas created, and like an iceberg only a tiny part of it was ever seen ... [W]hat appeared on the screen were fleeting, fabulous glimpses of a mind-made universe that was backed up by data mountains of fantastic detail.
>
> (Burchill 1986: 63, original italics)

The tendency towards hyperdiegesis is also noted by Roger Hagedorn (if not labelled as such) in his brief history of serial narrative (and see also Sara

Gwenllian Jones's (2000: 12–13) reworking of Eco 1995b). Hagedorn observes of *Star Trek: Deep Space Nine* that:

> its writers often refer to elements of one episode in subsequent ones and, even more significantly, link episodes with characters and events from the original *Star Trek* and *Star Trek: The Next Generation* series, the effect of which is to create a sense of fictional space, history and character development that is far more sophisticated and intricate than that of classic series programming.
>
> (Hagedorn 1995: 39)

This overarching intricacy of the cult narrative typically displays such a coherence and continuity that it can be trusted by the viewer, presenting the grounds for 'ontological security'. Issues of fan trust being central to the creation and maintenance of the cult. If one considers the fan as 'playing' with the cult object (as per chapter 4) then one reason for such a concern with continuity becomes apparent. The fan-viewer treats the hyperdiegetic world as a space through which the management of identity can be undertaken, such a process only becoming possible where a relationship of security has been established through the fantasy of the destruction of the object, it having survived these processes unscathed and unchanged (Winnicott 1971). Breaches in continuity threaten the security of the viewer–text play relationship.[17]

The hyperdiegetic world may, as Jenkins (1992a) notes, reward re-reading due to its richness and depth, but its role is, I would suggest, also one of stimulating creative speculation and providing a trusted environment for affective play. Particular genres or modes may be best suited to the maintenance of endlessly deferred narrative and hyperdiegesis.[18] The predominance of science fiction, horror, fantasy, comedy and camp[19] texts within cult forms is far from accidental.[20] In the following section I want to consider the cult icon; I will suggest that the mechanism of endlessly deferred narrative is central to understanding both cult texts and icons.

Cult icons: death and its mysteries

Discussing the 'cult icon' poses one immediate problem. For, unlike the text which does not presuppose the reader's attachment as such, *the icon is always already a focus for the fan's attachment*. This raises the issue of *how we can distinguish between the 'icon' and the 'cult icon'*.

Possibly the most significant difference between the icon or celebrity and the cult icon relates to the distinction between commodity manufacture and contingency. The celebrity is often considered to be a synthetic creation, made for the purposes of audience appeal and subject to the transient and fleeting touch of 'fame'. Boorstin's critique of the celebrity as a 'human pseudo-event' (1963: 55) which has replaced the true lineage of the 'hero' is one of the most scathing pieces in this vein. If celebrity is manufactured then it is often also realised through the minimum of product differentiation, being a commodity through and through. The absurdity of this system has been exposed by a series of interviews with PR personnel, agents and tabloid journalists which were undertaken by Joshua Gamson: 'Marla Keane tells of her boss's determination that the key to the selling of a female client – who in fact became a major television star – was nipples. "So she had nipples in every poster", says Keane. "In every photo session, she wore little rubber bands around her nipples so that they were always sticking out" ' (Gamson 1994: 73).

The icon is manufactured, mapped out as a limited set of connotations. It is the poverty of this associative framework which enables the celebrity to act as a housing of the fan-audience's affect:

> The active play with affect by the strands of the entertainment industry is also an attempt at producing viable differentiated categories of popular taste. The work on distinction and differentiation is the industrial construction of audiences ... [v]iability of a celebrity can be translated as the celebrity's capacity to appeal to an audience through a specific array of commodities or services. The various social constructions of taste intersect with the industrial construction of celebrity figures to produce a system of 'functioning' public personalities.
>
> (Marshall 1997: 186)

Marshall's analysis concludes that the celebrity functions to discipline the irrationality and affect of the mass, splitting this mass into social and cultural collectivities of 'taste'. The icon is thus akin to the concept of genre, acting as an individualised and embodied linkage between pre-existing social codes and audience fractions.

Allen (1997) analyses lesbian fans' responses to kd Lang and Martina Navratilova. Allen concludes that the lesbian star/fan relationship – 'a subculture *within a subculture*' (1997: 128) – challenges the heterosexuality of the star system and allows for the reproduction of lesbian identity: 'Heterosexual fandom closes down identity options for fans through securing heterosexuality as an ideal and dominant identity; lesbian fandom, conversely, opens up the range of identities available to the individual ... the media popularity of kd and Martina has had a powerful influence on how possible it is to be a lesbian in the 1990s' (*ibid.*: 130). However, Allen's argument neglects that dimension highlighted by Marshall, namely that the icon acts as a focal point for the stratification and organisation of consumption-based identities.

Allen's study does not convincingly illustrate radical subversion, but rather furnishes the acid test for Marshall's hypothesis; kd and Martina represent the viable embodiment of an audience fragment (the lesbian audience), and are precisely viable insofar as they act as an industrial conduit for a 'specific array of commodities and services'. The structural place of the lesbian icon – for whom muscular arms and hands rather than rubber-banded nipples are apparently the focus of fetishistic attention – naturalises lesbian identity only to the extent that it recognises such an identity as a lifestyle option within the marketplace. Such a process may well culturally empower lesbian identity and allow for the reproduction of lesbian culture (to this extent Allen's conclusions are perfectly fair) but this affective process also reproduces, enlarges and stabilises its embodied audience as a target market.[21]

Obviously, the cult icon similarly articulates social meaning and affect: Monroe embodied a combination of sexuality and innocence which housed the affect related to social shifts in the US:

> Monroe's image has to be situated in the flux of ideas about morality and sexuality that characterised the fifties in America and can here be indicated by such instances as the spread of Freudian ideas in post-war America ... the Kinsey report, Betty Friedan's *The Feminine Mystique*, rebel stars such as Marlon Brando, James Dean and Elvis Presley, the relaxation of cinema censorship in the face of competition from television etc.
>
> (Dyer 1979: 36)

And yet Monroe possesses a very different meaning within contemporary culture: '[in] to-day's cult of ... Monroe – do we see more ... tragic consciousness in her?' (Dyer 1979: 71). Baty observes of Marilyn-as-icon that 'Icons are culturally resonant units that convey a familiar set of "original" meanings and images. Because they represent content as form – Marilyn's image contains and conveys her "story" – they also provide a surface on which struggles over meaning can be waged' (Baty 1995: 59). In this sense, then, the distinction of the cult icon is that it might be considered as an icon which moves continuously across social-historical frames, being re-mapped and reworked in this process: it is an iteration, or an accreting set of iterations of the original moment of audience-mapping (cf. Bennett and Woollacott 1987) whereas the 'icon' remains locked into a given set of social and cultural co-ordinates. The opening-out of the icon – its temporal persistence across markedly different economies of meaning and affect – produces the moment of cult formation.[22]

What is it, however, which determines not only the successful, but also the *persistent* remapping of the icon? Why does Marilyn Monroe persist within what Baty (1995: 14) terms 'mass-mediated rememberings'?. Why is Elvis Presley subject to similar processes of remembrance and extensive mediation? Greil Marcus catalogued an astounding variety of Elvis references, citations and reworkings in *Dead Elvis* (1991); Gilbert B. Rodman (1996) also focused his cultural study of the Elvis phenomenon around 'The Posthumous Career of a Living Legend'; Rogan Taylor (1985) includes Presley in his study of the entertainment industry as a functionalist replacement for religion, *The Death and Resurrection Show: From Shaman to Superstar*, and Neal and Janice Gregory consider what happened 'When Elvis Died: Enshrining a Legend' (in Chadwick 1997).

It is the pure, unpredictable contingency of how and when Elvis's death occurred which looms large in 'Elvis Studies', time and time again. The vulnerability, frailty and mortality of the cult icon overwrites the mapping of industrial pressure, shattering the construction of minimal difference and annihilating the work of audience-generation:

> When ... [Elvis] died, the event was a kind of explosion that went off silently, in minds and hearts; out of that explosion came many fragments, edging slowly into the light, taking shape, changing shape again and again as the years went on. No-one, I think, could have predicted the ubiquity, the playfulness, the perversity, the terror and the fun of this, of Elvis Presley's second life: a great, common conversation, sometimes, a conversation between spectres and fans.
>
> (Marcus 1991: xiii)

Through his death, Elvis moved for a time beyond the direct concern of the culture industries. At least he – as an embodied, unique individual – could no longer be subjected to the manipulatory schemes of Colonel Parker. In a sense, death cleansed Elvis – even the scandalous type of death which claimed him – replacing the grotesque narrative of an excessive and, in many ways, foolish life, with an absolutely anarrational and enigmatic end-point. Spigel has argued that

> Elvis's untimely demise was responsible for the shift in his status from being a capitalist-controlled commodity to being a fan-controlled icon: 'Whereas in life Elvis was the epitome of the mass-market celebrity – packaged and repackaged by the Colonel – in death he is truly a popular medium – a vehicle through which people tell stories about their past and present day lives.'
>
> (quoted in Rodman 1996: 13)

I agree absolutely with Spigel's general sentiments, though not with the totality of her claims. While Elvis has shifted from celebrity to cult icon, and while this movement can indeed be aligned with the wresting of his image away from producers and towards audiences, this process cannot be explained solely by a cartoonish contrast between the living and the dead Elvis.

What remains important cannot be the 'untimely demise' of Elvis *per se* (since this much of the scenario is surely open to counterfactual invalidation: has each and every star who has suffered an 'untimely demise' merited cult status?). The supposedly democratising separation of image and referent cannot entirely explain away Elvis's posthumous cult status: Elvis becomes a cult icon

141

by virtue of his image's persistence and his reproduction or reiteration across generations and across social-historical contexts. His image persists not simply because of an untimely demise, or an absurdly notable demise, but rather *because his demise cannot be assigned a meaning and therefore remains essentially enigmatic.*

It is this fact more than any other which serves to explain the distance which Elvis has travelled from the controlling forces of capitalist entertainment. His demise was neither simply nor vastly untimely (Elvis lived to demonstrate his burger-enhanced loss of youthful vigour). It *did* simply and vastly disturb the systems of meaning and the sets of minimal difference through which the celebrity system otherwise operates (see Williamson (1998) for a similar point in relation to the death of Diana, Princess of Wales). Elvis's death was not just a loss, (see Brottman (2000: 11) on 'the celebrity death') it was also an enigma and a catastrophic tear in the fabric of celebrity space-time.

Despite having moved from analysis of the cult text to that of the cult icon, the issue of the enigma remains crucial. *Just as the cult text typically demonstrates an endlessly deferred narrative – endless interpretation and speculation predicated upon a point of identity or closure at which the narrative will expire, and a point which is endlessly warded off – so too does the cult icon.* Monroe; JFK; Presley; James Dean, and more recently the disappearance of the Manics' Richey Edwards as well as the death of Princess Diana – every cult icon has their own unending textuality of irresolvable conspiracy theories, with undecidable oscillations between narratives of homicide/suicide, accidental death/murder or real/faked death all which represent the perfection of minimised and encapsulated perpetuated hermeneutics. In the absence of decisive evidence such endlessly deferred narratives are able to operate without constraint, proliferating across different media with varying degrees of irony (see Bird (1992) on 'supermarket tabloid' narratives which deal with the continuing and secret 'lives' of Elvis and JFK; see also Chaney (1994: 202–3) on 'funary cults').

Insofar as these icons' deaths cannot be located within systems of meaning they also represent a free-flow of affect which is wholly contrary to the mechanism of the celebrity, intended in large part to organise the 'irrational' affect and desire of the crowd/mass. As such, it is not the fact of the icon's death, it is the fact of the intrusive contingency of this death which poses such a threat. So much for packaging, marketing and control, such an event screams out; so much for the ritualisation of production and consumption. Edgar Morin observes in *The Stars* that: 'The mythological hero encounters death in his quest for the absolute. His death signifies that he is broken by the hostile forces of the world, but at the same time, in this very defeat, he ultimately gains the absolute: immortality' (Morin 1960: 123). Stars and celebrities, though, are not mythological heroes, however much Morin might indulge in this functionalist metaphor, and their being 'broken by the hostile forces of the world' assures a very specific form of 'immortality'; the persistent recreation and extension of an endlessly deferred narrative. They are limit-cases; instances where the system cannot expand to contain the absolute and annulling difference of death.

As I will go on to explore in the final three chapters, another way in which both cult texts and icons can be differentiated from other forms in popular culture is by virtue of the geographical, somatic and technological dimensions which contribute to cult status. Media cults may be centrally concerned with text–audience relationships, but these relationships are *not* restricted to the immediate encounter between text and audience. Media cults support forms of affective attachment which can generate and sustain longer-term symbolic projects of the self (Thompson 1995).

Summary

- I have suggested that 'cult' texts and icons are not entirely arbitrary (see the previous chapter); they share 'family resemblances' such as endlessly deferred narrative, hyperdiegesis, auteurism and contingent denarration. This implies that cult status cannot be viewed as entirely extratextual or fan-led:

  > The processes by which fans choose to poach one thing and not another are complex and still not very well understood, but this choice obviously *must involve factors* both *in the text* and in the individual. All texts are not equally susceptible to this process of poaching, although the text itself cannot exclusively determine whether or not it will be poached.
  >
  > (Smith 1999: 68, my italics)

  However, neither can cult texts or icons be too obviously 'manufactured' by producers. Attempts at cult production can be counteracted by the 'gatekeeping' functions of cult niche media, and by cult fans' anti-commercial ideologies of romanticism.
- Cult status is recurrently linked to ideologies of romanticism, either through notions of 'uniqueness' and 'art' (via the figure of the *auteur*), or through endlessly deferred narrative which, as an 'unfinished-focused' type of narrative structure, reconstructs a sense of romantic 'excess' and 'unknowability'.
- Endlessly deferred narrative is, I would argue, the leading 'family resemblance' which links otherwise seemingly unrelated cult texts and icons. 'Cult' status therefore seems to hinge on a certain 'undecidability', a space for interpretation, speculation and fan affect which cannot be closed down by final 'proof' or 'fact'. Even texts which appear to offer closure or resolution can be mined by fans for endlessly deferred narrative.
- I have therefore argued in this chapter that 'cult' cannot be thought of as a genre, although certain genres (sf, fantasy, horror and comedy) can more readily give rise to the 'family resemblances' which are linked to cult status.

7

CULT GEOGRAPHIES

Between the 'textual' and the 'spatial'

In this chapter I will analyse how the cult fan's affective experience is quite literally mapped onto spatial relations.[1] This produces a 'sacred' place which can serve to anchor and legitimate the cult fan's attachments.[2] *'Cult geographies' are diegetic and pro-filmic spaces (and 'real' spaces associated with cult icons) which cult fans take as the basis for material, touristic practices.*[3] This definition, and my case study dealing with *The X-Files*, form a mirror image to Roger C. Aden's (1999) work, *Popular Stories and Promised Lands: Fan Cultures and Symbolic Pilgrimages.* Aden considers fans' 'symbolic pilgrimages' as 'the interaction of story and individual imagination' (1999: 10). For Aden, then, geography is considered as a textual representation and, ultimately, as a metaphor. Having already addressed academic and fan metaphors (in chapters 2 and 5) I will shift positions here, examining cult geography *literally*. The 'inhabitation' of extratextual spaces, I will suggest, forms an important part of cult fans' extensions and expressions of the fan–text relationship, something that Aden's metaphorical 'symbolic pilgrimage' neglects.

I will approach the 'sacred' focal point of the cult fan's touristic pilgrimage not as a matter of social/communal ritual which produces semiotic or psychical effects (Durkheim (1995); Couldry (1998a); see also my arguments in chapter 2),[4] but rather as an affective-interpretive process which spills into and redefines material space.[5] In this view, the structural and social constraints of supposedly 'subcultural' rituals emerge out of experiences of affective play rather than logically preceding these experiences.[6] It is vital to restore:

> emotional influences and responses [which] have perhaps too often ... been treated ... as little more than parts of a mass, collective phenomenon ... It is right that the testimonies of pilgrims should be utilised to draw attention to the social processes of pilgrimage, but this should not be at the expense of forgetting the personal and individual meanings of pilgrimage ... If more attention is paid to what *individual pilgrims think and feel* [my emphasis], our understandings of pilgrimage as an individual *and* as a social phenomenon simultaneously will be significantly deepened.
>
> (Reader 1993: 239)

At stake here is the need to introduce a consideration of space into any theorisation of cult media. I will argue that the fan–text affective relationship cannot be separated from spatial concerns and categories. Media reception is simply one moment within cult fans' repertoire of practices – with each type of practice relating in specific ways to the originating affective relationship. Through visiting cult geographies, the cult fan is able to extend an engagement with a text or icon by extratextually 'inhabiting the world' (Bukatman 1998: 266), in a restricted or imaginary sense, of the media cult. This material extension of the cult's hyperdiegesis also advances my argument by indicating that *the media cult cannot be entirely reduced to metaphors of textuality.* Dean MacCannell (1992) considers the Piercean 'icon' through examples such as Marilyn Monroe and Madonna, and develops a theory of the icon as inherently relating to a cult of members. MacCannell concludes that '*the cult-icon articulation is antecedent to any interpretation that might subsequently be performed*' (1992: 241, my italics). Opposing a premature 'textualisation' of the cult-icon articulation, MacCannell continues:

> The association of icons ... with human feelings suggests the participation of beings *not as external interpreters but as internal to the sign itself* ... *The relationship of the cult to its icon is one of inborn complicity, a never explicit articulation of feelings, attitudes and objects.*
> (MacCannell 1992: 241–2, my italics)

Exploring such extratextual complicity and 'practical unconsciousness', the first section of this chapter will draw on my own tourist experiences as a visitor to Vancouver.[7] I will then move on to consider cult geography in relation to arguments dealing with 'hyperreality'.

The truth was out there (in Vancouver)

Any consideration of what I am calling here 'cult geography' begins not only with a 'tourist gaze' coloured by mediated preconceptions but also with a 'tourist gaze' which is thoroughly determined by media products:[8]

> A series of new place names has been invented for the tourist. In the north of England there is 'Last of the Summer Wine Country', 'Emmerdale Farm Country', 'James Herriot Country', ... 'Brontë Country' and so on. Space is divided up in terms of signs which signify particular themes – but not themes which necessarily relate to actual historical or geographical processes ... Even stranger is the case of the recently opened Granada Studios in Manchester. Part of the display consists of a mock-up of certain sets from the soap opera *Coronation Street*, including the famous Rover's Return public house.
> (Urry 1990a: 145)

In relation to cult geography, we are all 'outsiders' in a sense since the notion of the 'inside' is displaced here into a mediatised point which, by definition, cannot arrive: the mediated 'reality' ('Last of the Summer Wine country') and the reality of the physical space or place cannot be made to thoroughly intersect; despite visiting Holmfirth we cannot ever get 'inside' the originating text. 'Reality' and 'fantasy' cannot be fused, but nor are they conspicuously 'confused';[9] it is rather the permeable boundaries between these two realms which are redefined and recontextualised by cult geography.[10]

However, although cult fans do not confuse the text ('fantasy') and its related diegetic or profilmic geographical markers ('reality'), many cultural critics have refused to view the fantasy/reality opposition as permeable, and have used this to construct a moral dualism between 'us' (who recognise 'geographical reality') and 'them' (fans who cannot separate out imaginary and actual geographies). Even in work centrally concerned with the imaginary nature of tourist activity, Urry continues to find tourism based on media texts 'even stranger' than the typical relationship between mediation and tourist experiences,[11] which he characterises as a 'hermeneutic circle':

> What is sought for in a holiday is a set of photographic images, as seen in tour company brochures or on TV programmes. While the tourist is away, this then moves on to a tracking down and capturing of those images for oneself. And it ends with travellers demonstrating that they really have been there by showing their version of the images that they had seen originally before they set off.
>
> (Urry 1990a: 140)

In this sense, Urry's work is marked by the anti-media/anti-fantasy bias that might be expected of a modernist sociologist, since an interest in 'visiting' The Rover's Return is deemed to be purely a matter of 'fantasy' as opposed to the 'reality' of, say, the Eiffel Tower as a tourist destination. The first exists only as a fictional location, while the second is an actual physical entity. It is precisely this valorisation of the 'real' versus the 'fantastic' which cult geography inevitably challenges. And yet this challenge has been dismissed within modernist criticism as a failure to recognise 'reality' on the part of deluded fan-tourists.[12]

In such cultural criticism, then, the status of 'outsider' belongs not so much to the English fan of *The X-Files* visiting Vancouver, nor to the Canadian fan of *Coronation Street* visiting Granada Studios, or even the Japanese fan visiting 'Brontë Country', but rather to the critic who dismisses, in advance, these fans' pleasures in, and experiences of, cult geography.[13]

Both Hewison (1987) and Urry (1990a) specifically dismiss soap opera fans. The intense emphasis upon both community and regionality which is typical both of the soap opera form (and the romantic saga, see Taylor 1989: 67) has led these texts and their fans to become the obvious (feminine) candidates for critical distaste among (masculine) cultural geographers and sociologists.

However, the set of texts which I defined in the previous chapter as possessing 'cult' qualities have been rendered largely invisible in tourist debates due to the notion that since fantasy and science fiction texts are based on imaginary spaces then they can possess no real-life geographical referents.[14] The sf/fantasy cult text therefore disappears beneath the 'bottom line' of geographical enquiry.[15]

Restoring cult fans' sense of place to visibility within cultural geography also means engaging with dimensions of the 'globalisation' debate. The multinational information flow of media texts clearly does not, in this instance, result in a necessary loss of local differences. Quite the reverse is in fact demonstrably true. This makes the 'tourist gaze' of the cult fan into an *unheimlich* manoeuvre (Freud 1919) insofar as Vancouver can be at once both familiar (the initial or original 'home' of *The X-Files*; the climatic double of the UK; the repetition of brands and products) and exotic (the site of the other'; the linguistic double of the US; a displacement of brands and products). Following Morley and Robins (1995) we might refer to this tense counterbalancing of difference and similarity as being indicative of the contradictory forces at work in the 'place race':

> [H]eritage, or the simulacrum of heritage, can be mobilised to gain competitive advantage in the race between places. When Bradford's tourist officer, for example, talks about 'creating a product' – weekend holidays based around the themes of 'Industrial Heritage' and 'In the Steps of the Brontës' – he is underlining the importance of place-making in placeless times, the heightened importance of distinction in a world where differences are being effaced.
>
> (Morley and Robins 1995: 119–20)

For the X-Phile, Vancouver represents a place of distinction 'in a world where differences are being effaced'. Morley and Robins's recognition of the importance of place-branding is apposite, but tells only half the story where cult geography is concerned. There has been, to date, no direct attempt on the part of organised tourism to 'cash in' upon the distinction which has been generated for Vancouver by the international success of *The X-Files*. Scouting for *X-Files* locations remains an 'underground' activity in the sense that one cannot simply join a guided tour. Neither can one readily purchase tourist souvenirs which link Vancouver with *The X-Files*, although unofficial T-shirts (proclaiming '*Vancouver: X-Treme City*' and appropriating the graphic design of the series' logo) can be discovered in souvenir emporiums scattered along Robson.

There are bleak and blatant exceptions to the advantaged status of Vancouver; parts of the city that tourists will not visit as a rule, and which tend not to feature in glossy brochures.[16] On one very early morning trip through the district of East Hastings – a ghettoised area characterised by urban decay, drug-taking, apparent prostitution and vagrancy – I happened upon a delivery of obviously pirated T-shirts, reading only 'Vancouver' in low-grade black printed on white, the *Millennium* logo on the front, and *The X-Files* 'X' on the back. In the midst of poverty, social and psychological distress, these media text 'brand-names' certainly appeared strangely anomalous: they clearly represented a desperate bid to convert (without official sanction) the cultural and informational capital of that 'other' mediatised Vancouver into economic capital. Sex, drugs and television programmes were apparently the only recognised currencies. Bootleg X-Files souvenirs were the order of the day, converting the place itself into a point within the multinational flow of images, information, affect and capital.

That the appeal of Vancouver as a tourist destination could be supplemented (or even determined) by its role within The X-Files underlies an article published in Starburst, 'X-Perience The X-Files Set', by Marcus Purvis.[17] This piece is also a personal travelogue, seemingly written in the detective-thriller genre as the author attempts to track down the then current X-Files filming location. As a quest narrative based upon a quest narrative (the Ur-text of The X-Files itself) Purvis's piece quickly reveals that 'the truth is out there' in Vancouver, positioning its author as the purveyor of 'inside' information:

> The X-Files is based at Brooksbank, Northshore studios, North Vancouver City. Normally they won't let people in, so to avoid disappointment it is a good idea to ring the studio (phone number: Canada 604 983 5500) and talk to staff in their X-Files offices. They ... are very unlikely to tell you where the current location shooting is taking place.[18] The easiest and most enjoyable way of finding the location is to spend time being a tourist and asking in shops, cafes, pubs, taxis and tourist information etc. ... A good fact to remember is that when location shooting takes place, the studio informs residents and businesses in and around the surrounding area beforehand – which of course means there are many people who know when and where they are filming.
>
> (Purvis 1997: 17–18)

Location filming therefore remains 'underground'. The 'tracking down' of sites hence replicates the narrative structure of the programme: the experience is not thoroughly commodified, packaged and offered up to be bought, but has to be (skilfully) worked at via the discovery of hidden information (Purvis 1997 and MacIntyre 1996). This transformative semiotic process turns Vancouver's residents into potential informers and makes the streets of Vancouver a site for obscure and deliberately encoded signs.[19] The 'tourist gaze' is thereby transformed into a focused and knowledgeable search for authenticity and 'reality'; the truth is literally supposed to be found right here.

The manner of this quest replays the 'hiddenness' of The X-Files' own tropes and secrets: 'signs' and 'informants' leak out of the text, as if it provided a guide for the cult fans' creative transposition. This transposition is one of the key aspects of 'cult geography'. The cult fans' pursuit of distinctive places and

148

spaces depends upon these *not* being convincingly commodified or prepackaged, and therefore allowing for the fans' projection of 'genres of self'; the fantasies which these places materialise are always to some degree dependent upon the generic and other formal qualities of the source text. This lack of commodification (which could cause the relationship between fan and place to become merely compliant)[20] means that underlying fantasies can operate in an unrestricted or loosely characteristic way, rather than being rigidly imposed. One might argue that since such fantasies are dependent upon a source text they are imposed in this sense, but this patently ignores the creative transposition which occurs in the movement from text-proper to the fans' cultural and material relationship with specific places and spaces. It is precisely this transposition which means that the use of 'cult geography' is not simply a matter of 'reliving' an already established affective relationship (Taylor 1989: 220). By seeking out the actual locations which underpin any given textual identity, the cult fan is able to extend the productivity of his or her affective relationship with the original text, reinscribing this attachment within a different domain (that of physical space) which in turn allows for a radically different object-relationship in terms of immediacy, embodiment and somatic sensation which can all operate to reinforce cult 'authenticity' and its more-or-less explicitly sacralised difference. The audience–text relationship is shifted towards the monumentality and groundedness of physical locations.[21] These locations may themselves be thoroughly banal: a back-street alleyway, a university building, a shopping precinct escalator,[22] but they may also be locations which, to an extent, reproduce the geographical distinctiveness of an area, and hence certain locations may become privileged over others. The privileging of locations will also depend on the extent to which they relate back to factors which have already been identified within the fan culture as particularly characteristic of the original text. This confluence of cultural geographies and fan preoccupations is what gives rise to the functioning of certain locations as short-hand for the 'cult geography' in question:[23] for example, Grouse Mountain is synecdochal in relation to Vancouver's place within *The X-Files*, being specifically mentioned in both Purvis (1997) and MacIntyre (1996), and also featuring in the following anecdote concerning fan practice:

> *uber*-fan Stephanie Davis scored highest on the weirdness counter when she and her family went to Vancouver, where the show is shot, on holiday. They visited the spot where Scully was kidnapped [Grouse Mountain] and put in a car boot in the episode 'Duane Barry'. To recreate the scene she tied up her young son and placed him in the boot of their rental car and then photographed him there.[24]

Although scoring 'highest on the weirdness counter', this relationship between image and tourist is a close recapitulation of the standard tourist 'hermeneutic circle' described by Urry (1990a), and is also in line with Susan Sontag's examination of the 'image world' in *On Photography*: 'Needing to have reality confirmed and experience enhanced by photographs is an aesthetic consumerism ... Industrial societies turn their citizens into image-junkies ... Today everything exists to end in a photograph' (Sontag 1977: 24). And yet in this instance it is not a mediated image of a cultural and material artefact which is sought out and reproduced by the tourist. It is the mediated image of a diegetic space which is materially restaged and *re*-mediated by the cult fan.[25] Hoggett (1992) would perhaps characterise such a thing as: 'the madness of normal life [where we could] ... consider this in terms of ... the development of intimate attachments to inanimate commodity objects' (*ibid.*: 71). This fan's 'normal madness' is, however, rather more normal than mad since it can be viewed as an instance of creative transposition. The cult image is re-'played' not as a repetition but as an extension of the family's attachment to the original text, thereby being appropriated within the social and psychical economy of the family. This also identifies the fan concerned, Stephanie Davis, as director of her own familial production of *The X-Files*.

Vancouver is now 'the industry's second largest producer of episodic television' (MacIntyre 1996: 2) and its production benefits – beyond the weak Canadian dollar – depend largely upon an assumed lack of identity (see Miller in Delany 1994: 282). This exaggerated lack of identity, however, can also be recuperated as a distinctive feature by cult fans: the city is then valued precisely for its combinatory matrix of urban/ethnic/suburban/mountainous/forested landscapes. Vancouver offers a gateway to innumerable other places and settings. It is not necessarily unique in this regard, drawing its flexibility in part from the Canadian cultural geography of the 'mosaic' rather than the melting pot, with this in turn being dependent upon Canada's historical status as a gateway between European, American and (most recently) Pacific Rim sensibilities. Canada's cultural critics have long been concerned with the national sense of place: 'Writing in the late 1960s [Northrop] Frye declared that Canadian sensibility has been "less perplexed by the question 'Who am I?' than by some such riddle as 'Where is here?'" ' (McNaught 1988: 393). The extreme flexibility of Vancouver's 'ambiences' or locales – the 'where is here?'-ness of the city – also stems from Canada's geographical dichotomy between the frontier and the urban, with urban centres displaying an advanced 'postmodernity' (see Delany 1994). Vancouver is, after all, the physical and cultural home of both William Gibson and Douglas Coupland; it is thus the birthplace of both 'Cyberpunk' and 'Generation X' as well as that non-place masked by the diegesis of *The X-Files*. Delany notes that in spite of expectations to the contrary, Vancouver's status within representations of the 'postmodern condition' is firmly one of marginality rather than centrality.[26] And yet this 'feeling of marginality' also functions as an open invitation to the recuperating and revalorising processes of cult fandoms surrounding *The X-Files*, Gibson and Coupland.

'Cult geography', as I have shown through this case study, offers a physical focus for the cult's sacredness.[27] It reinforces the media cult's difference, seeking to legitimate the fan's activities by drawing on the cultural notion of place as unmediated and authentic 'reality', while this 'anchoring' process is contested by non-fan critics. However, 'cult geography' does not merely map out a cultural space. The materiality of the 'actual' may place an emphasis upon the externality and the 'objective reality' of distinct locations, but these locations are privileged by fans not solely because of the cultural legitimation which they might provide. Cult geographies also sustain cult fans' fantasies of 'entering' into the cult text, as well as allowing the 'text' to leak out into spatial and cultural practices via fans' creative transpositions and 'genres of self'. Therefore cult texts are never merely textual artefacts; they also migrate through physical and geographical spaces (see Jackson 1994: 3).

A question which remains, is whether or not the spectre of 'hyperreality' can be rejected in theories of 'cult geography'. This is an issue which I have deflected by suggesting that 'cult geography' is best considered as a fan attachment to non-commodified space, or at the very least, to space/place which has been indirectly or unintentionally commodified so that the fan's experience of this space is not commercially constructed. However, given the prevalence of commodified fan-tourist experiences, this consumption/'authenticity' separation seems impossible to maintain. Can it be argued that Graceland is not, for example, an instance of 'cult geography'? This seems like a king-sized invalidation of my argument so far, and it is to this intricacy that I will now turn.

Graceland and other tales of hyperreality

Jim Collins's work provides a useful starting point here. Collins notes that the media has typically either been written out of accounts of physical and social space, or has instead been considered via a 'totalisation scenario' (1995: 38). This scenario is one where physical space has been overwritten by mediation and no longer exists in any meaningful sense. Collins cites Michael Sorkin's collection *Variations on a Theme Park* as a prime instance of such theorising: 'Sorkin's insistence that everything is now part of a singular "TV system" is a perfect example of a master-narrative which must totalise at all costs, a totalisation scenario that fails to recognise how categories of cultural difference might affect meanings generated by any landscape' (Collins 1995: 38). The notion that we are now all doomed to inhabit an essentially 'ageographical' world is one which also haunts the work of Joshua Meyrowitz, as exemplified by his infamously entitled *No Sense of Place: The Impact of Electronic Media on Social Behaviour* (1985). Sorkin and Meyrowitz both prematurely divorce space from information (see Meyrowitz (1985: 36) in particular) and thereby fail to see that culture is always unavoidably spatial, and likewise that space is always already cultural. Geography – much like 'reality' in the work of Baudrillard – can only be said to 'disappear' on the basis that it can first be identified once-and-for-all within the argument which laments its apparent death knell. This is a sleight-of-hand in which the only 'disappearance' of cultural space belongs within the critic's univocal theorising, and not in the material circumstances which supposedly prompt that work.

However, against such a weak thesis, Collins can find little to trumpet other than the 'polyphony' of spatial use and self-definition which can be enabled by image systems and the *imageability* of locations such as Los Angeles. This is a postmodernist manoeuvre which carries its own nominally 'feel-good' factor, but amounts to very little. What are we supposed to make of 'nostalgia, television, theme parks and shopping malls' now that 'easy' demonisation is off the agenda? Collins seems to hint at an uncritical celebration of these forms, something which could only be as foolhardy as the situation which he has already dismissed. It surely makes little sense to criticise Sorkin *et al.* on the basis of their totalisation and to replace this with what amounts to an opposed totalisation. Furthermore, it is possible that these cultural forms – demonised or not – should not be addressed as if they constituted an inevitable ensemble.[28]

A further difficulty is the manner in which the work of Umberto Eco is typically misapplied in work concerned with the postmodern commodification of touristic space:

> central to the balance between the fake and the real is the issue of authenticity; yet this does not seem of great importance to the visitor. This lack of concern is recognised by Umberto Eco, who suggests in *Travels in Hyperreality* that there is a more casual attitude towards the problem of authenticity in present society.
>
> (Rice and Saunders 1996: 91)

Here Eco's work is first denuded of context: a limited analysis of specific American sites (those found distasteful by Europeans) becomes general confirmation that 'there is a more casual attitude towards the problem of authenticity in present society'. Second, Eco's work is authoritatively appropriated without any consideration of the fact that Eco does not propose the notion of 'hyperreality' as if it were a binary either/or, but rather uses it as a comparative term: that is to say, cultural phenomena can be more or less 'hyperrealistic':

> Disneyland *is more hyperrealistic* than the wax museum, precisely because the latter still tries to make us believe that what we are seeing reproduces reality absolutely, whereas Disneyland makes it clear that within its magic enclosure it is fantasy that is absolutely reproduced.
>
> (Eco 1995a: 43, my italics)

Yet this comparative dimension seems to have been lost in subsequent critical thought, while the tactical and rhetorical groupings established by the 'totalisation scenario' have been carefully preserved. Neither fact is likely to move us closer to the less univocal approach to the spatiality of culture which Collins has advocated.

That the commodification or theming of places can be more or less conflictual – the 'authenticity' of this relationship not being knowable in advance – is evident, however, from sites where the commercial process has failed to disturb values which attracted devotees in the first instance: Stamford, for example 'goes beyond the TV series [*sic*: refers to a serialised adaptation of *Middlemarch*] and draws on our nostalgic images of Britain's past' (Rice and Saunders 1996: 93). The same might be said for Castle Howard (*Brideshead Revisited*) and Holmfirth (*Last of the Summer Wine*): in each case the originating text and the commodified location are saturated with nostalgic sets of social myths. The fundamentally social and binding function of these sets of ideas and images means that, unlike the romantic-solipsistic fantasies of 'a world for me' which are put into play by Disneyland, Disney World and Haworth, the value systems of nationalistic nostalgia ('our world for us') are not essentially threatened by processes of mass tourism. This is true because the originating texts are similarly fixated upon establishing the grounds for communal memory.

Alternatively, the commodification of place may also occur directly within fan cultures, with guided tours being run by fans for fans and thereby continuing to feed into values of 'Britishness' and 'eccentricity', as Toby Miller relates in the case of *Avengers* fans:

> *Avengers* weekends are held annually for keen followers ... Excursion organisers Anthony McKay and Annette McKay have published a guide to locations used for British TV drama series that is named after *The Avengers* ... The guide was 'compiled after years of detective work' so that we can 'drive down the same roads as Steed and Mrs Peel'. Each site is detailed by the episode and action that took place there.
>
> (Miller 1997: 156–7)

The commodification versus 'authentic experience' argument (Eco 1995a; Hewison 1987; Rojek 1990) denies the contextualised complexity of these examples, just as it would deny the cult geography of Graceland, considering it as nothing other than a vast and hyperreal themed space; a space so brutally and transparently commercialised that no cultural criticism worth the name could fail to find it lacking. According to this theoretical narrative, there can be nothing to separate Graceland from Disneyland.

However, Graceland can be usefully distinguished from the *bêtes noires* of cultural critiques of hyperreality, for while the commodification of, say, Disneyland presents a space which inevitably exists in tension with the values of the originating Disney texts – hyper-romantic values of child-like freedom, 'magic' and sentiment – Graceland's commodification reiterates *the already hyper-commodified values of its icon's own life and death*. It re-presents themes and realities which are central to fans' experiences of Elvis, meaning that its commodification does not represent an inherent disruption of 'authentic' Elvis cultism:

> While Graceland certainly didn't make Elvis into a star ... the house has had a significant – and largely unacknowledged – impact on the shape of Elvis's stardom ever since he purchased it in March 1957. Graceland gave Elvis something no other US celebrity of the twentieth century had: a permanent place to call 'home' that was as well known as its celebrity resident. ... Perhaps the single most important effect that Graceland had on Elvis's public image is that it gave his stardom a stable, highly visible, physical anchor in the real world.
>
> (Rodman 1996: 99)

Rodman's point is well taken, and reflects my own interest in the monumental-ising distinctiveness of cult fans' relationships with space and place. Through Graceland, the significance of Elvis – something which would otherwise tend to be free-floating, and incidental to processes of signification – can be contained or 'anchored' in a visible, physical and public fashion. This process of anchorage is important since it provides a form of permanence to what would otherwise be a potentially fleeting pre-verbal experience. Hence the repeated importance of physical spaces and architectures within all forms of organised religion. Sacred spaces do not simply reproduce sacred/profane oppositions, neither are they merely 'containers' for the purity of the sacred, as these forms of behavioural legislation emerge after the fact. The 'church' is first and foremost a physical anchor for the 'oceanic feelings' of the devout; it serves to 'hold' the original emotional experience which prompts a sense of sacredness:

> Whether this moment occurs in a Christian's conversion experience, a poet's reverie with a landscape, a listener's rapture in a symphony, or a reader's spell with his poem, such experiences crystallise time into a space where subject and object appear to achieve an intimate rendezvous ... such moments ... are fundamentally wordless occasions, notable for the density of the subject's feeling and the fundamental non-representational knowledge of being embraced by the aesthetic object. Once experienced, these occasions can sponsor a profound sense of gratitude in the subject that may lead him into a lifelong quest for some other reacquaintance with the aesthetic object. The Christian may go to church and there hope to find traces of his experience ... Such moments feel familiar, sacred, reverential, but are fundamentally outside cognitive coherence. They are registered through an experience in being, rather than mind.
>
> (Bollas 1987: 31–2)

Rodman's work resonates with this argument, as he suggests that '(
isn't simply a passive and neutral space where Elvis's already construc.
stardom just happened to make itself visible over the years' (1996: 99).
Unfortunately, Rodman then uses this insight to unjustifiably position Elvis
cultism as 'other' to similarly 'popular-culture-centred communities'. Promoting
the 'uniqueness' of all things Elvis, Rodman contends that:

> For all their affective similarities ... these other popular-culture-centred
> communities and Elvis's differ in significant ways. In particular, the
> community of Elvis fans is far more *fixed*, both in space and time, than
> are other fan communities, and this heightened sense of permanence
> helps not only to render Elvis's stardom unique, but also to make his
> posthumous career possible.
>
> (Rodman 1996: 123)

One particular target for Rodman's machinery of Elvis distinction is the
'Trekkie' (1996: 124) fan group. Suggesting that there is no site on the US
map which is sufficiently linked to the originating cult text to act as a gathering
point for *Star Trek* fans, Rodman dismisses *Trek* conventions as lacking fixity.
Convention sites, it is said, also lack any 'special significance' (1996: 124) for
the fan community. In apparent contrast to Elvis fans, then, *Star Trek* fandom is
deemed to rely upon fleeting and transient fan collectivities. Rodman cites S.
Paige Baty's 1995 *American Monroe* in defence of his disparagement of
'Trekkies'. Baty's work negates the significance of geographical location within
cult formations, analysing the fan community as a purely discursive construct.
This blind spot is evident from the fact that in a book-length study of Marilyn
Monroe as a cultural icon, Baty's index does not include a single reference to
either Brentwood or Westwood Cemetery. Baty's devaluation of physical space
is not incidental to her study; it forms part of a hierarchical devaluation of fan
'communities' which, since they exist *in media res* are 'linked across time and
space through viewing, reading and listening practices that substitute for what
Bellah *et al.* term "practices of commitment"' (1995: 42–3).

Rodman seems to forsake his usual perspicacity upon realising that the only
fan community which Baty exempts from her moralistic dismissal is that of Elvis
fans who commune at and through Graceland. At this point, Rodman happily
imports her thesis virtually untouched. However, Rodman notably neglects to
consider the extent to which, even in the supposed absence of a Graceland-like
location, *Star Trek* and other media fandom conventions may nevertheless relate
their gathering in communal space to a specific and 'sacred' date (often the
anniversary of a text's first transmission) or to the commemoration of a mile-
stone anniversary (1998 represented '35 years of *Doctor Who*', for example) and
so on. In this way, even the 'rented' and transient space of a hotel conference
suite can spatialise a precise temporality. Rodman also neglects to consider the

way that, over time, specific hotels may come to take on their own histories of convention-hosting such that the contingency and alien-ness of the hotel space may actually become a necessary part of a given convention's identity (see Porter 1999 for an excellent study of *Star Trek* convention attendance which draws on Victor Turner's theories of pilgrimage). However, Rodman's chief objections have in fact been directly superseded: Las Vegas now plays host to 'The *Star Trek* Experience' (see Mead 1998), a form of *Star Trek* Theme Park/Ride,[29] which reproduces sets from the programme and hence materialises the fan's fantasised 'entry' into the text (recall Bukatman (1998: 266) on this extratextual desire to 'inhabit the world' of the text). If nothing else, this highlights the danger of seeking to valorise one's object of study, transforming forms of culture into 'unique' phenomena as a type of auto-legitimation for their study.

This chapter has advanced my general argument in two ways. First by conceptualising cult fans' practices as extensions of fan–text affective relationships, affect has been considered not as an abstract and context-free quality, but rather as a component (seeking legitimation) within the social and individual contexts of fan 'pilgrimage' or tourism. Second, by stressing the extratextuality of this process, I have illustrated that media cults cannot be reduced to metaphors based around 'reading', 'meaning' or interpretation.

In the next chapter I will close in on the final extratextual object which is used within cult practices to mediate affect. This is the fan's body, simultaneously the most private/subjective and the most socially spectacularised or 'objective' component of the media cult.

Summary

- I have argued in this chapter that cult formations are realised through extratextual spatial relations. Such cult geographies accrue their 'sacredness' from association with the originating texts and icons. Adapting Horton and Wohl (1956), we might term these cult geographies 'para-spatial' interactions, in that the meaning and value ascribed to specific places depends entirely upon their role within mediated texts.

- I have stressed that 'cult geography' is distinct from the processes of contemporary tourism which have been examined by Urry (1990a, 1990b). Touristic mediation generally intervenes *between* material artefacts and their (travelling) audiences, whereas in this case, it is mediation which *primarily* determines the fan-tourist's valorisation of specific places.

- I have also argued that the geographies which are derived from media cults reproduce the generic characteristics and values of their originating texts; considering Vancouver as an example, this 'leaking out' from text to materiality and material practices involves the cult fans' replication of textual emphases on investigation and 'hiddenness'.

- Finally, I have argued that cult spaces are approached by fans in ways which are prestructured by points of textual and narrative significance within the originating text (Grouse Mountain in Vancouver occupying a potentially synecdochal position within X-Philes' tourist accounts). This 'creative transposition' of the cult text suggests that cult geographies allow fans to fantasise extratextually 'inhabiting the world' of the text in precise and detailed ways. However, I have argued that this does not presage the 'hyperreal' breakdown of divisions between 'reality' and 'fantasy', but indicates instead an attempt to legitimate and ground the fan-text affective relationship through ideologies of 'objectivity'.

8

CULT BODIES

Between the 'self' and the 'other'

In this chapter I want to explore the role of the fan's body within fan cultural practices of costuming and impersonation. The site of the body has been largely neglected in previous work on fan cultures. I will suggest that the cult fan's costumed and/or impersonating body can be usefully explored both through theories of performativity and consumption. Uniting these areas, I will introduce the concept of 'performative consumption' in what follows. To begin with, however, it is worth observing that at least one theorist has viewed 'performativity' as a theoretical 'solution' to the religious metaphors or discourses which tend to circulate around fan cultures:

> In researching the [audience-text] relation as improvisation, the 'Church' analogy for fan communities should be replaced by a focus on performance as enactment of the contradictions of capitalism fetishistically represented in the lived textual performances of the [audience-text] relation.
>
> (Nightingale 1994: 1)

Nightingale definitively rejects all metaphors of religiosity, seeking to replace these with (suitably secular) theoretical narratives; performativity *should* replace notions of the fan culture as 'cult' or as 'church' according to her argument. However, I am not convinced that the theoretical concept and narrative that Nightingale relies on – performativity, although Nightingale blurs this with the term 'performance' – can entirely displace the metaphors of religiosity that fans have used to make sense of fan experiences. I say this because fans' use of religious discourses (within self-absent imagined subjectivities) are related to one key distinction of the performative: 'There is no volitional subject behind the mime who decides, as it were, which gender it will be today ... gender is not a performance that a prior subject elects to do, but gender is *performative*' (Butler cited in Gallop 1995: 15).

While 'performance' presupposes a wilful and volitional subject, the performative is always a citation, always a reiteration: 'the account of agency ... [in relation to gender performativity] cannot be conflated with voluntarism or individualism, much less with consumerism, and in no way presupposes a choosing subject' (Butler 1993: 15). But this separation of 'performance' and 'performative' is perhaps itself an untenable moment of splitting which works to support a moral dualism between the (delusional) voluntarist and the (right-thinking) theorist of 'Butler-performativity' (itself an academic commodity). How can we choose between choosing and not-choosing? The concept-name[1] of 'Butler-performativity' installs a moment of theoretical clarity, vision and choice – on the basis of rigorous philosophical argument, of course, and in line with academic imagined subjectivity – which it otherwise denies to 'ordinary' social agents.

J.L. Austin's distinction between 'performative' (utterances that are 'doing something as opposed to just saying something', Austin 1986: 133) and 'constative' (utterances which refer to a state of affairs and can be 'true' or 'false') begins to look rather wobbly on occasions (see Austin 1986, lecture XI). And so too does the separation of 'performative' and 'performance' when these terms are linked to fan cultures. (However, this does not mean that the two terms can simply be used interchangeably; instead it suggests that their separation needs to be reconsidered without dissolving entirely into non-meaning.)

The 'problem' for performative theory is that fans display a type of 'non-volitional volition' (Frankfurt 1988) which disrupts Butler's poststructuralist separation of voluntarist 'agency' and 'power/knowledge'. Fans are 'self-absent' to the extent that they are unable to account, finally, for the emergence of their fandom, but they are also highly self-reflexive and wilfully/volitionally committed to their objects of fandom. Each and every expression of fan identity is hence both a non-volitional citation *and* the (consumerist) 'choice' of a volitional fan-subject. The *performative consumption* which characterises media fandom – i.e. media fandoms presuppose consumption and are expressed through consumption – is hence both an act and an iteration-without-origin. This is only a problem if we expect a clear 'philosophical' logic to tidy away, once and for all, the matter of 'agency'. If, following the dialectic of value, we do not expect to resolve fandom's essential contradictoriness, then this is less of a problem.

My interest in the term 'performative consumption' is that it seems to hold open the matter of agency; it does not dismiss fans as dupes whose belief in their own agency is mistaken (*contra* the (1988) Derridean point developed in Butler 1993: 13), but neither does it reduce fandom to an iterated and repeated discourse in which the fan agent vanishes altogether (for a related attempt to theorise fandom in the doubled light of Derridean iterability and sociological co-ordinates, see Gilbert 1999).[2] Through the notion of 'performative consumption' it is also possible to view the question of agency not as a determinate or definite property which fans do or do not 'possess' (this remains one possible implication of Butler's argument), but rather as a claim that can be made at certain points in time but not at others. Fans do not claim agency in their 'becoming-a-fan' stories, but they do claim agency through their later 'performances' of fan identity. It seems highly unhelpful to read one of these claims as 'true' and the other as 'false'. Arguing that fans are *really* constantly self-absent and non-volitional would equate fans with addicts, while arguing that fans are *really* constantly volitional and active social agents busy making meanings would have to selectively ignore fans' inability to rationalise fully the origins of their fandoms. Instead, I am suggesting here that both types of claim need to be respected within fan studies. Extremely ironically, these doubled fan claims also seem to reverse Butler's view of the 'performative' and 'performance'; fans are 'performative' (i.e. lack voluntarism) when they describe the beginnings of their fandoms. But these beginnings are precisely points of non-iteration which *precede* any iterable fan identity. Fan voluntarism and choice is therefore not disrupted *tout court*, only in relation to specific moments of non-iteration. And when fans occupy a more comfortably iterable space of fan cultural identity, they seem able (or willing!) to claim fan agency and thus volitionally 'perform' and express their (now communal) fandom. This situation raises a significant problem for Butlerian and Derridean approaches to 'performativity'. Fandom, perhaps unlike gender, possesses a moment of 'emergence' rather than always already being citational, and this appearance cannot be readily placed within specific theoretical narratives of performativity, despite sharing their emphasis on the loss of individual 'agency'.

Returning to the work of Virginia Nightingale on fan impersonators, we find that Nightingale defines two 'significant performative modes' (1994: 1) of fan engagement with texts and icons, namely 'improvisation' and 'impersonation':

> *impersonation generates another experience* [the experience of 'improvisation'], *a re-creation of the star not as an image but as a story about capitalism, often as the story of a contradiction in capitalism.* As the 'star's' personal narrative is recreated and explored by the impersonator, another performance, another personal narrative is pursued – the impersonator's life as the star.
>
> (Nightingale 1994: 11, my italics)

For Nightingale, the impersonator's experience therefore becomes a case of 'improvisation' only when it allows for the opening up of knowledge – either about the capitalist system or about the self – and when it allows the fan 'to occupy a ground from which to speak' (Nightingale 1994: 15). 'Improvisation' is not the slavish citation of consumer products: it literally makes a difference, whereas impersonation either remains dependent upon the culture industry, replaying and reinforcing its mechanisms, or extends and 'improvises' only to the extent of finding itself once again structurally enclosed by the industry from which it hoped to escape:

> Priscilla Presley opens Graceland to the tourists and the trustees of the Elvis Estate police the impersonations, ensuring that they sound suffi-

ciently like the original to keep selling the original records. Entrepreneurs make impersonation a business proposition, and the impersonators generate their own fan clubs. New commodities – like *Dead Elvis* (Marcus 1991), like recordings of new music by tribute bands or performers – become commonplace. Impersonation points to its related mode of cultural engagement, improvisation.

(Nightingale 1994: 15)

It 'points', but it doesn't quite get there. Despite simplistically pinning 'progressive' and 'complicit' audience practices to the clearly valued/devalued terms of improvisation/impersonation, Nightingale explores an essential aspect of what I have termed the dialectic of value; the internal contradictions of the commodity are re-enacted through cult fans-as-impersonators' acts of *performative consumption*. These practices can *simultaneously* intensify the commodity's contradictions between use and exchange-value, *and* allow the extension of commodified exchange-value. However, Nightingale's apparent desire to create a moral dualism between 'impersonation' and 'improvisation' replaces the dialectic of value with abstractions which stress the movement from one distinctive regime ('impersonation') to another ('improvisation'). This defuses the dialectic of value by holding contradictions apart rather than recognising their coexistence.

Considering the cult body as written through a process of commemoration and impersonation suggests that this body is not broken down and recomposed 'retail' in the sense suggested by Foucault's disciplinary procedures; the body of the cult fan reverts very much to the 'wholesale' remembrance of pre-disciplinary models. The 'wholeness' of the body is celebrated via the 'wholeness' of an impersonation which at times may threaten a complete loss of self-identity in the face of the powerful other:

the fear of the replacement of the real world by the world of the image, by simulacra, is repeated as cautionary tale in acts of Elvis and Marilyn impersonation. The impersonation exceeds repetition or commemoration and points to the deeper psychic dangers of a world in which the image has assumed disproportionate power. The psychic power of the impersonator is linked to the courage with which they address such dangers.

(Nightingale 1994: 13)

By treading that knife-edge between the complete loss of self and the 'wholesale' writing of the body, the impersonator's life-as-the-star threatens to reproduce those very contradictions inherent in the original star's existence as a component within capitalism's fantasy of pure exchange-value. The repetition of a 'cautionary tale' can therefore, at worst, attain precisely the original tragedy of the cult icon, and the Vermorels recount one such infamous case, that of Kay

Kent, a Marilyn Monroe lookalike who 'in a meticulous re-enactment of Monroe's own suicide ... took her own life with a cocktail of drink and drugs while lying naked over the pink coverlet of her bed' (Vermorel and Vermorel 1989: 68). Media cult history repeats itself here: the first time as tragic iconicity and the second time as tragic impersonation. It is the ultimate commodification of self which farcically underpins such repetition, a commodification which impersonation always plays across, but here collapses into entirely.

'Returning to the body', we can place the cult body as a negation of the following: it is not recomposed through the subtle coercion of part-objects (Foucault 1991), nor is it a legitimating sign system of the 'real' worked upon by mediating tools (de Certeau 1988). However, if the cult body facilitates 'wholesale' remembrance then the physicality and wholeness of this process cannot be considered apart from the processes through which gender difference is iterated, mapped and stabilised or destabilised in a variety of ways. The moment of the body cannot remain outside systems of social signification for anything more than a moment. What becomes significant, finally, is not the fact of the body's brute physicality, but the manner in which this materiality acts simultaneously as a 'relay' for the systems of meaning which hope to exhaust it (Foucault and De Certeau), while also producing a *citational act of consumption* that replays 'as cautionary tale' the essential contradictions of the commodified and gendered 'real' under late capitalism.

Gender and impersonation

The term 'impersonation', when used in the analysis of stars and cult icons, is typically dependent upon an implied notion of the 'immersed' feminine. This ideological and industrial presupposition has been examined in the work of Mary Ann Doane and Charles Eckert among others (see Doane 1987: 1; Eckert 1991: 34). And yet the cult fan-text attachment is far from being gender-specific, even if it continues to replay the gendering of textual forms and genres: the 'cult' audience for science fiction (far from monolithically male or ideologically masculine; cf. Bacon-Smith 1992 and Penley 1997) is paralleled by the cult status of texts such as *Gone With the Wind* (Taylor 1989). What these fan-text attachments share across genders is their status as mediators of gender identity within the family, as possible openings for communication and/or impersonation/emulation of gendered identities across and between generations – from father to son, or from mother to daughter:

> Many women with growing daughters (but few with sons) say they can hardly wait to introduce them to *GWTW*, and a few who were apprehensive have been rewarded with a new generation of fanatics. For a handful of correspondents *GWTW* provided a kind of neutral territory on which a mother and daughter could safely meet ... One cannot generalise as to how mothers and daughters share such an enthusiasm,

though its rarity is commented on by one or two correspondents ... it appears that several women resisted falling for *GWTW* precisely *because* their mothers recommended it.

(Taylor 1989: 32)

This is not to claim that all cult fans will share their cult interest with family members (although there is often a familial rhetoric within the fan group itself as a 'family of choice'), but rather that the family is one persistently privileged social grouping which can act to shape and organise the contingencies of the child's early (and continuing) object relationships, particularly where the cult text is encountered initially in the private sphere (on television, video, radio or as a novel) – see, for instance, Joseph-Witham (1996) on *Star Trek* fans (both men and women) whose intense and lived-out attachments to the text involve costuming and hence 'impersonation'. *Star Trek* costuming traverses family networks which are combined with fan networks (*ibid.*: 12–13), and facilitates the relaxation of standards which might otherwise apply to female roles, e.g. using the impersonation or emulation of a Klingon identity to avoid being seen as a slut:[3]

> Tiger [Manning] further explains the lifestyle of the Klingon female: 'You can wear push-up bras and fishnets and you're not like a slut. You're a Klingon. Klingon women ... have power over themselves. Dressing like this isn't dressing for men ... It's your own thing.[4] I couldn't go out on the street dressed like this and feel like I was actually in charge of myself.'
>
> (Joseph-Witham 1996: 24)

However, Joseph-Witham's study does not explicate a similar function for the men who engage in costuming, although the militaristic and hierarchical nature of the Star Fleet/Klingon/Romulan uniforms may facilitate a sense of identity and authority for participants of both genders.

Specifically theorising the 'impersonation' of the cult audience, it is important not to simply leave highly abstract gender codings in place. If the media cult always relates to the social experience of gender as well as to the iteration of gender codes (I am like/unlike my father – I am like/unlike my mother) then its gendering *cannot* be decided in advance. And yet it is insistently assumed in 'common sense' (Gramsci 1996: 324) that where the media cult is concerned, issues of gender can be decided in advance.

The flexibility of such hegemonic articulations is evident in the case of Elvis impersonators. One might think that it would be difficult to align 'the King's men' with a feminised stereotype of emulation, but the equation between 'impersonation' and 'femininity' is so ingrained at an *a priori* level that discussions of Elvis impersonators almost inevitably revolve around discussions of the feminine. The work of Marjorie Garber clearly illustrates this trajectory. Garber suggests that mimicry and impersonation are intrinsic to the phenomenon of stardom; it is not only fans who impersonate their idols: the stars themselves also self-consciously borrow from prior celebrities. This chain of an impersonation of an impersonation of an impersonation results in disembodied hyper reality:

> To put it another way, Elvis mimicking Little Richard is Elvis *as* female impersonator – or rather as the *impersonator* of a female impersonator … Elvis was the white 'boy' who could sing 'black', the music merchandiser's dream. And that cross-over move was … a cross-over move in gender terms: a move from hypermale to hyperfemale, to, in fact, *hyperreal* female, female impersonator, transvestite.
>
> (Garber 1992: 367)

Elvis as the '*impersonator* of a female impersonator' represents an absolute exorcism of the body. Impersonation is so insistently connected with femininity (with the signs of femininity and with the femininity of signs) that '[i]t is almost as if the word "impersonator", in contemporary popular culture, can be modified *either* by "female" *or* by "Elvis" '(*ibid.*: 372).

Garber thus essentialises the sign system of gender such that there is nothing beyond its ever-replicating and proliferating multiplicity of empty displays: gender is always already transgendered, simply a trick of the staging. Femininity and representation/impersonation are so firmly locked together that the space of empirical identity and its negotiations becomes utterly irrelevant to Garber's totalising project.[5]

Garber's *a priori* feminisation of impersonation – a desired eradication of the flesh in the name of transgender freedom – also extends to the Elvis impersonator, who following Garber's judgement on Elvis would logically have to be discussed as an impersonation of an impersonation of a female impersonator. One wonders if the value of 'impersonation' as a concept is beginning to fray at the edges here. Nevertheless, Garber again attempts to exorcise the body – this time by figuring impersonation as mechanical reproduction: 'The impersonator is something alive that seems almost like a machine … Some were even surgically reconstructed, like the man in Florida who had his nose, cheeks, and lip altered to look like the King' (1992: 371). Like the Vermorels' anecdote concerning Kay Kent, the scandal of these Elvis impersonators lies in their pursuit of a 'wholeness' of the re-embodied other.

By immediately citing the 'surgical Elvis', Garber illustrates the process of impersonation through one of its most extreme instances. The 'cyborgification' of the impersonator can only be treated as an implicit value judgement, since if we are all inherently transgendered via the femininity of representation, then it is difficult to ascertain how the 'machinic' body of the impersonator is in any way distinctive. The trope of the 'machinic' remains a way to ward off the threat of the biological body: it is a way of reconceiving the flesh as Idea and as perfected instrumentality. The Elvis impersonator's remaking of the flesh is, by contrast, not a denial of the body, but is exactly part of that process which Baudrillard (1993: 23) believes we no longer have time for: 'to search for an identity for ourselves in the archives, in a memory, in a project or a future'. The fan's writing of Elvis upon his or her (see Henderson 1997: 125) body *is* that search, not for a 'look' or visuality (an 'I want to look like Elvis') which Baudrillard (1993: 23) diagnoses as the condition of contemporary consumer culture, but for a *being* (an 'I want to be (like) Elvis'). Elvis impersonation is a project; it represents recourse to an archive (the precisely catalogued set of jumpsuits and outfits worn on-stage by Elvis; images of Elvis; set-lists and conventionalised details of his stage show), and recourse to a powerful set of memories; those of the fan's lived experience *as a fan*.

William McCranor Henderson's (1997) *I, Elvis: Confessions of a Counterfeit King* presents a record of his own endeavours as an Elvis impersonator; rehearsing, practising, and ultimately performing at an impersonator's contest.[6] This work highlights the manner in which Elvis impersonators do not only 'replicate' the King – leading impersonators display no particular psychological transference or over-identification with Elvis as a figure – they use the vehicle of Elvis 'to occupy a ground from which to speak' in Nightingale's words (1994: 15); or, as Henderson puts it:

> Watching him [Japanese Elvis, Mori Yasumasa], I realised he was the best example yet of Rick Marino's dictum [Marino is president of the Elvis Presley Impersonators' International Association, the EPIIA] that the top impersonators use Elvis as a platform for their own personality. He made no attempt to look like Elvis. Mori was always Mori. Elvis was the medium for his work, the language he was speaking – a starting point and constant reference, sometimes a distant reference.
>
> (1997: 251–2)

When Henderson first encounters Rick Marino and informs him of his interest in becoming an Elvis impersonator, Marino's immediate response is to stress that the impersonator always has his (or her) own identity. Such a defensive response is necessary not only as a counter to the wider culture's short-sighted insistence on impersonation as absolute replication but also due to the 'psychic danger' of over-identification which the impersonator entertains (Nightingale 1994: 9). Marino notes:

> trying to be more exactly like Elvis than Elvis himself is one of the stages. And then it leaches out into your life. You start to walk around thinking you're Elvis. I counsel guys not to go around trying to look like Elvis all the time ... I tell 'em: guys, there's a switch – you turn it on, you turn it off. Once you learn that, you're okay.
>
> (Henderson 1997: 23–4)

Replication, then, is not the end of the story: it is a moment (or a stage) in the impersonator's dynamic career trajectory. Reproducing a 'wholeness' of the other, the successful impersonator finally returns to his or her own body and their own expressive idiom: ideally, the other is used as an object to assist in the unfolding of self and subjectivity. This object-use can be viewed neither as a pure replication of the cult icon, nor as a matter of 'passive' impersonation on the part of the cult fan. The cult fan's sense of self is not subordinated to the other, being *realised through this process of attachment*. This process is captured in the essay 'Social Mimesis' (Gebauer and Wulf 1995b: 13–24; see also Gebauer and Wulf 1995a) which revitalises the concept of mimesis by freeing it from the chains of imitation. Gebauer and Wulf, bring the notion of mimesis into closer affinity with philosophies such as Ricoeur's hermeneutics and Adorno's negative dialectics. In both cases it is the mimetic 'loss of self' which can actually facilitate an expansion of self:

> to understand oneself is to understand oneself *in front of the text* ... To appropriate is to make what was alien become one's own. What is appropriated is indeed the matter of the text. But the matter of the text becomes my own only if I disappropriate myself, in order to let the matter of the text be. So I exchange the *me, master* of itself, for the *self, disciple* of the text.
>
> (Ricoeur 1981: 113)

It is in this sense that Elvis impersonators – and cult fans more generally, given the extratextual impulse to inhabit the world of the text which I have examined in this and the preceding chapter – could be considered as 'disciples of the text' or, indeed, as disciples of the icon.

By considering the cult body within cultural and social processes, it becomes necessary not only to examine the impersonator's 'writing on the body' and the subjective, affective and physical significance which this can have in terms of gender articulations. It is also important to consider the cult body as an object, and thus as a sign for others. This immediately raises the issue once more of fan stereotypes and the external meanings which are commonly attributed to the fans' concrete practices of costuming (in relation to fictional characters) and impersonation (in relation to cult icons). Why, perhaps more than any other fan practice, is fan impersonation and costuming a source of non-fan derision?

Impersonation and the 'threat' of performative consumption

With their midnight processions of costumed spectators, of look-alikes duplicating the main character in the film; with the collective singing, dancing, miming by which their audience greets the sequences displayed on screen, cult movies [and *The Rocky Horror Picture Show* in particular here] start as fiction texts but move from mere spectacle toward the realm of performance. They are turned into ceremony.

(Dayan and Katz 1996: 118)

This description – of texts rendered as ceremonial and necessarily embodied performances, of characters remade as 'lookalikes' – partially demonstrates how the 'aura of publicity' inherent in 'the look of some admired ... figure' (Braudy 1986: 481) has been remade by the media cult through a confluence of Romantic ideologies which in turn are framed by 'postmodern' social conditions: 'midnight processions of costumed spectators' replace more general social ideals of emulation, and a 'large audience' is consciously and romantically rejected in favour of a smaller audience which is minutely self-defined and self-reflexive as a participatory group. The primary historical difference of the media cult is, then, one of intense self-reflexivity regarding the constant management of fluid boundaries between self (cult impersonator) and other (icon). And yet this self-reflexivity – Spigel (1990: 184) describes Elvis impersonators as 'one set of especially self-conscious fans' – nevertheless fails to produce conclusive or conscious self-knowledge regarding the origins of the cult impersonator's affective attachment to a specific icon: 'In ... childhood memories, Elvis is represented as an overriding influence, a kind of "calling" (whether secular or spiritual) to which the impersonators succumbed "by accident", without conscious deliberation' (Spigel (1990: 189) – consider this in the light of my retheorisation of the 'transitional object' in chapter 4). As set out in the introduction to this chapter, the cult fan's impersonation raises the matter of performative consumption whereby fans are both intently and volitionally self-reflexive as well as being 'self-absent' (i.e. unable to account for their fandom which is described non-volitionally, for example, as occurring 'by accident').

The question that I want to explore is why the cult fan's costuming and impersonation appears to be so threatening to hegemonic and non-fan culture. What is it about taking the body as a site for displaying fan identity that seems 'automatically' to condemn the fan to ridicule? So far, I have explored the extent to which fan impersonation and costuming blurs the borders and boundaries of the self. I have suggested that fan impersonation can re-stage the contradictions between use-value and exchange-value which characterise the originating text or icon as a commodity (Nightingale 1994). And I have suggested that the impersonator's 'loss of self' is ultimately an expansion of self; it is only by passing through moments of self-absence that our sense of self can be re-narrated and expanded (Ricoeur 1984). However, these dimensions of performative consumption pose a cultural challenge to the notion of the 'invested body':

current structures of production/consumption induce in the subject a dual practice, linked to a split (but profoundly interdependent) representation of his/her own body: the representation of the body as *capital* and as *fetish* (or consumer object). In both cases, it is important that, far from the body being denied or left out of account, there is deliberate *investment in* it (in the two senses, economic and psychical, of the term).

(Baudrillard 1998: 129)

The body that is invested in comes to represent a form of capital, and a fetish, only to the extent that it is worked on by a volitional subject trapped in a total-ising consumer system/code. In Baudrillard's discussion of the body as 'the finest consumer object' (the title of chapter 8 of *The Consumer Society*), this body's narcissism is always 'managed' (1998: 131) and always acts 'in terms of an enforced instrumentality that is indexed to the codes and norms of a society of production and managed consumption' (*ibid.*). The body seemingly cannot evade this circuit; instead it seems to act either as the mediating and completing point of the system (which takes us back to Foucault and de Certeau), or else it displays its failure as a badly managed and a poorly invested in body. However, Baudrillard's argument should not provoke us to describe the cult body simply as a 'mismanagement' or a 'bad investment'; this would accept Baudrillard's characterisation of a totalising consumer 'code'. One problem is that Baudrillard's model is resolutely non-dialectical.[7] It allows for no possibility that the privatised intensities of the 'body-fetish' may struggle against, disrupt, and become recontained by, the exchangeable 'body-capital'.

Contra Baudrillard's 'invested body', performative consumption indicates that the cult body does not simply become trapped in an all-encompassing discursive or capitalist system – the cult body is neither a product of an entirely volitional subject, nor is it the product of such a subject trapped in a total consumer code.[8] The threat that performative consumption poses to 'common sense' (both academic and non-academic) is precisely that it cannot be reduced to such narratives, or to narratives of self and other. Viewing Baudrillard's work as an academic transposition of 'common sense',[9] the cult body of the imper-sonator is also an affront to shared academic and non-academic 'common sense' because it indicates that there is no one authoritative consumer 'system', *and* that there is no singularly 'volitional' consumer whose opposition to this 'monolithic' system can be championed, or whose consumer 'choice' can be solicited. Furthermore, the impersonator is not a clearly fixed and bounded 'self', but neither are they lost in the 'other'. By opening an irresolvable space for playing, spectacularly and physically, between these two supposedly fixed terms, fan impersonation violates 'common sense'. Cultural work therefore has to be done to represent impersonation as a 'bad' (feared and feminised) if not *abject* loss of self, and hence to ridicule fan impersonators as 'addicts' or as pathological instances of 'weak' or dependent subjectivity. Such narratives emphasise the fan's self-absence or lack of volition, and are therefore to an extent 'correct', but through their (falsifying and non-dialectical) emphasis they seek to regenerate a sense of normative and 'good' consumer will/choice.[10] The self/other permeability that is staged and embodied as a 'to-be-looked-at-ness' by male and female impersonators also raises the related matter of communal/individual permeability. That is to say, cult impersonators cannot simply be interpreted as part of a 'regulative discourse' or an 'interpretive community', but neither can they be counter-interpreted as individuals choosing to represent their fandom through their bodies. Consider, for example, these two competing descriptions of the same 1990 'EP' International Impersonators' Association convention:

> Impersonating Elvis, I'd soon decide, was deeply embedded in restoring the memory of an authentic experience – it was, that is, all about recovering one's historical identity through the literal em'body'-ment of a spirit from the past. [These fans] are excessively aware of their pretence even as they hope to recover something true about themselves and their world.
>
> (Spigel 1990: 179)

> According to Spigel, the use to which fans put Elvis is in establishing a set of shared values with which to construct a continuity of tradition and a common sense of the American past. ... the knowledges surrounding Elvis seem to me to be very far removed from 'common sense'. Rather than providing fans with a stable ground for meaning, Elvis seems instead to allow for its free play.
>
> (Joyrich 1993: 79)

Joyrich characterises her 'differences' from Spigel via her account of Elvis impersonators as displaying 'not just a desire for knowledge [but rather a] ... knowledge *for* desire' (1993: 80). In Spigel's case, it is the fans' 'exchange-value' of Elvis impersonation which is emphasised via the manner in which Elvis impersonators cite and reiterate a specific set of codes and values. But for Joyrich,[11] this 'communal' approach undervalues the fans' use-value of impersonation, in which knowledge about Elvis is produced in and through the body rather than merely being inscribed upon it:

> allowed to invest in any detail within an endless circle of knowledge and desire, the 'Elvisophile', far from being chained to an oppressive addiction, is empowered to revel in the pleasure of speculation without subjecting [him/]herself to the frustration provoked by an actual lack.
>
> (Joyrich 1993: 86)

Joyrich's approach reinforces my own emphasis on the 'endlessly deferred narratives' which circulate around cult texts and icons,[12] but it is also important to consider that, as we have seen in previous chapters, this specific debate polarises into moral dualisms in which either the fan community or specific fan knowledge are valued. And just as I criticised the polarity of the Jenkins–Bacon-Smith argument in chapter 3, this Spigel–Joyrich splitting of academic positions also requires rereading so that we can avoid siding with 'the individual' fan versus the fan 'community' or vice versa. As I argued in chapter 4, it is important to consider how fan communities can be reworked through the patternings of subjective (emotional) intervention, as well as addressing how 'subjective' fan practices are produced through communal co-ordinates. Such is the nature of fandom's dialectic of value: both Spigel and Joyrich are correct in the sense that they focus on aspects of Elvis impersonation, but to the extent that they isolate or prioritise *either* 'knowledge for desire' (a bodily-affective reading of impersonation; Joyrich) *or* the 'desire for knowledge' (a cognitive-interpretive reading; Spigel), these approaches cut a dialectic into two non-contradictory moments of conventional logic, hence falsifying it.

The contemporary media cult appears to be distinctive in terms of its rigorous self-objectification. As Braudy observes: 'there have now grown up several generations of fans who in their turn have become looked at themselves' (Braudy 1986: 571–2). The contemporary cult fan, then, is no less subject to those very processes of objectification and spectacular 'to-be-looked-at-ness' which have traditionally been examined as a feature of stardom or iconicity. The costumier or impersonator does not only imitate a specific cult icon or character taken from a cult text: he or she embodies the processes of stardom and textuality, self-reflexively presenting the body-as-commodity. Yet this complex form of fan display and expression, which I have termed performative consumption, doesn't only dramatise and spectacularise the fan's affective relationship to a text/icon, it also dramatises the fans' self-absence, blurring moments of the volitional subject ('master of the text') and the non-volitional 'disciple' of the text. Performative consumption enacts the dialectic at the heart of the fan cult(ure). It is simultaneously a matter of communal and cultural 'exchange-value' and a matter of intensely private or cultic 'use-value'. And this simultaneity cannot be carved up into either/or narratives of fan cult(ure) as either 'challenging' commodification, or as being wholly 'complicit' with consumer culture (*contra* the Spigel–Joyrich debate and Nightingale's 'improvisation'–'impersonation' dualism). Nor can one aspect of fan cult(ure)'s contradictoriness be taken as real or as primary: exchange-value is not structurally real compared to delusional use-value (or vice versa). 'Secondary' use-value cannot be read off from 'primary' exchange-value (and, again, the reversal of this relationship does not hold either). Performative consumption involves not only essential tensions; it involves essential contradictions which academic study closes down and 'resolves' at its peril and to its own detriment. In the concluding chapter, I will address how new media technologies, specifically the world wide web, have reconfigured fan cultures. I will consider online fan cult(ure)s as a further instance of the performance of fan identity.

Summary

- In this chapter I have introduced the term 'performative consumption' as a way of capturing the contradictions between use-value and exchange-value which fan cult(ure) represents and stages.
- I have also argued that performative consumption is a useful term because it refers to the oscillation between intense 'self-reflexivity' and 'self-absent' which is characteristic of fan cult(ure)s. Although 'self-absence' can be discursively dealt with or warded off via discourses of aesthetics and religiosity, I have suggested here that practices such as impersonation and costuming can embody and physically replay the self-reflexive/self-absence contradictions of fandom.
- By blurring the lines between self and other, fan impersonation challenges cultural norms of the fixed and bounded self. Criticisms of fan impersonation tend to be produced within 'common sense' notions of 'good' voluntarist individualism, therefore dismissing fan-impersonators as lacking a 'strong enough' self-identity.
- I have argued that impersonation also tends to be culturally linked to femininity. The abstract gendering of this linkage needs to be contested in order to avoid the rather odd conclusion that Elvis impersonators are *a priori* feminised by virtue of being impersonators. Problematically, such abstract gender codings seem to produce forms of analysis that are more gender-blind or gender-fixed than the cultural phenomena they seek to analyse.

CONCLUSION

New media, new fandoms, new theoretical approaches?

In this chapter I will argue that Internet newsgroups which appear to offer constant access to a fan identity and community (thereby partially deconstructing the sacred/profane social divisions informing fandom; see chapter 5) intersect with fans' affective relationships in such a way as to alter fan practices. This indicates that online fandoms cannot merely be viewed as a version or reflection of 'offline' fandoms. The mediation of 'new *media*' must be addressed rather than treated as an invisible term within the romanticised 'new'. Furthermore, *this particular alteration of fan practices through new media technologies also indicates that we cannot consider the dialectic of value purely as a romanticisation of cult media and fans: cult fandom doesn't merely 'escape' or 'resist' the processes of commodification, it also intensifies – and is increasingly caught up in – these same processes.*

Alt.tv.X-Files: the serialisation of the audience

In this section, I will examine the phenomenon of the Usenet newsgroup, analysing a corpus of postings to the US-oriented newsgroup alt.tv.X-Files (hereafter, abbreviated on some occasions to 'atx', a term used by newsgroup members).[1] The season four cliffhanger – 'Gethsemane' – was broadcast in the US on Sunday, 18 May 1997, enabling me to examine the speculation which preceded this significant event, and to track X-Philes' immediate responses to the episode.[2]

Usenet and its wide diversity of newsgroups – as well as the many listservers and mailing lists to which one can subscribe online – offer up a constantly proliferating plethora of interest groups, 'elective affinities' and fan-bases. Newsgroups in particular could be considered as a form of public space since by definition they are open to anonymous, unseen lurkers who need not post nor actively contribute to discussion in order to be able to follow the various 'threads' of information available at any one time:

> lurkers … are embraced as legitimized participants. The only people ostracized are those who attack the legitimacy of soap opera fandom.

172

These invaders, but not the lurkers, might be considered unratified. The nature of the network, however, is such that eavesdroppers are granted the same access to messages that full-fledged members are, and posters know this when they write. The relational possibilities between posters and lurkers have yet to be systematically examined.

(Baym 1995b: 51–2)

The inevitability of 'lurkers' might be figured in different ways within the symbolic resources of the newsgroup: lurkers may be discursively constructed and fantasised as parasitic, as invasive, as lacking motivation or the ability to engage, or they may be simultaneously welcomed as a form of friendly readership. Indeed, all of these motifs and fantasised identities can coexist within a single newsgroup; certain fragments of the 'outside' readership might be highly desirable – for example, members of *The X-Files'* production team, who it is suspected occasionally lurk on the atx news group. Other lurkers may be far less welcome, such as those who might exploit the group as a resource in terms of copyright infringement, and others again may be tolerated or partially disavowed, such as those contributing to the massive volume of posts which immediately followed the US broadcasting of 'Gethsemane':

I just got back from Texas: 2437 ATX newsgroup messages since Sunday at 8 PM EST. Who the heck are these people and where have they been all year? If I recognise maybe 10–14 posters I'm lucky. What do they do, just watch the season finale? Well, excuse me while I plow through them.

(laura capozzola, atx, 20 May 1997)

Over the period of study, academic surveillance of the newsgroup itself constituted an insistent newsgroup presence, soliciting fan testimony as ethnographic data. As such, those posting to the newsgroup could not fail to be aware of their status as an 'object of study', or as a resource in the production of academic work:

I've decided to do a paper that will be presented in a folklore/popular culture/ethnography conference this fall. I've already gathered mucho information, but now would like your insights – not just why you like it here, why you do it, and how it's done! ... This should take your collective minds off of the finale. What goes on behind the scenes? How and why did you find atx? Who do you think has more 'power' on atx, and why? What buzzwords do you use, and where'd you pick them up? ... Are there cliques/divisions behind atx? Infamous threads and/or posters? ... Self-referential terms?

(rae, atx, 16 May 1997)

It is undoubtedly the newsgroup's status as an informational resource which has struck scholars of cult fandom most forcefully. Henry Jenkins has observed that:

> The problem working with the net becomes not how to attract suffi-
> cient responses to allow for adequate analysis but how to select and
> process materials from the endless flow of information and commen-
> tary. What's so exciting is that the net discussion tends to center on
> those issues that are of the most interest to media researchers; ...
> attempts to develop aesthetic criteria for the evaluation of television
> and other popular texts; speculations about media authorship; critiques
> of ideology; and self-analysis of the netters' own involvement with the
> broadcast materials ... the computer net groups allow us to observe a
> self-defined and ongoing interpretive community ... [whose] discus-
> sions occur without direct control or intervention by the researcher,
> yet in a form that is legitimately open to public scrutiny and analysis.
>
> (Jenkins 1995: 52–3)

The ethnography of the cult audience therefore threatens to switch from enduring a poverty of communication, to suffering its exact antithesis: a welter of opinions, fan expression and debate which cannot be subjected to any controlling or synthesising gaze. Confronting the mass of data which is available online, it becomes immediately clear that no *a priori* meaningful or internally coherent corpus can be identified: one can only extract artificially bounded sets of information (such as my own focus here on a temporally fixed corpus of postings) which even then may remain virtually unmanageable in terms of the sheer weight of communications traffic.[3] Posing seemingly intractable difficulties of selection and generalisability, Internet research may presage an academic crisis in confidence, provoked by the very 'massification' of Internet discussion and interpretation. This is the dark side to Jenkins's enthusiasm: far from revealing the cultural processes which academics have been positing, the proliferation of interpretations might in fact threaten to destroy the conceptual space or distance required for the formulation of academic meta-readings, leaving no viable cultural 'outside' for the academic deconstruction and hierarchical reconceptualisation of contemporary social life.

To date, ethnography as it has been practised within cultural studies has continued, all claims to the contrary, to construct a position of authority and detachment for the researcher able to read his or her respondents' 'everyday life' symptomatically in order to expose the deeper workings of cultural hegemony below the surfaces of discursive and supposedly trivial meaning-constructions. It is my contention here that the advent of 'cyberspace ethnography' (Bernardi 1998: 155) should force a reconsideration of ethnographic practices: we cannot proceed as if nothing has changed, and as if Usenet has merely solved all the prior difficulties of data acquisition. The 'embarrassment of riches' enthusiastically posited by Jenkins cannot be transformed into an unproblematic wealth of textual data without this very 'embarrassment' being carefully thought through. The newsgroup is evidently embarrassing for processes of ethnography in a number of ways.

Significantly, it offers the oft-fantasised position of non-interventionist data-gathering (see Ruddock (1998: 301–2) for a particularly clear statement regarding unobtrusive/obtrusive Internet research strategies in relation to media audiences). By extending what would previously have been deemed private discussion into a public forum, alt.tv.X-Files does indeed make visible those very processes which researchers have been interested in studying.[4] However, this immediate plenitude masks a profound banality; what drops out of the picture here is the technology itself. The rather bizarre assumption is that *the newsgroup is supposedly a perfectly transparent form of mediation*. The 'transparency fallacy' so roundly condemned in relation to television culture (Fiske 1991) is in constant danger of Usenet reactivation. The 'transparency fallacy' seduces critics into supposing that the Internet can unproblematically unveil those cultural processes and mechanisms which cultural studies has been positing for the past two decades.[5] For instance, in an otherwise sensitive study of the potential gendering of ('masculine') newsgroups as opposed to ('feminine') listservs, Susan Clerc comments that:

> although cmc has increased the amount of contact between fans and producers, it has not changed the essence of fan activities. Analysis, interpretation, and speculation, building a community through shared texts and playfully appropriating them for their own ends – these are the defining features of fandom both online and off. Fans are fans because they engage in these practices.
>
> (Clerc 1996b: 51)

In other words, fans are fans are fans, and the Internet simply holds this 'essence' up to the academic gaze.[6] It is as if the cyberspace ethnographer's own desire to attain the position of a 'lurker' – invisible and supposedly all-seeing – overwhelms or displaces any interest in the technological, social and historical processes through which this 'invisibility' has itself been constructed as a specific nodal point within mediation:

> The influence of the World Wide Web on the conduct of social life within the Internet is an indication of the effect 'lurking' can have upon the construction of social spaces.... The claimed advantages of the World Wide Web, particularly the visual orientation of its interface, allowed people to treat the Internet as a type of slow-moving television set, or, alternately, as a series of pages to be 'turned', enabling them to adopt a more familiar role as an audience member rather than a partici-pant.... In the construction of new media as unthreateningly

television-like, a range of culturally and generationally specific knowl-edge has been utilised to invent its interactive space.

(Fletcher and Greenhill 1996: 187)

The ethnographic 'lurker' is itself an interpellated position which hinges on reproducing the net as neo-televisual and/or literally textual, and therefore as familiar and controllable within a generationally specific set of practices. 'Cyberspace ethnography', then, becomes a media-hybridised form in which the 'viewer' carries out a textual analysis not of the isolated originating media text, but rather of the constructed 'text' of cult fandom which nevertheless unfolds with as much scheduled regularity and predictability as its point of origin/attachment.[7] This 'shadow-text' composed of X-Philes' responses remains exactly that: in thrall to the scheduling of *The X-Files*, alt.tv.X-Files is necessarily built up out of topical and timely posts which march onwards to the rhythms of *The X-Files* as an established media commodity:[8]

> laura capozzola wrote:
> I just remembered why I liked the X-Files on Friday night. I didn't wish away my weekend like I do when it's on Sunday. I'm also thinking if this season finale is going to be one humungous (spelling?) spectac-ular episode I'm going to wind up wishing the summer away.
> Is it Sunday yet?

> No goddamn it. We still have hours and hours and hours to go. For once I just wish time would 'Tempest Fugit' already.

> The wolf
> who's going absolutely 'bleepin' crazy waiting for sunday.
>
> (The Wolf, atx, 17 May 1997)

Falling out of step with this spatio-temporal rhythm means falling out of the newsgroup's mutually reinforcing spheres of anticipation and speculation, or indeed revealing a geographical difference which marks the poster as inevitably and informationally 'alien' to the group's US-based composition:

> What about people who read newsgroups that aren't in the US or Canada??? I live in England and if I was to wait until the end of the 4th season and then write about it on this NG I would look stupid as by the time it gets to the cliffhanger, the 5th season probably would've started over in the US etc. All I, and most other people I believe, want is for people to a put simple word in the header, SPOILER. It only takes a second to write it.
>
> (Adam Carter, atx, 21 May 1997)

In either case, the result is identical: the poster is subordinated within the hier-archy of the group, if not flamed or ignored. Off-line temporal structures therefore dictate the unfolding text of alt.tv.X-Files: 'Temporal norms of rele-vance are an important dimension of temporal structure not previously addressed. The evidence ... suggests that such norms may be related to the external contexts in which interaction is situated' (Baym 1995a: 144).

To consider the newsgroup as merely 'revealing' the essential practices of offline fandom is hence to miss the point that the newsgroup participates in a doubled interpellation, both on the basis of its neo-televisual and magazine-like format, which allows for the relative audience security and 'passivity' of lurking, and on the basis of its nesting within – and intensification of – external temporal structures. 'Cyberspace ethnography' therefore becomes more accurately a process through which the 'audience' can be approached as a mediated product or performance itself, and through which the lines between performance and audience are minutely reconfigured (see Abercrombie and Longhurst 1998: 96–7). This represents what I would term *a serialisation of the fan audience itself.* The term is intended to indicate that the online *X-Files* audience cannot merely offer a 'window' on the programme's offline, socially atomised fandom; it must, instead, perform its fan audiencehood, knowing that other fans will act as a read-ership for speculations, observations and commentaries. This self-representation and self-performance of the audience-as-text therefore creates a second-order or implied commodification insofar as the online fan audience consumes a textual construction of itself alongside the originating commodity-text, with the valued novelties of the latter crossing over into the equally novel and similarly valued speculations, rewritings, and framings of the former. The online audience is hence serialised insofar as the 'secondary text' of fans' detective work uncannily parallels the hyperdiegetic narrative space of the primary text.

Such a mimetic collapsing together of commodity-text and audience is a key theme within Adorno's work, being especially evident in the general claim that '[m]imesis explains the enigmatically empty ecstasy of the fans in mass culture' (1991: 82). Adorno writes sarcastically, but not entirely contemptuously, of fans; he perceives the figure of the 'raving autograph-chaser at the film studio' as 'the citizen who has come to consciousness of himself ... [and] whose apparent insanity merely confirms the objective insanity which men have finally succeeded in catching up with' (1991: 74).

My extension of this formulation hinges on Adorno's ambivalence. The online fan not only exemplifies the colonising spatiotemporal processes of timely and information-saturated commodity exchange, s/he also self-consciously 'catches up with' these objective processes. As such, the serialisation of the fan audience does not simply illustrate the 'duping' of this audience, but in fact demonstrates the critical significance of information within both the cult audience of alt.tv.X-Files and the textual construction of *The X-Files.* In 'The Schema of Mass Culture' Adorno perceives information as being solely a matter of 'pseudo-activity', but elsewhere he suggests that:

No matter to what extent modern mass media tend to blur the difference between reality and the aesthetic, our realistic spectators are still
aware that it is 'all in fun' ... What is more important is the interpretation of reality in terms of psychological carry-overs, the preparedness
to see ordinary objects as though some threatening mystery were
hidden behind them. Such an attitude seems to be syntonic with mass
delusions such as suspicion of omnipresent ... corruption and
conspiracy.

(Adorno 1991: 152)

In relation to *The X-Files* such a 'psychological carry-over' – more accurately
addressed as a 'semiotic carry-over' from the codes of the originating text to the
codes of exegesis – allows for the possibility that 'delusions of conspiracy' might
be projected not at 'ordinary objects', but at the very production of the text
itself, and the informational processes of the culture industry underpinning this
mode of production. As one poster commented after viewing 'Gethsemane':

My darling husband's truly awful theory: THERE IS NO FIFTH
SEASON. DD and GA are getting paid a year's pay in exchange for
keeping quiet about the whole hoax and the death of Mulder. The
movie will be a pre-quel.

I love that man, but sometimes he gives me nightmares.

(Layna Ayre Andersen, atx, 19 May 1997)

Whether or not serial fictions have become more responsive to their audiences,[9]
cult fans have themselves also become more responsive to the scheduling
patterns of these serials, exhibiting what could be termed a form of *'just-in-time
fandom'*. By this, I mean that practices of fandom have become increasingly
enmeshed within the rhythms and temporalities of broadcasting, so that fans
now go online to discuss new episodes immediately after the episode's transmission time – or even during ad-breaks – perhaps in order to demonstrate the
'timeliness' and responsiveness of their devotion.[10] Rather than new media
technology merely allowing fans to share their speculations, commentaries,
thoughts and questions, then, cmc has seemingly placed a premium not only on
the quality of fan response (i.e. there is a social pressure not to be too far 'off-
thread', unless this situation is inverted due to a huge influx of newsgroup
non-regulars) but also on the timing of fan response. Much like the post-
Fordist production process where inventory stock is ordered as and when
needed, sociotechnological pressures indicate here that the fan should respond
as and when it is relevant, rather than entering into a relationship with the text
that is not purely dictated by transmission time (however significant this may
remain both as a subjective point of anticipation and as a ritualised space and
time). Despite in some sense allowing fans to share their ritualisations of trans-

mission time (see the final posting cited in this chapter), alt.tv.X-Files neverthe-less produces a performance of fandom which is cut to the specific temporalities of the commodity-text. It is the commodity-text's delivery of fan responses within specific and highly predictable temporal rhythms that I want to draw attention to via the notion of just-in-time fandom. Describing the temporality of just-in-time fandom as a techno-evolution towards fuller 'interactivity', which is deemed superior to the prior 'time-lag' involved in writing to and reading niche magazines' letters pages,[11] therefore neglects the extent to which this eradication of the 'time-lag' works ever more insistently to discipline and regu-late the opportunities for temporally-licensed 'feedback', and the very horizons of the fan experience.

The ways in which online fandom can mirror processes of textual or iconic commodification have been considered by Frances Wasserlein. Using the world wide web to conduct research on Madonna and, by implication, her fans (contained in the Appendix to Faith (1997)), Wasserlein was led to the following observation:

> Nowhere have I been able to locate a list which includes the names of the players and technical people on Madonna's recordings. I think this is remarkable, on the one hand, and entirely consistent with the Madonna business, on the other. The Madonna business is about marketing Madonna, not about building the reputation of back-up singers ... session musicians, and producers. ... There isn't, apparently, a purpose in a fan collecting that information. Otherwise, I'm certain it would have been done by now.
>
> (Wasserlein 1997: 187)

Wasserlein's research indicates that these fan practices carry their own distinctive criteria of relevance; given the possibility of putting information on the web, Madonna fans have compiled vast discographies indicating variant releases in different countries (Wasserlein in Faith 1997: 186), and written fantasies and fictions revolving around Madonna – but production details such as *who actu-ally plays on the records* are clearly irrelevant for these fans.[12] In this case, fan categorisations of relevance/irrelevance reproduce the information flow which characterises the commodification of Madonna-as-pop-icon, just as the emphasis on timely commentary and speculation on alt.tv.X-Files participates in the staged information flow which characterises the commodification of *The X-Files*. Both of these examples illustrate that the intense attachments of fans cannot be assumed to resist or transcend commodification; online fan practices such as just-in-time fandom and the newsgroup's serialisation of the audience are complicit with the commodity-text, functioning within the dialectic of value as an intensification rather than a transcendence of commodification.

I am suggesting here that rather than using Usenet and the web merely to confirm academic hypotheses (of audience 'activity', of subcultural 'identity' etc.), it may be more significant to address *online spatiotemporal transformations in what it means to be part of a 'cult audience' as a commodity-based community.* Rather than addressing alt.tv.X-Files as an imagined community, then, I believe that it may be more adequately considered as a *community of imagination*.[13] This is a community which, rather than merely imagining itself as coexistent in empty clocked time, constitutes itself precisely through a common affective engagement, and thereby through a common respect for a specific potential space. As Winnicott has observed: 'We can share a respect for illusory experience, and if we wish we may collect together on the basis of the similarity of our illusory experiences. This is a natural root of grouping among human beings' (1971: 3). Alt.tv.X-Files offers one such instance in which similar imaginative experiences form the basis of group identity. This common respect for imaginative material determines the particular narratives which remain constitutive of the group: narratives of anticipation and speculation, narratives of information, dissemination and status, narratives of detection, and narratives of conspiracy.

The coincidence which defines the 'community of imagination' therefore occurs on a very different level to that which defines the imagined community: rather than a coincidence in the temporality of information and consumption (the 'mass ceremony'), the defining coincidence here is affective. Unlike imagined communities, which can function in a mechanical and taken-for-granted fashion, being resecured for as long as their routinised repetitions ground their narratives of commonality, the community of imagination constantly threatens to fragment. Routinisation and repetition do not afford the same protective weight, exactly because this is a community based on the assumption that its respondents can experience *a common affective tie and not merely a common and therefore immediately visible instance of media consumption.* Such a development moves beyond the routinised visibility attested to by Anderson: 'the newspaper reader, observing exact replicas of his own paper being consumed by his subway, barbershop or residential neighbours, is continually reassured that the imagined world is visibly rooted in everyday life' (1991: 35–6). What if one seeks the community of a cult fan of our exemplary 'newspaper'? Merely observing a fellow reader does not suffice as evidence of a common affective tie: how can we ascertain that a meaningfully shared experience has occurred in this context?

The community of imagination therefore acts as a specific defence against the possible 'otherness' or even 'alienness' of the discursively inexplicable intensity and emotionality of fandom (see Harrington and Bielby 1995). Reassuringly, by going online this intense but somehow 'almost' non-verbalisable fan experience can be picked over, restaged, and reperformed through self-reflexive and humorous analogies:

Ok ... it's early friday morning and I am slightly inebriated. My hands are shaking, my heart is pounding. I have what many would call a sickness. I am insanely obsessed. I hope to NEVER be cured. Here among the similarly afflict [*sic*] I am comfortable with my illness. I can step forward and proudly say 'My name is Piper and I am a philoholic'. Please let my addiction forever flourish, and please oh please oh please let Sunday come as fast as lightning. Ok what are the other 11 steps?

(Piper Maru, atx, 16 May 1997)

In short, to perceive information technology only as a technology of information flow (Jenkins 1995) is to neglect the affective flow and intensification which can accompany this process. Alt.tv.X-Files does not only celebrate and validate the fan's knowledge, it also mirrors the fan's attachment back to him or her, validating this affective experience itself. The newsgroup therefore presents an inverted Durkheimian scene since unlike the 'religious thought' analysed by Durkheim, the 'state of effervescence that alters the conditions of psychic activity' (Durkheim 1995: 424) stems here not from the periodic and ritualised misrecognition of social forces, but from the constantly-available and social recognition of subjective 'rituals' – namely those belonging to media reception and consumption:

You watch the X-Files with other people? Am I the only one who refuses to let people be with me when the X-Files is on? What do you do if they talk while it's on? Don't you have like a special place where you sit? Special X-Files watching clothing that you wear? A particular snack or beverage that you MUST have when the show is on? ... Do you run the VCR through a practice drill just to make sure both you and the machine are ready?

... People with me? Like the ones who ask 'how come she calls him Mulder instead of Fox?' 'What titles are you talking about. I don't see any titles' ... 'Don't tell me to be quiet. Honestly, you're obsessed with this show.'

(camgib, atx, 18 May 1997)

Summary

- I have argued here that the dialectic of value cannot be viewed simply as an escape from commodification, and have sought to illustrate this by considering the 'serialisation' of the fan audience on alt.tv.X-Files. *It is the fan's 'filling-in' of commodity-provision (occupying the time-frame of the commodity's immediate novelty in the case of atx) which extends and intensifies the logic of commodification.*
- I have also suggested that the audience becomes a commodity-text in its own right given that *the newsgroup audience constructs itself extensively as a mediated and textual performance of audiencehood.*

• I have argued that it is important not to lose sight of differences introduced by the phenomenon of the 'audience-as-mediation', since cultural critics are otherwise in danger of replicating the 'transparency fallacy' in relation to new media technologies.

Suspending 'fan vs. academic' moral dualisms?

It may well be difficult to reduce this book to a singular set of recommendations, conclusions or directions for future study. Throughout, my emphasis has been on the ways that previous academic approaches to fandom and cult media have produced singular narratives of their 'object' of study.[14] These academic narratives have persistently implied moral dualisms, granting activity to some audiences and not to others, seeing 'resistance' in some audiences and not in others, and either working to separate out 'fan' and 'academic' cultural identities, or to model fans on academics. My approach has been to emphasise what I have called the 'dialectic of value' of fan cult(ure)s. By this, I mean the *essentially contradictory process* through which fan cult(ure)s:

i   both challenge and intensify commodification (see chapter 1 and this chapter especially);

ii   display self-reflexivity and what might be termed *reflexive pre-reflexivity*, drawing on discourses of aesthetics and religiosity to cover over moments of pre-reflexivity or self-absence (chapters 3 and 5);

iii function as 'interpretive communities' while also providing a shared cultural space for intensely private sentiments and attachments (chapter 4);

iv   construct hierarchical forms of internal and external cultural distinction/difference while preserving ideals of the 'fan community' (chapter 2).

I have also examined the specific 'between-ness' of cult fandoms which focus on specific sets of texts and icons while preserving a sense of cult status as fan-led (chapter 6), and which dispute the text-reader model that has been dominant in film, tv and cultural studies by performing cult fandom through modes of geographical pilgrimage (chapter 7), embodiment (chapter 8) and through the performed 'textualisation' of the cult audience (this chapter). My guiding metaphor and guiding narrative has, paradoxically, been *one of doubleness*, of seeking to keep open the 'actual' or 'empirical' contradictions of fan cult(ure)s rather than closing down these many and varied contradictions by prematurely mapping 'philosophical' logic onto the practical reasons of fandom.

If this book does amount to anything like a prescriptive approach to fandom, then its own structuring moral dualism could perhaps be described as pitting 'decisionism' against 'suspensionism'. Decisionist approaches want to police fan cultures, warding off the supposedly negative taints of religiosity, irrationality or pre-reflexivity and hence overwriting the imagined subjectivity of fandom (self-absence) with an academic imagined subjectivity. Suspensionist approaches, which I favour, do not seek to protect fandom, to link fan experiences to a series of positive values, but neither do they seek to protect academic imagined subjectivity from its others. For ultimately, the 'duly trained' and 'good' subject of the academic cannot be fully separated out from the 'untrained' and 'deficient' figure of the fan, despite the discursive, cultural and institutional mechanisms and legitimations that work to enforce this distinction. By constructing fans as being like academics, we have studiously avoided the reverse question and possibility, that of constructing academics like fans (and not just as 'fans of fans'). If pushed to indicate one future direction for fan studies, I would suggest that it starts to look beyond cultural groups which self-identify as 'fans', or which have conventionally been described as 'fans'; groups, for example, such as academic subcultures (and for an intriguing start here, see Lacey 2000). Where fandom has leaked into the academy, this process has typically been represented as a matter for grave concern, with academics becoming the 'fans' of other 'star' academics: 'an essay on "The Star System in Literary Studies" ... places you and me in a relationship with Jacques Derrida that resembles a fifteen-year-old girl's relationship with Leonardo DiCaprio or Keanu Reeves' (O'Dair (2000: 47); see also Caesar (2000: 75n4) and Nash and Lahti (1999) for an excellent study of DiCaprio fans). Such concern locates fandom in an artificially restricted space within academia, and then proceeds to demonise this fannish infection of academic imagined subjectivity. But a more sensitive approach to fandom within the academy would continue to tease out the many ways in which fan attachments, affects and passions permeate 'academic' work, institutions and the *embodied*, rather than imagined, subjectivities of academia.

The battle to place fandom on the cultural studies agenda has long since been won.[15] In this sense, Henry Jenkins's 'tactical' portrayal of fandom in *Textual Poachers* (1992a) has been eminently successful, but in its wake it leaves new battles and questions, which focus on the roles of 'rationality' and 'religiosity' in both fan and academic activities. Prior work on fandom should not be seen as the end of one academic story arc, or as the beginning of another. As ever, we remain stuck in the middle, picking up loose threads, unravelling earlier conclusions while failing to arrive at new points of closure. But certain types of narcissistic and narrative closure (chapter 3) can and should be challenged. Academia is more reliant on forms of subcultural agreement and 'common sense' than it likes to suppose, and the academic performance of 'rationality' and 'reflexivity' is one of these sticking points. Curiously, academic work might be able to adopt greater cultural authority (which is after all what it imagines that it purchases through performing rationality) by surrendering some of its moral dualisms and repositioning itself. However, this is not a call for greater 'accessibility' or for the jettisoning of 'jargon'. Instead it is a call for *impassioned thought* rather than the parroting of academic discursive mantras. It is a call for an academic 'affective reflexivity' which admits its own neoreligiosities, its own fandoms, and its own 'reflexive pre-reflexivities' or self-absences. It is a call for academic commitment which is modelled on fan commitment. And it is a call which is unlikely to be heard as long as the situation I have described here persists, and where fan and academic imagined subjectivities mirror one another and contribute to the cultural reproduction of types of 'good' authority and 'good' rationality.

Just how 'rational' and 'enlightened' *is* academic subculture? Look back at the quote on page vi of this book, and join me in wondering. Cultural studies may be keen to critique and remake the world, but it has become amazingly adept at ignoring its own power relationships, its own exclusions (of which fandom is, finally, only one) and its own moral dualisms.

NOTES

Introduction

1   While this position could be related to Michel Foucault's view of subjectivity, the problem which it poses rather more acutely than Foucauldian-influenced work is how academia itself participates in and reproduces a specific value system. The difficulty with simply accepting a Foucauldian version of 'critical psychology' is that this approach seeks to unveil the operations of discourse in all sites other than its own. This means that 'critical psychology', for example, cannot account for its own attachment to the notion of detached and 'critical' academic work other than as an instance of the very 'power/knowledge' that it seeks to diagnose elsewhere.

2   See also Roberts (1990: 6):

> a *fan club* says, 'What we love you should, too', but a *discipline* says, 'What we are discovering about what we love will be useful in your investigations of what you love'. If one of the many groups studying the oeuvre of John Milton or of the detective story or of the oral culture of the Ashanti makes no larger claim than that it finds that oeuvre deeply rewarding and that we others are at fault for not recognising its merits also, then that group – be it ever so learned and ever so honoured and ever so wise – is a fan club and only that.

3   See also Rowe (1995: 14) and Brunsdon (2000: 212).

4   Self-authored in Kermode (1997), and presented ethnographically in Harrington and Bielby (1995), Barker and Brooks (1998) and Cavicchi (1998).

5   There are also other intriguing parallels at work in terms of academics and their 'imagined subjectivities'. For example, Craib (2001: 2–3) identifies a stand-off between psychoanalytic clinicians and psychoanalytic academic theorists which is analogous to that which I have suggested exists between fans and academics. As Craib (*ibid.*: 2) puts it: '[f]rom the psychoanalytic consulting room the academic world seems populated by "brainboxes on sticks", people who use their intellectual abilities to avoid contact with the complexities and difficulties of their humanity.' Again, academic imagined subjectivity is devalued here as overly rationalising.

6   Cynthia Erb posits a similar situation in her excellent (1991) PhD dissertation, where she analyses 'Academic' versus 'Cultist' reading formations (see Erb 1991: 101–213). Unfortunately, this groundbreaking work on cult fans is not included in the revised, published version of Erb's PhD (1998). I have considered fan and academic 'imagined subjectivities' rather than fan/academic reading formations because the latter approach seems, to me, to pay insufficient attention to the moral dimensions and positionings that characterise fan and academic versions of 'self' and 'other'.

7   It may well be the case that the 'use' of cultural practices, processes and artefacts by cultural studies' scholars is inevitable. Perhaps this use can be justified by referring to

politicised aims and tactics. Indeed, given his testimony to the US Senate Commerce Committee on the subject of media violence (Jenkins 1999) there can be no doubting Jenkins's interest in political intervention. However, my concern with the academic 'use' of fandom is that, regardless of political aim, fan cultures are thereby constructed (and potentially *falsified*) in line with highly specific disciplinary and theoretical valorisations, e.g. 'the active audience' or 'the resistive reader'.

8 This question is posed by Doty (2000: 13).

9 Although Doty (2000: 11) rightly notes that these norms can be challenged, and can shift over time, as has arguably happened since the 'personal is the political' banners of 1970s feminism.

10 See Ruddock (2001: 153) and Jensen (1992).

11 For more on this, see Hills (2000a), especially my case study of journalistic representations of X-Philes as opposed to cultural studies' representations of *The X-Files*.

12 By which I mean the emotional colouration of the fans' engagement with their favoured fan object: see Grossberg (1992a and 1992b) and chapter 4 of this book.

13 On this debate, see for example Miller (1997: 146) and Brooker (1998: 120).

14 Or indeed historians: see Verba (1996).

15 John Tulloch has used the work of sociologist Anthony Giddens to explain the way that fandom makes use of academic analyses such as *The Unfolding Text* and *Textual Poachers* (see Tulloch in Tulloch and Jenkins 1995: 145). Giddens's term, the 'double hermeneutic', refers to a double interpretation (hermeneutics being the 'science of interpretation'). Interpretation is doubled because while academics produce knowledge about fans (first interpretation), the fans then read this work, which is about them, and absorb parts of it back into their fan culture while rejecting others (second interpretation). Although Tulloch and Jenkins (1995) therefore conceptually consider the fans' take-up of academic studies, they do not engage in any detail with actual fan-scholar interpretations.

16 As Jane Shattuc (1997: 187) puts it: 'when cultural studies does ethnographic studies of complex readings by fans ... the subjects tend to be from the educated bourgeoisie. Henry Jenkins readily admits that the sophisticated fans described in his [1992a] book come out of his participatory community, which happens to be white and educated.' This observation neglects the fact that despite focusing on educated fans, the work of fan-scholars specifically remains under-represented.

17 This is apparent in Jancovich (2000: 30–1) where fandom is admitted into academic discussion, and where the academic theorist of horror also speaks '*as* a horror fan rather than *for* the horror fan' (*ibid.*: 30). But the version of fandom recounted is one that is very much aligned with sociological accounts of cultural distinction (see chapter 2). This writes fandom into academically and institutionally acceptable norms.

18 Consider, for example, Hartley (1996: 65, 66):

> Some researchers, for example Henry Jenkins, have decided simply to refuse the protocols of academic distance (controlling gaze), despite the apparent 'danger of overidentification with the research subject' ... such an understanding defers too much to informal, experiential knowledge, and belittles too much the practice of formal knowledge production with its attempts to be scrupulous, testable and open.

1 Fan cultures between consumerism and 'resistance'

1 As Hal Niedzviecki has written: 'In their much-revered ... essay, first published in 1947, called "The Culture Industry: Enlightenment as Mass Deception", Adorno and Horkheimer lay the sophisticated groundwork for what later becomes an increasingly unsophisticated argument against mass entertainment' (2000: 32).

2 A number of pieces in Lisa Lewis's (1992) edited collection *The Adoring Audience* take this antagonistic line, especially those by Fiske and Brower.

3 The latter has been termed 'curatorial consumption' by Tankel and Murphy (1998); see also Fiske (1992) and Hills (1999b).

4 Abercrombie and Longhurst (1998: 144) examine what they term 'technical', 'analytical', and 'interpretative' skills.

5 Michael R. Real (1996: 43) makes the same move when he attempts to describe fans, and media receivers more generally, as 'co-authors', having determined that alternative labels (readers, receivers, audiences, spectators, consumers, decoders) are all too problematic. Again, the taint of consumption and consumerism is neatly done away with, and 'productivity' is *a priori* valorised.

6 And especially when these binaries are mapped on to gender; see Huyssen (1986).

7 See, for example, a recent media studies A-level textbook, Nicholas and Price (1998: 62).

8 Where 'past experiences, academic or personal, can never be directly reclaimed ... they can only be comprehended through the construction of narratives that reshape the past in response to current needs, desires and perspectives' (Spigel and Jenkins 1991: 118).

9 For reappropriations of Adorno's work which are less one-sidedly critical than the cultural Studies' populists, see Miklitsch's excellent *From Hegel to Madonna: Towards a General Economy of 'Commodity Fetishism'* (1998), McGee's (1997) *Cinema, Theory, and Political Responsibility in Contemporary Culture* and Ben Watson's (1996) *Frank Zappa: The Negative Dialectics of Poodle Play*.

10 As Johnson (2001) has quite rightly pointed out, cult fans do not form an unproblematic niche audience in relation to the discourses and aims of British public service broadcasting, especially where 'prime-time' is concerned. Cult fans have, however, formed a desirable target audience for UK satellite and cable schedulers. And within the BBC's public service remit, such fans have also been targeted as Internet communities, e.g. via the BBC's release of a new (audio) episode of *Doctor Who* which was made available exclusively on the web from Friday, 13 July 2001.

11 This appropriation of fandom within commercial discourses is particularly clear in the publication of a 1998 HarperCollins-Business book entitled *Raving Fans: A Revolutionary Approach to Customer Service*, and co-written by Ken Blanchard, one of the authors of the totemic business management text *The One Minute Manager*. Fandom is significant for Blanchard and Bowles (1998) only insofar as it can function as a way of retaining customers.

12 This process has also been repeated in US TV programming and scheduling, where attempts to create cult fan 'loyalty' have been prevalent within the 'new' networks such as Fox (*The X-Files*) and Warner Brothers (*Buffy the Vampire Slayer*).

13 Although Buchanan (2000: 86–107) argues that the romanticisation of 'poaching' belongs not to de Certeau, whose model of cultural power is in fact pessimistic, but rather to some of those who have poached from de Certeau, such as Jenkins (1992a). Buchanan suggests that 'concepts like 'strategy' and 'tactics' have been let become unruly orphans, while de Certeau's unwavering religiosity ... has been quietly dropped from view altogether' (2000: 2) in cultural studies readings and disseminations of his work. And Jeff Lewis (forthcoming) argues intriguingly and persuasively that de Certeau's reliance on psychoanalysis has also been written out of the de Certeau-esque work of John Fiske and Henry Jenkins. Although not centred on the figure of de Certeau, both religiosity and psychoanalysis return in my work here; see chapters 4 and 5.

14 See also Lehtonen (2000: 149): 'Provided that fans are poachers and hunters, are not writers those very things as well? What else is this book, for instance, than a new entity put together out of ideas and excerpts gathered from here and there, thus

gaining new meanings?' Like Altman (1999), Lehtonen challenges the idea that consumer-poachers can be contrasted to producer-strategists.

15 Of course, it could be argued that not all fan-consumers can so readily or easily become fan producers in this way. Although such a move has occurred in *Doctor Who* fandom, this fandom is predominantly male, and its official fan-producers are also predominantly male. *Star Trek* fandom, on the other hand, where fan writers are far more likely to be women, has been confronted by a situation where 'Paramount has decreed that anything that's televised as *Star Trek* is "Star Trek fact", whereas anything that's printed is "Star Trek fiction"' (Pearson 1999: 4). This means that even if *ST* fans are able to cross over into professional writing – a difficult step given that, unlike the policy established by the BBC for *Doctor Who* novels, unsolicited manuscripts/proposals are not read – their efforts are still not seen as possessing quite the same legitimacy as those of fan writers of *Doctor Who* novels and audios. Quite what the role of gender is in these differential processes, and whether gender is a contingent rather than 'determining' issue in relation to fan professionalism, remain questions to be explored. My thanks to Una McCormack for raising this issue.

16 This is similar to a conclusion that I reach in chapter 7, although there I draw on the work of object-relations psychoanalyst Christopher Bollas.

17 A question which I attempt to consider in chapter 4 by applying and modifying the work of D.W. Winnicott.

18 And it is tempting to recall Blackman and Walkerdine's commentary on the work of David Morley here:

> Morley (1992) ... presents an audience theory resolutely set against what he sees as 'psychology' or, more particularly, a universalistic reading of psychoanalysis. While it is important and admirable that he attempts to understand the production of meaning as a dynamic process, he nevertheless invokes a pregiven psychological subject in a given social position, one who is being 'active'. In other words, like many media theorists who refuse the terrain of the psychological on the grounds of universalism or essentialism, those very features in fact return by the back door.
>
> (Blackman and Walkerdine 2001: 59)

19 Lancaster also potentially operates with an impoverished view of the 'cultic', automatically assuming that this implies irrationality, delirium and excessive (i.e. delusional) belief: 'UFO cultists believe in the reality of their myth. Science fiction fans know that their myths are stories' (1999: 146). This distinction may be reasonable enough, although it is probably open to further argument over what it means to 'know' that a myth is a story, versus what it means to 'believe' a myth. But as I argue in chapter 5, any overly rigorous separation of the 'fan' and the 'cultist' runs into problems when it tries to account for the appropriation of discourses of 'cult' *within* science fiction fandom. And any such binary opposition also appears to replay a secularist/rationalist distaste for religiosity *per se*, in which 'good' fandom must be removed not only from the taint of consumerism but also from that of religiosity.

2 Fan cultures between community and hierarchy

1 Given my emphasis on fan culture as simultaneously *both* community *and* hierarchy, it is interesting to note that Ganz-Blättler (1999: 10) effectively splits apart these meanings when she observes that fan

> communities ... most certainly contain more 'dominant' fans or groups of fans trying to use their cultural capital ... to gain or maintain status, while other fans/other groups of fans deliberately invest their cultural capital to put it to use

to the mutual benefit of the community. ... Both strategies are highly political: the use of knowledge as prestigious privilege or as shareware.

This is also a highly legible moral dualism, but it is hard to see it as sustainable – would our 'heroic' shareware fans not derive some measure of status through their apparent selflessness? And wouldn't our 'villainous' fans possessing prestigious privilege also be in a position to produce benefits for the community? Rather than being wholly invisible or private, their privilege and status would need to be recognised by those with lesser fan cultural capital. This means that 'privileged' fan knowledge would have to circulate socially and textually in forms of fan production, say, hence *accruing benefits to the fan 'community' at the same time as reinforcing a sense of 'hierarchy'*. In short, Ganz-Blättler's view is insufficiently dialectical.

2 As Philip Auslander has argued, '[w]ithin fan cultures ... cultural capital does translate into symbolic capital: the more you know about a particular rock group, for example, the more prestige you will have among fans of that group' (Auslander 1999: 58n38).

3 This is cited in Sanjek (2000: 315); the first line is also cited in Sconce (1995: 383) and Watson (1997: 70), and the second line and continuation of the quote as per Sanjek is also cited in Hawkins (2000: 30).

3 Fan cultures between 'knowledge' and 'justification'

1 See Barker and Brooks (1998: 74) on the counter-discourses of 'sadness' which are attributed to fans and which need to be managed in fan-talk.

2 Huntington's criticisms of Radway 1984 (UK edition 1987) make a similar point, since he notes that 'Radway presumes that what people say about their preferences is adequate and true' (1989: 23).

3 As opposed to a fan-ethnography that draws on 'situated knowledge' (Jenkins 1996: 264), which is Jenkins's description of his own work. This marks a clear distinction between the 'ethnographies' of Jenkins (1992a) and Bacon-Smith (1992). However, I would argue that Jenkins doesn't emphasise the situatedness of his hybridised fan and academic knowledge as much as he might or could have done in *Textual Poachers*. It is for this reason – rendering the details of one's fan investments explicit rather than implicit – that I carry out an autoethnography later in this chapter.

4 See Game and Metcalfe (1996: 62–86) for a particularly insightful discussion of the use of narrative form in sociology. Game and Metcalfe observe that '[s]ociology, history and anthropology have all been traditionally motivated by a horror of disorder. Social analysis is often a story of the heroic quest into chaos from which the analyst emerges with order. To make their achievement seem the greater, all three disciplines emphasise the dangers they encounter and the strangeness they strive to tame' (*ibid.*: 85).

5 This may seem like a dangerous move for me to make, especially as I am writing as an academic. How, then, can I challenge the special legitimacy of academic knowledge? My point here is that academic knowledge is aligned with academic imagined subjectivity: 'we' (academics) assume an ability to account for ourselves as fully rational and self-present human beings, whilst we do not always extend this courtesy to others (fans). The usual way out of this problem is to argue that academics must imagine social and cultural others as equally rational and sensible. For me, this rather defeats the object of the exercise, since it creates an *a priori* 'rationalisation' of social and cultural forces, actions and subjects.

The reverse project would be more useful, since it would contest the resolute 'rationality' of academic imagined subjectivity. This is not, of course, the same thing as arguing that academics cannot possess forms of expertise. The difference lies in rejecting the aura of the 'subject-who-is-supposed-to-know', a position that academics tend to occupy when they engage with, and are engaged by, the cultural politics of the public sphere. Academics aware of the potential deficiencies in their own legitimating accounts would be necessarily driven to challenge the subcultural politics of the academy as well as politics 'out there'. They might also seek to engage with social and cultural issues as expert-consumer-participants rather than as distanced or objective 'experts'.

Addressing academia as a matter of subcultural difference and potential self-absence would certainly challenge the cultural legitimacy that is (residually) accorded to academic study. But it would also draw academia out of the disdainful 'othering' that it is simultaneously subjected to, e.g. in the accounts of fans or clinical psychoanalysts.

Such thinking could, of course, be marshalled against academia; i.e. academics are 'frauds', they claim to know but don't; academic subcultural difference lacks 'objective' authority and is therefore illegitimate, i.e. it shouldn't be supported or funded. But such representations would be a matter of appropriation and dissemination – of cultural politics at work – rather than foregone conclusions.

6 Although it does draw heavily on feminist work on 'standpoint epistemology': see Clough (2000: 173).

7 Autoethnography has no value as an expression of what Bourdieu (2000: 10) has termed the 'intimist' self. Its value lies in confronting the ego (puffed up with a sense of uniqueness) with its own cultural constitution and formation (see Bourdieu 2000: 33–4; Hunter 2000: 197; Couldry 2000b: 52–8).

8 For a potential example of this see Kendall and Wickham (2001: 78) who favour 'one-step reflexivity' in order to avoid the 'danger of collapsing into a confessional morass, whereby honest statements by honest researchers about their roles in their research projects and their feelings about their roles come to swamp the descriptions of appearances that are supposedly at the core of these projects.' However, it is in no way clear that 'feelings' would automatically swamp 'description' were they to be allowed a significant place in academic writing and research. The danger that is so emotively conjured up by Kendall and Wickham (2001) is nothing less than a threat to academic 'objectivity', authority and cognition. The 'common sense' of academic subculture is momentarily threatened here, but rather than following or developing this challenge, Kendall and Wickham promptly close it down. Their 'one-step reflexivity' thus works to reinstate a resolutely 'rational' academic imagined subjectivity, forming a premature narrative closure in their account.

9 For further discussion which relates fan subcultural identities to feminist subcultural identities, see Thomas (1995 and forthcoming).

10 Wolff even provides a flurry of references when claiming rock 'n' roll's direct appeal to the body (see 1995: 29), perhaps in an attempt to make this fannish value judgement appear theoretically solid, stable and respectable.

11 This, and the following two paragraphs, were added in the third draft of this chapter. If nothing else, autoethnography also disrupts the smooth or assumed singularity of writing.

4 Fan cultures between 'fantasy' and 'reality'

1 See, for example, Smith (1995); Grodal (1999); Plantinga and Smith (1999); Freeland (2000); see also Hallam with Marshment (2000: 122–42).

2 I have already suggested that the affect/cognition opposition results in a situation where theorists side 'with' one term 'against' the other and thereby participate in a moral dualism (which also extends along modernist/postmodernist lines). Although it is true to say that 'the difficulty at the heart of emotion theory has been to marry … the affective and the cognitive … in some effective and plausible way' (Redding

1999: 2), this difficulty has only been exacerbated by its theoretical transformation into a powerful moral dualism.

3 As Jeanne Randolph has observed: 'It would seem that at some point one must reflect upon these questions subjectively, that one must take advantage of the fact that art and entertainment presuppose a subjective audience' (1991: 56).

4 Compare, for example, the following two claims: 'It is no exaggeration to say that, in psychoanalysis as it is practised today, work on the affects commands a large part of our efforts. There is no favourable outcome which does not involve an affective change. We would like to have at our disposal a satisfactory theory of affects, but that is not the case.' (Green 1996: 174). And: 'psychoanalysis is ... the theory *par excellence* of the affects' (Silverman 1996: 1).

5 Winnicott's work, and that of Christopher Bollas which develops a broadly Winnicottian perspective on aesthetics, has recently moved into favour in areas of cultural studies; see, for example, Elliott (1996); Minsky (1998); Campbell (2000) as well as Bollas (1987, 1989, 1992, 1995, 1999, 2000). I do not have the space here to develop a discussion of Bollas's developments of 'Winnicottian' theory (see Hills 1999a), nor to focus on the recent work of Jean Laplanche (1999a, 1999b). However, my own reworking of Winnicottian theory is very much indebted to the work of 'Winnicottians' such as Christopher Bollas and Adam Phillips (1993, 1994, 1995, 1998).

6 It is also worth noting that my own account of moral dualisms, and the many and varied splittings between the 'good' self and the 'bad' other, possesses Kleinian overtones. But the splittings that I have referred to are more-or-less conscious, relating as they do to 'imagined subjectivities'. These 'good' and 'bad' objects are moral precisely because they are available in people's self-accounts and self-valuations of 'the good'. Moral dualisms, in short, do not operate through processes of unconscious fantasy, although I would not rule out the possibility that they involve unconscious elements. Moral dualisms are also always socially and culturally located: they depend on cultural concepts of the 'good' (the 'duly trained' good subject) rather than on lived experiences of 'goodness' or 'badness'; again, this indicates that moral dualisms relate to imagined subjectivities, and thus to versions of ourselves that we realise do not correspond to our lived selves, but which are retained because of the cultural value that we can claim as a result. Although the 'goodness' of the self may be threatened at the level of unconscious fantasy, moral dualisms always work to support the consciously 'good' self versus a 'bad' other. By contrast, fans' claims of ownership over texts are often less available in self-accounts, suggesting that fans' implicit sense of ownership is closer to unconscious processes.

7 The psychoanalytic narrative of this process runs as follows: the child's distress is responded to by the mother, who then 'becomes a container for the baby's unbearable experiences' (Segal 1992: 122). The child is then able to introject, take back inside, in fantasy 'the mother with her ability to contain the baby's distress and to make good sense of it' (*ibid.*). Strengthening containment in this way means that the baby is better able to sustain a sense of hope and to deal with emotional frustrations.

8 One of their essays, 'Fantasy and the origins of sexuality', has even been described as 'a cult text among people working on fantasy and culture' (Rose in Fletcher and Stanton 1992: 55).

9 Russ (1985); Lamb and Veith (1986); Bacon-Smith (1992); Jenkins (1992a); Penley (1991, 1992); Cicioni (1998); Green, Jenkins and Jenkins (1998); Cumberland (2000).

10 See McDougall (1985: 67) and (1989: 82) for a consideration of 'pathological transitional objects' which lead to addictive rather than affective play, and which McDougall therefore terms 'transitory objects' because of their fleeting and unsatisfactory ability to allow inner and outer worlds to be inter-related. My argument here

is that what might appear to be a form of 'addictive play' among fans is actually affective play. This should not be taken to imply that fandom cannot become 'addictive play' in specific cases, but it remains important to avoid tainting the 'normal' or 'little madnesses' of fandom with grand theoretical assumptions of pathology, as Elliott and Hoxter seem to.

5 Fandom between cult and culture

1 As Mark Gottdiener has argued: 'With Dead Elvis, the boundary ... between a popular cultural obsession and a religious obsession has become blurred' (1997: 189).

2 Note that even while restoring 'religious sentiment' to the agenda of cultural studies, Frow nevertheless relies on a functional model of a settled 'thing' called 'religion' which 'migrates' from its expected cultural locations into 'strange and unexpected' places seemingly without being reconfigured or altered in the process.

3 The 'cult'-proper or NRM (New Religious Movement) is readily amenable to examination in the light of theories of 'moral panic' as set out in Cohen (1987): the cultist-proper and the fan (cultist-metaphorical) may then be said to share a structural position as 'other' within such media discourse – a discourse which suggests that the 'good' viewer is always a rational and self-present agent.

4 And note that such a notion would be alien to an 'academic imagined subjectivity' in which academic readings and engagements would be legitimated through 'the rational public good'.

5 Practical unconsciousness, much like Giddens's notion of 'practical consciousness', cannot readily be related to psychoanalytic concepts of repression. 'Non-knowledge' might exceed discourse without being entirely or reductively 'psychoanalytic' in tone. But this possibility serves to illustrate the paucity of theories of 'unconsciousness' in cultural studies and sociology. Such a lack isn't surprising, given that sociological-cultural-studies versions of subjectivity tend to emphasise cognitive or 'false' (common sense) knowingness rather than addressing forms of unknowingness.

6 See also Strausbaugh (1995) for a further equation of Elvis fandom and religion. Rodman (1996: 113) offers a scathing critique of Ted Harrison's work on Elvis before reclaiming it as evidence of 'a crucial set of differences between Elvis and other stars' (ibid.). Rodman therefore reproduces an opposition between 'religion-proper' and 'empty' religious discourses. This separation is used to promote the supposed 'uniqueness' of Rodman's object of study, Elvis, and hence falls into the same trap as Jindra (1994). Promoting the 'uniqueness' of *Star Trek* fans' 'religiosity' (Jindra 1994) or Elvis fans' 'religiosity' (Rodman 1996) – quite apart from the fact that this 'uniqueness' is therefore doubled and non-unique! – unhelpfully devalues the more general circulation of religious and 'cult' discourses in other fan cultures.

7 See Harrison (1998: 230–43) on the 'cult' surrounding Princess Diana after her death.

8 The term 'cult' has not only been applied to media reception. It has also formed a pejorative term within – and in relation to – academic circles that are deemed to be insufficiently 'rational': see Noll (1996) in general and Noll (1996: 4) on Tonnies's (1897) discussion of the 'Nietzsche Cult', as well as Shaviro (1993: ix). The academic 'cult' replays the connotations of the media cult and the cult-proper, implying that an irrational influence acts on and distorts weakened or vulnerable thought processes.

9 It is worth noting that the sociology of religion has not been immune to charges that it devalues religiosity and religious experience (see Flanagan 1999: 27–30). This suggests that Frow's (1998) call for a cultural studies which uses the sociology of religion may not entirely displace the 'embarrassment' of religion.

10 My use of Durkheim's *The Elementary Forms of Religious Life* in this chapter has at least one notable precursor in cult film criticism: James Hoberman and Jonathan Rosenbaum begin chapter 2 of *Midnight Movies* – 'Cults, Fetishes and Freaks' – with a quote from Durkheim and the observation that 'the movies are surely the universal secular faith of the twentieth century' (1991: 15).

11 And it also characterises the use of the term 'cult' in the phrase 'cult of celebrity'; see Rose (1999) for a discussion of this.

12 The dangers of this are evident in Klapp (1969), in which the author discusses 'cult' in relation to such an all-inclusive set of diverse cultural practices, both institutionally religious and secular – covering drug-taking, holiday-making, fashion, hero worship and the counterculture among other topics – that the term 'cult' becomes virtually meaningless. 'Cultic' activity thus appears to become wholly synonymous with cultural activity *per se*.

6 Media cults: between the 'textual' and the 'extratextual'

1 It must be noted that 'texts' cannot easily be conceptualised here as fixed or bounded 'units', given the ultimately extratextual derivation of cult status and its related fan performance/immersion (Lancaster 2001; Jones 2001). Continuing to think of 'texts' at all therefore becomes problematic, but I would argue that it remains a necessary moment in analysis. This is so precisely because fan valorisation (or performance/immersion) occurs in relation to privileged and favoured textualities, and not in relation to any old series of texts or meta-texts. Textual specificity remains very important (to fans and to textual analysts) even when a concept of the 'text' as detached/distanced from the 'reader' is problematised. And while seeking to account for the process of textual fetishisation or over-valuation that marks the fan's move into performance/immersion or other modes of extratextual engagement (such as cult geography and impersonation), textual analysis inevitably *repeats* this same fetishisation.

2 Bignell (2000: 52) suggests that Eco 'does not explicitly call *Casablanca* a postmodern film, though he does parallel it with more recent self-reflexive and pastiching films'. Given that Eco distinguishes between *Casablanca* and 'more recent' films in a number of ways, it seems curious that Bignell would choose to emphasise a 'parallel' relationship in his reading of the essay. If Eco does indeed parallel *Casablanca* with *Raiders* or *ET* then this can only be described as a rather divergent parallelism!

3 Jenkins (2000: 167–8) compares Eco's 'textual' approach to cult status to Timothy Corrigan's (1991) perspective which argues that audience appropriation produces cult status. This text–audience debate is replayed in Telotte (1991a) and Kawin (1991), as well as being developed in Mendik and Harper (2000). Jenkins (2000) concludes that both Eco and Corrigan 'describe an exchange of meanings which is partially determined by the film text and partially by the film-goer' (*ibid.*: 168). Although I agree with Jenkins's move to a third position in the debate, I am not convinced that 'meaning' exhausts the created and found dimensions of the cult film. This approach neglects the affective and interpretive dimensions of what I will term 'endlessly deferred narrative', whereby fan interpretations cannot ever be closed down by 'official' textual knowledge. My approach here emphasises that cult texts are marked by textual absences and the withholding of information which does not simply allow for an 'exchange' of meaning, but which instead calls certain fan affective-interpretive strategies into being.

4 Working implicitly against Eco's third definition of cult status, Greg Taylor (1999) has produced an impressive study of the recurrent links between 'cult' readings and attributions and discourses of auteurism (see especially Taylor (1999), chapter 5).

5 Cult films are often marked by fans' emphasis on their *auteurs*. This creates a situation where a 'series' of films can be produced out of titles which, diegetically, may be unrelated, and where each film may offer narrative closure. Through the figure of the *auteur* a type of 'endlessly deferred narrative' can be produced by cult film fans which focuses on the *auteur*'s unfolding career. The same cult 'family resemblances' – e.g. 'endlessly deferred narrative' – can hence be produced through fan reading strategies and publicity discourses, as well as through 'textual' attributes. And if auteurism can give rise to a specific type of ongoing (extratextual) fan narrative without closure, then this also suggests that cult 'family resemblances' cannot be thought of as entirely separable 'qualities', despite my analytical separation in this chapter of auteurism, endlessly deferred narrative and hyperdiegesis.

6 See Suarez (1996) for an interesting account of the role of auteurism within the 'film cults' of the 1960s: 'Auteurism was officially "imported" to the United States by Andrew Sarris ... The title of Sarris's compilation of his 1960s reviews, *Confessions of a Cultist*, underlines the parallels between auteurism and the passionate, almost religious [popular] reception of Hollywood films' (Suarez 1996: 118). I think Suarez is correct to identify 'parallels' between what he terms 'intellectual' (auteurist) and 'popular' (star/genre-based) film cults, but he fails to consider the ways in which 1960s auteurism, rather than merely paralleling popular film cults at an elevated level, itself began to reconstruct the discursive possibilities of 'cultism' such that film (and media) cults could cut across 'popular' and 'intellectual' formations, rendering auteurism available as a cultural legitimation within the so-called 'popular' space of cultism.

7 Although soap fans may well discriminate between favoured and disliked writers/producers and so on. The principle of decentred non-authority does not always hold true for soaps, especially when formats (and casts) are being reworked in order to modernise a flagging TV institution. In such an atypical case, specific producers may be named in extratextual publicity by way of guaranteeing and 'securing' this textual overhaul; cf. the example of producer Brian Park in relation to *Coronation Street*.

   The more usual tension between officially-licensed extratextual representations of soaps as 'unauthored' and soap fans' interest in production personnel is captured in Mumford's 1995 discussion of US soap fan magazines: 'this area marks one of the most noticeable differences between a network-produced ['fan'] magazine and an "independent" one, reinforcing the networks' attempts to represent soaps as in some sense "unauthored"' (Mumford 1995: 126).

8 Especially the issue of cult geographies in relation to Shakespeare's ideological 'grounding' through the tourist industry surrounding Stratford-upon-Avon. This industry anchors cultural value-systems of 'Bardolatry' in supposedly innocent and 'objective' (but often constructed) physical 'realities'. See Holderness (1988a) on Stratford-upon-Avon; and see the following chapter for a full discussion of cult geography.

9 Although, as the case of Princess Diana has shown, the disruption of predictable narrative frameworks and the fantasised installation of a subject-who-is-supposed-to-know by virtue of proliferating conspiracy theories can produce a form of cult iconicity.

10 And here I am belatedly following Peter Wollen's (1982: 48) rallying call for work on the hermeneutic code, agreeing that 'There is a need for much more precise knowledge of narrative'.

11 Despite this apparent commonality, *Babylon 5* stands out when set against other cult shows, as its narrative is self-consciously constructed in an 'epic' format, with its narrative arc designed to move towards a predetermined authorial pattern and closure: see especially Keane (1998a) in the collection on *Babylon 5* edited by James

and Mendlesohn. Despite lacking a perpetuated hermeneutic, *Babylon 5* displays other 'family resemblances' of the media cult such as a romantic ideology of authorial creation and a potential disruption of cultural value-systems (the novelistic attained within the televisual).

12 This coverage of *Nowhere Man* in *Cult Times* illustrates the extent to which cult status may depend upon the role of cult 'experts' and upon the 'gatekeeping' functions of niche or secondary media dealing with media cults. In one sense, then, we might conclude that cult texts are, tautologically, merely those texts which are labelled as 'cults'! However, this conclusion neglects the cult expert's surprisingly delimited position within a cult formation. Despite occupying an 'elite' position in terms of access to media production and personnel, as part of the circuit of 'cult' ascription and contestation such expert coverage is far from sufficient in and of itself to determine cult status. It merely acts as one moment within the biography of a potentially cult text; a moment which requires the corroborative evidence of ongoing fan valorisation and socially organised fandom. Similarly, we cannot conclude that any text is a cult simply because marketing and/or journalistic discourses proclaim that this is so; the term 'cult' has become almost meaningless in these mainstream contexts, carrying a self-contradictory and thoroughly co-opted (Hebdige 1979) hint of 'the subversive'.

13 Attributes of 'quality' and 'uniqueness' which are used to value cult texts also operate as self-descriptions of and for cult audiences. An ideology of romanticism therefore allows the cult audience to recognise its own 'qualities' through its favoured texts. On this anti-mass culture process see Bennett and Woollacott (1987: 42 and 260); see also Schelde (1993: 21n) on the 'cult' audience as a 'specialised, intellectual' fraction of media consumers. Although it could be argued that the cult audience is also significantly gendered as masculine, many studies have contested and complicated this monolithic assumption (Bacon-Smith 1992; Jenkins 1992a; Studlar 1991; Austin 1981), while other studies have focused on the masculine gendering of specific fandoms, e.g. Tarantino (Brooker and Brooker 1996) and comic book fan culture (Bacon-Smith and Yarborough 1991). Given the complex demographics of cult fandoms, it seems unhelpful to contain fan cultures by portraying them as *a priori* 'gendered' or 'middle-class'. One of the most significant 'doublings' within cult fandoms is that they often contain a mix of child and adult fans (Tulloch and Alvarado 1983: 56). The cult's 'double reading position' raises the possibility that adult cult fans may be portrayed as 'regressive' or 'infantile', but it also raises a possible counter-accusation, from moral campaigners, that such texts may not be suitable for children. Cult texts are hence often drawn into 'generational' discourses, being used to mark out the 'appropriately' childish or adult (see Inglis (1982: 191–7) on the Tolkien cult, and Jameson (1983) on *Star Wars*, discussed in Keane 1998b).

14 The expanding viability of endlessly deferred narrative can also be related to a set of institutional and historical forces, whereby the fall of the episodic series (Buxton 1990) and the rise of the sequential series (Dolan 1995) presuppose both a 'media (or series) memory' and a degree of audience sophistication not previously programmed-for outside of soap opera. These elements are tied into the greater institutional need to secure loyal audiences in a fragmented media environment (Hagedorn 1995).

15 Which might help to explain why a title like *The Metaphysics of Star Trek* (Hanley 1997) could make sense as a publishing venture, beyond the mere vagaries of merchandising. *Star Trek* evidently presents narrative possibilities (what I have referred to here as 'epistemological eclipse' and 'ontological operation') which, functioning as perpetuated hermeneutic, are especially inviting to philosophical exploration, contextualisation and exegesis.

16 This form of implied narrative world has been identified by Murray (1997: 83) as an instance of 'encyclopedic' narrative (see also Murray and Jenkins 1999). Discussing the future of narrative in cyberspace, Murray posits the notion that 'encyclopedic' narrative will become increasingly common:

> In the past this kind of attention [to detail, scope and continuity of the hyper-diegetic space] was limited to series with cult followings like *Star Trek* or *The X-Files*. But as the Internet becomes a standard adjunct of broadcast television, all program writers and producers will be aware of a more sophisticated audience, one that can keep track of the story in greater detail and over longer periods of time.
>
> (Murray 1997: 85)

While I would question this positioning of the cult's 'encyclopedic' narrative as a teleological precursor to a seemingly technologically-determinist view of 'digital narrative' (and see Elsaesser (1998: 146, 148) for a similar claim in relation to cult 'serialization' and 'interactive storytelling'), Murray's discussion of cult narrative otherwise follows my own here.

17 Although as Pustz (1999: 133) notes in relation to very 'tight' comic book continuity: 'stories that obviously break continuity by putting familiar characters into new situations or by putting different heroes into familiar settings ... give fans a chance to recognise their expertise by seeing how different the divergent story is'. This argument – that 'playful' continuity violation allows fans to read textual 'variation' in relation to established continuity, does not involve the type of continuity violation that I am referring to. In 'parallel universe' style narratives, original continuity forms a pleasurable fan inter-text rather than being 'seriously' disrupted. Such playful 'continuity violations' are, in fact, often highly popular with fans, since they rework textual conventions without threatening them; see also Gregory (2000) on 'parallel narratives' in the later *Star Trek* franchises.

18 Soap opera seemingly exhibits hyperdiegesis: both cults and soaps will tend to run for considerable periods of time, generating vast stores of relevant programme knowledge which can be drawn upon to make sense of any single episode. It has been argued (Geraghty 1981, 1991) that this knowledgeable mode of viewing is one of soap's key pleasures. However, although soaps can, and do, generate relationships of trust, familiarity and security through their hyperdiegesis (and their representations of 'real' time) and can become available as 'play' objects, they lack the 'religious' and expansive (but contained) endlessly deferred narrative of the cult.

19 The relationship between 'cult' and 'camp' is one of the more troubling aspects of any attempt to define the media cult, especially given the contested versions of 'camp' in the first place (see Flinn 1995: 54–5). Cult and camp are often assumed to be closely related, although the mechanism of this relationship appears to be extremely flexible: it is politicised as a common concern with 'coming out' in Gross's (1991: 144) discussion of *The Rocky Horror Picture Show* as being among 'camp cult favorites'; it is a common concern with 'the perceived inappropriateness of their object to the critical attention and adulation which is heaped upon [it]' in Ellis (1992: 275) and it is a common concern with textual 'surfaces' rather than 'depths' which renders cult artefacts 'close cousins of camp' for Flinn (1995: 61).

I would argue that cult and camp share a number of dimensions – one is the indecisiveness as to whether either term represents a textual quality or an audience evaluation/valorisation: I have already suggested that 'cult' is both of these simultaneously, but I will reserve judgement in the matter of 'camp'. Cult and camp are both concerned with creating distinctions of cultural identity in unexpected spaces of leisure and consumption, or as Andrew Ross puts it in his essay 'Uses of Camp':

'Camp, in this respect, is the *re-creation of surplus value from forgotten forms of labour*' (1989: 151, original italics). And of course many cult texts are known for their representations of camp, especially the TV series of *Batman* (see Medhurst 1991).

Despite these similarities, I would suggest that Ellis runs together 'the vagaries of camp and cult' somewhat prematurely (1992: 275). Although both cult and camp are marked by an interest in 'inappropriate' or 'low' cultural forms, *'camp' deliberately revalues the obsolete and the out-moded* (Flinn 1995: 57–8) *by accepting that it is working with the devalued detritus of popular culture, whereas enduring 'cult' attachments refuse to accept that their objects of attachment are obsolete or out-moded*. This may seem to be a subtle difference, but it is important to realise that cult fandom constitutes more of a protective 'holding' of texts and icons, unlike the aggressive revaluations of 'camp'. Where 'camp' is theatrically combative, 'cult' is rather more seduced by its own marginality.

20 Martin Barker has noted the need to consider why it is that science fiction texts inspire such devoted cult fan followings. Barker (1993b: 672, 1996: 365) criticises Jenkins (1992a) and Tulloch and Jenkins (1995) for their apparent lack of interest in this textual issue. I have suggested that specific textual forms may be highly significant in determining the high incidence of cult sf and fantasy since these genres presuppose the creation of detailed, internally logical and extensible worlds.

21 This commodification of the icon – such that it articulates social codes and audience fractions – is akin to the model of the text-as-commodity that the cult text both intensifies and contests. Just as the cult text's audience cuts across typical lines of demographic division rather than merely delivering a specific audience demographic to advertisers (hence the failure of *Nowhere Man* which transparently conceived of, and courted, the cult audience as a subculture in its own right), so too does the cult icon distinguish itself from the icon by virtue of its increased semiotic, social and cultural mobility. And as with the cult text, this increased semiotic fluidity both *contests the force of commodification* (uniting diverse audience demographics, class fractions and interest groups around a single figure, and through intensely-felt consumption practices) and *extends the logic of commodification* (seeking to link pre-decided target audiences to prejudged semiotic codes and conventions and seeking to create specific temporalities of consumption).

22 It is worth noting here that some commentators have referred to the 'cult of the celebrity' in a far more generalised sense than the notion of the 'cult icon' which I am seeking to establish here (see, for example, Gardiner (1998) discussing the 'Cult of (Eric) Cantona', and Dixon (1999) fulminating on a globalised 'cult of celebrity'). The notion of a celebrity 'cult' in this sense appears to be coterminous with my earlier discussion of the icon; it is part of a system of affective containment and part of the mapping of audience segments and markets through the systematic (and minimal) 'differences' of embodied personalities.

7 Cult geographies: between the 'textual' and the 'spatial'

1 'The root of semiotic and semiology is the Greek semeion, which means sign, mark, spot or point in space. You arrange to meet someone at a semeion, a particular place. The significance of this connection between semiotics and spatiality is too often forgotten' (Soja 1989: 246).

2 This legitimation operates through the objective 'monumentality' of the location: see MacCannell (1976: 14) on the ideological 'authenticity' of tourist sites/sights.

3 These links between text, space and cult status cannot be described as entirely 'postmodern'. Bakhtin (1986: 47) argues that 'unique "local cults" engendered by literary works are a typical feature of the second half of the eighteenth century'.

Bakhtin links an emergent aesthetic interest in conveying 'a direct geographical reality' to the fact that readers 'made a pilgrimage' (*ibid.*) to textually-represented sites. However, Bakhtin's argument cannot hold for the cult geographies I am discussing, since the 'geographical realism' of cult texts is not distinctive in itself. Despite this, Bakhtin's work suggests that cult status and 'cult geography' have been interwoven at least since the romantic cults of Goethe's *Werther* and Rousseau's *La nouvelle Heloïse*.

4   See Bauman (1996) and Horne (1984) for opposed views of the tourist-as-pilgrim. Bauman contends that the social world of the identity-building pilgrim, in which 'saving for the future' makes sense, is alien to the post-pilgrim and postmodern social context which frames the 'aesthetic spacing' of the tourist. (Bauman 1996: 30). Horne, by way of contrast, perceives tourists as being essentially 'the new pilgrims' (Horne 1984: 9). Neither position is particularly helpful. Horne is thoroughly dismissive of tourism as a non-intellectual practice, and his rhetoric of pilgrimage clearly aims to reduce tourism to a singular and (for Horne) evaluative dimension excluding it from rational activity. Bauman's separation of tourism and pilgrimage seems to overplay the 'solidity' and the fluidity associated with pre-modern and post-modern epochs respectively. Neither author attempts an adequate form of differentiation within tourist practices.

5   I have excluded geographies which are purely internal to cult texts, despite the secondary commodification of hyperdiegetic geographies such as Terry Pratchett's Discworld: 'In 1993 we produced a map of Ankh-Morpork. The map of a fictional city entered the non-fiction bestseller lists. After all, it was a *real* map' (Pratchett and Briggs 1997; see Briggs and Pratchett 1993). It should be noted that this commodification of diegetic space also extended to the 1996 publication of the *Official Map of The X-Files*, designed like Briggs and Pratchett (1993) to mimic an actual map in its fold-out format. The *Official Map of The X-Files* places episode events in their primary diegetic locations across the US.

6   Although this is not to deny the possibility that (considered purely at the level of individual biography rather than at the level of logical relationships) 'subcultural' rituals can precede private play experiences in the sense that a non-fan may be inspired to become involved in the media cult precisely because of an interest in the ritual practices which are perceived to distinguish the cult! This constitutes a biographical 'inversion' of the logical relations which pertain between psychical processes and social relations in the initial social formation of the media cult. Such an inversion is therefore only possible when the specific cult formation exists at a certain moment in its history, confronting the subject as a set of already defined and ritual-istic practices.

7   Vancouver was the shooting location for *The X-Files* until the end of season 5, doubling for the US locations of the show's diegesis. Subsequent to my visit, the final episode filmed in Vancouver was entitled 'The End' – seemingly a reference both to diegetic and extratextual events – and featured Vancouver as a diegetic site by way of acknowledging its significance within the programme's mise-en-scène. The programme has since relocated to LA.

8   By this I mean the 'outsider syndrome' which typically functions on the basis of nationality: see Urry (1990a: 7).

9   John Hartley's apposite neologism 'Portmeirionization' seems both to imply and lament this confusion of 'reality' and 'fantasy', as if 'real' geography is somehow led astray by a new-found adherence to its own 'fictionalization':

> Portmeirion ... was the setting for the cult TV show of the 1960s ... *The Prisoner*. Portmeirionization refers to the tendency in real towns to paint them-selves up as a set, to present themselves as their own simulacrum, to change

from a locality to a location. Places start to look real, authentic and genuine only when they approximate most accurately to their fictionalization on TV.

(Hartley 1999: 220)

10 It should also be noted that this recontextualisation of 'reality' and 'fantasy' may be achieved in a variety of ways by and through a wider range of geographies, e.g. through fictions and spaces of 'the nation'. Although I will not offer a full typology of geographical fantasy-reality redefinitions here, I will suggest that cult geography remains distinct insofar as its recontextualisations of 'reality' and 'fantasy' are located around specific diegetic 'models' (e.g. Portmeirion and *The Prisoner*, Vancouver and *The X-Files*, Snoqualmie and *Twin Peaks*) or around the work of specific cult authors (e.g. New Orleans and Anne Rice). The relationship between 'fantasy' and 'reality' which is redefined through cult geography is therefore precisely locatable in terms of its singular (textual/*auteurist*) origins. National geographies, to continue my example, may operate through a far more diffused, and therefore much less apparent, redefinition of 'fantasy' and 'reality' in which no single textual source, diegesis, or writer is discernible.

11 Consider, as a further example, this tirade from Robert Hewison:

> Increasingly, real experiences are over-taken by pseudo-events ... As television swallows its own tail with repeats and revivals, the time lapse between the event and its nostalgic reprise becomes shorter and shorter ... Drama and real life become so indistinguishable that every summer weekend the inhabitants of Washburn Valley in Yorkshire are plagued with sightseers seeking the mirage of Emmerdale Farm.
>
> (Hewison 1987: 135)

12 Taylor's study of *Gone With The Wind* (1989) is unusual in that it refuses to align the fans' redefined sense of place wholly with an absolute collapse into hyperreality, instead viewing the fans' sense of place as a product of the desire to continue inter-acting – and to extend and refine the quality of this interaction – with the textual object:

> Many people are drawn to places associated with writers *in an attempt to under-stand, or in some ways to relive the fiction* ... Reader-viewers find endlessly fascinating the relationship between writer and his or her region, between real and fictional place.
>
> (Taylor 1989: 220, my italics)

13 See Couldry (1998a, 1998b, 2000a) for a more sensitive consideration of the fan viewpoint. Although resolutely sociological and non-psychoanalytic in its under-standing of the fan-tourist, Couldry's work shares many points of intersection with my own, particularly an interest in approaching grand narratives of hyperreality with caution.

14 This argument is reproduced in Rodman (1996) in relation to Elvis fans as opposed to *Star Trek* fans: the former possessing a precise relationship with geographical space and place and the latter being placeless. Cult icons can clearly be more readily placed within a realist epistemology of space and place given their one-time flesh-and-blood existence within precise spatial and temporal limits. Nevertheless, as I will endeavour to demonstrate, I believe that Rodman prematurely replicates a point of geographical 'common sense' without interrogating its ideological preconceptions. Furthermore, the 'placelessness' of particular genres such as telefantasy cannot be assumed in advance. For example, *The Prisoner* is associated with its distinctive filming location,

199

Portmeirion (see Gregory 1997), which this year hosted the annual 'Six of One' [*The Prisoner* Appreciation Society] convention for the final time, its owners having refused to continue the arrangement (see *The Sunday Times*, 3 May 1998; this fact has also been debated within cult niche media). *The Avengers* is similarly – though less obviously – associated with geographical filming locations by its cult fans.

15 As Peter Jackson has observed:

> Geographers have ... shown little interest in the symbolic representation of place in literature or in what those representations tell us about the non-literary world. Why, for example, are James Bond movies always set in such obviously 'exotic' locations, and how do science fiction novels, like all utopian works, project contemporary social relations on to the imagined geographies of the future? Our experience of place is now thoroughly mediated by what we read and what we see on television, yet the media have only recently received any serious treatment from geographers.
>
> (Jackson 1994: 22)

16 See Castells (1998: 162) on 'the black holes of informational capitalism'; spaces which are ignored and 'switched off' by flows of global capital and which therefore become structurally irrelevant to capital's systemic and symbolic processes.

17 *Starburst Special* No. 33 (1997: 17). See also Gradnitzer and Pittson (1999).

18 In other words, this author's inclusion of a contact telephone number is pointless. But such a detail arguably functions as a marker of fan cultural capital – see chapter 2.

19 Such as cards bearing the letters *XF* which direct production trailers and staff to current locations: see MacIntyre (1996: 6).

20 '[T]he fans might prefer to celebrate the birth of Elvis in January. Graceland executives do not encourage that practice, however. The date falls too close to Christmas to be good for sales or travel.... The timetables of tourism determine the ways in which Elvis is remembered' (Marling 1997: 211).

21 Horne (1984: 30) views the 'overwhelming transformation of objects into monuments' as a profoundly negative process in which historical processes are replaced by hegemonic constructions of the past, and therefore also of the present. Horne's specific definition of 'the monument' is a cognitive and rationalist one, in which the tourist has a moral duty to accurately apprehend 'the past'. My use of monumentality here is meant only to indicate that the ideology of 'the monument' as a material, intersubjective commemoration of significance can be adopted by the cult fan in an attempt to extend these legitimating connotations of solidity from the monument to the attachments of the self.

22 Burgess and Gold have written that:

> the products of popular media fictions and entertainments, through indirect and symbolic means, engage with social existence. The use of real locations in these fictions is a fascinating area for geographical research ... It is highly probable that the places get caught up in the ideological web underpinning these ... series.
>
> (Burgess and Gold 1985: 24)

The 'ideologies' involved in Vancouver's case are those of investigation and truth allied to meanings of significance and secrecy. However, as Burgess and Gold note elsewhere (1985: 1) this process is not simply a matter of ideology, since research also needs to be aware of the characteristic 'emotional experiences' which places can thereby generate or sustain. The notion of a singular 'ideological web underpinning' the text fails to mark the multiplicity of ways in which individual responses – however keenly structured by textual forms – may nevertheless be realised *as emotional responses* which cannot be clearly regulated on the basis of the encoding/decoding model.

23 Another good example would be the interest displayed by *Doctor Who* fans in actual locations used in the filming of the programme. Two notable points of emphasis have been produced by the text itself: first, an interest in the location of actual police boxes prior to their obsolescence (the TARDIS being stuck in the form of a police box) and second, an interest in quarries, given the frequency with which these locations doubled for alien landscapes, and equally given the ideology of English eccentricity and amateurism versus US high gloss and production values that such an interest could reproduce (see Airey and Haldeman 1986: 115; Daniels and Bignell 1989: 20).

24 'We just want to be like Scully: The lengths fans will go to just to be an X-Phile' (*Focus*, October 1997: 59; no author credited).

25 On this desire to restage the mediated diegetic image extratextually, consider a similar example offered by Jarvis:

> The tourist industry in Snoqualmie, the setting for *Twin Peaks*, wasted little time before cashing in on its recognisability. Since Lynch's visit, tourists have flocked to sample 'Dale Cooper coffee' and cherry pie *and to be photographed on the banks of the Columbia river wrapped in plastic like Laura Palmer.*
>
> (Jarvis 1998: 184, my italics)

This restaging again illustrates that such attempts are likely to coalesce around images marked as significant within the originating text. By 'becoming' Laura Palmer's corpse the fan of *Twin Peaks* reproduces probably the most widely publicised image of the programme; an image which encapsulated the programme's stylistic intensity and its (ultimately unsustainable) perpetuated hermeneutic.

26 For an example of such thinking see Jameson (1995a: 24) on *Videodrome*. See also Berland (1992) on the theorisation of centre/margin in Canadian communications theory.

27 Another good example of these processes concerns the cult author Anne Rice, whose 'Vampire Chronicles' are a blend of 'horror' and 'family saga' genres marked by a powerful New Orleans' regionality (see Allen-Mills, *The Sunday Times*, 26 October 1997: 21; Marcus 1997; Williamson 1998).

28 This remains a central assumption of the 'totalisation scenario' given its attempt to reductively align cultural spaces, the experience of which might otherwise be considered as radically divergent. In *Place and Placelessness* Edward Relph (1976) considers a tripartite schema of Disneyfication, Museumification and Futurization, while in *Ways of Escape* Chris Rojek (1990) examines what he terms tourist 'black spots', heritage sites, literary landscapes and theme parks.

29 This blatant commodification is not the only *Star Trek* tourist experience on offer. Rather more idiosyncratically, and without corporate might, there is also 'the real Vulcan [Alberta, Canada: '60 miles south-east of Calgary']' (Hall 1997: 9) as well as the case of Riverside, Iowa which sought to promote itself as the 'unofficial birthplace' of James T. Kirk (see Gibberman 1991: 33). Kirk's place of 'death' has also been promoted as a tourist destination: 'An easy three-mile ... trail from Rainbow Vista leads to yet more spectacular and colourful rocks at Fire Canyon, from where you can see the spot where Captain Kirk met his doom in the movie *Star Trek: Generations*' (*Time Out Guide: Las Vegas*, 2000: 258).

8 Cult bodies: between the 'self' and the 'other'

1 By this description – the 'concept-name' – I mean to indicate that academic practices of citation link concepts to the proper names of their 'creators'. This preserves a link

between practices of citation and practices of individualist agency. Ironically, then, Butler's work is cited within a set of practices which, I would argue, regenerate and use the theorist's proper name in a non-performative and individualist sense (see also Bell 1999). Butler (1993: ix, 208–18) tackles the issue of the proper name, although the proper name of 'Judith Butler' as a 'theory-star' is not explored (see English 2001; Moran 2000: 155–61). Remedying this absence, Duncombe (1997) analyses the graduate fanzine *Judy!* which is

> devoted to hotshot academic Judith Butler. Through gently teasing sexual fantasies about Butler [and] gossip on the personal exploits of celebrity academics ... the authors effectively deflate celebrity academics and in doing so close – if again, only symbolically – the gulf between their 'loser' status as graduate students and the elite world of the tenured superstar.
>
> (Duncombe 1997: 109)

2   My use of 'performative consumption' in relation to socially and historically specific fan practices is also a possible corrective to Butler's over-abstraction of agency: 'insofar as it appears to be primarily a capacity of symbolic structures rather than of individuals, Butler's idea of agency lacks social and historical specificity' (McNay 1999: 178; see also Threadgold 1997: 84).

3   See also Bradby (1994: 67–95) on similar issues which have been raised by young female Madonna fans and lookalikes.

4   A similar claim is made by a respondent in Jennifer Porter's study of costuming as 'ludic masquerade' at *Star Trek* conventions; see Porter (1999: 251–2).

5   Sarah Groenewegen contends that Garber's theorisation of impersonation and transvestism does not apply only to the impersonation of stars or cult icons by their fans, but is also relevant in the costuming (and the performances 'in character') of *Doctor Who* fans:

> The biggest problem that the media seems to have with SF fans is our cross-dressing. Double-take on my choice of words: we don't cross-dress, we dress as our favourite characters. Well, that is precisely what drag acts, female-to-male cross-dressers, and transvestites ... generally do. The difference is that their (to create a false dichotomy) characters are internal fantasies about themselves as the 'opposite' sex, and we dress as recognisable characters from a TV series.
>
> (Groenewegen 1997: 74–5)

Groenewegen attempts to account for the disturbance which such costuming causes, provoking stereotypical media reportage of lunatic fans. Her conclusion is that it is not the act of fan costuming itself which is so provocative, but rather the transformative intentionality which can be attributed to the fan: 'The costumier is doing something that "society" says is bad. The costumier is being whom they want to be, and to hell with what society says. And they're doing it for their own reasons!' (1997: 76). Although Groenewegen evidently blurs together transvestism and costuming, this depends on an alignment of the fan and the transvestite based purely on common intentionality of self-transformation rather than on Garber's essentialist view of representation.

6   See also Rubinkowski (1997) for a more general and less personalised discussion of Elvis impersonators: both titles were, I would suspect not coincidentally, published in the 'twentieth anniversary' year of Elvis's death.

7   In Baudrillard's formulation, despite the body-as-capital and the body-as-fetish being 'profoundly interdependent', these two moments seem to remain cut adrift. The body's 'exchange-value' (acting as capital) is deplored, but its function as a type of

fetish (acting as a configuration of use-value here, since the fetish is always private and non-exchangeable) seems to issue from the body-as-capital.

8 This is not to argue that the costumier and the impersonator won't embody a level of fan cultural capital (see chapter 2) within the situated locale of the convention event. This type of exchange-value is indeed produced by the iteration of codes which constitute what it means to perform as a good 'Elvis', or a good Klingon. However, this does not exhaust the fan's act of performative consumption.

9 A similar argument has been made by Jeffrey Sconce in relation to Baudrillard's discussion of postmodernism; see Sconce (2000: 170).

10 It could be suggested that a shared academic/non-academic 'common sense' has contributed to misreadings of Butler's 'performativity' thesis as implying a wilful or voluntarist/volitional subject; see Gallop (1995: 15).

11 Clearly the Elvis impersonator can open up a space for academic epistemophilia (the desire for knowledge) if critics can read impersonation in such opposed, and even mimetically doubled ways:

> I asked if Lynne Joyrich might be acting like a Lynn Spigel impersonator ...
> When the one Lynne quoted the other Lynn about how Elvis impersonators are
> 'excessively aware of their pretence' ... I was reminded of the 'slight insecurities
> about the intellectual and cultural status of this essay' that Lynne presented in
> her opening lines ... [T]he way that she assumed, and yet differentiated herself
> from, Spigel's position seemed to somehow enact – or impersonate – the
> pretense that Joyrich feared might appear in her own intellectual position.
>
> (Crane 1995: xi)

12 Simon Frith has suggested that cultural studies' response to the question of 'who wrote' Elvis is 'a simple answer ...: his fans' (Frith 1996d: 108). However, Frith's enthusiasm for a 'simple' version of cultural studies ignores the fact that his own question – 'is Elvis the author or a character in such readings?' – revolves around the issue of the volitional subject. To the extent that fans' endlessly deferred narratives may tackle this same Frithian question (e.g. discussing Elvis as undecidable *auteur*/victim, or creator/commodity), then fans cannot be thought of as simply 'writing' Elvis. Rather, they engage with the same structuring absences and puzzles that drive forward the 'academic Elvis'. Unlike academics, fan-impersonators respond to the question of Elvis as self-absent/volitional by restaging this undecidability through (reflexively) self-absent/volitional fan bodies. Academic imagined subjectivity would not permit such a response.

Conclusion

1 I downloaded all postings between 12 May 1997 and 28 May 1997; dejanews would allow for a more diachronic study via searches for references to 'season finale', but this thematic approach would lack my focus here on the variety of postings which circulate at any one time around major threads and topics.

2 Although I have suggested that cult audiences properly gather around 'defunct' programmes, the dedicated fan audience for *The X-Files* is interesting insofar as the programme (still in its original run) and its fans have been repeatedly described as 'cult' within niche media such as *Cult Times* and the now defunct *Cult TV*. This implies that the cult criteria previously identified (fan-text affective relationships enduring beyond original transmission; self-ascription of cult status within niche media; the social organisation of fandom) can become conflictual. I would tentatively explain this conflict by suggesting that the label 'cult' is now increasingly applied immediately to programmes during their first transmission. The purist's division between 'Fad TV' and 'Cult TV' suggested by Geairns (1996) is perhaps becoming

increasingly untenable, with the notion of the cult-as-commodity (i.e. the mainstreaming of the cult) being embraced within sections of fandom. This hypothesis implies that industrial definitions of the 'instantaneous' media cult may be hegemonically displacing notions of the 'grass-roots' cult.

3   A printout of the postings I am examining here runs to some 1,828 pages. Clearly exhaustive study therefore becomes impossible, as does any exhaustive participation in the newsgroup conceived of as a singular or rigorously communal communicative environment. Even within the newsgroup, then, posters and lurkers continue to navigate precise pathways according to their particular interests, however predominant certain topics may become. In this case, posters themselves testified to the difficulties of negotiating the newsgroup's communication traffic:

> Just ignore all the ones with the header 'MULDER'S DEAD??????' 'Is this the last season' or some equivalent fly-by-night post. That'll drop it down to about a third :).

> (pusher, atx, 21 May 1997)

4   See, for example, the work produced by Street (2000) on online Ewan McGregor fans, and Brooker (1999b) on online *Star Wars*, *Blade Runner* and *Alien* fans.

5   Jenkins (1995: 66) draws attention to the specificity of 'computer culture' in terms of its modification of the *Alt.tv.twinpeaks* fan culture. The implication is that netbased fan culture cannot be taken to represent offline interactions with offline 'preferred texts': i.e. online and offline fan cultures are disarticulated. This complicates Jenkins's earlier assertion that net discussions can be of use to media researchers concerned with general processes of audience activity, indicating a possible tension between interest in the newsgroup as a contextualised specificity *and* as a teleological site of wider theoretical validation. Of course, it could be argued that Jenkins is merely clarifying and correcting his own position in this essay, hence his movement from the general to the specific, but I would claim that there remains a tension between Jenkins's initial *celebration* of academic access to online fans (where these fans implicitly represent offline fan activities) and his later *caution* over the specificity of online fandom (where these fans cannot be taken to represent offline fan activities).

6   It is only relatively recently that academic work has focused directly on 'differences and similarities between traditional fans and fans on the Web' (Pullen 2000: 52). Pullen suggests that the web has allowed fan cultures to spring up more quickly around a wider variety of texts than in the past (*ibid.*: 55), leading to a 'mainstreaming' of fandom (*ibid.*: 60). Although I wouldn't quibble with these broad conclusions, Pullen's analysis does not engage with how online fans (temporally) perform their fandom, underplaying the 'differences' between online and offline fans.

7   'Cyberspace ethnography' is therefore centrally a matter of textual analysis, with audience interpretation and discussion constituting the 'text' under examination. The textual dimensions of this fan activity are – unlike the academic solicitation of textual material such as correspondence or transcripts of interviews – primarily constitutive of the fans' interactions and interpretations. These interactions are thoroughly rather than contingently textual insofar as they are composed with an imagined audience in mind (cf. Abercrombie and Longhurst 1998: 88) and are thus always already claims for attention prior to any academic scrutiny. Cultural studies' stand-off between 'textual analysis' and 'ethnographic' methodologies finds itself potentially superseded here by technocultural modes of engagement and mediatised experience.

8   The reconstruction of time via the Internet is usefully covered in Hine (2000). Hine argues that temporality can be 'internal' to a newsgroup, but also that 'it is important to position a statement as temporally relevant, as a reaction to some external event,

rather than an idly expressed passing speculation. Message content, particularly in new threads, was frequently temporally marked in relation to events occurring outside the newsgroup' (2000: 102).

9 See Jenkins (1995); Clerc (1996a, 1996b); Hayward (1997); Harrington and Bielby (1995); Cohan (2001); Baym (2000) and Hills (2001b).

10 Cf. Poster (1998):

> watching a television show like *The X-Files* and, during the commercial break, connecting by computer modem to a Usenet group on that subject to enter one's comments or see what others are saying and finally going to a mall to buy an 'X Files' T-shirt are each differential engagements that constitute subjects in highly heterogeneous ways.
>
> (1998: 200)

Poster's view of the 'highly heterogeneous' seems strained here; and one is tempted to ponder what he might view as homogeneous. Rather than seeming to contrast commodified T-shirt purchasing to somehow more authentic or romanticised Usenet use, I am interested, *contra* Poster, in tracing the lines of continuity across these 'differential engagements', given that they are engagements which cannot be entirely differential insofar as they typically coalesce in and through my object of study here: the cult formation. And it is commodification – in more-or-less embedded and intensified guises – which links these engagements; the T-shirt is a paid-for display of fandom, but then so too is the use of a relevant Usenet group, especially 'during the commercial break' when the temporality of fan practices can be directly harmonised with (that is to say, indicated by) the temporality of the commodity-text's transmission time.

11 The 'letters page' is commonly invoked in order to be surpassed within a meta-narrative of technological progress: 'One user explains that Usenet is like a newspaper where "everyone's letter to the editor is printed"' (Hauben and Hauben 1997: 59). Such narratives of freedom and plenitude – see also Harrington and Bielby (1995: 169) and MacKinnon (1995: 117) – ignore the temporal restructurations of the newsgroup. It is worth noting that fan-historians have linked the formation of the earliest cult fandoms to the appearance of letters pages (see Moskowitz 1990: 16). This only serves to emphasize the point that cult fan practices cannot be considered outside the mediated spatiotemporal context within which they arise.

12 Whereas fans of LA session guitarists such as Michael Landau and Steve Lukather (also a member of the US rock group Toto) devote their time, and websites, to compiling details of the sessions on which these particular musicians have played. Thus 'devalued' information on music industry production is therefore recuperated, but only within specific fan groups with their own distinct (and one could argue, marginalised) criteria of relevance.

13 For more on the 'community of imagination' see Hills (2001a).

14 I have challenged the previous academic tendency to produce fandom within 'singular narratives' throughout this book. However, Una McCormack has suggested that I place the Internet within just such a 'singular narrative' in this final chapter. To an extent, I think McCormack's criticism is fair. However, I would defend my account of 'the Internet' here on at least two counts: first, I do not refer to 'the Internet' as a global 'entity'; such commentary would constitute an absurd over-generalisation and would be difficult to sustain, given the many different types of interaction (synchronous/asynchronous; websites or MUDs, MOOs, MUSHs; chat-rooms or newsgroups) that are possible on the Internet. And second, although I may seem to provide a predominantly negative account of the Internet *newsgroup*'s place within rhythms of commodification, this account needs to be read as part of an

academic commentary on fandom where, although I am also a cult fan and newsgroup lurker, I am nevertheless criticising online *mediations* of fandom.

This criticism refers to an aspect of the 'dialectic of value' and therefore cannot form part of a 'singular narrative'. My argument here implies that in the very moment online X-Philes claim fan ownership and perform fan activity they simultaneously become more closely enmeshed in the rhythms of commodification. But as I have stated before, this does not mean that one of these dimensions is 'false' and the other is 'true'; it does not mean that fans are *really* 'passive' because caught up in commodification or that they are *really* 'active' in their online fan activities. What it *does* mean is that we cannot univocally celebrate or denigrate fandom's dialectic of value as this emerges through new media forms such as the newsgroup.

I recognise that fans, especially those involved in newsgroups, may strongly disagree with my conclusions here, or even that I – as a fan – may want to dispute my thoughts as a scholar-fan. In a sense, then, the argument hinges on whether I wish to give 'special treatment' to the fan newsgroup, allowing my position as a fan to colour my theoretical framework. And, as I argue in chapter 3, the scholar-fan must take great care not to distort theoretical frameworks in line with pre-theoretical commitments and affective engagements. Writing as a scholar-fan carries two obligations: theoretical agendas should not be used to distort fandom (a key part of my argument in the Introduction), and fan agendas should not be used to distort theoretical frameworks (see chapter 3). I leave it to others, who may share Una McCormack's concerns, to assess whether my work has lived up to the twin standards that I have struggled to establish and defend.

15 And when revisiting *Textual Poachers* in a 1998 article, Jenkins observes that 'when I published my first work on fans as "textual poachers", I was describing a subculture that was oddly alien to a good percentage of the audience I was addressing ... Today, thanks to the Internet, fan sites are much more visible; fan traditions are discussed on the front page of the *New York Times*, and aspects of fan practice are influencing commercial media in a much more direct fashion' (1998: 2–3).

BIBLIOGRAPHY

Abbott, A. (2001) *Chaos of Disciplines*, Chicago: University of Chicago Press.

Abercrombie, N. and Longhurst, B. (1998) *Audiences: A Sociological Theory of Performance and Imagination*, London: Sage.

Adams, R.G. and Sardiello, R. (eds) (2000) *Deadhead Social Science*, New York: AltaMira Press.

Aden, R.C. (1999) *Popular Stories and Promised Lands: Fan Cultures and Symbolic Pilgrimages*, Tuscaloosa: University of Alabama Press.

Adorno, T.W. (1978) *Minima Moralia: Reflections from Damaged Life*, London: Verso.

—— (1991) *The Culture Industry: Selected Essays on Mass Culture*, London: Routledge.

——(1994) *The Stars Down to Earth and other essays on the irrational in culture*, London: Routledge.

—— (1996) *Negative Dialectics*, London: Routledge.

Adorno, T.W., Frenkel-Brunswik, E., Levinson, D.J. and Sanford, R.N. (1982) *The Authoritarian Personality*, London: W.W. Norton.

Airey, J. and Haldeman, L. (1986) *'Doctor Who': Travel Without the Tardis*, London: Target.

Allen, L. (1997) *The Lesbian Idol: Martina, Kd and the Consumption of Lesbian Masculinity*, London: Cassell.

Allen, R.C. (ed.) (1992) *Channels of Discourse, Reassembled: Television and Contemporary Criticism*, London: Routledge.

Allen-Mills T. (1997) 'Hallowe'en turns into US horror show', *The Sunday Times* 26 October: 21.

Althusser, L. (1971) *Lenin and Philosophy and other essays*, New York: Monthly Review Press.

Altman, R. (1999) *Film/Genre*, London: BFI Publishing.

Amesley, C. (1989) 'How to watch *Star Trek*', *Cultural Studies* Vol. 3 No. 3 October: 323–39.

An, J. (2001) '*The Killer*: cult film and transcultural (mis)reading', in Yau, E.C.M. (ed.) *At Full Speed: Hong Kong Cinema in a Borderless World*, Minneapolis: University of Minnesota Press.

Anderson, B. (1991) *Imagined Communities: Reflections on the Origin and Spread of Nationalism*, London: Verso.

Andrew, D. (1993) 'The unauthorized auteur today', in Collins, J., Radner, H. and Preacher Collins, A. (eds) *Film Theory Goes To The Movies*, London: Routledge.

Appadurai, A. (ed.) (1986) *The Social Life of Things: Commodities in Cultural Perspective*, Cambridge: Cambridge University Press.

Atkinson, M. (1998) *The Secret Marriage of Sherlock Holmes and Other Eccentric Readings*, Ann Arbor: University of Michigan Press.

Auslander, P. (1999) *Liveness: Performance in a Mediatized Culture*, London: Routledge.

Austin, B.A. (1981) 'Portrait of a cult film audience: *The Rocky Horror Picture Show*', *Journal of Communications* 31: 450–65.

Austin, J.L. (1986) *How to do Things with Words*, Oxford: Oxford University Press.

Austin, T. (1999) ' "Desperate to see it": straight men watching *Basic Instinct*', in Maltby, R. and Stokes, M. (eds) *Hollywood and Cultural Identity*, London: BFI Publishing.

Bacon-Smith, C. (1992) *Enterprising Women: Television Fandom and the Creation of Popular Myth*, Philadelphia: University of Pennsylvania Press.

—— (2000) *Science Fiction Culture*, Philadelphia: University of Pennsylvania Press.

Bacon-Smith, C. with Yarborough, T. (1991) 'Batman: the ethnography', in Pearson, R.E. and Uricchio, W. (eds) *The Many Lives of the Batman: Critical Approaches to a Superhero and his Media*, London: BFI Publishing.

Bakhtin, M.M. (1981) *The Dialogic Imagination*, Austin: University of Texas Press.

—— (1986) 'The Bildungsroman and its significance in the history of realism (Toward a Historical Typology of the Novel)', in *Speech Genres and Other Late Essays*, Austin: University of Texas Press.

Barbalet, J.M. (1998) *Emotion, Social Theory and Social Structure*, Cambridge: Cambridge University Press.

Barker, E. (1984) *The Making of a Moonie: Brainwashing or Choice?*, Oxford: Basil Blackwell.

Barker, M. (1989) *Comics: Ideology, Power and the Critics*, Manchester: Manchester University Press.

—— (1992) *A Haunt of Fears: The Strange History of the British Horror Comics Campaign*, Jackson: University Press of Mississippi.

—— (1993a) 'Seeing how far you can see: on being a "fan" of *2000 AD*', in Buckingham, D. (ed.) *Reading Audiences: Young people and the media*, Manchester: Manchester University Press.

—— (1993b) 'The Bill Clinton fan syndrome: Review article on Lisa A. Lewis (ed.) *The Adoring Audience* and Henry Jenkins *Textual Poachers*', *Media, Culture and Society* Vol. 15 No. 4: 669–74.

—— (1996) 'Review of John Tulloch and Henry Jenkins, *Science Fiction Audiences*', *Media, Culture and Society* Vol. 18 No. 3: 364–7.

—— (1997) 'Taking the extreme case: understanding a fascist fan of Judge Dredd', in Cartmell, D., Hunter, I.Q., Kaye, H. and Whelehan, I. (eds) *Trash Aesthetics: Popular Culture and its Audience*, London: Pluto Press.

Barker, M. and Brooks, K. (1998) *Knowing Audiences: Judge Dredd – Its Friends, Fans and Foes*, Luton: University of Luton Press.

Barker, M. and Sabin, R. (1995) *The Lasting of the Mohicans: History of an American Myth*, Jackson: University Press of Mississippi.

Barnes, B. (2000) *Understanding Agency*, London: Sage.

Barrett, M. (1999) *Imagination in Theory*, Cambridge: Polity Press.

Barrett, M. and Barrett, D. (2001) *'Star Trek': The Human Frontier*, Cambridge: Polity Press.

Barthes, R. (1974) *S/Z: An Essay*, New York: Hill and Wang.

—— (1982) *Mythologies*, London: Granada Publishing.

—— (1990) *Image–Music–Text*, London: Fontana Press.

Bartolovich, C. (2000) 'To boldly go where no MLA has gone before', in Herman, P.C. (ed.) (2000) *Day Late, Dollar Short: The Next Generation and the New Academy*, New York: SUNY Press.

Baty, S.P. (1995) *American Monroe: The Making of a Body Politic*, Berkeley: University of California Press.

Baudrillard, J. (1988) *Selected Writings*, Cambridge: Polity Press.

—— (1993) *The Transparency of Evil: Essays on Extreme Phenomena*, London: Verso.

—— (1996) *The System of Objects*, London: Verso.

—— (1998) *The Consumer Society*, London: Sage.

Bauman, Z. (1996) 'From pilgrim to tourist', in Hall, S. and du Gay, P. (eds) *Questions of Cultural Identity*, London: Sage.

Bayard, P. (2000) *Who Killed Roger Ackroyd?*, London: Fourth Estate.

Baym, N.K. (1995a) 'The emergence of community in computer-mediated communication', in Jones, S.G. (ed.) *Cybersociety: Computer-Mediated Communication and Community*, London: Sage.

—— (1995b) 'From practice to culture on Usenet', in Leigh Star, S. (ed.) *The Cultures of Computing*, Oxford: Blackwell Publishers.

—— (2000) *Tune In, Log On: Soaps, Fandom, and Online Community*, London: Sage.

Beckford, J. (1989) *Religion and Advanced Industrial Society*, London: Unwin Hyman.

Bell, V. (1999) 'On speech, race and melancholia: an interview with Judith Butler', in Bell, V. (ed.) *Performativity and Belonging*, London: Sage.

Benjamin, W. (1992) *Illuminations*, London: Fontana Press.

Bennett, T. and Woollacott, J. (1987) *Bond and Beyond: The Political Career of a Popular Hero*, London: Macmillan.

Bennett, T., Emmison, M. and Frow, J. (1999) *Accounting for Tastes: Australian Everyday Cultures*, Cambridge: Cambridge University Press.

Berger, P. (1967) *The Sacred Canopy: Elements of a Sociological Theory of Religion*, New York: Anchor Books.

—— (1971) *A Rumour of Angels: Modern Society and the Rediscovery of the Supernatural*, London: Penguin.

Berger, P. and Luckmann, T. (1979) *The Social Construction of Reality*, London: Penguin.

Berland, J. (1992) 'Angels dancing: cultural technologies and the production of space', in Grossberg, L., Nelson, C. and Treichler, P. (eds) *Cultural Studies*, London: Routledge.

Bernardi, D.L. (1998) *'Star Trek' and History: Race-ing Toward a White Future*, New Jersey: Rutgers University Press.

Bettelheim, B. (1978) *The Uses of Enchantment: The Meaning and Importance of Fairy Tales*, London: Penguin.

Bignell, J. (2000) *Postmodern Media Culture*, Edinburgh: Edinburgh University Press.

Billig, M. (1992) *Talking of the Royal Family*, London: Routledge.

Bird, S.E. (1992) *For Enquiring Minds: A Cultural Study of Supermarket Tabloids*, Knoxville: University of Tennessee Press.

Blackman, L. and Walkerdine, V. (2001) *Mass Hysteria: Critical Psychology and Media Studies*, London: Palgrave.

Blanchard, K. and Bowles, S. (1998) *Raving Fans*, London: HarperCollins.

Bloom, C. (1996) *Cult Fiction: Popular Reading and Pulp Theory*, London: Macmillan.

Bollas, C. (1987) *The Shadow of the Object: Psychoanalysis of the Unthought Known*, London: Free Association Books.

—— (1989) *Forces of Destiny: Psychoanalysis and Human Idiom*, London: Free Association Books.

—— (1992) *Being a Character: Psychoanalysis and Self Experience*, London: Routledge.

—— (1995) *Cracking Up: The Work of Unconscious Experience*, London: Routledge.

—— (1999) *The Mystery of Things*, London: Routledge.

—— (2000) *Hysteria*, London: Routledge.

Boorstin, D. J. (1963) *The Image or What Happened to the American Dream*, London: Penguin.

Bordwell, D. (1989) *Making Meaning: Inference and Rhetoric in the Interpretation of Cinema*, Massachusetts: Harvard University Press.

Bourdieu, P. (1984) *Distinction: A Social Critique of the Judgement of Taste*, London: Routledge.

—— (1990) *The Logic of Practice*, Stanford: Stanford University Press.

—— (1991) *Language and Symbolic Power*, Cambridge: Polity Press.

—— (2000) *Pascalian Meditations*, Cambridge: Polity Press.

Bourdieu, P. and Eagleton, T. (1992) 'In conversation: *Doxa* and common life', *New Left Review* 191: 111–21.

Bourdieu, P. and Passeron, J.-C. (1977) *Reproduction in Education, Society and Culture*, London: Sage.

Boyne, R. (2001) *Subject, Society and Culture*, London: Sage.

Bradby, B. (1994) 'Freedom, feeling and dancing: Madonna's songs traverse girls' talk', in Mills, S. (ed.) *Gendering the Reader*, Hemel Hempstead: Harvester Wheatsheaf.

Branston, G. (2000a) 'Why theory?', in Gledhill, C. and Williams, L. (eds) *Reinventing Film Studies*, London: Arnold.

—— (2000b) *Cinema and Cultural Modernity*, Buckingham: Open University Press.

Braudy, L. (1986) *The Frenzy of Renown: Fame and Its History*, Oxford: Oxford University Press.

Briggs, S. and Pratchett, T. (1993) *The Streets of Ankh-Morpork*, London: Corgi.

Bristol, M.D. (1996) *Big-time Shakespeare*, London: Routledge.

Brooker, P. and Brooker, W. (1996) 'Pulpmodernism: Tarantino's affirmative action', in Cartmell, D., Hunter, I.Q., Kaye, H. and Whelehan, I. (eds) *Pulping Fictions: Consuming Culture across the Literature/Media Divide*, London: Pluto Press.

Brooker, W. (1997) 'New hope: the postmodern project of *Star Wars*', in Brooker, P. and Brooker, W. (eds) *Postmodern after-images*, London: Arnold.

—— (1998) *Teach Yourself Cultural Studies*, London: Hodder and Stoughton.

—— (1999a) 'Batman: one life, many faces', in Cartmell, D. and Whelehan, I. (eds) *Adaptations: From Text to Screen, Screen to Text*, London: Routledge.

—— (1999b) 'Internet fandom and the continuing narratives of *Star Wars, Blade Runner* and *Alien*', in Kuhn, A. (ed.) *Alien Zone II*, London: Verso.

—— (2000) *Batman Unmasked: Analysing a Cultural Icon*, London: Continuum.

Brottman, M. (2000) 'Star cults/cult stars: cinema, psychosis, celebrity, death', in Mendik, X. and Harper, G. (eds) *Unruly Pleasures: The Cult Film and its Critics*, Guildford: FAB Press.

Brower, S. (1992) 'Fans as tastemakers: viewers for quality television', in Lewis, L.A. (ed.) *The Adoring Audience*, London: Routledge.

Brown, M.E. (1996) 'Desperately seeking strategies: reading in the postmodern', in Grodin, D. and Lindlof, T.R. (eds) *Constructing the Self in a Mediated World*, London: Sage.

Brown, S. (1995) *Postmodern Marketing*, London: Routledge.

Brubaker, R. (1993) 'Social theory as habitus', in Calhoun, C., LiPuma, E. and Postone, M. (eds) *Bourdieu: Critical Perspectives*, Cambridge: Polity Press.

Brunsdon, C. (2000) *The Feminist, the Housewife, and the Soap Opera*, Oxford: Clarendon Press.

Buchanan, I. (2000) *Michel de Certeau: Cultural Theorist*, London: Sage.

Buckingham, D. (ed.) (1993) *Reading Audiences: Young people and the Media*, Manchester: Manchester University Press.

—— (2000) *After the Death of Childhood*, Cambridge: Polity Press.

Bukatman, S. (1993) *Terminal Identity: The Virtual Subject in Post-modern Science Fiction*, Durham: Duke University Press.

—— (1994) 'X-Bodies (the torment of the mutant superhero)', in Sappington, R. and Stallings, T. (eds) *Uncontrollable Bodies: Testimonies of Identity and Culture*, Seattle: Bay Press.

—— (1998) 'Zooming out: the end of offscreen space', in Lewis, Jon (ed.) *The New American Cinema*, Durham: Duke University Press.

Burchill, J. (1986) *Damaged Gods: Cults and Heroes Reappraised*, London: Century Hutchinson.

Burgess, J. and Gold, J.R. (eds) (1985) *Geography, The Media and Popular Culture*, London: Croom Helm.

Burt, R. (1998) *Unspeakable Shaxxxspeares*, London: Macmillan.

Butler, J. (1993) *Bodies That Matter*, London: Routledge.

—— (1999) *Gender Trouble (10th anniversary edn)*, London: Routledge.

Buxton, D. (1990) *From The Avengers to Miami Vice: Form and Ideology in Television Series*, Manchester: Manchester University Press.

Caesar, T. (2000) 'Phantom narratives: travel, jobs and the next generation', in Herman, P.C. (ed.) (2000) *Day Late, Dollar Short: The Next Generation and the New Academy*, New York: SUNY Press.

Cameron, S. and Collins, A. (2000) *Playing the Love Market*, London: Free Association Books.

Campbell, J. (2000) *Arguing with the Phallus*, London: Zed Books.

Campbell, S. (1997) *Interpreting the Personal: Expression and the Formation of Feelings*, Ithaca: Cornell University Press.

Carraze, A. and Oswald, H. (1990) *The Prisoner: A Televisionary Masterpiece*, London: W.H. Allen.

Carpenter, H. (1977) *J.R.R. Tolkien: A Biography*, London: George Allen and Unwin.

Carroll, N. (1990) *The Philosophy of Horror or Paradoxes of the Heart*, London: Routledge.

Cartmell, D., Hunter, I.Q., Kaye, H. and Whelehan, I. (eds) (1996) *Pulping Fictions: Consuming Culture across the Literature/Media Divide*, London: Pluto Press.

—— (eds) (1997) *Trash Aesthetics: Popular Culture and its Audience*, London: Pluto Press.

Castells, M. (1998) *End of Millennium (The Information Age: Economy, Society and Culture, Vol. III)*, Oxford: Blackwell Publishers.

Caughey, J.L. (1984) *Imaginary Social Worlds: A Cultural Approach*, Lincoln: University of Nebraska Press.

Cavell, S. (1981) *Pursuits of Happiness: the Hollywood Comedy of Remarriage*, Massachusetts: Harvard University Press.

Cavicchi, D. (1998) *Tramps Like Us: Music and Meaning Among Springsteen Fans*, Oxford: Oxford University Press.

Chadwick, V. (ed.) (1997) *In Search of Elvis: Music Race Art Religion*, Oxford: Westview Press.

Chaney, D. (1994) *The Cultural Turn: Scene-Setting Essays on Comporary Cultural History*, London and New York: Routledge.

Chibnall, S. (1997) 'Double exposures: observations on *The Flesh and Blood Show*', in Cartmell, D., Hunter, I.Q., Kaye, H. and Whelehan, I. (eds) *Trash Aesthetics: Popular Culture and its Audience*, London: Pluto Press.

Church Gibson, P. (2001) ' "You've been in my life so long I can't remember anything else": into the labyrinth with Ripley and the Alien', in Tinkcom, M. and Villarejo, A. (eds) *Keyframes: Popular Cinema and Cultural Studies*, New York: Routledge.

Cicioni, M. (1998) 'Male pair-bonds and female desire in fan slash writing', in Harris, C. and Alexander, A. (eds) *Theorizing Fandom: Fans, Subculture and Identity*, Cresskill: Hampton Press.

Clerc, S. (1996a) 'Estrogen brigades and "big tits" threads: media fandom online and off', in Cherny, L. and Weise, E.R. (eds) *Wired_Women: Gender and New Realities in Cyberspace*, Seattle: Seal Press.

—— (1996b) 'DDEB, GATB, MPPB, and Ratboy: *The X-Files*' media fandom, online and off', in Lavery, D., Hague, A. and Cartwright, M. (eds) *Deny All Knowledge: Reading the X-Files*, London: Faber and Faber.

Clough, P.T. (2000) *Autoaffection*, Minneapolis: University of Minnesota Press.

Cohan, S. (2001) 'Judy on the net: Judy Garland fandom and "the gay thing" revisited', in Tinkcom, M. and Villarejo, A. (eds) *Keyframes: Popular Cinema and Cultural Studies*, New York: Routledge.

Cohen, S. (1987) *Folk Devils and Moral Panics: The Creation of Mods and Rockers*, Oxford: Basil Blackwell.

Collins, J. (1992) 'Postmodernism and Television', in Allen, R.C. (ed.) (1992) *Channels of Discourse, Reassembled: Television and Contemporary Criticism*, London: Routledge.

—— (1993) 'Genericity in the nineties: eclectic irony and the new sincerity', in Collins, J., Radner, H. and Preacher Collins, A. (eds) *Film Theory Goes To The Movies*, London: Routledge.

—— (1995) *Architectures of Excess: Cultural Life in the Information Age*, London: Routledge.

Collins, J., Radner, H. and Preacher Collins, A. (eds) (1993) *Film Theory Goes To The Movies*, London: Routledge.

Collins, R. (1998) *The Sociology of Philosophies*, Massachusetts: Harvard University Press.

Conrich, I. (1997) 'Seducing the subject: Freddy Krueger, popular culture and the *Nightmare on Elm Street* films', in Cartmell, D., Hunter, I.Q., Kaye, H. and Whelehan, I. (eds) *Trash Aesthetics: Popular Culture and its Audience*, London: Pluto Press.

212

Coombe, R.J. (1998) *The Cultural Life of Intellectual Properties: Authorship, Appropriation, and the Law*, Durham: Duke University Press.

Cornell, P. (ed.) (1997) *Licence Denied: Rumblings from the 'Doctor Who' Underground*, London: Virgin Books.

Corrigan, T. (1991) 'Film and the culture of the cult', in Telotte, J.P (ed.) *The Cult Film Experience: Beyond All Reason*, Austin: University of Texas Press.

Couldry, N. (1996) 'Speaking about others and speaking personally', *Cultural Studies* 10(2): 315–33.

—— (1998a) 'The view from inside the "simulacrum": visitors' tales from the set of *Coronation Street*', *Leisure Studies* 17: 94–107.

—— (1998b) 'Towards a radical geography of television'; paper presented at the Screen Studies Conference, Glasgow University 3–5 July 1998.

—— (2000a) *The Place of Media Power*, London: Routledge.

—— (2000b) *Inside Culture: Re-imagining the Method of Cultural Studies*, London: Sage.

Coupland, D. (1992) *Generation X*, London: Abacus Books.

—— (1997) 'Brentwood notebook', in *Polaroids from the Dead*, London: Flamingo.

Cowie, E. (1997) *Representing the Woman: Cinema and Psychoanalysis*, London: Macmillan.

Craib, I. (2001) *Psychoanalysis: A Critical Introduction*, Cambridge: Polity Press.

Crane, D. (1995) 'A personal postscript, an impostured preface', in Gallop, J. (ed.) *Pedagogy: The Question of Impersonation*, Bloomington: Indiana University Press.

Creed, B. (1993) *The Monstrous-Feminine*, London: Routledge.

Cult Times (1995) 'Nowhere man' [no author credited] Nov 1995: 10.

Cumberland, S. (2000) 'Private uses of cyberspace: women, desire and fan culture', available HTTP: <http://media-in-transition.mit.edu/articles/cumberland.html> (accessed 20 July 2001).

Daniels, G. and Bignell, R. (1989) 'On location', *'Doctor Who' Magazine* No. 151 August 1989: 20.

Davidhazi, P. (1998) *The Romantic Cult of Shakespeare: Literary Reception in Anthropological Perspective*, London: Macmillan.

Davis, L.J. (1987) *Resisting Novels: Ideology and Fiction*, London: Methuen.

Dawson, G. (1994) *Soldier Heroes*, London: Routledge.

Dayan, D. and Katz, E. (1996) *Media Events: The Live Broadcasting of History*, London: Harvard University Press.

de Certeau, M. (1988) *The Practice of Everyday Life*, London: University of California Press.

Delany, P. (ed.) (1994) *Vancouver: Representing the Postmodern City*, Vancouver: Arsenal Pulp Press.

—— (1994) ' "Hardly the center of the world": Vancouver in William Gibson's "The Winter Market" ', in Delany, P. (ed.) *Vancouver: Representing the Postmodern City*, Vancouver: Arsenal Pulp Press.

Derrida, J. (1988) *Limited Inc*, Evanston: Northwestern University Press.

—— (1998) 'Faith and knowledge: the two sources of "religion" at the limits of reason alone', in Derrida, J. and Vattimo, G. (eds) *Religion*, Cambridge: Polity Press.

Dika, V. (1990) *Games of Terror: Halloween, Friday the 13th, and the Films of the Stalker Cycle*, New Jersey: Associated University Presses.

Dixon, W.W. (1999) *Disaster and Memory: Celebrity Culture and the Crisis of Hollywood Cinema*, New York: Columbia University Press.

Doane, M.A. (1987) *The Desire to Desire: The Woman's Film of the 1940s*, London: Macmillan.

Dolan, M. (1995) 'The peaks and valleys of serial creativity: what happened to/on *Twin Peaks*', in Lavery, D (ed.) *Full of Secrets: Critical Approaches to* Twin Peaks, Detroit: Wayne State University Press.

—— (1996) *Modern Lives: A Cultural Re-reading of 'The Lost Generation'*, Indiana: Purdue University Press.

Donald, J. (ed.) (1989) *Fantasy and the Cinema*, London: BFI Publishing.

—— (ed.) (1991) *Psychoanalysis and Cultural Theory: Thresholds*, London: Macmillan.

Doss, E. (1999) *Elvis Culture: Fans, Faith and Image*, Lawrence: University Press of Kansas.

Doty, A. (2000) *Flaming Classics: Queering the Film Canon*, London: Routledge.

Dreyfus, H. and Rabinow, P. (1999) 'Can there be a science of existential structure and social meaning?', in Shusterman, R. (ed.) *Bourdieu: A Critical Reader*, Oxford: Blackwell Publishers.

Duncombe, S. (1997) *Notes from Underground: Zines and the Politics of Alternative Culture*, London: Verso.

Durkheim, E. (1964) *The Rules of Sociological Method*, New York: The Free Press.

—— (1984) *The Division of Labour in Society*, London: Macmillan.

—— (1995) *The Elementary Forms of Religious Life*, New York: Free Press.

Dyer, R. (1992 [1979]) *Stars*, London: BFI Publishing.

—— (1987) *Heavenly Bodies: Film Stars and Society*, London: BFI Publishing.

—— (1991) '*A Star is Born* and the construction of authenticity', in Gledhill, C. (ed.) *Stardom: Industry of Desire*, London: Routledge.

Earle, W. (1999) 'Bourdieu nouveau', in Shusterman, R. (ed.) *Bourdieu: A Critical Reader*, Oxford: Blackwell Publishers.

Eckert, C. (1991) 'The Carole Lombard in Macy's window', in Gledhill, C. (ed.) *Stardom: Industry of Desire*, London: Routledge.

Eco, U. (1995a) 'Travels in hyperreality', in *Faith in Fakes: Travels in Hyperreality*, London: Minerva.

—— (1995b) '*Casablanca*: cult movies and intertextual collage', in *Faith in Fakes: Travels in Hyperreality*, London: Minerva.

Elliott, A. (1996) *Subject to Ourselves: Social theory, Psychoanalysis and Postmodernity*, Cambridge: Polity Press.

—— (1999) *The Mourning of John Lennon*, Berkeley: University of California Press.

Ellis, J. (1982) *Visible Fictions*, London: Routledge.

—— (1992) 'Postface', in *Visible Fictions: Revised Edition*, London: Routledge.

Elsaesser, T. (1998) 'Fantasy Island: dream logic as production logic', in Elsaesser, T. and Hoffman, K. (eds) *Cinema Futures: Cain, Abel or Cable? The Screen Arts in the Digital Age*, Amsterdam: Amsterdam University Press.

English, J.F. (2001) 'Afterword: bastard *Auteurism* and academic *Auteurs*: a reflexive reading of Smithee studies', in Braddock, J. and Hock, S. (eds) *Directed by Allen Smithee*, Minneapolis: University of Minnesota Press.

Erb, C. (1991) 'Film and reception: a contextual and reading formation study of *King Kong* (1933)', Indiana University, PhD dissertation, Michigan: UMI Dissertation Services.

—— (1998) *Tracking King Kong: A Hollywood Icon in World Culture*, Detroit: Wayne State University Press.

Everman, W. (1993) *Cult Horror Films*, New York: Citadel Press.

Faith, K. (1997) *Madonna: Bawdy and Soul*, Toronto: University of Toronto Press.

Feuer, J. (1995) *Seeing Through the Eighties: Television and Reaganism*, London: BFI Publishing.

Feuer, J., Kerr, P. and Vahimagi, T. (eds) (1984) *MTM 'Quality Television'*, London: BFI Books.

Fields, K. E. (1995) 'Introduction' to Durkheim, E. *The Elementary Forms of Religious Life*, New York: Free Press.

Fiske, J. (1990) 'Ethnosemiotics: some personal and theoretical reflections', *Cultural Studies* Vol. 4 No. 1: 85–99.

—— (1991) *Television Culture*, London: Routledge.

—— (1992) 'The cultural economy of fandom', in Lewis, L.A. (ed.) *The Adoring Audience*, London: Routledge.

Flanagan, K. (1999) *The Enchantment of Sociology*, London: Macmillan.

Fleming, D. (1996) *Powerplay: Toys as Popular Culture*, Manchester: Manchester University Press.

Fletcher, G. and Greenhill, A. (1996) 'The social construction of electronic space', *Social Semiotics* Vol. 6 No. 2: 179–98.

Fletcher, J. and Stanton, M. (eds) (1992) *Jean Laplanche: Seduction, Translation, Drives*, London: ICA.

Flinn, C. (1995) 'The deaths of camp', *Camera Obscura* No. 35: 53–84.

Focus (1997) 'Bending the Truth' containing 'We just want to be like Scully: The lengths fans will go to just to be an X-Phile' October issue [no author credited]: 54–60.

Foucault, M. (1977) 'What is an author?', in *Language, Counter-Memory, Practice*, New York: Cornell University Press.

—— (1991) *Discipline and Punish: The Birth of the Prison*, London: Penguin.

Frankfurt, H.G. (1988) *The Importance of What We Care About: Philosophical Essays*, Cambridge: Cambridge University Press.

Freeland, C. (2000) *The Naked and the Undead*, Boulder: Westview Press.

French, K. and French, P. (1999) *Cult Movies*, London: Pavilion Books.

French, S. (1996) *BFI Modern Classics: The Terminator*, London: BFI Publishing.

Freud, S. (1907, reprinted 1991) 'Obsessive actions and religious practices', in *Penguin Freud Library 13: The Origins of Religion*, London: Penguin.

—— (1982 [1915]) 'The unconscious', in *Penguin Freud Library 11: On Metapsychology*, London: Penguin.

—— (1991 [1919]) 'The uncanny', in *Penguin Freud Library 14: Art and Literature*, London: Penguin.

—— (1991 [1921]) 'Group psychology and the analysis of the ego', in *Penguin Freud Library 12: Civilisation, Society and Religion*, London: Penguin.

—— (1991 [1930]) 'Civilisation and its discontents', in *Penguin Freud Library 12*, London: Penguin.

Frith, S. (1990) 'Review article', *Screen* 31 (2): 231–5.

—— (1992) 'The cultural study of popular music', in Grossberg, L., Nelson, C. and Treichler, P. (eds) *Cultural Studies*, London: Routledge.

—— (1996a) 'Music and identity', in Hall, S. and du Gay, P. (eds) *Questions of Cultural Identity*, London: Sage.

—— (1996b) *Performing Rites: On the Value of Popular Music*, Oxford: Oxford University Press.

—— (1996c) 'Youth culture/youth cults', in Frith, S. and Gillett, C. (eds) *The Beat Goes On: The Rock File Reader*, London: Pluto Press.

—— (1996d) 'The academic Elvis', in King, R.H. and Taylor, H. (eds) *Dixie Debates: Perspectives on Southern Culture*, London: Pluto Press.

Frith, S. and Goodwin, A. (eds) (1990) *On Record: Rock, Pop and the Written Word*, London: Routledge.

Frith, S. and Horne, H. (1987) *Art into Pop*, London: Methuen.

Frow, J. (1995) *Cultural Studies and Cultural Value*, Oxford: Clarendon Press.

—— (1998) 'Is Elvis a God? Cult, culture, questions of method', *International Journal of Cultural Studies* Vol. 1 No. 2: 197–210.

Fuller, K.H. (1996) *At The Picture Show: Small-Town Audiences and the Creation of Movie Fan Culture*, Washington: Smithsonian Institution Press.

Gallop, J. (1995) 'Im-personation: a reading in the guise of an introduction', in Gallop, J. (ed.) *Pedagogy: The Question of Impersonation*, Bloomington: Indiana University Press.

Game, A. and Metcalfe, A. (1996) *Passionate Sociology*, London: Sage.

Gamson, J. (1994) *Claims to Fame: Celebrity in Contemporary America*, London: University of California Press.

Ganz-Blättler, U. (1999) 'Shareware or prestigious privilege? Television fans as knowledge brokers', available HTTP: <http://media-in-transition.mit.edu/articles/ ganz.html> (accessed 20 July 2001).

Garber, M. (1992) *Vested Interests: Cross-Dressing and Cultural Anxiety*, London: Routledge.

Gardiner, S. (1998) 'The law and hate speech: "Ooh Aah Cantona" and the demonisation of "the other"', in Brown, A. (ed.) *Fanatics! Power, Identity and Fandom in Football*, London: Routledge.

Garnham, N. with Williams, R. (1990) 'Pierre Bourdieu and the sociology of culture: an introduction', in Garnham, N. *Capitalism and Communication*, London: Sage.

Garratt, S. (1984) 'All of us love all of you', in Steward, S. and Garratt, S. *Signed, Sealed and Delivered: True Life Stories of Women in Pop*, London: Pluto Press.

—— (1994) 'All of me loves all of you', in Aizlewood, J. (ed.) *Love is the Drug: Living as a Pop Fan*, London: Penguin.

Geairns, A. J. (1996) 'WHO ARE YOU CALLING A CULT?', *Infinity* Issue 4 November 1996: 21.

Gebauer, G. and Wulf, C. (1995a) *Mimesis: Culture, Art, Society*, London: University of California Press.

—— (1995b) 'Social mimesis', *Paragrana* Band 4 Heft 2: 13–24.

Gelder, K. and Thornton, S. (eds) (1997) *The Subcultures Reader*, London: Routledge.

Geraghty, C. (1981) 'The continuous serial: a definition', in Dyer, R. *et al Coronation Street*, London: BFI.

—— (1991) *Women and Soap Opera: A Study of Prime Time Soaps*, Cambridge: Polity Press.

Gershuny, J. (2000) *Changing Times: Work and Leisure in Postindustrial Society*, Oxford: Oxford University Press.

Gibberman, S.R. (1991) '*Star Trek*': *An Annotated Guide to Resources on the Development, the Phenomenon, the People, the Television Series, the Films, the Novels and the Recordings*, Jefferson: McFarland.

Giddens, A. (1988) *Central Problems in Social Theory: Action, Structure and Contradiction in Social Analysis*, London: Macmillan.

Gilbert, J. (1999) 'White light/white heat: *jouissance* beyond gender in the Velvet Underground', in Blake, A. (ed.) *Living Through Pop*, London: Routledge.

Gilbert, J. and Pearson, E. (1999) *Discographies: Dance Music, Culture and the Politics of Sound*, London: Routledge.

Giles, D. (2000) *Illusions of Immortality: A Psychology of Fame and Celebrity*, London: Macmillan.

Gillatt, G. (1996) 'Editorial', *'Doctor Who' Magazine* Issue 239, 1996: 3.

Gottdiener, M. (1997) 'Dead Elvis as other Jesus', in Chadwick, V. (ed.) *In Search of Elvis: Music Race Art Religion*, Oxford: Westview Press.

Gradnitzer, L. and Pittson, T. (1999) *X Marks the Spot: On Location with 'The X-Files'*, Vancouver: Arsenal Pulp Press.

Gramsci, A. (1971) *Selections from the Prison Notebooks*, London: Lawrence and Wishart.

Gray, A. (1992) *Video Playtime: The Gendering of a Leisure Technology*, London: Routledge/Comedia.

Green, A. (1996) *On Private Madness*, London: Rebus Press.

Green, D. and Bodle, A. (1995) 'Living in a TV timewarp', *Focus* December 1995: 16–20.

Green, S., Jenkins, C. and Jenkins, H. (1998) 'Normal female interest in men bonking: selections from *The Terra Nostra Underground* and *Strange Bedfellows*', in Harris, C. and Alexander, A. (eds) *Theorizing Fandom: Fans, Subculture and Identity*, Cresskill: Hampton Press.

Gregory, C. (1997) *Be Seeing You ...: Decoding 'The Prisoner'*, Luton: University of Luton Press.

—— (2000) *'Star Trek': Parallel Narratives*, London: Macmillan.

Gregory, N. and Gregory, J. (1997) 'When Elvis Died: Enshrining a Legend', in Chadwick, V. (ed.) *In Search of Elvis: Music Race Art Religion*, Oxford: Westview Press.

Grodal, T. (1999) *Moving Pictures*, Oxford: Clarendon Press.

Groenewegen, S.J. (1997) 'Frocks, Coats and Dress (Non)Sense', in Cornell, P. (ed.) (1997) *Licence Denied: Rumblings from the 'Doctor Who' underground*, London: Virgin Books.

Gross, L. (1991) 'Out of the mainstream: Sexual minorities and the mass media', in Seiter, E., Borchers, H., Kreutzner, G., Warth, E.-M. (eds) *Remote Control: Television, Audiences and Cultural Power*, London: Routledge.

Grossberg, L. (1988) 'It's a sin: politics, post-modernity and the popular', in Grossberg, L., Curthoys, A., Fry, T., Patton, P. *It's A Sin: Essays on Postmodernism, Politics and Culture*, Sydney: Power Publications.

—— (1992a) *We gotta get out of this place*, London: Routledge.

—— (1992b) 'Is there a fan in the house?: The affective sensibility of fandom', in Lewis, L.A. (ed.) *The Adoring Audience*, London: Routledge.

—— (1996) 'Identity and cultural studies: Is that all there is?', in Hall, S. and du Gay, P. (eds) *Questions of Cultural Identity*, London: Sage.

—— (1997a) *Bringing It All Back Home: Essays on Cultural Studies*, Durham: Duke University Press.

—— (1997b) *Dancing in Spite of Myself: Essays on Popular Culture*, Durham: Duke University Press.

Hagedorn, R. (1995) 'Doubtless to be continued: A brief history of serial narrative', in Allen, R.C. (ed.) *To Be Continued... Soap Operas around the World*, London: Routledge.

217

Hall, M. (1997) 'Kling on to great TREKSPECTATIONS: Little town on the prairie is cashing in on the *Star Trek* mania', *XS* (*Sunday Mail* magazine) 4 May: 9.

Hallam, J. with Marshment, M. (2000) *Realism and popular cinema*, Manchester: Manchester University Press.

Halton, E. (1992) 'The cultic roots of culture', in Munch, R. and Smelser, N.J. (eds) *Theory of Culture*, Berkeley: University of California Press.

Hanley, R. (1997) *The Metaphysics of 'Star Trek'*, New York: Basic Books.

Harrington, C. L. and Bielby, D. (1995) *Soap Fans: Pursuing Pleasure and Making Meaning in Everyday Life*, Philadelphia: Temple University Press.

Harris, C. and Alexander, A. (eds) *Theorizing Fandom: Fans, Subculture and Identity*, Cresskill: Hampton Press.

Harrison, Ted (1992) *Elvis People: The Cult of the King*, London: Fount Paperbacks.

—— (1998) *Diana: Icon and Sacrifice*, Oxford: Lion Publishing.

Harrison, Taylor, Projansky, S., Ono, K.A. and Helford, E.R. (eds) (1996) *Enterprise Zones: Critical Positions on 'Star Trek'*, Oxford: Westview.

Hartley, J. (1996) *Popular Reality*, London: Arnold.

—— (1999) *Uses of Television*, London: Routledge.

Harvey, D. (1989) *The Condition of Postmodernity*, Oxford: Blackwell Publishers.

Haslett, M. (1994) 'Only the ones we love', *Skaro* No. 9 Summer 1994: 10.

Hauben, M. and Hauben, R. (1997) *Netizens: On the History and Impact of Usenet and the Internet*, London: IEEE Computer Society Press.

Hawkins, J. (2000) *Cutting Edge: Art-Horror and the Horrific Avant-garde*, Minneapolis: University of Minnesota Press.

Hayward, J. (1997) *Consuming Pleasures: Active Audiences and Serial Fictions from Dickens to Soap Opera*, Kentucky: University Press of Kentucky.

Hebdige, D. (1979) *Subculture: The Meaning of Style*, London: Methuen.

Hegel, G.W.F. (1977) *The Phenomenology of Spirit*, Oxford: Oxford University Press.

Heinich, N. (1996) *The Glory of Van Gogh: An Anthropology of Admiration*, Princeton: Princeton University Press.

Henderson, W.M. (1997) *I, Elvis: Confessions of a Counterfeit King*, New York: Boulevard Books.

Herman, P.C. (ed.) (2000) *Day Late, Dollar Short: The Next Generation and the New Academy*, New York: SUNY Press.

Hermes, J. (1995) *Reading Women's Magazines*, Cambridge: Polity Press.

Hewison, R. (1987) *The Heritage Industry: Britain in a Climate of Decline*, London: Methuen.

Hills, M. (1999a) 'The dialectic of value: the sociology and psychoanalysis of cult media', unpublished PhD dissertation, University of Sussex.

—— (1999b) 'Virtual community and the virtues of continuity', *New Media and Society* Vol. 1 No. 2: 251–60.

—— (2000a) 'Media fandom, Neoreligiosity and Cult(ural) Studies', *The Velvet Light Trap* No. 46: 73–84.

—— (2000b) 'Mapping narrative spaces', in Butler, A., James, E. and Mendlesohn, F. (eds) *Terry Pratchett: Guilty of Literature*, Reading: Science Fiction Foundation.

—— (2001a) 'Virtually out there: strategies, tactics and affective spaces in online fandom', in Munt, S.R. (ed.) *Technospaces: Inside the New Media*, London: Continuum.

—— (2001b) 'Review of *Tune In, Log On* (Baym 2000)', *New Media and Society* Vol. 3 No. 1: 115–19.

Hine, C. (2000) *Virtual Ethnography*, London: Sage.

Hinerman, S. (1992) ' "I'll Be Here With You": fans, fantasy and the figure of Elvis', in Lewis, L.A. (ed.) *The Adoring Audience*, London: Routledge.

Hinton, C. (1995) untitled in *Cult Times* No. 2 Nov 95: 46.

Hoberman, J. and Rosenbaum, J. (1991) *Midnight Movies*, New York: Da Capo Press.

Hobson, D. (1982) *Crossroads: The Drama of a Soap Opera*, London: Methuen.

Hoggett, P. (1992) *Partisans in an Uncertain World: The Psychoanalysis of Engagement*, London: Free Association Books.

Holderness, G. (ed.) (1988a) *The Shakespeare Myth*, Manchester: Manchester University Press.

—— (1988b) 'Bardolatry: or, The cultural materialist's guide to Stratford-upon-Avon', in Holderness, G. (ed.) *The Shakespeare Myth*, Manchester: Manchester University Press.

Hollway, W. and Jefferson, T. (2000) *Doing Qualitative Research Differently*, London: Sage.

Horkheimer, M. and Adorno, T. (1973) *The Dialectic of Enlightenment*, London: Allen Lane.

Hornby, N. (1993) *Fever Pitch*, London: Victor Gollancz.

Horne, D. (1984) *The Great Museum*, London: Pluto Press.

Horton, D. and Wohl, R.R. (1956) 'Mass communication and para-social interaction', *Psychiatry* Vol. 19: 215–29.

Hoxter, J. (1998) 'Anna with the Devil Inside: Klein, Argento and "The Stendhal Syndrome" ', in Black, A. (ed.) *Necronomicon Book Two*, London: Creation Books.

—— (2000) 'Taking possession: cult learning in *The Exorcist*', in Mendik, X. and Harper, G. (eds) *Unruly Pleasures: The Cult Film and its Critics*, Guildford: FAB Press.

Hunter, I.Q. (2000) 'Beaver Las Vegas! A fan-boy's defence of *Showgirls*', in Mendik, X. and Harper, G. (eds) *Unruly Pleasures: The Cult Film and its Critics*, Guildford: FAB Press.

Huntington, J. (1989) *Rationalizing Genius: Ideological Strategies in the Classic American Science Fiction Short Story*, New Jersey: Rutgers University Press.

Huyssen, A. (1986) 'Mass culture as woman: Modernism's Other', in Modleski, T. (ed.) *Studies in Entertainment*, Bloomington: Indiana University Press.

Inglis, F. (1982) *The Promise of Happiness: Value and Meaning in Children's Fiction*, Cambridge: Cambridge University Press.

Jackson, P. (1994) *Maps of Meaning*, London: Routledge.

James, E. and Mendlesohn, F. (eds) (1998) *The Parliament of Dreams: Conferring on 'Babylon 5'*, Reading: Science Fiction Foundation.

Jameson, F. (1991) *Postmodernism, or, The Cultural Logic of Late Capitalism*, London: Verso.

—— (1995a) *The Geopolitical Aesthetic: Cinema and Space in the World System*, London: BFI Publishing.

—— (1995b) 'On cultural studies', in Rajchman, J. (ed.) *The Identity in Question*, London: Routledge.

Jancovich, M. (1990) *Horror*, London: Batsford.

—— (2000) ' "A Real Shocker": authenticity, genre and the struggle for distinction', *Continuum: Journal of Media and Cultural Studies* Vol. 14 No.1: 23–35.

Jarvis, B. (1998) *Postmodern Cartographies: The Geographical Imagination in Contemporary American Culture*, London: Pluto Press.

Jenkins, H. (1991) 'Star Trek Rerun, Reread, Rewritten: Fan Writing as Textual Poaching', in Penley, C., Lyon, E., Spigel, L. and Bergstrom, J. (eds) Close Encounters: Film, Feminism, and Science Fiction, Minneapolis: University of Minnesota Press.

—— (1992a) Textual Poachers: Television Fans and Participatory Cultures, London: Routledge.

—— (1992b) ' "Strangers No More, We Sing": Filking and the social construction of the science fiction fan community', in Lewis, L.A. (ed.) The Adoring Audience: Fan Culture and Popular Media, London: Routledge.

—— (1995) ' "Do You Enjoy Making the Rest of Us Feel Stupid?": alt.tv.twinpeaks, the Trickster Author and Viewer Mastery', in Lavery, D. (ed.) Full of Secrets: Critical Approaches to 'Twin Peaks', Detroit: Wayne State University Press.

—— (1996) 'Interview with Henry Jenkins', in Harrison, T., Projansky, S., Ono, K.A. and Helford, E.R. (eds) Enterprise Zones: Critical Positions on 'Star Trek', Oxford: Westview.

—— (1997) ' "Never Trust a Snake": WWF Wrestling as Masculine Melodrama', in Baker, A. and Boyd, T. (eds) Out of Bounds: Sports, Media, and the Politics of Identity, Bloomington: Indiana University Press.

—— (1998) 'The Poachers and the Stormtroopers: cultural convergence in the digital age', available HTTP: <http://commons.somewhere.com/rre/1998/The.Poachers. and.the.Sto.html> (accessed 20 July 2001).

—— (1999) 'Congressional testimony on media violence', available HTTP: <http://media-in-transition.mit.edu/articles/dc.html> (accessed 20 July 2001).

—— (2000) 'Reception theory and audience research: the mystery of the vampire's kiss', in Gledhill, C. and Williams, L. (eds) Reinventing Film Studies, London: Arnold.

—— (2001) 'Foreword' to Lancaster, K. Interacting with 'Babylon 5': Fan Performances in a Media Universe, Austin: University of Texas Press.

—— (forthcoming) 'Quentin Tarantino's Star Wars?: digital cinema, media convergence, and participatory culture', in Cheever, B. (ed.) d.film, Cambridge: MIT Press. Available HTTP: <http://web.mit.edu/21fms/www/faculty/henry3/starwars.html> (accessed 20 July 2001).

Jenkins, R. (1992) Key Sociologists: Pierre Bourdieu, London: Routledge.

Jerslev, A. (1992) 'Semitoics by instinct: "cult film" as signifying practice between audience and film', in Skovmond, M. and Schrøder, K.C (eds) Media Cultures: Reappraising Transnational Media, London and New York: Routledge.

Jensen, J. (1992) 'Fandom as pathology: the consequences of characterisation', in Lewis, L.A. (ed.) The Adoring Audience, London: Routledge.

Jensen, J. and Pauly, J.J. (1997) 'Imagining the audience: losses and gains in cultural studies', in Ferguson, M. and Golding, P. (eds) Cultural Studies in Question, London: Sage.

Jewett, R. and Lawrence, J. S. (1977) The American Monomyth, New York: Anchor Press.

Jindra, M. (1994) 'Star Trek Fandom as a Religious Phenomenon', Sociology of Religion Vol. 55 No. 1: 27–51.

—— (1999) ' "Star Trek to Me is a Way of Life": Fan Expressions of Star Trek Philosophy', in Porter, J.E. and McLaren, D.L. (eds) 'Star Trek' and Sacred Ground, New York: SUNY Press.

Johnson, C. (2001) 'Primetime Fantasies: the scheduling and production of contemporary telefantasy in Britain'; paper presented at 10th 'Console-ing Passions' conference, Bristol University 5–8 July 2001.

Jones, Sara G. (2000) 'Starring Lucy Lawless?', *Continuum: Journal of Media and Cultural Studies* Vol. 14 No. 1: 9–22.

—— (2001) 'Conflicts of interest? The folkloric and legal status of cult TV characters in online fan culture'; paper presented at Society for Cinema Studies Annual Conference 2001, Washington DC, 24–7 May.

Jones, Steve G. (ed.) (1995) *Cybersociety: Computer-Mediated Communication and Community*, London: Sage.

—— (ed.) (1997) *Virtual Culture: Identity and Communication in Cybersociety*, London: Sage.

Joseph-Witham, H.R. (1996) *'Star Trek' Fans and Costume Art*, Jackson: University Press of Mississippi.

Joyrich, L. (1993) 'Elvisophilia: knowledge, pleasure, and the cult of Elvis', *differences* 5.1: 73–91.

Kawin, B. (1991) 'After midnight', in Telotte, J.P. (ed.) *The Cult Film Experience: Beyond All Reason*, Austin: University of Texas Press.

Keane, S. (1998a) 'Time past/time future: reading "Babylon Squared"', in James, E. and Mendlesohn, F. (eds) *The Parliament of Dreams: Conferring on 'Babylon 5'*, Reading: Science Fiction Foundation.

—— (1998b) 'Recycling *Star Wars*: What's so special about the Special Edition?'; paper presented at 'Consumption, Fantasy, Success and Desire' conference, November 1998, Liverpool John Moores University.

Kelly, R.G. (1998) *Mystery Fiction and Modern Life*, Jackson: University Press of Mississippi.

Kendall, G. and Wickham, G. (2001) *Understanding Culture: Cultural Studies, Order, Ordering*, London: Sage.

Kermode, M. (1997) 'I was a teenage horror fan: or, "How I learned to stop worrying and love Linda Blair"', in Barker, M. and Petley, J. (eds) *Ill Effects: The Media/Violence Debate*, London: Routledge.

Kinder, M. (1991) *Playing with Power in Movies, Television and Video Games – From Muppet Babies to Teenage Mutant Ninja Turtles*, Berkeley: University of California Press.

King, C. (1993) 'His truth goes marching on: Elvis Presley and the pilgrimage to Graceland', in Reader, I. and Walter, T. (eds) *Pilgrimage in Popular Culture*, London: Macmillan.

Klapp, O.E. (1969) *Collective Search for Identity*, New York: Holt, Rhinehart and Winston.

Lacey, J. (2000) 'Discursive mothers and academic fandom: class, generation and the production of theory', in Munt, S.R. (ed.) *Cultural Studies and the Working Class: Subject to Change*, London: Cassell.

LaFollette, H. (1996) *Personal Relationships: Love, Identity, and Morality*, Oxford: Blackwells Publishers.

Lamb, P.F. and Veith, D.L. (1986) 'Romantic myth, transcendence, and *Star Trek* zines', in Palumbo, D. (ed.) *Erotic Universe*, New York: Greenwood Press.

Lancaster, K. (1996) 'Travelling among the lands of the fantastic: the imaginary worlds and simulated environments of science fiction tourism', *Foundation – The Review of Science Fiction* No. 67: 28–47.

—— (1999) *Warlocks and Warpdrive: Contemporary Fantasy Entertainments with Interactive and Virtual Environments*, Jefferson: McFarland.

—— (2001) *Interacting with 'Babylon 5': Fan Performances in a Media Universe*, Austin: University of Texas Press.

Lancaster, K. and Mikotowicz, T. (eds) (2001) *Performing the Force: Essays on Immersion into Science Fiction, Fantasy and Horror Environments*, Jefferson: McFarland.

Langley, R. (1990) 'Prisoner of *The Prisoner*', in Carraze, A. and Oswald, H. *The Prisoner: A Televisionary Masterpiece*, London: W.H. Allen.

Laplanche, J (1989) *New Foundations for Psychoanalysis*, Oxford: Blackwell Publishers.

—— (1999a) *Essays on Otherness*, London: Routledge.

—— (1999b) *The Unconscious and the Id*, London: Rebus Press.

Laplanche, J. and Pontalis, J.-B. (1986) 'Fantasy and the origins of sexuality', in Burgin, V., Donald, J. and Kaplan, C. (eds) *Formations of Fantasy*, London: Methuen (translation first published in *International Journal of Psychoanalysis* vol. 49, 1968).

Lavery, D. (ed.) (1995) *Full of Secrets: Critical Approaches to 'Twin Peaks'*, Detroit: Wayne State University Press.

Lavery, D., Hague, A. and Cartwright, M. (eds) (1996) *Deny All Knowledge: Reading the X-Files*, London: Faber and Faber.

Lebeau, V. (1995) *Lost Angels: Psychoanalysis and Cinema*, London: Routledge.

Lehtonen, M. (2000) *The Cultural Analysis of Texts*, London: Sage.

Lewis, J. (forthcoming) *Cultural Theory and Cultural Studies*, London: Sage.

Lewis, J. E. and Stempel, P. (1993) *Cult TV: The Essential Critical Guide*, London: Pavilion Books.

—— (1996) *Cult TV: The Essential Critical Guide – Second Edition*, London: Pavilion Books.

Lewis, L.A. (ed.) (1992) *The Adoring Audience*, London: Routledge.

Lindlof, T.R., Coyle, K. and Grodin, D. (1998) 'Is there a text in this audience? Science Fiction and Interpretive Schism', in Harris, C. and Alexander, A. (eds) *Theorizing Fandom: Fans, Subculture and Identity*, Cresskill: Hampton Press.

Lindner, R. (2001) 'The construction of authenticity: the case of subcultures', in Liep, J. (ed.) *Locating Cultural Creativity*, London: Pluto Press.

Luckhurst, R. (1997) *'The Angle Between Two Walls': The Fiction of J.G. Ballard*, Liverpool: Liverpool University Press.

Luckmann, T. (1967) *The Invisible Religion*, London: Collier-Macmillan.

Lupton, D. (1998) *The Emotional Self*, London: Sage.

Lury, C. (1993) *Cultural Rights: Technology, Legality and Personality*, London: Routledge.

Lyon, D. (1985) *The Steeple's Shadow: On the Myths and Realities of Secularization*, London: Third Way Books.

McCann, G. (1988) *Marilyn Monroe: the body in the library*, New Jersey: Rutgers University Press.

—— (1991) 'Biographical boundaries: sociology and Marilyn Monroe', in Featherstone, M., Hepworth, M. and Turner, B.S. (eds) *The Body: Social Process and Cultural Theory*, London: Sage.

MacCannell, D. (1976) *The Tourist: A New Theory of the Leisure Class*, London: Macmillan.

—— (1992) *Empty Meeting Grounds: The Tourist Papers*, London: Routledge.

McClure, J. (1977) 'Book One: To Be Continued?', in *Murder Ink: The Mystery Reader's Companion* (perpetrated by Winn, D.), Newton Abbot: Westbridge Books.

McCormack, U. (2000) 'Negotiating subjectivities in fan communities: a study of online fans of *Blake's 7*'; paper presented at Third International Crossroads in Cultural Studies Conference, Birmingham University, 21–5 June.

McDonagh, M. (1991) *Broken Mirrors, Broken Minds: The Dark Dreams of Dario Argento*, London: Sun Tavern Fields.

MacDonald, A. (1998) 'Uncertain Utopia: science fiction media fandom and computer mediated communication', in Harris, C. and Alexander, A. (eds) *Theorizing Fandom: Fans, Subculture and Identity*, Cresskill: Hampton Press.

McDougall, J. (1985) *Theatres of the Mind*, London: Free Association Books.

—— (1989) *Theatres of the Body*, London: Free Association Books.

McGee, P. (1997) *Cinema, Theory, and Political Responsibility in Contemporary Culture*, Cambridge: Cambridge University Press.

McGoohan, P. (1993) 'Foreword' to Lewis, Jon E. and Stempel, P. *Cult TV: The Essential Critical Guide*, London: Pavilion Books.

MacIntyre, K. (1996) *Reel Vancouver: An Insider's Guide*, Vancouver: Whitecap Books.

McKee, A. (2001) 'Which is the best *Doctor Who* story? A case study in value judgements outside the academy', in *Intensities: The Journal of Cult Media* Issue 1, available HTTP: <http://www.cult-media.com/issue1/Amckee.htm> (accessed 20 July 2001).

McKinley, E.G. (1997) *Beverly Hills 90210: Television, Gender and Identity*, Philadelphia: University of Pennsylvania Press.

MacKinnon, R.C. (1995) 'Searching for the Leviathan in Usenet', in Jones, Steve G. (ed.) *Cybersociety: Computer-Mediated Communication and Community*, London: Sage.

McLaughlin, M.L., Osborne, K.K. and Smith, C.B. (1995) 'Standards of conduct on Usenet', in Jones, Steve G. (ed.) *Cybersociety: Computer-Mediated Communication and Community*, London: Sage.

McLaughlin, T. (1996) *Street Smarts and Critical Theory: Listening to the Vernacular*, Wisconsin: University of Wisconsin Press.

MacLeod, E. (1997) 'Generation E', in Chadwick, V. (ed.) *In Search of Elvis: Music Race Art Religion*, Oxford: Westview Press.

MacLeod, P. (1997) 'Why I'm the World's Number One Elvis Fan', in Chadwick, V. (ed.) *In Search of Elvis: Music Race Art Religion*, Oxford: Westview Press.

McNaught, K. (1988) *The Penguin History of Canada*, London: Penguin.

McNay, L. (1999) 'Subject, psyche and agency: the work of Judith Butler', in Bell, V. (ed.) *Performativity and Belonging*, London: Sage.

McRobbie, A. (1990) 'Settling accounts with subcultures: a feminist critique', in Frith, S. and Goodwin, A. (eds) *On Record: Rock, Pop and the Written Word*, London: Routledge.

—— (1996) 'Psychoanalytic conversations: the writing of Adam Phillips', *Soundings* Issue 3 Summer: 103–8.

Maffesoli, M. (1996) *The Time of the Tribes: The Decline of Individualism in Mass Society*, London: Sage.

Marcus, G. (1991) *Dead Elvis: A Chronicle of a Cultural Obsession*, New York: Doubleday.

Marcus, G.E. and Fischer, M.M.J. (1986) *Anthropology as Cultural Critique: An Experimental Moment in the Human Sciences*, Chicago: University of Chicago Press.

Marcus, J. (1997) *In the Shadow of the Vampire: Reflections from the World of Anne Rice*, New York: Thunder's Mouth Press.

Marling, K.A. (1997) *Graceland: Going Home with Elvis*, London: Harvard University Press.

Marshall, P.D. (1997) *Celebrity and Power: Fame in Contemporary Culture*, London: University of Minnesota Press.

Marty, M.E. (1969) 'Sects and cults', in Birnbaum, N. and Lenzer, G. (eds) *Sociology and Religion*, New York: Prentice-Hall.

Marx, K. (1976) 'The fetishism of the commodity and its secret', in *Capital Volume 1*, London: Penguin.

Massumi, B. (1996) 'The autonomy of affect', in Patton, P. (ed.) *Deleuze: A Critical Reader*, Oxford: Blackwell Publishers.

Mead, R. (1998) 'The *Star Trek* experience: there may be Tribbles ahead', *Cult TV*, Season 2 Episode 4, April 1998: 15–16.

Medhurst, A. (1991) 'Batman, deviance and camp', in Pearson, R.E. and Uricchio, W. (eds) (1991) *The Many Lives of the Batman: Critical Approaches to a Superhero and his Media*, London: BFI Publishing.

Meehan, E. (1990) 'Why we don't count: the commodity audience', in Mellencamp, P. (ed.) *Logics of Television: Essays in Cultural Criticism*, London: BFI Publishing.

—— (1991) ' "Holy commodity fetish, Batman!": the political economy of a commercial intertext', in Pearson, R.E. and Uricchio, W. (eds) *The Many Lives of the Batman: Critical Approaches to a Superhero and his Media*, London: BFI Publishing.

Mendik, X. and Harper, G. (eds) (2000) *Unruly Pleasures: The Cult Film and its Critics*, Guildford: FAB Press.

Merck, M. (ed.) (1998) *After Diana: Irreverent Elegies*, London: Verso.

Messenger Davies, M. (1989) *Television is Good for Your Kids*, London: Hilary Shipman.

Meyrowitz, J. (1985) *No Sense of Place: The Impact of Electronic Media on Social Behaviour*, Oxford: Oxford University Press.

Michael, J. (2000) *Anxious Intellects: Academic Professionals, Public Intellectuals, and Enlightenment Values*, Durham: Duke University Press.

Miklitsch, R. (1998) *From Hegel to Madonna: Towards a General Economy of 'Commodity Fetishism'*, New York: SUNY Press.

Mikulak, B. (1998) 'Fans versus Time Warner: who owns Looney Tunes?', in Sandler, K.S. (ed.) *Reading the Rabbit: Explorations in Warner Bros. Animation*, New Jersey: Rutgers University Press.

Miles, S. (2001) *Social Theory in the 'Real' World*, London: Sage.

Miller, C. and Thorne, J. (eds) (1997) *Wrapped in Plastic* Vol. 1 No. 29.

Miller, S.E. (1994) 'The Grid: living in Hollywood North', in Delany, P. (ed.) *Vancouver: Representing the Postmodern City*, Vancouver: Arsenal Pulp Press.

Miller, T. (1997) *The Avengers*, London: BFI Publishing.

Minsky, R. (1998) *Psychoanalysis and Culture*, Cambridge: Polity Press.

Mitra, A. (1997) 'Virtual commonality: looking for India on the Internet', in Jones, Steve G. (ed.) *Virtual Culture: Identity and Communication in Cybersociety*, London: Sage.

Modleski, T. (1986) 'The terror of pleasure', in Modleski, T. (ed.) *Studies in Entertainment*, Bloomington: Indiana University Press.

Moores, S. (1993) *Interpreting Audiences: The Ethnography of Media Consumption*, London: Sage.

Moorhouse, H.F. (1991) *Driving Ambitions: An Analysis of the American Hot-rod Enthusiasm*, Manchester: Manchester University Press.

Moran, J. (2000) *Star Authors*, London: Pluto Press.

Morin, E. (1960) *The Stars: An Account of the Star-System In Motion Pictures*, London: John Calder.

Morley, D. (1980) 'Texts, readers, subjects', in Hall, S., Hobson, D., Lowe, A. and Willis, P. (eds) *Culture, Media, Language*, London: Hutchinson.

—— (1992) *Television, Audiences and Cultural Studies*, London: Routledge.

Morley, D. and Chen, K.-H. (eds) (1996) *Stuart Hall: Critical Dialogues in Cultural Studies*, London: Routledge.

Morley, D. and Robins, K. (1995) *Spaces of Identity: global media, electronic landscapes and cultural boundaries*, London: Routledge.

Morris, M. (1990) 'Banality in cultural studies', in Mellencamp, P. (ed.) (1990) *Logics of Television: Essays in Cultural Criticism*, London: BFI Publishing.

Moskowitz, S. (1990) 'The origins of science fiction fandom: a reconstruction', *Foundation: The Review of Science Fiction* 48: 5–25.

Muggleton, D. (2000) *Inside Subculture: The Postmodern Meaning of Style*, Oxford: Berg.

Mumford, L.S. (1995) *Love and Ideology in the Afternoon: Soap Opera, Women and Television Genre*, Bloomington: Indiana University Press.

Murdock, G. (1994) 'Tales of expertise and experience: sociological reasoning and popular representation', in Haslam, C. and Bryman, A. (eds) *Social Scientists Meet the Media*, London: Routledge.

Murray, J.H. (1997) *Hamlet on the Holodeck: The Future of Narrative in Cyberspace*, Cambridge: MIT Press.

Murray, J. and Jenkins, H. (1999) 'Before the Holodeck: translating *Star Trek* into digital media', in Smith, G.M. (ed.) *On a Silver Platter*, New York: New York University Press.

Napier, S. J. (2001) *Anime from 'Akira' to 'Princess Mononoke': Experiencing Contemporary Japanese Animation*, New York: Palgrave.

Nash, M. and Lahti, M. (1999) ' "Almost Ashamed to Say I Am One of Those Girls": *Titanic*, Leonardo DiCaprio, and the paradoxes of girls' fandom', in Sandler, K.S. and Studlar, G. (eds) *Titanic: Anatomy of a Blockbuster*, New Jersey: Rutgers University Press.

Nicholas, J. and Price, J. (1998) *Advanced Studies in Media*, Surrey: Thomas Nelson.

Niedzviecki, H. (2000) *We Want Some Too: Underground Desire and the Reinvention of Mass Culture*, Toronto: Penguin Books Canada.

Nightingale, V. (1994) 'Improvising Elvis, Marilyn and Mickey Mouse', *Australian Journal of Communication* Vol. 21 (1): 1–20.

—— (1996) *Studying Audiences: The Shock of the Real*, London: Routledge.

Nimoy, L. (1995) *I Am Spock*, London: Century.

Nochimson, M. (1997) *The Passion of David Lynch: Wild at Heart in Hollywood*, Austin: University of Texas Press.

Noll, R. (1996) *The Jung Cult: Origins of a Charismatic Movement*, London: Fontana Press.

O'Dair, S. (2000) 'Stars, tenure, and the death of ambition', in Herman, P.C. (ed.) (2000) *Day Late, Dollar Short: The Next Generation and the New Academy*, New York: SUNY Press.

Official Map of 'The X-Files' (1996) [No author given], London: HarperCollins.

Osborne, P. (2000) *Philosophy in Cultural Theory*, London: Routledge.

Parker, I. (1997) *Psychoanalytic Culture*, London: Sage.

Parsons, T. (1997) 'Alex Through the Looking Glass', in French, K. (ed.) *Screen Violence*, London: Bloomsbury Publishing.

Pearson, L. (1999) *I, Who: The Unauthorised Guide to 'Doctor Who' Novels*, New York: Sidewinder Press.

Pearson, R.E. (1997) ' "It's Always 1895": Sherlock Holmes in Cyberspace', in Cartmell, D., Hunter, I.Q., Kaye, H. and Whelehan, I. (eds) *Trash Aesthetics: Popular Culture and its Audience*, London: Pluto Press.

Pearson, R.E. and Uricchio, W. (eds) (1991) *The Many Lives of the Batman: Critical Approaches to a Superhero and his Media*, London: BFI Publishing.

Peary, D. (1981) *Cult Movies*, New York: Delta Books.

—— (1983) *Cult Movies 2*, New York: Delta Books.

Penley, C. (1991) 'Brownian Motion: women, tactics and technology', in Ross, A. and Penley, C. (eds) *Technoculture*, Minneapolis: University of Minnesota Press.

—— (1992) 'Feminism, psychoanalysis and the study of popular culture', in Grossberg, L., Nelson, C. and Treichler, P. (eds) *Cultural Studies*, London: Routledge.

—— (1997) *Nasa/Trek: Popular Science and Sex in America*, London: Verso.

Penzler, O. (1977) 'A few (million) words about my good friend Holmes', in *Murder Ink: The Mystery Reader's Companion* (perpetrated by Winn, D.), Newton Abbot: Westbridge Books.

Phillips, A. (1988) *Fontana Modern Masters: Winnicott*, London: Fontana Press.

—— (1993) *On Kissing, Tickling and Being Bored: Psychoanalytic Essays on the Unexamined Life*, London: Faber and Faber.

—— (1994) *On Flirtation*, London: Faber and Faber.

—— (1995) *Terrors and Experts*, London: Faber and Faber.

—— (1998) *The Beast in the Nursery*, London: Faber and Faber.

Plantinga, C. and Smith, G.M. (eds) (1999) *Passionate Views: Film, Cognition and Emotion*, Baltimore: Johns Hopkins University Press.

Porter, D. (ed.) (1997) *Internet Culture*, London: Routledge.

Porter, J.E. (1999) 'To boldly go: *Star Trek* convention attendance as pilgrimage', in Porter, J.E. and McLaren, D.L. (eds) *'Star Trek' and Sacred Ground*, New York: SUNY Press.

Porter, J.E. and McLaren, D.L. (eds) (1999) *'Star Trek' and Sacred Ground*, New York: SUNY Press.

Poster, M. (1995) 'Postmodern virtualities', in Featherstone, M. and Burrows, R. (eds) *Cyberspace, Cyberbodies, Cyberpunk: Cultures of Technological Embodiment*, London: Sage.

—— (1998) 'Virtual ethnicity: tribal identity in an age of global communications', in Jones, Steve G. (ed.) *Cybersociety 2.0: Revisiting Computer-Mediated Communication and Community*, London: Sage.

Pratchett, T. and Briggs, S. (1997) *The Discworld Companion*, London: Vista.

Pullen, K. (2000) 'I-love-Xena.com: creating online fan communities', in Gauntlett, D. (ed.) *web.studies*, London: Arnold.

Purvis, M. (1997) 'X-Perience the X-Files set', *Starburst* Special No. 33: 17–19.

Pustz, M.J. (1999) *Comic Book Culture: Fanboys and True Believers*, Jackson: University Press of Mississippi.

Radway, J. (1987) *Reading the Romance*, London: Verso.

Randolph, J. (1991) *Psychoanalysis and Synchronized Swimming*, Toronto: YYZ Books.

Rapaport, H. (1994) *Between the Sign and the Gaze*, Ithaca: Cornell University Press.

Reader, I. (1993) 'Conclusions', in Reader, I. and Walter, T. (eds) *Pilgrimage in Popular Culture*, London: Macmillan.

Reader, I. and Walter, T. (eds) (1993) *Pilgrimage in Popular Culture*, London: Macmillan.

Real, M.R. (1996) *Exploring Media Culture: A Guide*, London: Sage.

—— (2001) 'Cultural theory in popular culture and media spectacles', in Lull, J. (ed.) *Culture in the Communication Age*, London: Routledge.

Redding, P. (1999) *The Logic of Affect*, Ithaca: Cornell University Press.

Redhead, S. (1997) *Post-Fandom and the Millennial Blues: The Transformation of Soccer Culture*, London: Routledge.

Reeves, J.L., Rodgers, M.C. and Epstein, M. (1996) 'Rewriting popularity: the cult files', in Lavery, D., Hague, A. and Cartwright, M. (eds) *Deny All Knowledge: Reading the X-Files*, London: Faber and Faber.

Relph, E. (1976) *Place and Placelessness*, London: Pion.

Rheingold, H. (1994) *The Virtual Community: Finding Connection in a Computerized World*, London: Secker and Warburg.

Rice, J. and Saunders, C. (1996) 'Consuming *Middlemarch*: the construction and consumption of nostalgia in Stamford', in Cartmell, D., Hunter, I.Q., Kaye, H. and Whelehan, I. (eds) *Pulping Fictions: Consuming Culture across the Literature/Media Divide*, London: Pluto Press.

Rickels, L. (1999) *The Vampire Lectures*, Minneapolis: University of Minnesota Press.

Ricoeur, P. (1981) *Hermeneutics and the Human Sciences*, Cambridge: Cambridge University Press.

Ritzer, G. (2001) *Explorations in Social Theory: From Metatheorizing to Rationalization*, London: Sage.

Robbins, D. (1991) *The Work of Pierre Bourdieu*, Buckingham: Open University Press.

—— (2000) *Bourdieu and Culture*, London: Sage.

Roberts, T.J. (1990) *An Aesthetics of Junk Fiction*, Athens: University of Georgia Press.

Robertson, J. (1998) *Takarazuka: Sexual Politics and Popular Culture in Modern Japan*, London: University of California Press.

Robins, K. (1995) 'Cyberspace and the world we live in', in Featherstone, M. and Burrows, R. (eds) *Cyberspace, Cyberbodies, Cyberpunk: Cultures of Technological Embodiment*, London: Sage.

—— (1996) *Into the Image: culture and politics in the field of vision*, London: Routledge.

Rodman, G.B. (1996) *Elvis After Elvis: The Posthumous Career of a Living Legend*, London: Routledge.

Rojek, C. (1990) *Ways of Escape*, London: Macmillan.

Rose, J. (1999) 'The cult of celebrity', *New Formations* No. 36: 9–20.

Ross, A. (1989) *No Respect: Intellectuals and Popular Culture*, New York: Routledge.

Ross, J. (1993) *The Incredibly Strange Film Book*, London: Simon and Schuster.

Rowe, D. (1995) *Popular Cultures*, London: Sage.

Rubinkowski, L. (1997) *Impersonating Elvis*, London: Faber and Faber.

Ruddock, A. (1998) 'Active Netizens: television, realism and the *ER* website', in Moody, N. and Hallam, J. (eds) *Medical Fictions*, Liverpool: ARPF and MCCA/Liverpool John Moores University Press.

—— (2001) *Understanding Audiences: Theory and Method*, London: Sage.

Russ, J. (1985) *Magic Mommas, Trembling Sisters, Puritans and Perverts*, New York: Crossing.

Sabal, R. (1992) 'Television executives speak about fan letters to the networks', in Lewis, L.A. (ed.) *The Adoring Audience*, London: Routledge.

Sanjek, D. (1990) 'Fans' notes: the horror film fanzine', *Literature/Film Quarterly* Vol. 18 No. 3: 150–9; reprinted in Gelder, K. (ed.) (2000) *The Horror Reader*, London: Routledge.

Savage, J. (1996) 'The doors of perception? What makes a cult book cult?', *W: The Waterstone's Magazine* Winter/Spring 1996, Volume 4: 12–19.

Schatz, T. (1993) 'The New Hollywood', in Collins, J., Radner, H. and Preacher Collins, A. (eds) *Film Theory Goes to the Movies*, London: Routledge.

Schelde, P. (1993) *Androids, Humanoids and other Science Fiction Monsters: Science and Soul in Science Fiction Films*, New York: New York University Press.

Schodt, F.L. (1996) *Dreamland Japan: Writings on Modern Manga*, Berkeley: Stone Bridge Press.

Sconce, J. (1995) ' "Trashing" the academy: taste, excess, and an emerging politics of cinematic style', *Screen* 36 (4): 371–93.

—— (2000) *Haunted Media*, Durham: Duke University Press.

Segal, J. (1991) *Phantasy in Everyday Life*, London: Penguin.

—— (1992) *Melanie Klein*, London: Sage.

Shattuc, J.M. (1997) *The Talking Cure: TV Talk Shows and Women*, New York: Routledge.

Shaviro, S. (1993) *The Cinematic Body*, Minneapolis: University of Minnesota Press.

Silverman, K. (1996) *The Threshold of the Visible World*, London: Routledge.

Silverstone, R. (1994) *Television and Everyday Life*, London: Routledge.

—— (1999) *Why Study the Media?*, London: Sage.

Silverstone, R. and Hirsch, E. (eds) (1992) *Consuming technologies: Media and Information in Domestic Spaces*, London: Routledge.

Smith, B.H. (1988) *Contingencies of Value: Alternative Perspectives for Critical Theory*, Massachusetts: Harvard University Press.

Smith, G.M. (1999) ' "To Waste More Time, Please Click Here Again": Monty Python and the quest for film/CD-ROM adaptation', in Smith, G.M. (ed.) *On a Silver Platter*, New York: New York University Press.

Smith, M. (1995) *Engaging Characters*, Oxford: Clarendon Press.

Soja, E. (1989) *Postmodern Geographies: the Reassertion of Space in Critical Social Theory*, London: Verso.

Sontag, S. (1977) *On Photography*, New York: Dell.

Sorkin, M. (ed.) (1992) *Variations on a Theme Park: The New American City and the End of Public Space*, New York: Hill and Wang.

Spigel, L. (1990) 'Communicating with the dead: Elvis as medium', *Camera Obscura* 23: 176–205.

Spigel, L. and Jenkins, H. (1991) 'Same Bat Channel, Different Bat Times: mass culture and popular memory', in Pearson, R.E. and Uricchio, W. (eds) *The Many Lives of the Batman: Critical Approaches to a Superhero and his Media*, London: BFI Publishing.

Stabile, C.A. (1995) 'Resistance, recuperation, and reflexivity: the limits of a paradigm', *Critical Studies in Mass Communication* Vol. 12 No. 4: 403–22.

Stacey, J. (1994) *Star Gazing: Hollywood Cinema and Female Spectatorship*, London: Routledge.

Staiger, J. (1992) *Interpreting Films: Studies in the Historical Reception of American Cinema*, Princeton: Princeton University Press.

—— (2000) *Perverse Spectators: The Practices of Film Reception*, New York: New York University Press.

Strausbaugh, J. (1995) *E: Reflections on the Birth of the Elvis Faith*, New York: Blast Books.

Street, S. (2000) *British Cinema in Documents*, London: Routledge.

Studlar, G. (1991) 'Midnight S/Excess: Cult Configurations of "Femininity" and the Perverse', in Telotte, J.P. (ed.) *The Cult Film Experience: Beyond All Reason*, Austin: University of Texas Press.

—— (1997) ' "Out-Salomeing Salome": dance, the new woman, and fan magazine orientalism', in Bernstein, M. and Studlar, G. (eds) *Visions of the East: Orientalism in Film*, New Jersey: Rutgers University Press.

Suarez, J.A. (1996) *Bike Boys, Drag Queens, and Superstars: Avant-Garde, Mass Culture and Gay Identities in the 1960s Underground Cinema*, Bloomington: Indiana University Press.

Sudjic, D. (1985) *Cult Objects*, London: Andre Deutsch.

—— (1989) *Cult Heroes: How to Be Famous for More Than Fifteen Minutes*, London: Andre Deutsch.

Sunday Times [no author given] (1998) 'Prisoner barred', 3 May 1998: 24.

Tankel, J.D. and Murphy, K. (1998) 'Collecting comic books: a study of the fan and curatorial consumption', in Harris, C. and Alexander, A. (eds) *Theorizing Fandom: Fans, Subculture and Identity*, Cresskill: Hampton Press.

Taylor, G. (1999) *Artists in the Audience: Cults, Camp and American Film Criticism*, Princeton: Princeton University Press.

Taylor, H. (1989) *Scarlett's Women: Gone With the Wind and Its Female Fans*, London: Virago Press.

Taylor, L. and Willis, A. (1999) *Media Studies: Texts, Institutions and Audiences*, Oxford: Blackwell Publishers.

Taylor, R. (1985) *The Death and Resurrection Show: From Shaman to Superstar*, London: Blond Publishing.

Telotte, J.P. (ed.) (1991) *The Cult Film Experience: Beyond All Reason*, Austin: University of Texas Press.

—— (1991a) 'Beyond all reason: the nature of the cult', in Telotte, J.P. (ed.) *The Cult Film Experience: Beyond All Reason*, Austin: University of Texas Press.

Tepper, M. (1997) 'Usenet communities and the cultural politics of information', in Porter, D. (ed.) *Internet Culture*, London: Routledge.

Thomas, L. (1995) 'In love with *Inspector Morse*: feminist subculture and quality television', *Feminist Review* No. 51: 1–25.

—— (forthcoming) *Fans, Feminism and Popular Media*, London: Routledge.

Thompson, J.B. (1995) *Media and Modernity*, Cambridge: Polity Press.

Thompson, R.J. (1990) *Adventures on Prime Time: The Television Programs of Stephen J. Cannell*, New York: Praeger.

Thornham, S. (1997) *Passionate Detachments*, London: Arnold.

Thornton, S. (1995) *Club Cultures: Music, Media and Subcultural Capital*, Cambridge: Polity Press.

Threadgold, T. (1997) *Feminist Poetics*, London: Routledge.

Time Out Guide – Las Vegas: Second Edition [no author given] (2000), London: Penguin.

Tudor, A. (1997) 'Why horror? The peculiar pleasures of a popular genre', *Cultural Studies* 11(3): 443–63.

Tulloch, J. (1990) *Television Drama: Agency, Audience and Myth*, London: Routledge.

—— (2000) *Watching Television Audiences: Cultural Theories and Methods*, London: Arnold.

Tulloch, J. and Alvarado, M. (1983) *'Doctor Who': The Unfolding Text*, London: Macmillan.

Tulloch, J. and Jenkins, H. (1995) *Science Fiction Audiences: Watching 'Doctor Who' and 'Star Trek'*, London: Routledge.

Tulloch, J. and Moran, A. (1986) *'A Country Practice': 'Quality Soap'*, Sydney: Currency Press.

Tulloch, J. and Munro, R. (1999) ' "Whose stories you tell": writing "Ken Loach" ', in Bignell, J. (ed.) *Writing and Cinema*, Essex: Longman.

Turkle, S. (1984) *The Second Self: Computers and the Human Spirit*, London: Granada Publishing.

—— (1996) *Life On The Screen: Identity in the Age of the Internet*, London: Weidenfeld and Nicolson.

Turner, V.W. (1969) *The Ritual Process: Structure and Anti-structure*, London: Penguin.

Uricchio, W. and Pearson, R.E. (1991) 'I'm not fooled by that cheap disguise', in Pearson, R.E. and Uricchio, W. (eds) *The Many Lives of the Batman: Critical Approaches to a Superhero and his Media*, London: BFI Publishing.

Urry, J. (1990a) *The Tourist Gaze: Leisure and Travel in Contemporary Societies*, London: Sage.

Urry, J. (1990b) 'The "consumption" of tourism', *Sociology: The Journal of the British Sociological Association* Vol. 24 No. 1: 23–35.

Vale, V. and Juno, A. (1986) 'Introduction', in Vale, V. and Juno, A. (eds) *Re/Search # 10 Incredibly Strange Films*, San Francisco: Re/Search Publications.

Van Maanen, J. (1988) *Tales of the Field*, Chicago: University of Chicago Press.

Verba, J.M. (1996) *Boldly Writing: A Trekker Fan and Zine History, 1967–1987*, Minnesota: FTL Publications.

Vermorel, F. and Vermorel, J. (1989) *Fandemonium! The Book of Fan Cults and Dance Crazes*, London: Omnibus Press.

—— (1990) 'Starlust', in Frith, S. and Goodwin, A. (eds) *On Record: Rock, Pop and the Written Word*, London: Routledge.

—— (1992) 'A glimpse of the fan factory', in Lewis, L.A. (ed.) *The Adoring Audience*, London: Routledge.

Vikan, G. (1994) 'Graceland as *Locus Sanctus*', in DePaoli, G. (ed.) *Elvis + Marilyn: 2 x Immortal*, New York: Rizzoli.

Walkerdine, V. (1987) 'Video replay: families, films and fantasies', in Donald, J. and Kaplan, C. (eds) *Formations of Fantasy*, London: Methuen.

Waller, G.A. (1991) 'Midnight Movies, 1980–1985: a market study', in Telotte, J.P. (ed.) *The Cult Film Experience: Beyond All Reason*, Austin: University of Texas Press.

Wasserlein, F. (1997) 'Selected works of Madonna', appendix in Faith, K. (1997) *Madonna: Bawdy and Soul*, Toronto: University of Toronto Press.

Watson, B. (1996) *Frank Zappa: The Negative Dialectics of Poodle Play*, London: Quartet Books.

Watson, N. (1997) 'Why we argue about virtual community: a case study of the Phish.Net fan community', in Jones, Steve G. (ed.) *Virtual Culture: Identity and Communication in Cybersociety*, London: Sage.

Watson, P. (1997) 'There's no accounting for taste: exploitation cinema and the limits of film theory', in Cartmell, D., Hunter, I.Q., Kaye, H. and Whelehan, I. (eds) *Trash Aesthetics: Popular Culture and its Audience*, London: Pluto Press.

Weldon, M. (1994) 'Intro', *Psychotronic Video* No. 19: 2–3.

Westfahl, G. (1996) 'Where no market has gone before: "The Science Fiction Industry" and the *Star Trek* Industry', *Extrapolation* 37 (4): 291–301.

Whissen, T.R. (1992) *Classic Cult Fiction: A Companion to Popular Cult Literature*, New York: Greenwood Press.

Williams, L. (1999) 'Film bodies: gender, genre and excess', in Thornham, S. (ed.) *Feminist Film Theory*, Edinburgh: Edinburgh University Press.

Williams, S. (2001) *Emotion and Social Theory*, London: Sage.

Williamson, J. (1998) 'A glimpse of the void', in Merck, M. (ed.) *After Diana: Irreverent Elegies*, London: Verso.

Williamson, M. (1998) 'Vampire fans and vampire fan clubs: "official" and "unofficial" practices', paper presented at Screen Studies Conference, Glasgow University 3–5 July 1998.

Winn, M. (1985) *The Plug-In Drug: Television, Children and the Family*, London: Penguin.

Winnicott, D.W. (1971) *Playing and Reality*, London: Penguin.

—— (1988) *Human Nature*, London: Free Association Books.

—— (1990) *Home Is Where We Start From: Essays by a Psychoanalyst*, London: Penguin.

—— (1993) 'Communicating and not communicating', in Goldman, D. (ed.) *In One's Bones: The Clinical Genius of Winnicott*, New Jersey: Jason Aronson.

Wise, S. (1990) 'Sexing Elvis', in Frith, S. and Goodwin, A. (eds) *On Record: Rock, Pop and the Written Word*, London: Routledge.

Wittgenstein, L. (1988) *Philosophical Investigations*, Oxford: Basil Blackwell.

Wolff, J. (1995) *Resident Alien: Feminist Cultural Criticism*, Cambridge: Polity Press.

Wollen, P. (1982) 'The Hermeneutic Code', in *Semiotic Counter-Strategies: Readings and Writings*, London: Verso.

Wood, R.E. (1991) 'Don't dream it: performance and *The Rocky Horror Picture Show*', in Telotte, J.P. (ed.) *The Cult Film Experience: Beyond All Reason*, Austin: University of Texas Press.

Wright, E. (1987) *Psychoanalytic Criticism: Theory in Practice*, London: Routledge.

Wright, S.A. (ed.) (1995) *Armageddon in Waco: Critical Perspectives on the Branch Davidian Conflict*, Chicago: University of Chicago Press.

Young, R. (1991) 'Psychoanalysis and political literary theories', in Donald, J. (ed.) *Psychoanalysis and Cultural Theory: Thresholds*, London: Macmillan.

Young, R.M. (1989) 'Transitional phenomena: production and consumption', in Richards, B. (ed.) *Crises of the Self: Further Essays on Psychoanalysis and Politics*, London: Free Association Books.

Zizek, S. (1996) *The Indivisible Remainder: Essays on Schelling and Related Matters*, London: Verso.

—— (1997) *The Plague of Fantasies*, London: Verso.

INDEX

Printed in the United Kingdom by
Lightning Source UK Ltd., Milton Keynes
139049UK00001B/42/A